Exit, Voice, and Solidarity

Exit, Voice, and Solidarity

Contesting Precarity in the US and European Telecommunications Industries

VIRGINIA DOELLGAST

Oxford University Press is a department of the University of Oxford. It furthers
the University's objective of excellence in research, scholarship, and education
by publishing worldwide. Oxford is a registered trade mark of Oxford University
Press in the UK and certain other countries.

Published in the United States of America by Oxford University Press
198 Madison Avenue, New York, NY 10016, United States of America.

© Oxford University Press 2022

All rights reserved. No part of this publication may be reproduced, stored in
a retrieval system, or transmitted, in any form or by any means, without the
prior permission in writing of Oxford University Press, or as expressly permitted
by law, by license, or under terms agreed with the appropriate reproduction
rights organization. Inquiries concerning reproduction outside the scope of the
above should be sent to the Rights Department, Oxford University Press, at the
address above.

You must not circulate this work in any other form
and you must impose this same condition on any acquirer.

Library of Congress Cataloging-in-Publication Data
Names: Doellgast, Virginia Lee, 1976– author.
Title: Exit, voice, and solidarity : contesting precarity in the US and
European telecommunications industries / Virginia Doellgast.
Description: New York, NY : Oxford University Press, [2022] |
Includes bibliographical references and index.
Identifiers: LCCN 2022027303 (print) | LCCN 2022027304 (ebook) |
ISBN 9780197659779 (hardback) | ISBN 9780197659786 (paperback) |
ISBN 9780197659809 (epub)
Subjects: LCSH: Telecommunication—Employees—Labor unions—United States. |
Telecommunication—Employees—Labor unions—Europe. | Industrial management—
Employee participation—United States. | Industrial management—Employee participation—Europe. |
Precarious employment—United States. | Precarious employment—Europe.
Classification: LCC HD6515.T24 D64 2022 (print) | LCC HD6515.T24 (ebook) |
DDC 331.88/11621382—dc23/eng/20220714
LC record available at https://lccn.loc.gov/2022027303
LC ebook record available at https://lccn.loc.gov/2022027304

DOI: 10.1093/oso/9780197659779.001.0001

Contents

Preface and Acknowledgments   vii

   Introduction   1

1. Theorizing Exit, Voice, and Solidarity   20
2. Mapping Exit, Voice, and Solidarity in the Case Studies   50
3. Downsizing   105
4. Performance Management   143
5. Externalization: Outsourcing, Agency Work, and Subsidiaries   190
6. Conclusions   244

References   261
Index   279

Preface and Acknowledgments

Under what conditions do employers create and sustain high quality jobs? We generally think of "good jobs" as those offering pay high enough to allow a decent standard of living, some degree of job and income security, reasonable working hours that allow for work-life balance, and the ability to take paid time off when needed for illness, vacation, and family. Added to this are the more intangible qualities of interesting work with opportunities to learn and advance in your career and some control over how you do your job. The idea of a bad job evokes the opposite characteristics: low pay at poverty wages, precarity based on fear of being fired or not having one's contract renewed, unpredictable working hours, no paid time off, "dead end" work lacking the prospect of better pay, and routine tasks with little control.

Business leaders often argue that they will create good jobs out of self-interest, as happy employees are likely to also be more motivated and productive. I have heard this conventional wisdom often in my fifteen-some years of teaching on human resource management degrees. A few years ago, I was talking with a team of corporate human resource managers who had come to speak to my class about their outsourcing strategies. The head of the team told me that his favorite book was *Joy, Inc: How We Built a Workplace People Love* by Rich Sheridan (2015), written by the CEO of a small software company, Menlo Innovations. He had visited Menlo and was trying to model his organization's own practices on theirs, following Sheridan's advice to remove "the fear and ambiguity that typically make a workplace miserable"—with "joy" as the ultimate goal. They were also seeking to extend this model to their subcontractors. He asked me to organize a workshop for his team to discuss my research on worker well-being in call centers, as part of a project to encourage their business process outsourcing (BPO) call center vendors to reduce turnover and improve service quality.

A few years later the company faced a crisis, with lower than expected earnings and a plunging share price. As a result, the strategic focus had shifted from investing in human resources to cutting costs. When the same team came again to talk with my class, they described how they were outsourcing more work and switching to cheaper vendors, while downsizing their own internal workforce. The commitment to worker joy seemed difficult to sustain in the face of these restructuring pressures, which were largely beyond the control of the human resource team.

This example captures a dynamic I saw often in the course of my research for this book: the optimism for a human-centered future of work, and the reality of financial and restructuring pressures that, in the words of Paul Thomson (2003), make it quite hard for employers to "keep their side of the bargain." The result, seen at a global scale, is expanded precarity and inequality, with a shrinking number of workers actually able to access and hold on to good-quality jobs.

Even where we would expect employers to have a strong self-interest in taking the proverbial high road, they often have trouble sticking to these practices. This is particularly the case for jobs that are easily rationalized and restructured, in companies facing steep pressures to cut labor costs. In 2012, I wrote a report with Lisa Sezer on worker stress in call centers, commissioned by UNI-ICTS, the global union for IT and telecom workers, for their annual "Call Center Action Month" (Doellgast and Sezer 2012). The report summarized research on the management practices that contribute to worker stress, anxiety, and burnout, as well as their performance consequences. Not surprisingly, investments in worker skills, autonomy, and job security produce both better psychosocial health for workers and improved organizational outcomes.

The report was intended in part as a resource for unions to use in negotiations with management, to present the performance case for investing in their employees. However, many of the unionists I spoke with at UNI-ICTS meetings told me that call center managers were increasingly reluctant to discuss alternatives to their technology-driven, discipline-based model for motivating workers, even when they came out of pilot projects funded by the companies themselves. Unions' target audience for this kind of research was thus shifting to workers and the public. Organizing and campaigning focused on employers' broader social responsibilities to their employees and communities. Their goals were to negotiate collective agreements that institutionalized those commitments, or to encourage governments to pass binding minimum standards that improved wages, employment security, and health and safety standards.

While both employers and workers stand to benefit from improved job quality, accelerating pressures in global and financial markets tend more often to encourage restructuring strategies that drive up insecurity while degrading pay and working conditions. As argued in this book, the trend toward increasing precarity at work can best be reversed through building more inclusive and democratic social institutions. And this requires worker power—based on constraints on employer exit, support for collective worker voice, and strategies of inclusive labor solidarity. The chapters that follow explain what this means, and why strengthening the social regulation of work is so important for creating and sustaining good jobs.

PREFACE AND ACKNOWLEDGMENTS   ix

This book has taken a decade to research and write, and so I have many people to thank. The study was funded by the Economic and Social Research Council (grant number RES-061-25-0444) in the United Kingdom, while I was a faculty member at the London School of Economics and Political Science (LSE). David Marsden was my faculty mentor on this "First Grant" for junior scholars, Katja Sarmiento-Mirwaldt was the Research Officer, and Chiara Benassi and Elisa Pannini were Research Assistants. Katja and I worked closely together in developing the research design, interview protocols, and questionnaires, as well as compiling archival data, developing timelines of restructuring events, and analyzing findings. She also carried out all or most of the research in Austria, the Czech Republic, Poland, and the UK. Chiara conducted the field research in Italy, and also played a central role in compiling and interpreting findings. Elisa helped to write the country report for France based on coding and analysis of the French interviews and archival data. David provided support and advice throughout.

I coauthored articles based on the project findings with these colleagues, as well as with Peter Berg and Maxime Bellego. After the official conclusion of the research project, Christian Ibsen, Lisa Sezer, and I worked together on a study of telecom employer associations in Denmark and Sweden, which gave me an opportunity to carry out follow-up interviews—including at a UNI-ICTS conference in Sweden that I attended with Lisa, and during visits to employer and union offices in Copenhagen with Christian.

This book draws heavily on the joint work of this research team and community of colleagues, who together helped me both to understand very different national institutional contexts and union traditions, and to puzzle through the salient lessons from our comparative findings. They were kind enough to give me permission to use our joint work in this sole-authored book. I try to acknowledge their specific contributions throughout—as this book owes a huge debt to their insights, ideas, and findings "in the field."

The research reported on here would not have been possible without the many unionists, managers, and workers with whom I and my colleagues spoke over the course of this study, and who helped provide access to workplaces and interviewees across many countries. I cannot name most of them for confidentiality reasons. A few to whom I owe a personal debt of thanks include Marcus Courtney, Kornelia Dubbel, Nell Geiser, Debbie Goldman, Christoph Heil, Alex Hogback, Louise Novatny, Lutz Päge, Alan Tate, and Tomas Wellejus. Many of these individuals have already seen and commented on some of the results of this research, in the form of reports, research articles, or presentations at conferences and meetings. I hope this book can be of use in giving a "bigger picture" comparative view of the work that labor unions are doing across countries to fight back against restructuring pressures, as well as the possibilities for companies to accomplish similar goals with very different (more or less precarious) management models.

My research benefited from financial and logistical support and exchanges with colleagues at different universities and institutes in Europe. I carried out field research and wrote portions of this book while a visiting scholar at the Freie Universität (FU) in Berlin, Germany; the Laboratoire d'Economie et de Sociologie du Travail (LEST) in Aix-en-Provence, France; Institutions et Dynamiques Historiques de l'Economie et de la Société (IDHES) in Paris, France; and Forskningscenter for Arbejdsmarkedsog Organisationsstudier (FAOS) in Copenhagen, Denmark. Gregory Jackson, Ariel Mendez, Claude Didry, and Søren Kaj Andersen were generous hosts. And many colleagues shared their knowledge, contacts, and ideas during research seminars and over lunches, dinners, and drinks.

My intuition for comparative research owes much to discussions and workshops organized through international research institutes and partnerships. I have been a Senior Research Fellow since 2018 at the Hans Böckler Stiftung's (HBS) Wirtschafts- und Sozial-wissenschaftliches Institut (WSI), a leading center for research on German industrial relations. My participation in the Centre de recherche interuniversitaire sur la mondialisation et le travail (CRIMT) network has given me the opportunity to test out my ideas, while thinking through the meaning of "better work" and institutional experimentation. A particularly important collaboration started with a book project organized by Jan Drahokoupil at the European Trade Union Institute (ETUI), on union responses to outsourcing in Europe—*The Outsourcing Challenge* (Drahokoupil 2015). Exchanges with Jan and the other chapter authors led to a second co-edited book with Nathan Lillie and Valeria Pulignano, *Reconstructing Solidarity* (Doellgast, Lillie, and Pulignano 2018). The framework and analysis developed with my co-editors and the chapter authors are the starting point for my arguments in this book. The Transatlantic Social Dialogue organized annually by the ILR School, HBS, and the ETUI gave me a regular opportunity to discuss the themes that are at the center of this book with international academics and unionists.

Of course, the bulk of my research and writing happened while I was based at LSE's Department of Management and then Cornell University's ILR School. Both institutions provided very generous support. An Einaudi International Faculty Fellow award at Cornell funded follow-up research and travel. My colleagues are too numerous to name individually, but I owe much to them as mentors and friends. Rose Batt deserves particular mention for setting me down the path of studying the telecommunications industry and cheering me on along the way. Sophie Mace (LSE), Michael Hall (Cornell), and Katrina Ferreira (Cornell) provided able research assistance. The PhD students and postdocs

I worked with across these institutions have been my best critics. A special thanks to Dario Azzellini, Chiara Benassi, Elodie Béthoux, Jörg Flecker, Jérôme Gautié, Nell Geiser, Ursula Holtgewe, Nick Krachler, Adam Mrozowicki, Sean O'Brady, Elisa Pannini, Sid Rothstein, Ole Sørensen, and Chris Tilly, who read and commented on the book manuscript. Their feedback contributed greatly to both improving its coherence and fixing mistakes.

My children Ada and Uli were born while I was conducting the field research for this book, and my ability to write a long and reasonably coherent manuscript was helped by their growing ability to feed, clothe, and entertain themselves. I started drafting the introduction during a summer in Europe with my mother, who kept the kids busy while I attended conferences and wrote in cafés across several countries. Mamaw Janet, Granddad Terry, and Grama Jill together provided many years of support, traveling around the world to spend time with their grandkids. The COVID-19 pandemic lockdowns began in the early spring of 2020, when I was somewhere in the middle of drafting chapters. I could not have accomplished much without Jessica and David Custer-Bindel, and Veronica and Mike Matsuda-Martinez—my co-parents in a "pandemic bubble." Finally, my husband Ian Greer is my best sounding board, critic, and source of good ideas—all while keeping me and the kids well fed and loved.

I enjoy many supports and privileges that keep me on the secure side of the precarity divide. This divide has been thrown into sharper relief during the pandemic. I hope this book can help in a small way to inspire policies and strategies that both constrain the risks of exit and extend the benefits of voice and solidarity more broadly.

Introduction

Work is becoming more precarious and insecure. The stylized facts of these trends are well rehearsed. The future looks increasingly bleak for the bulk of the workforce as they are forced to compete in a brave new global market undergoing rapid creative destruction, spurred on by financialization and digitalization. Employers are able to take advantage of growing opportunities to cut labor costs through downsizing, outsourcing, and offshoring. Inequality expands, as profits are redistributed up toward shareholders, corporate CEOs, and the finance sector, while risk is redistributed down to workers in the form of insecure jobs, stagnating wages, and shrinking welfare states.

At the same time, employers do not all make the same choices when it comes to investing in (or disinvesting from) their workers. Downsizing can lead to unemployment and sudden loss of income and job opportunities. Or employers can respond to changes in demand through reducing working hours, retraining workers for new business areas, or investing in voluntary plans with generous redundancy payments. Performance management can transfer risk to workers, through tying their pay or continued employment to meeting sales and productivity goals. Or it can seek to improve performance through good pay, training, and interesting work with some degree of discretion or control, while ensuring that workers will not be fired arbitrarily. Employers can use the threat of outsourcing to demand concessions and to shift jobs to lower paid contracts. Or subcontractors and temporary agencies can sell their services based on flexibility and technical expertise, rather than cheaper labor costs.

In this book, I ask why similar employers take these different approaches to restructuring—most simply summarized as the high road providing wider access to high-quality jobs, or the low road leading to expanding inequality and precarity. My answer is that they are more likely to take the high road where worker interests and rights—to stable and secure jobs, control over their schedules and work, and adequate pay and benefits—are viewed as legitimate outcomes that should be pursued alongside market-based objectives focusing on cost, productivity, and profit. The logic of seeking mutual gains for labor and capital, or investing in workers because it is good for business, is unlikely on its own to produce sustained investments in good-quality jobs. Within capitalist economies, the social responsibility of companies to a broad set of stakeholders must be enforced through workers' countervailing power. That power, in turn, is grounded in three factors: constraints on employer exit from encompassing labor market institutions, support for collective worker voice in management decisions, and strategies of inclusive labor solidarity based on bridging divides among workers and in the labor movement.

My findings and analysis are based on ten case studies of incumbent (former monopolist or state-owned) telecommunications companies in the United States and Europe. A comparison of the micro-politics of restructuring across these cases shows that they all experienced expanding worker precarity as a result of downsizing, new performance management practices, and outsourcing. At the same time, workers and their unions drew on different sources of power to build or maintain inclusive institutions that reduced precarity. While unions are the main actors capable of mobilizing this power, they need strong institutions to back them up, based on worker rights to participate in organizational decisions and inclusive minimum standards established through law and collective bargaining. This book is about how those institutions are built, used, and sustained. Workers advance a social logic based on worker voice and solidarity when they organize against, and help design alternatives to, restructuring measures that are guided by a market-based logic of employer exit.

My Argument in Brief

Seen from above, there is a global trend toward expanding precarity and declining job quality. Employers are restructuring work in ways that shift risk onto workers. Seen from below, however, these trends are not inevitable or irreversible. Alternative management models are forged every day through social partnership, negotiation, and compromise. They are also steered by changes in law and public policy that hold employers to minimum standards and require them to negotiate or consult with their workers. Through looking at both these micro-politics and public campaigns for policy change within similar companies, across different institutional settings, we can better understand not only why restructuring so often leads to increased labor market insecurity, but also the conditions that support alternatives.

My argument has two parts. First, restructuring decisions involve contested choices concerning the social value versus the market value of work. Restructuring drives down pay and conditions to the extent that it is market-oriented—involving a shift in the employment relationship away from social concerns with internal coordination and equity, and toward market-based concerns that prioritize maximizing short-term profit. A central mechanism in market-oriented restructuring is intensifying competition based on the replacement of worker voice with employer exit as a means of securing worker cooperation (Doellgast, Lillie, and Pulignano 2018; Greer and Doellgast 2017).

My second argument concerns the conditions under which market-oriented restructuring can be contested, based on (re)asserting the legitimacy of social values and outcomes in the employment relationship. Labor's power in negotiations or in conflicts over restructuring rests on three different factors, summarized as constraints on employer exit, support for collective worker voice, and strategies of inclusive labor solidarity—inspired by Hirschman's (1970) "exit, voice, and loyalty" framework.

Most fundamentally, workers and their unions have more power to contest market-oriented restructuring where employers face negotiated or legal restrictions on their ability to exit internal employment relationships. When employers find it more difficult or expensive to downsize employment and to move work to subcontractors or to groups of workers with cheaper employment contracts, they are more likely to engage with the social demands of their own internal workers. Inclusive institutions setting minimum employment standards and social protections at the national level, within industries, and along companies' supply chains or supplier networks are necessary to constrain organizational exit from these inclusive standards (Bosch, Mayhew, and Gautié 2010). On the other hand, the presence of institutional loopholes or exit options are more likely to encourage market-oriented strategies. Where employers are not constrained by inclusive institutions, they are more likely to externalize work via outsourcing or workplace fissuring (Weil 2014). These strategies are particularly attractive where externalized jobs and employers have lower labor costs—due to poor coverage by or weak compliance with labor laws, social insurance programs, and collective agreements.

The second factor affecting labor power in contests over restructuring concerns institutional support for collective worker voice. Wilkinson et al. (2020, 5) define worker voice as "the ways and means through which employees attempt to have a say [...] potentially to influence organizational affairs relating to issues that affect their work, their interests, and the interests of managers and owners." Collective voice grounds this attempted influence in more broadly democratic or representative structures, such as collective bargaining with unions or other worker representatives. Institutions supporting expanded collective voice can include bargaining or participation rights, which encourage negotiation and consultation over management decisions at workplace, company, or industry level (Doellgast 2012). They also include worker rights to representation on company boards (Ferreras 2017), or state support for tripartite social dialogue and social pacts over social, labor market, and training policies (Avdagic, Rhodes, and Visser 2011). The common factor linking these institutions is that they integrate workers and their unions into democratic decision-making structures at multiple levels.

Together, these constraints on exit and supports for voice are sources of *institutional power*. Unions are better able to insist on strengthened social commitments from employers where those employers find it more difficult to move jobs beyond the reach of established social and labor market regulations, collective agreements, welfare supports, and minimum employment standards. Worker representatives rely on legal rights and formal bargaining structures to directly challenge and craft alternatives to restructuring measures that would increase the precarity of their members and the broader workforce.

The third factor that is central to reasserting the legitimacy of social over market values is labor strategies based on inclusive forms of solidarity—which seek to bridge divides in the labor movement, across the workforce, and within societies. Solidarity is undermined by market-based competition for jobs or investment across groups of workers (Greer and Doellgast 2017). It is also weakened by historic divides within the labor movement, based on ideology, racism, or narrow construction of interests (Lee and Tapia 2021) and often is reflected in or reinforced by the structure of union representation and collective bargaining (Benassi, Dorigatti, and Pannini 2019). Labor strategies based on inclusive forms of solidarity that bridge these divides are needed to strengthen *associational power* within the workforce, and ideally at the level of civil society. They are also crucial to expanding access to democracy at work and to building more inclusive institutions.

The combination of perfectly inclusive and encompassing constraints on employer exit, supports for worker voice, and strategies of labor solidarity are unlikely to be found in a pure form in any national or industry case. However, this ideal type model can be used as a benchmark to judge how close or far away a country, industry, or employer is from conditions encouraging organizational strategies that balance social with market concerns. In this book, I show that these three factors play a central role in the form that restructuring conflicts take, as well as in labor's (potential) sources of bargaining power, as workers and their representatives seek to influence management strategies and their outcomes.

Restructuring in Telecommunications: Introduction to the Case Studies

The telecommunications industry is in many ways the ideal setting for studying the politics of restructuring. Until the 1990s, telecom markets in most countries were highly regulated, with most major market segments serviced by domestic companies that were protected from international competition. The large incumbent public telecommunications operators (PTOs) controlled fixed-line telephone markets and dominated mobile services. In the United States and Europe, these incumbents were also highly unionized, with good pay and working conditions, including high levels of job security. In Europe, they were state owned, and their workers were typically on civil-service or public-sector employment contracts.

Then, between the early and late 1990s, governments radically overhauled regulation and ownership structures in the telecom sector. Incumbent companies were fully or partially privatized, and their markets were opened up to competition. As a result, they faced new pressures to cut costs and improve service quality—to retain or grow market share and to increase returns to shareholders. Employers responded with a range of often radical restructuring strategies.

In this book, I compare changing approaches to downsizing, performance management, and externalizing employment across ten incumbent telecom companies in Denmark (TDC), Sweden (Telia), Austria (A1), Germany (Deutsche Telekom), France (France Telecom), Italy (Telecom Italia), the United Kingdom (BT), the United States (AT&T), the Czech Republic (O2 Czech Republic), and Poland (Orange Polska). Nearly all of these companies were state owned (with the exception of AT&T) until the 1980s or 1990s; and all operated until the mid-1990s within largely protected, nationally or regionally bounded markets. By the 2010s, when I started the research for this book, all ten companies had been adjusting to radically changing markets and ownership structures over some fifteen to twenty years. They faced similar challenges from falling prices and market share, as well as new, activist shareholders who expected quick returns on their investments. However, they developed their strategic responses to these challenges within different industrial relations, legal, and policy environments.

To set the stage for my analysis, I first give a short summary of restructuring trajectories, conflicts, and their (at least partial) resolution at three of my case study companies: France Telecom (France), Deutsche Telekom (Germany), and Telia (Sweden). I then draw on these examples to explain the book's argument and framework.

France Telecom (France)

In the spring of 2010, I visited one of France Telecom's call centers in southern France. The large glass and steel building was a short walk from the city's tourist district, tucked behind boutiques selling lavender sachets, almond calissons, and bottles of pastis. The call center manager invited me into his office for a coffee with the local human resource manager before I began a round of interviews with workers and supervisors.

The conversation quickly turned to the "social crisis," or *crise sociale*. Over the past year, the company had been the focus of global news headlines due to what was widely referred to as a *vague de suicides*: a wave of close to forty employee suicides. Some involved spectacular actions, such as workers throwing themselves out of the windows of their office buildings. In many cases, workers had left suicide notes blaming management for their distress. The large number of suicides came to be attributed to the company's multi-year restructuring plan, dubbed "NExT"—*Nouvelle expérience des télécommunications*. Managers were encouraged to meet aggressive goals to downsize 22,000 employees (around 20% of the workforce) and encourage 14,000 job changes, including a requirement that employees change their job every three years.

Union representatives had long argued against the unilateral and draconian way in which layoffs and relocations were being carried out, asserting that management was privileging shareholder value at the expense of worker health. However, they faced steep challenges in trying to change these policies. One challenge was the weak formal rights of workplace representatives. Works councils could consult over restructuring policies, but ultimately management decided whether to take their advice or not. A second challenge was the significant ideological divisions among the multiple union confederations that represented France Telecom's workers. While conservative unions typically favored partnership and compromise, more radical and leftist unions tended to take a more oppositional stance in negotiations.

However, these unions worked together to develop what became a remarkably coherent critique of the NExT plan. One coalition of unions established an Observatory of Stress and Forced Mobility that documented the negative impact of restructuring on workers, based on surveys carried out by a scientific committee and publicized via company-wide meetings and discussions. Another group of unions used the works council's social funds to sponsor a theatre project that dramatized conflicts over restructuring to large audiences of workers and union representatives.

When the number of workers committing suicide began rising in 2009, the unions were able to bring their own research findings to the media while organizing mass demonstrations led by an already mobilized workforce. In late 2009, the chief human resources officer, Didier Lombard, was asked to resign, and management negotiated a series of eighteen social accords with the unions that ended forced relocations, committed management to improving work-life balance, and established a tripartite committee to regularly monitor worker stress and well-being. From 2010, any organizational change had to pass a psychosocial risk analysis at the regional level to prevent a new crisis.

The union campaigns at France Telecom had a larger impact in France, through strengthening legal and policy support for social dialogue on workers' psychosocial health (Palpacuer and Seignour 2020; Doellgast, Bellego, and Pannini 2021). From 2010, a national collective agreement on harassment and violence at work required employers to evaluate psychosocial risks and develop a plan to address them. The unions also used the courts to hold managers to account for their "unsocial" actions. In 2009, in the midst of the crisis, the unions brought a complaint to the Paris prosecutor's office, accusing France Telecom's management of engaging in a systematic campaign of moral harassment (*harcèlement moral*) against the workforce. In 2019, a criminal court ordered the company to pay 3 million euros in damages, and the former management team faced jail time and fines. This decision set an important legal precedent in France, while the trial kept public attention on the company and its management practices.

In the call center I visited, the social accords had filtered down to a series of new initiatives to reduce stress and improve job quality. The manager asked me to help with the design of a survey he was planning to carry out in the center, to evaluate different options for scheduling practices that gave workers more control over their working time. The biggest change he saw was in the culture of labor relations: "I used to see the local union representatives as mostly an obstacle—to meeting my goals, to improving flexibility. We had endless meetings, to present our strategies and study their effects. But ultimately, we did things our way. Now we are trying to see the unions as partners, in changing the orientation of the company."

This change was even more significant in the field technician units. Union representatives had long opposed deskilling, as management designed narrower job titles and broke up once integrated tasks. They argued that this was undermining professional identity and driving inefficiency, based on their own experience trying to coordinate work between a growing number of specializations. After the social crisis, a new department was established within some of the units based on multi-skilled teams. This was then rolled out company-wide, with the decision to implement the new team structure decided within each technician unit in consultation with local union representatives.

My coauthor Maxime Bellego interviewed more than fifty technicians as part of a company evaluation of psychosocial stress, in the wake of the social crisis (Bellego 2013). A few years later, he was invited back to study the effects of the multi-skilled teams and other changes negotiated with the unions. One of the most significant differences he found was the increased respect and trust between union representatives and managers. This mutual respect was rooted in fear that the unions could bring new problems to the media. "They can threaten to re-mediatize stress at France Telecom: to bring this to the media, that management is not respecting worker rights. And that is an ongoing source of power."

In 2016, my family and I returned to southern France for the summer. I noticed that our neighbor drove a France Telecom van and asked him if he would talk with me about his work. We shared a bottle of wine on the hill behind our house, and he told me his own story while reflecting on how the company (and his role in it) had changed over some forty years he had worked as a field technician. He described the shift of many jobs to subcontractors, which he felt had been one of the biggest stressors for his co-workers. "For many, they experienced it as an insult; as something that wasn't honest. Because these teams, these companies [the subcontractors] worked in a way that was inferior. It was said that with growing competition between operators, the main winners would be the customers. They haven't won. To get a service that works well, you have to have four, five, six service call-outs."

He said things had gotten better in the period following the social crisis and social accords. Multi-skilled teams helped to break down communication barriers between different groups of technicians and to give them more control over how they did their work. He and his co-workers did not have to fear losing their jobs or being relocated. Relations with managers were more open, and there was less conflict or distrust. Still, he felt like this more cooperative culture was fragile, in the face of ongoing pressure from increasingly competitive markets. The attempt to compete for customers and satisfy shareholders with expanding profits introduced a kind of permanent instability that, in his (translated) words, "brings the capitalist market into our working lives and the whole logic of how we are managed, how we do our work."

Deutsche Telekom (Germany)

I had spent several weeks in Deutsche Telekom call centers during my PhD research in the early 2000s. I returned to one of these centers in 2010, located in a bright office building with large windows that overlooked a business park. On the surface, not a lot had changed. Collective agreements still protected workers from being fired if they did not meet performance goals and limited how management monitored workers and used data on their sales and time taken to resolve calls. Workers had formal control over their schedules, with flexible starting and ending times and working time accounts that allowed them to build up hours through voluntary overtime and then take time off when they needed it. There was a lot of investment in coaching, and a formal process for workers to ask for changes in sales goals they could not meet. A joint labor-management committee met regularly to review these requests and decide on adjustments in goals.

The works councilor with whom I was meeting felt this stability in formal practices was largely superficial. "It may look like we have a lot of the same policies, if you look at our agreements, but this is not the same company. Things have gotten a lot worse: the workers are scared to use their rights." When I asked why, she told me there was a simple answer. "Outsourcing. They tell us, the vendors can do your jobs for half the money. And we don't want to lose more work to them. So we have to be more flexible, and always prove that we can save them money or sell more products."

Like France Telecom, Deutsche Telekom had adopted its own approach to radical restructuring. In 2007, after close to a decade of incremental downsizing and outsourcing, managers announced that all remaining call center and field technician services, employing around 50,000 workers, would be spun off into two new dedicated service subsidiaries. At that time, they demanded a new collective agreement that brought pay and conditions more in line with those at the company's subcontractors. Management threatened to sell the subsidiaries if the union did not agree. The union mobilized a six-week strike, but union representatives eventually accepted a series of concessions in exchange for commitments not to outsource the jobs. Employees were required to work more hours without a comparable increase in their monthly salaries, the percentage of variable pay linked to performance increased, starting pay was cut, and call center agents were required to work weekends.

While the concessions saved the company money, Deutsche Telekom's own workforce was still more expensive compared to its mostly non-union subcontractors. Employment shrunk over time in both the call centers and technician units, and managers were threatening to shift more work to third-party firms. This was constantly hanging over the heads of workers, who were discouraged from using flexible working time policies, due to worries that more jobs would be outsourced if they could not be available to take calls, handle repairs, or connect customers to the network. Supervisors were under pressure to meet increasingly high performance targets in their teams and started pressuring lower performers to quit. In the call centers, workers handling sales and customer retention saw their "pay at risk" increase to close to 30%. This meant if they did not make sales goals, they could lose over €7,000 Euros from their €24,000 annual salary.

In the few years following my 2010 visit, the works councils made an aggressive push to turn around the trend toward growing precarity. In 2012, the union negotiated an agreement that raised pay for all workers, with a 3% increase for those in the lowest pay group. They also succeeded in raising the "fixed" (non-variable) percentage of salary, after several days of strikes. In 2014, based on the success of a pilot project, a new agreement with the works council gave workers the choice between three different "working time models," with different options for more flexibility or fixed working hours. Those opting into the more flexible model got extra payments and days off. In exchange, management reduced the use of subcontractors and temporary agencies, from close to 50% to 15% of total employment.

In 2015, I emailed the works councilor I had interviewed five years earlier, to ask her how it was possible that she and her colleagues had succeeded in negotiating these strong agreements. She replied: "The underlying reason was the Works Constitution Act, which provides local co-determination rights for works councils in the organization of working time." These legal bargaining rights made a crucial difference in bringing management to the table, making it possible to negotiate compromises that protected job quality while giving management some flexibility to match the workforce with demand.

When I returned to Germany to do follow-up interviews in 2019, this agreement was still in place—leading to a further shrinking of the percentage of jobs outsourced. At the same time, the union and works councils were fighting ongoing battles to save jobs in anticipation of the next big wave of restructuring. In the call centers, management was adopting new AI-based technology that automated responses to customer calls and texts and that reduced offline or back-office work. The works council had started a project on digitalization, focusing on regulating the use of algorithmic management tools, protecting employee data, and identifying training and qualification needs. But union and works council representatives anticipated that there would be more conflict on the horizon as they tried to protect jobs and job quality in the face of these new challenges.

Telia (Sweden)

In February 2014, I attended a Global Call Center Conference in Orlando, Florida, that was co-sponsored by the Communications Workers of America (CWA) and Union Network International–Information, Communications, Technology, and Related Services (UNI-ICTS), the global trade union for the IT and communications sector. Some 500 union delegates from over forty countries and a range of industries had gathered to discuss strategies for improving job quality in call centers, from global campaigns in multinational companies and local organizing efforts at call center subcontractors to case studies of unions that had succeeded in raising standards through bargaining and legislation.

Midway through the conference, I had lunch with a group of Swedish union officials and shop stewards. We moved from discussing the obvious cultural differences between unions at the conference, to their own experience with cultures and practices of solidarity in Swedish workplaces. Sweden is known for its inclusive collective agreements and universalist welfare state, supporting high equity in pay and working conditions. In the telecom and call center sectors, maintaining the solidarity that underpins these institutions has not always been easy. Workers are represented by several different union confederations, which often compete for members, while disagreeing on how much conflict or social partnership is appropriate when dealing with employers bent increasingly on cost cutting.

Still, the union reps were optimistic about their ability to work together in a united front to keep bargaining coverage high and to stop the growth of precarious and low-wage employment. In most countries represented at the conference, outsourced call centers had little or no union presence. However, in Sweden nearly all were covered by collective agreements, with relatively good terms and conditions coordinated through pattern bargaining with established industries like telecom. I asked how this was possible. A union representative who worked at one of these subcontractors explained that the main reason was fear that if a call center remained non-union, it would face strikes or blockades. "If the larger companies are going to start outsourcing to a call center and the call center starts up and they don't have a collective agreement, it's a gamble for the company. Because they don't know—if there's going to be a strike here, our customers can't get the support."

This was a legitimate fear. One small call center company in northern Sweden, Focus CRS, was operating without a collective agreement, with very low pay and no notice period for dismissals or layoffs. In 2013, after a colleague was refused sick pay, a group of workers organized with one of the unions and sought to negotiate an agreement with management. The company refused, and the workers went out on strike. The Swedish media reported intensively on the strike, and the Swedish Minister of Industry and Trade responded to public pressure by denouncing the company's anti-union practices. The call center started losing customers and eventually closed. The union reps saw this as a victory, as it showed other subcontractors and their clients the risk of operating without a collective agreement in Sweden.

High bargaining coverage and strong bargaining coordination had also been resources for workers and their unions at the former state-owned operator Telia to stem the growth of precarious work as the company restructured. In one example, Telia set up and then sold a series of subsidiary companies responsible for business services and for installation and network maintenance activities between 2001 and 2007—affecting close to 11,000 workers. As a result, nearly all of the company's network and field technicians were transferred to subcontractors. These subcontractors then replaced around a quarter of their workforce with agency workers. However, unlike the case of Deutsche Telekom described above, these organizational changes did not involve renegotiation of collective agreements or a major change in terms and conditions of employment.

I spoke with one union representative who had gone through this transition as a network technician. In the space of a few years, she had moved from Telia to a subcontractor and then to a temporary staffing agency, which hired her back to her former employer. However, her pay and working conditions had largely stayed the same across these transitions. Her collective agreement with the agency required it to pay temporary workers the same salary as permanent employees doing similar work, and she received 90% of her pay when she was not working. Her union had recently negotiated a new collective agreement with the subcontractor requiring that they rehire their own redundant employees before bringing in more agency workers.

In 2015, a year after the Orlando conference, I was invited to UNI-ICTS's World Conference, at the Djurönäset conference center outside of Stockholm, Sweden. This was a very different environment from Orlando: a sprawling complex of buildings on a bay, with guest houses, saunas, and trails through the countryside. A colleague explained that this center was itself the product of the Swedish model of industrial relations. It had been built as a union training center in the 1970s by the Council for Negotiation and Cooperation (PTK)—a joint organization of twenty-seven member unions, which negotiates, among other things, an occupational pension plan covering 80% of Swedish workers.

At the conference, I was able to meet with representatives from different Swedish unions. Over lunches and coffees, I heard many examples of how telecom employers had tried to introduce more flexibility in pay and conditions to save costs—often seeking to play different unions off each other. However, the unions had consistently managed to present a united front, relying on a combination of militant organizing and strategic use of Sweden's labor laws. In one example, representatives from Telia talked about their battle with management to reinstate a program of retraining and job security that the employer had unilaterally terminated around 2008, while at the same time announcing close to 2,000 redundancies. This meant that Telia had to follow the national law on managing layoffs: in Sweden, you can circumvent these often much stricter legal requirements through negotiating a collective agreement.

Meanwhile, the unions worked together to fight against individual redundancies in the courts, arguing that management was not properly following the law. This brought managers back to the table, and the unions were able to negotiate a stronger agreement, with double redundancy payments and a strengthened role for union reps in overseeing retraining and ensuring due process. "So in 2011, they [management] were softer. They came to us and said, 'we want to do something, if you are interested.' We came together in the unions, all three, and said: 'okay, our only chance to get a good agreement is to stick together.' We worked on our side of the table to get a good agreement, we were always agreed on what we should demand from the management, and we talked with one voice."

In 2020, I interviewed representatives from several different unions to ask about recent developments in Sweden. They were again divided—this time over a proposed change in national employment protection legislation, which would weaken just cause provisions for redundancies in exchange for training investments, as well as over the structure and backdating of pay increases in the telecom sector collective agreement. One interviewee observed that both of these conflicts were incited by increasingly aggressive employer tactics to weaken social protections, coordinated by the employer association. As part of this push, employers were benchmarking pay between similar jobs in telecom and subcontractor companies, and using this information to argue for concessions. At the same time, the unions were continuing to work together to coordinate bargaining and political responses, to bring up conditions across networked workplaces. "Ultimately, our greatest strength comes from solidarity. We have this tradition in Sweden, and we have to hold on to it, even in challenging times."

The Politics of Restructuring and Conditions for Solidarity

These three cases illustrate the themes and argument that I will develop in more detail across the chapters in this book. They all follow a common trajectory. First, the companies restructured jobs in a way that downgraded pay and working conditions and weakened job security, often reversing decades of gains hard fought and won by workers and their unions. In each case, the workers experienced a devaluing of their jobs and work, as well as growing precarity. At France Telecom, this was connected to a radical restructuring program that sought to downsize the workforce through "management by stress" and forced relocations. At Deutsche Telekom, management moved service jobs into separate subsidiaries and the unions were forced to negotiate concessionary collective agreements on pay and working conditions under threat of further outsourcing. At Telia, management stopped following a generous collective agreement on layoffs and downsizing, bringing it into conflict with its unions.

As a result of these changes, worker well-being moved from a legitimate concern of management policy—and certainly a central justification for union positions in collective bargaining—to a more peripheral or contested factor in decision-making. Even union arguments that workers' job satisfaction, engagement, and psychosocial health were crucial to company performance no longer were viewed as valid in negotiations. Instead, managers reoriented their rhetoric to "restructuring at any cost," with financial concerns and shareholder value taking precedence over longer-term investments in the workforce.

These political dynamics of restructuring led to expanding precarity through substituting a market-based logic of exit for an organizational logic of voice. Benchmarking of labor costs, particularly with more flexible and poorly organized groups of workers, was used to justify demands for concessions or cost-cutting measures.

However, in all three cases, worker representatives also contested these changes. Unions and works councils were often first on the defensive. But over time they all moved toward organizing and bargaining strategies that asserted the value of worker interests: in a healthy and safe workplace free from crippling stress and job insecurity (France Telecom), in control over variable pay and working time (Deutsche Telekom), and in pay and employment security and equity (Telia). Companies' restructuring strategies were based on reducing labor costs to a number in a spreadsheet or a cost to be minimized. In response, union campaigns sought to change that equation and reassert worker rights to safe, secure, and fairly compensated jobs.

In each of these cases, success in contesting precarity was based on mobilizing worker power from three main sources: constraints on employer exit from encompassing labor market institutions, support for collective worker voice in management decisions, and strategies of inclusive labor solidarity based on bridging divides among workers and in the labor movement.

Worker representatives used power from existing labor market and collective bargaining institutions—or *institutional power* (Dörre, Holst, and Nachtwey 2009)—to fight to extend protections for workers across organizational boundaries or to improve terms and conditions for internal workers. This power was strongest in Sweden, where collective agreements and national employment protections established encompassing minimum standards that followed Telia workers as they were outsourced and gave them a long period of retraining before being downsized. In Germany, Deutsche Telekom's union and works councils were able to use strong co-determination rights to rebuild some company-level restrictions on subcontracting, while improving worker control over working time and reducing pay insecurity associated with variable pay. In France, a dense network of social dialogue institutions became more useful once the unions mobilized against France Telecom's draconian restructuring measures and negotiated agreements that gave them an ongoing role in monitoring the impact of management practices on psychosocial health.

Worker representatives also sought to build or mobilize solidarity within the workforce and across civil society. This often involved bridging past divides, including across different unions. Strategies of inclusive solidarity were the basis for strengthening *associational power*, or power derived from workers' collective organization (Silver 2003). At France Telecom, the unions overcame their own ideological differences to develop shared projects that studied and dramatized how and why management practices were harming workers. At Deutsche Telekom, solidarity across works councils representing different workplaces and business units was necessary to build a common organized front in negotiations. At Telia, unions representing different occupations worked together to negotiate sectoral agreements and coordinate bargaining across companies linked in vertically disintegrated value chains.

In the three cases, institutional power and associational power were closely entwined but took different forms, depending on the social, legal, and industrial relations context. For example, the unions at France Telecom were able to mobilize around a dramatic and tragic event in the form of a wave of employee suicides to gain widespread media attention and state intervention, and eventually to shift the internal politics of the company. This was based in part on using existing institutions in creative, new ways. French employers have an extensive system of workplace committees or works councils, but their actual influence depends on management's willingness to engage in social dialogue. In addition, France's laws and judicial system have established the principle that companies can be held accountable for work-related suicides, related to a more expansive view of the social obligations of employers.[1] However, mobilizing these resources required a coordinated campaign. Solidarity between different unions, among workers, and with the public brought concerns with worker health and well-being into the public sphere: it changed the conversation about the high costs to workers from the single-minded pursuit of profits and shareholder value.

The sources of institutional power looked different in the other cases. In Germany, works councils used their strong co-determination rights to reverse a trend toward increasing pay precarity, and to negotiate alternative working time practices that gave workers more control and choice over their schedules. In Sweden, high bargaining coverage, coordinated bargaining, and union rights to organize solidarity strikes and blockades made it difficult for subcontractors to operate without a collective agreement, and protected workers' pay and conditions when their jobs were outsourced or moved to temporary agencies. Strong employment protection legislation discouraged employers from bypassing union agreements: if they tried to get out of a generous but more flexible union agreement, they had to follow the stricter national rules. In both cases, laws and industrial relations institutions did not on their own change employer behavior. Rather, unions and works councils could use these institutions as a source of power in their negotiations with management over restructuring.

---

[1] Article L. 4121-1 of the *code du travail* requires employers to take necessary measures for protecting the safety and physical and mental health of their employees. This has been applied by the courts from the mid-2000s to hold employers responsible for suicides connected to employees' conditions at work.

Accessing them required a well-organized workforce and cooperation across different unions or between unions and works councils.

My more recent interviews with union representatives in these three cases show that fights to defend the social rights and interests of workers are ongoing. Their employers are global companies seeking to maximize shareholder value in increasingly competitive markets and with access to rapidly changing digital and AI-based technologies. This book compares workers' past experiences with negotiation and industrial conflict, as well as public campaigns to change laws and policies. It thus provides some lessons for the challenges ahead, as well as possibilities to re-embed increasingly financialized, liberalized, and globalized markets within our societies.

Methodology and Case Selection

The analysis in this book draws on a mixed-method comparative study of incumbent telecom companies in ten countries. Six are European "social market economies" (Denmark, Sweden, Austria, Germany, France, and Italy) with traditions of strong unions and labor market protections (Pontusson 2005). Two (United Kingdom and United States) are often described as "liberal market economies" with more decentralized bargaining, lower bargaining coverage, and more weakly regulated labor markets. Poland and the Czech Republic fall between these two groups, as former state socialist, "embedded neoliberal economies" with some social dialogue institutions but liberal labor markets (Bohle and Greskovits 2007). Within the European social market group, I selected pairs with similar national models, based on the history and structure of industrial relations and welfare state development (see Chapter 2): Nordic or social democratic (Denmark and Sweden); Germanic or neo-corporatist (Austria and Germany); and Mediterranean or state-led (France and Italy).

To trace differences in employment practices and outcomes, I focus on two major employee groups: technicians and call center employees. These occupations represent a large share of employment at the case study companies and have been the target of restructuring and work reorganization. They also have different skill and task profiles (see Chapter 4). Technicians typically have engineering and technical degrees or training and are responsible for network and equipment construction, maintenance, and installation. Call center employees at telecom companies handle mostly inbound calls, requiring customer service and sales training, broad product knowledge, and often specialized expertise in areas such as technical support.

The primary data collection and analysis were carried out between 2010 and 2014 by me, a research officer (Katja Sarmiento-Mirwaldt), and two research assistants (Chiara Benassi and Elisa Pannini). First, we analyzed changes in organizational restructuring strategies and their impact on employment and pay structures at all ten case study companies. In each country, we created a database of major "restructuring events" between 1995 and 2010—including downsizing, subsidiary creation and spin-offs, relocation or consolidation, and outsourcing. These measures were identified through newspapers and trade publications, company annual reports, the Thomson Banker One database, and in-depth interviews with management and employee representatives. We distributed a survey to union, works council, and management representatives in which we asked about the numbers of jobs affected by these measures and accompanying negotiations or social plans. We also gathered data through this survey and our interviews on collective bargaining institutions at each company, change over time in labor conflict, and pay structures for call center and technician jobs.

Second, we carried out more in-depth case studies comparing work reorganization and human resource management practices in five case study companies—one from each national model described above. These included TDC (Denmark), Deutsche Telekom (Germany), France Telecom (France), BT (United Kingdom), and Orange Polska (Poland). In each of these cases, we conducted twenty to fifty interviews, including interviews with central or business unit management and union representatives, as well as site visits at technician and call center workplaces where we interviewed local management, worker representatives, and supervisors. Interviews focused on the recent evolution of work organization and skills, performance management, and working time or scheduling arrangements. This allowed us to analyze key differences in the overall approach to organizing similar jobs and motivating employees within these jobs.

In this first phase of the study (2010–2014), we conducted 235 interviews with management and employee representatives, supplemented by archival data, surveys, and institutional databases. Interviews in Austria, Germany, France, Italy, Poland, the United States, and the United Kingdom were in the native language; in Denmark and Sweden, they were in English; and in the Czech Republic, interviews were conducted with the assistance of a translator. I later added 37 follow-up interviews, at two UNI-ICTS meetings and over the phone, via video conference, or in person to track recent developments in the cases. Thus, in total, the book draws on 272 interviews, between 2010 and 2021.

Structure of the Book

In Chapter 1, I explain the three components of my framework: constraints on employer exit, support for collective worker voice, and strategies of inclusive labor solidarity. For each, I summarize theory and evidence on how each advances the social regulation of work; and factors that are contributing to a shift toward more market-oriented institutions and strategies.

In Chapter 2, I compare institutions across the ten countries, particularly those affecting the telecom sector and incumbent telecom companies. Constraints on exit take the form of legal or negotiated job security protections and inclusive minimum standards via equal pay rules, sectoral bargaining, and transfer of undertakings protections. Institutional support for collective worker voice is based on differences in participation rights and structures, as well as mobilization capacity associated with union membership and rules or rights concerning industrial action. The dynamics of labor solidarity are most difficult to summarize "from above," as they evolve within each of the cases. However, I am able to map broad differences in the structures and rules that support cooperation (or encourage competition) among worker representatives, as well as the identity or ideology of the national labor movement and major union federations. Each of these is important for understanding not only the institutional framework supporting or undermining inclusive solidarity, but also the most salient divides within the labor movement. I describe four general patterns across the cases: structural inclusive solidarity (Austria and Sweden), representation domain divides (Denmark and Germany), ideological divides (France, Italy, and Poland), and structural exclusive solidarity (United Kingdom, United States, Czech Republic, and Poland). I conclude by outlining a model that categorizes the cases, based on the intersection of exit, voice, and solidarity in each.

In Chapters 3–5, I compare restructuring politics and outcomes in three areas: downsizing, performance management, and externalization. Chapter 3 focuses on policies for managing collective redundancies. There were often strong social partnerships at the incumbents around the time of market liberalization and/or privatization, with generous voluntary redundancy and early retirement plans. However, after the mid-2000s, management came under increased pressure to reduce the cost of these plans. Market liberalization, growing competition from companies with lower labor costs, and changing ownership structures combined with high debt ratios pushed employers to pursue more aggressive cost-cutting. However, the cases differed significantly in the scale and pace of cuts, the overall generosity of redundancy payments, as well as the form and outcome of associated labor conflict. I divide them into two broad groups, based on constraints on employer exit from internal employment relationships. Overall, where constraints on exit were stronger, employers adopted more social approaches to downsizing. However, each case shows change over time, as management sought to exploit loopholes and cut costs. Unions had success in countering these trends where they were able to build solidarity across their membership, as well as among unions and with other actors in civil society.

In Chapter 4, I turn to negotiations over performance management in four of the case study companies: BT (United Kingdom), France Telecom (France), TDC (Denmark), and Deutsche Telekom (Germany). Performance management can contribute to precarious employment conditions, particularly based on pay insecurity (connected to variable pay) and job insecurity (connected to fears of losing your job if you do not meet performance goals). Collective worker voice plays a central role here, as a crucial resource for workers to negotiate alternative practices. Based on a comparison of call center and technician jobs, I show that constraints on exit via job security and support for voice via participation rights and structures together shaped the performance management model. Where both were strong, management was not able to use discipline to motivate workers, encouraging a focus on training and development; and performance targets were fairer and more transparent. Labor solidarity again was in the background, as a source of worker mobilization and countervailing power. But it played a particularly important role in campaigns to establish pay equity and reduce precarity for the most vulnerable groups of workers.

In Chapter 5, I compare externalization strategies across the ten case study companies, as they moved work to subcontractors, temporary agencies, and service subsidiaries. Different institutions structuring exit options and giving workers collective voice in negotiating alternatives to externalization played a central role in both strategies and outcomes. However, the dynamics of labor solidarity were particularly important in campaigns to extend or maintain protections across networked workplaces. I thus divide my discussion of the cases based on the four patterns of structural exclusive solidarity, representation domain divides, ideological divides, and structural inclusive solidarity identified in Chapter 2. I first discuss employer strategies and union responses in each group of cases. I then compare outcomes for workers, focusing on union success in reducing or reversing precarity. Findings show most success in the "structural inclusive solidarity" cases. However, unions across the four groups adopted new, creative approaches to raise the costs of exit through legal or negotiated extension of minimum terms and conditions, and to extend the benefits of voice through organizing and representing externalized workers.

In Chapter 6, I summarize the comparative findings and discuss implications for theory, policy, and labor strategy.

1
Theorizing Exit, Voice, and Solidarity

This book's title and framework are inspired by Hirschman's (1970) classic book: *Exit, Voice, and Loyalty: Responses to Decline in Firms, Organizations, and States*. Hirschman argues that customers, members, or citizens respond in two different ways when they perceive a decline in quality or benefits from membership. First, they can "exit" or escape the relationship, through, e.g., leaving an organization, not buying a company's products, or emigrating from a country. Second, they can use their voice to attempt to change (rather than to escape from) "an objectional state of affairs, whether through individual or collective petition to the management directly in charge, through appeal to a higher authority, or through various types of actions and protests, including those that are meant to mobilize public opinion" (p. 30). Loyalty, in turn, affects the cost–benefit analysis in choosing between the two courses of action. If you feel loyal to an organization or country, you will more often try to change what you find objectionable or wrong before giving up your membership, looking elsewhere for a job, or moving. This is more likely if you expect that you will actually be able to influence policies or decisions and improve outcomes.

Hirschman's framework is an attempt to work out the dynamic tension between market and society. Economists have a bias toward exit as the ideal (or most efficient) market-based mechanism for expressing preferences, pursuing interests, or allocating resources. Citizen or member voice has traditionally been of interest to political scientists studying organized "interest articulation" and protest as sources of collective power and policy change. The addition of loyalty suggests that beyond interests and power, there is an ideational dimension of collective or individual action, which can affect the cost–benefit analysis concerning whether (and how) to use exit or voice.

Hirschman's framework is a useful starting point for modeling the choices workers face in an employment relationship—and indeed, it has long been a central reference in industrial relations theory (e.g., Budd 2004; Freeman and Medoff 1984). This book builds on this past literature. However, rather than focusing on the choices of individual workers to "exit" their organization or "voice" their grievances and ideas, my central concern is with the actions of collective actors: employers and unions.

Employers or capital have traditionally been better able to exercise exit options vis-à-vis unions or labor. Employers exit employment relationships when they dismiss individual workers, downsize their workforce, or shift work to subcontractors and temporary agencies. When managers benchmark costs and threaten to outsource work, they are applying a market-based logic that exit threats are the best way of communicating to the workforce (and their unions) the need to improve efficiency or productivity vis-à-vis competitors. When they actually exit, shifting jobs to cheaper contracts or locations, fears of further disinvestment likewise discipline workers, undermining the legitimacy of social demands.

Alternatively, employers can adopt mechanisms and policies that encourage collective worker voice, or "democracy at work," through consultation and negotiation with the workforce. This can directly improve efficiency, through applying workers' knowledge and experience to problem-solving and innovation; or it can improve performance outcomes indirectly, through enhancing cooperation, commitment, and trust. However, collective voice can also be costly to establish and maintain. Resources must be invested in institutions like joint labor–management committees or works councils, decisions require discussion and debate, and both employers and worker representatives must make distributive trade-offs to balance their respective interests and goals. Employers may make these investments in the short term, to diffuse conflict or encourage cooperation. But in the longer term, it is inevitable that restructuring pressures, economic downturns, or activist shareholders demanding higher profit margins will lead management to view these institutions more as unwelcome limitations on managerial prerogative than as resources. Thus, effective collective worker voice is more likely where there are formal, legal, and negotiated constraints on employer exit. This tension between the first order preference of employers for exit and of workers for voice is expressed well by Hoffman:

> Companies' decisions on saving, investing part of their profits, closing plants or transferring certain operations elsewhere have always been exit options that have enabled capital to adopt a stance at times bordering on blackmail vis-à-vis the other side. By contrast, waged workers/trade unions are often left with only the "voice" option because human labour entails individuals with specific qualifications, emotional and material commitments, clearly defined jobs, specific employers and/or places of residence. (Hoffmann 2006, 610)

The central concern in this book is with analyzing how these trade-offs between employer exit and collective worker voice are shaped by institutions, such as collective bargaining, labor and employment law, and state welfare benefits and programs. These institutions structure exit options or establish constraints on exit; and they provide stronger or weaker support for organized worker voice.

The third factor in the framework is "solidarity." Solidarity has some relationship to Hirschman's concept of "loyalty" as both are ideational and shape how individuals interpret their interests or find meaning in their relationships. Some theorists describe solidarity as a category of loyalty—grounded in a "non-rational sense of belonging" (Kapeller and Wolkenstein 2013). However, according to most definitions, solidarity is collective, while loyalty is individual. Solidarity is based on mutual identification among individuals, or shared feelings of trust and social unity, rather than the "upward-facing" relationship of loyalty an individual would have with an employer or country: for example, as a dedicated organizational citizen or patriot.

The term "solidarity" has a wide range of definitions and uses (see, e.g., Stjernø 2009). It is used here in its more political or relational sense, as collective action aimed at social change and grounded in strategies of mutual aid. The focus in this book is on differences in the form and content of "strategies of solidarity" adopted by labor, broadly encompassing unions or other worker organizations, as they seek to challenge market- (and often exit-) based restructuring strategies. Solidarity is also closely bound up with the dynamics of employer exit and worker voice: undermined by the former and strengthened by the latter. Employer exit can exploit existing (or open up new) divisions between workers, while collective voice can be a tool for bridging those divisions and establishing a shared agenda based on asserting the social value of work.

In the sections below I discuss the different components of my framework—constraints on employer exit, support for collective worker voice, and strategies of inclusive labor solidarity. In each section, I summarize theory and evidence concerning how each dimension advances the social regulation of work, as well as the factors eroding or undermining this role.

Constraints on Employer Exit

Employers' ability to exit an employment relationship with their workers—or their exit options—depend at root on the framework of social and organizational rules in the labor market. Employment regulation and collective agreements limit employer exit, establishing a longer term mutual obligation between the worker and employer based on social aspects of employment.

A starting point for understanding the dynamics of employer exit is to ask how and why the weakening of social regulation and strengthening of markets leads to downgrading pay and conditions—particularly for lower skilled or more easily rationalized jobs. The popular perception that the expansion of markets impoverishes social relationships is expressed by Rifkin (2001, 112): "what is left for relationships of a noncommercial nature . . . when one's life becomes little more than an ongoing series of commercial transactions held together by contracts and financial instruments . . . ?" In classical political economy, social and market values are often theorized to be in contradiction or tension. According to Marx's theory of alienation, the connection between productive life and social being is destroyed within capitalism. Workers are alienated from their humanity, because they can only express their labor through a system in which they are an instrument.

That contradiction might lead to revolution; or, more moderately, it may inspire movements for social reform. Karl Polanyi (1944, 73) argued in *The Great Transformation* that where markets expand, they are met with a countermovement as society attempts to re-embed the economy through social protections:

> To allow the market mechanism to be sole director of the fate of human beings and their natural environment, indeed, even of the amount and use of purchasing power, would result in the demolition of society. For the alleged commodity, "labor power" cannot be shoved about, used indiscriminately, or even left unused, without affecting the human individual who happens to be the bearer of this peculiar commodity.

A dichotomy is set up between commodification, or expansion of a market logic and relations, and social values tied up with solidarity. If left to their own devices, markets tear apart the fabric of society. However, treating labor (solely or primarily) as a commodity is not viable in the long run, because workers and other members of civil society inevitably fight back against this kind of subordination of social demands to market mechanisms.

Social and labor market policy are thus at root motivated by taming the excesses of the market and encouraging the "constraint" of market logics by institutions that reflect social values and bind employers and capital to society. When seen in terms of the employment relationship, this involves establishing a framework of rules that require employers to treat their workers less as a factor of production and more as members or citizens with employment and labor rights. Put another way, the incomplete labor "contract" is replaced by a public "status" for workers, made up of "a complex of rights and duties" and grounded in industrial citizenship (Streeck 1992, 43). Central here is a recognition that companies in search of expanding profits and guided by the invisible hand of free markets are not likely to provide socially optimal levels of pay, worker discretion or control, health and safety, leisure and family time, and provision for sickness and old age. Markets need institutions if a race to the bottom is to be avoided.

Constraints on the use of market mechanisms to govern employment relationships are constraints on employer exit from these social protections. One form these constraints on exit can take are social entitlements through welfare states—for example, social welfare, unemployment insurance, pensions, healthcare, and housing support. According to Esping-Andersen (1990), the ability of workers themselves to exit exploitative or unfair employment relationships is a key measure of decommodification, defined as the "degree to which individuals, or families, can uphold a socially acceptable standard of living independently of market participation." Where social benefits are high, workers are less willing to accept low-wage jobs and so employers are forced to raise conditions above this social wage. Seen another way, employers' exit options are limited where they lack a "reserve army of labor" who depend on the labor market to satisfy their basic needs (Engels 1845).

Employer exit is also constrained by labor market legislation establishing minimum standards: minimum wages, maximum hours, safety standards, restrictions on child labor, rights for paid sick and vacation leave, and employment protections. In most countries, these kinds of standards were won through social and political movements, often led by workers and their unions. Above and beyond these minimum legislated standards, labor unions put in place additional constraints on exit through collective bargaining and social dialogue. Collective agreements at workplace, company, industry, and/or national level typically raise the bar on minimum conditions, while establishing social rules and supplemental welfare arrangements.

Over the past century or so, labor unions have been the primary advocates and instruments for restricting employers' ability to use market-based exit to discipline labor. Beatrice and Sydney Webb (1902) developed an oft-cited typology of trade union action, arguing that unions try to control labor markets through three methods: enforcing their own rules on labor supply, collectively negotiating common rules with employers, and demanding government regulation of labor standards. Important to the success of all these strategies (and a key motivation for collective action) is unions' capacity to take wages out of competition by regulating and controlling employer exit from minimum standards. John Commons's (1909) study of US shoemakers is a common reference for understanding how workers' own collective organization evolves as they seek to protect themselves from the "competitive menace" associated with the extension of markets. Commons (1909, 68) writes:

> Defining the "marginal producer" as the one with the lowest standards of living and cost and quality of work, he [sic] is the producer whose competition tends to drag down the level of the others toward his own. It is not necessary that he be able to actually supply the entire market or even the greater part of it. His effect on others depends on the extent to which he can be used as a club to intimidate others against standing out for their side of the bargain. He is a menace rather than an actual competitor.

Collective bargaining or industrial relations systems were built through collective action, but they have been institutionalized through national (and state or regional) laws that establish organizing and bargaining rights, freedom of association rules, and procedures and sanctions for carrying out industrial action or strikes. While these institutions can be an ongoing source of institutional power for unions, they also represent the crystallization of power hard won through organizing, campaigning, and striking (Brinkmann and Nachtwey 2010). The history of national social welfare systems is also closely tied to the development of collective bargaining institutions. Welfare states may be more or less private, liberal, or market oriented, depending on the historic role of employer-provided insurance (typical of the United States) or public, state-provided benefits (more common in Europe). This is to say that institutions are not rational and individual solutions to specific policy problems, but rather are established by the tightly linked politics of contestation and compromise.

Exit is most likely to be constrained when institutions are more encompassing or inclusive. Bosch, Mayhew, and Gautié (2010, 91) give a useful definition of "inclusive" and "exclusive" pay-setting systems. In exclusive systems, "the pay and other terms and conditions of employees with strong bargaining power have little or no effect on employees with weaker bargaining power within a company, within an industry, or across industries." In contrast, inclusive systems extend this bargaining power and its benefits from the relatively powerful to the relatively powerless. This can take different forms, either through centralized and coordinated collective bargaining or a high national minimum wage. They share in common encompassing social regulations, enforced by actors committed to reducing inequality.

Shrinking Constraints on Exit: Liberalization, Financialization, and Vertical Disintegration

Institutions are never perfectly encompassing, and they are always bounded within a defined and demarcated space—for example, within a workplace, company, industry, or country. The opening up of exit options is associated with growing institutional fragmentation, or declining coverage of protections provided by the welfare state, labor market legislation, collective agreements, and even organizations' own pay and benefit systems. The literature discussed above suggests that the history of capitalism is characterized by a "double movement," in Polanyi's terms, or a dialectical process where marketization inspires movements seeking social protections from markets. However, several recent trends have accelerated the expansion of market-driven exit options, as well as employers' willingness to take advantage of them. These are usefully categorized under three terms that describe related changes in state policy, markets, and organizational structure: liberalization, financialization, and vertical disintegration.

First, employer exit has been most directly enabled by *liberalization*, or the expansion of market mechanisms in different spheres of the national and international political economy. State-led liberalization has self-consciously freed markets from more encompassing social regulation—or has opened up exit options within and across national labor markets. Governments that once pursued growth based on investments in public services and infrastructure, expanded labor rights and welfare states, progressive taxation, and counter-cyclical Keynesian macroeconomic policies have embraced (if with different levels of enthusiasm) "neoliberal" policies. These policies broadly are oriented toward reducing barriers to trade and regulation of financial markets and encouraging fiscal discipline through cutting government expenditures.

Neoliberal policies mobilize state power to enable more competitive markets, or a "market order" (Biggart and Beamish 2003), involving what Streeck (2009, 149) describes as a common trend "away from centralized authoritative coordination and control towards dispersed competition." They are enabled by reforms that commodify labor markets, through weakening employment protections (Emmenegger 2014), reducing the generosity and duration of unemployment benefits, enacting "work first" welfare-to-work policies (Greer 2016), and rolling back social entitlements, including housing benefits and state pensions (McCarthy 2017). A number of liberalizing reforms have targeted industrial relations: for example, restricting bargaining rights or strike rules; altering conditions for extension of collective agreements in a sector; or encouraging deviation from central collective agreements.

Most accounts trace this neoliberal turn in state policy and industrial relations to the economic crises of the 1970s, which led to the collapse of Keynesian macroeconomic management. The following shift to monetarism sought to stop inflationary wage-price spirals via raising interest rates and reducing government spending. Labor unions in the United States and Europe lost key sources of bargaining power, as rising unemployment disciplined wage demands, while governments came to rely less on unions' capacity to promise wage restraint (Scharpf 1987). Globalization of production, services, and trade further undermined labor's bargaining power, as employers' dependence on domestic labor markets declined—particularly for manufacturing jobs and then for technology-enabled back-office service work (Peck 2017). Newly empowered employers could threaten exit through disinvestment and offshoring or tie promises of investment and job creation to favorable tax, subsidy, and labor market policies. Employer associations began to mobilize their own collective power to promote neoliberal reforms, even in countries with strong unions like Sweden and Germany (Kinderman 2017).

A second broad set of trends loosely grouped under the term *financialization* has increased employers' incentives to exploit exit options, as well as to lobby for liberalization policies. It is tightly bound up with these policies, most notably the liberalization of finance and privatization of formerly state-owned services, from public utilities to prisons and hospitals. Financialization is most often defined as the increasing importance of financial markets, institutions, and motives in the economy. The source of profits shifts from productive (e.g., trade and commodity) to financial activities—through both the growing importance of the financial sector in an economy and the growing share of corporate revenues from financial activities (Krippner 2011). This shift, in turn, can change the interests (or perceived interests) of companies and governments concerned with accumulation and economic growth. Governments themselves are increasingly financialized, as state actors manage public debt and assets via financial market practices (Schwan, Trampusch, and Fastenrath 2021). Meanwhile, household debt and mortgage credit have expanded across the United States and Europe, looping individual workers and citizens into increased dependence on volatile financial markets (Johnston, Fuller, and Regan 2021; Krippner 2017).

One trend accompanying financialization is the growing importance of shareholder value in corporate governance decisions, encouraged by changing ownership patterns, the decline of "cross-shareholding" in many countries, and regulatory reforms, for example of accounting and disclosure rules and competition law (Lazonick and O'Sullivan 2000). Often companies themselves are responsible for designing these changes in corporate regulation via "quiet politics" pursued through political committees and insider lobbying (Culpepper 2010). As part of this process, financial actors, including investment banks and other institutional investors, exert growing influence over organizational strategies— either indirectly through their own threatened exit via disinvestment or directly through using their disproportionate voice as owners and capital providers. One way of describing this is a process of rent extraction, as financial sector actors shift income from labor to capital, driving up inequality within companies and across sectors (Lin and Tomaskovic-Devey 2013). Non-financial companies themselves get into the game through diversion of profits from research and development (R&D) and productive investments to financial engineering tools such as stock buy-backs.

New investment funds, like private equity, hedge, and sovereign wealth funds, have received particular attention for their role in subjugating "the interests of firms, their employees, and the wider public to the pursuit of high financial returns by a small class of speculative investors" (Gospel and Pendleton 2014). Appelbaum and Batt (2014) carried out a comprehensive analysis of the role of private equity funds in the US economy. They found that a drive to generate above-average returns—to service high debt loads or meet inflated investment targets—often has encouraged companies acquired by these funds to pursue cost cutting through downsizing, outsourcing, and offshoring. At the same time, similar trends can be seen throughout increasingly financialized companies and economies, as scarce resources are invested in increasing short-term shareholder value or servicing high debts, rather than making sustainable investments in employees (Cushen and Thompson 2016; Thompson 2013).

Both liberalization and financialization are particularly relevant to the cases discussed in this book, as the telecom industry has been dramatically reshaped by changes in markets and ownership. The liberalization of national telecom markets over the 1990s introduced intensified price competition in formerly protected markets. Shareholder pressure increased within privatized (formerly public or state-owned) companies. Investment funds, including private equity funds, have also become a major new set of actors in the telecom industry. These funds own significant stakes in all of the case study companies, and in many cases they have been key players, diffusing certain "best practice" restructuring strategies across countries.

This brings me to the third trend, *vertical disintegration*, which involves shifting formerly internal functions or jobs to subcontractors, service vendors, temporary staffing agencies, and independent contractors. Vertical disintegration can be seen as both a response to liberalization and financialization, as well as a key development in its own right that increases opportunities and incentives for employer exit from internal employment relationships. It can involve global value chains, with offshoring to tiered subcontractors, but also often occurs through chains of domestic vendors, particularly where employers outsource services like cleaning, catering, and security that are performed on site by different companies. Advances in cloud computing and algorithmic management are particularly important in facilitating further outsourcing of service work to dispersed freelance contracts in the expanding gig economy, and offshoring of programming and data analysis tasks via online labor platforms (Boes and Langes 2019; Kellogg, Valentine, and Christin 2020; Wood et al. 2019).

The vertically integrated corporation is itself a historical artifact of the twentieth century, as companies internalized a range of production functions and processes, shifting them from coordination by market to coordination by hierarchy or bureaucracy. Alfred Chandler's (1977, 1) study of the rise of modern business enterprise in the United States describes how it "took the place of market mechanisms in coordinating the activities of the economy and allocating its resources," replacing the invisible hand of market forces with the visible hand of management. An important consequence, according to Chandler, was a particular approach to growth, based on horizontal integration into different product and service markets, that served management interests in long-term stability rather than profit maximization. The vertically integrated corporation also was a useful tool for securing labor's cooperation in exchange for economic or job security (Jacoby 1985).

The developments discussed above helped to reverse both the pressures and incentives that had encouraged management to vertically integrate. Liberalization of trade made it easier and cheaper to offshore production, while liberalization of service markets encouraged lead companies in formerly public services, including in the telecom sector, to seek cheaper options for performing service work. Financialization, and the growing role of new investment funds, put new pressures on managers to demonstrate short-term returns, and thus to seek new ways to downsize and drive down labor costs. Outsourcing was seen as a way to shed "less essential" activities, often justified by a business logic of focusing on core competencies, or activities providing the greatest value to customers or investors. New technologies also played an important role. Advanced computing permitted inventory tracking and coordination across complex subcontracting networks, while digital and satellite technologies reduced the costs of moving back-office work to outsourced or offshored business process outsourcing (BPO) vendors.

Employer strategies to externalize work have been increasingly used to exit previously encompassing employment and welfare state institutions (Bernhardt et al. 2016). Large international comparative studies in the mid-2000s to 2010s showed that outsourcing often allowed employers to bypass minimum employment standards set by collective bargaining and labor market legislation, contributing to the expansion of low-wage work (Batt, Holman, and Holtgrewe 2009; Gautié and Schmitt 2009; Grimshaw et al. 2015). Externalization also can allow employers to develop creative strategies to exploit uncertainty concerning which collective regulations or laws apply. One example in the European context is worker posting between countries, which has its own framework of rules at the EU level (Arnholtz and Lillie 2019). Wagner (2018) argues that the evolution of this framework of rules has created "spaces of exception" in which employers use a temporary migrant workforce to avoid collective agreements and labor laws. Another example is the misclassification of workers in new platform- or app-based jobs. The actions of employers like Uber and Instacart to classify their workers as independent contractors, and to lobby for legal changes to legitimize this, has been described by Collier, Dubal, and Carter (2018) as a strategy of "disrupting regulation."

To summarize, institutional constraints on employer exit have traditionally been the means to bind markets to society—preventing the "competitive menace" of the market from infringing on social values associated with fair pay, decent and healthy working conditions, and secure employment. Interconnected trends of liberalization, financialization, and vertical disintegration have expanded incentives and opportunities for employer exit from these constraints.

Thus, a key challenge that unions and other worker organizations face is how to defend, establish, or rebuild more encompassing institutions. The main tools are through the other two factors in my framework: collective worker voice and inclusive labor solidarity.

Support for Collective Worker Voice

Workers may influence organizational policies through their own exit decisions; for example, by quitting or refusing to work for employers with low pay and poor conditions. However, as described above, most individual workers have a rather weak ability to use threatened exit as any kind of tool of influence. The alternative is to use voice to improve conditions—in Hirschman's terms, to change rather than escape from an objectionable "state of affairs" at work. The main concern in this book is with collective forms of worker voice. These are described using a range of terms and can take multiple forms, including consultation, co-determination, and collective bargaining; or, more broadly, social dialogue, social partnership, and economic and industrial democracy. Governments, employers, and unions have legislated or negotiated different collective voice institutions, putting in place structures intended to promote democracy at work. These institutions are strongest where they give workers formal rights to participate in decision-making and where they are backed by worker power beyond an individual company or workplace—for example, at the national or industry level. Under these conditions, collective voice can serve as a constraint on market-oriented management decisions through allowing workers to assert social demands. If "exit" is primarily concerned with the shifting interests of different actors—capital, labor, the state—"voice" involves most centrally their power relations: Who holds power in the employment relationship, and what tools are available to express different interests and negotiate improvements in terms and conditions?

Demands for strengthening collective worker voice are grounded in arguments concerning the social value of extending democracy from the political to the economic and workplace spheres. Seen this way, demands for collective voice are part of movements for broadening political citizenship rights to more ambitious aspirations for universal social citizenship. According to Pateman (1970), democratic decision-making at work should have positive effects on civic democracy. As workers learn to voice their views and engage with others, they develop the practice and skill of citizenship they otherwise would not develop in more autocratic workplaces. Beatrice and Sydney Webb (1902, 844) write in *Industrial Democracy*:

It is the supreme paradox of democracy that every man [sic] is a servant in respect of the matters of which he possesses the most intimate knowledge, and for which he shows the most expert proficiency, namely, the professional craft to which he devotes his working hours; and he is a master over that on which he knows no more than anybody else, namely, the general interests of the community as a whole.

Collective participation at work has also been viewed as a form of education preparing workers to mobilize and exercise collective power within broader social movements. Gramsci (1919) argued not only that the right to participate in workplace and community decisions is essential for broader dignity and equality in democratic societies, but also that this participation itself transforms workers' psychology so that they are more capable of exercising collective power. Expressed similarly by Rosa Luxemburg (1899, 45), using the Marxist language of class struggle, "Democracy is indispensable to the working class, because only through the exercise of its democratic rights, in the struggle for democracy, can the proletariat become aware of its class interests and its historic task."

Important to the notion of collective voice is not simply the opportunity to speak but also to influence outcomes: the employer "must alter policies in a discernable way as a result of voice mechanisms" (Allen 2020, 41). Hyman (2010, 12–13) writes, "It is common to advocate employee 'voice' as an expression of industrial democracy. In principle this is correct, but unless voice is effective—unless it yields concrete results—it is no more than window-dressing for employer unilateralism." This again brings in the distribution of power as an important factor underpinning the effective exercise of collective worker voice—particularly where it comes to look less like consultation and more like democratic decision-making.

Indeed, collective voice is most effective where it involves a substantive change in the authority relations between labor and management. This idea is central to most definitions of industrial democracy, including that given by Poole et al. (2001, 491): the "exercise of power by workers and their representatives over decisions within their places of employment, coupled with *a modification of the locus and distribution of authority* within the workplace" (emphasis added). That power is built through collective action and organizing. However, it is institutionalized through laws and collective agreements that establish structures for workers to participate in decision-making—in a way that involves substantive deliberation based on a more equal balance of power, and that produces concrete results for workers in decisions about their pay and working conditions.

Institutional supports for collective voice take different forms. Some of the most meaningful differences concern the strength of participation rights, the structure of workplace representation—for example, through works councils, safety committees, or union-based shop stewards, and employee rights to participate on corporate boards. Chapter 2 compares these institutions more systematically across the ten countries that are the focus of this study. However, some broad observations can be made on how these differences have been described in the theoretical and research literature.

The first observation is that while movements to strengthen support for collective worker voice typically focus on distributional outcomes, scholars and policymakers have also often argued that voice has economic benefits. Freeman and Medoff (1984) described collective voice through unions as promoting both improved productivity and more equitable sharing of those productivity gains, through opening a direct line of communication between labor and management. When workers have job security through collective agreements, they are protected from management retaliation when they voice concerns; and they will be more willing to share their shopfloor knowledge to make improvements that might otherwise threaten their jobs. A similar logic runs through the US "mutual gains" literature on labor–management partnership (Kochan and Osterman 1994), and particularly in research on partnerships from the 1990s to the early 2000s over adoption of high-involvement work systems (Appelbaum et al. 2000; Batt, Colvin, and Keefe 2002; Rubinstein 2000). According to this view, collective voice institutions help to overcome market failures associated with underinvestment in skills, poor information exchange, and incomplete contracts. As unions partner over productivity-enhancing teams and training programs, backed by job security and high pay, they contribute to creating more competitive organizations—underpinned by cooperation rather than conflict (Bamber, Gittell, and Kochan 2009; Kochan et al. 2009).

This emphasis on the mutual gains benefits of collective voice can also be seen in research from the 1990s that sought to explain the rise and impact of different national production models in countries characterized by distinctive industrial relations institutions. An early concern in this literature was with the global diffusion of lean production from Japan, and its adaptation in different countries as "post-Fordist" models of work organization (Berggren 1993; Dore 2000). In Germany, Sorge and Streeck (1988) coined the term "diversified quality production" to describe a production model oriented to both high volume and customized, quality-competitive markets, but reliant on a particular industrial relations system that supported high wages, employment security, and strong collective worker voice (Sorge and Streeck 2018). They argued that these institutions could promote more efficient and productive organizational practices because they encouraged not only "redundant capacities" in the form of high and broad worker skills, but also social peace and decentralized decision-making.

Employers gained competitive advantage partially against their will, via "beneficial constraints" that were established and sustained by powerful and independent labor unions (Streeck 1997).

Hall and Soskice (2001) built their Varieties of Capitalism framework on a similar kind of logic concerning the economic benefits of non-market institutions. However, they argued that employer interests were central to recognizing these benefits, with collective worker voice theorized more as a resource than as a constraint. Complementary national systems of labor market, corporate governance and finance, welfare state, and industrial relations institutions provided companies with distinct resources for coordinating their activities, and thus different comparative advantages in global markets. Strong collective voice institutions like those in Germany underpinned non-market coordination, encouraging incremental innovation in "coordinated market economies." Meanwhile, weak voice institutions like those in the United States supported market-based coordination, encouraging radical innovation in "liberal market economies."

Throughout this literature, and in more general debates about the "European social model," collective worker voice played a central role in underpinning and sustaining alternative economic models that sought to balance equity and efficiency. These models were typically promoted by social democratic or labor parties, with a strong base of support from labor unions—but often relied on cross-class coalitions among groups that had diverse economic and political interests. The literature on corporatism or neo-corporatism in Europe described the tripartite arrangements that developed at national level as a form of political exchange that was necessary to secure union cooperation with wage moderation (Schmitter and Lehmbruch 1979). Europe's small, open economies, in particular, relied on these arrangements to remain competitive in global markets (Katzenstein 1985).

Trade unions and social democratic parties in Europe have continued to argue that collective voice produces broad economic and social benefits, particularly as institutionalized through social partnership. According to the European Trade Union Confederation (ETUC) (2006), the European Union "is built on the principle of social partnership: a compromise between different interests in society to the benefit of all." Institutions supporting social partnership—coordinated bargaining, consultation, and co-determination—were established and strengthened by binding legal and negotiated frameworks. These not only encouraged democratic worker voice but also restricted employer exit from minimum standards negotiated at different levels. While they may have been beneficial, they were nonetheless constraints; and their social or distributive effects depended on institutionalized rules requiring dialogue and compromise.

Shrinking Support for Collective Worker Voice: Declining Labor Power and Expanding Precarity

The developments described above that have increased incentives and opportunities for employer exit—liberalization, financialization, and vertical disintegration—have also undermined support for collective worker voice. As exit options expand, employers are better able to discipline workers and secure labor cooperation through the stick that is the threat of exit rather than with the carrot that is the promise of voice. But more directly, employers can bypass established collective voice institutions, like collective agreements with unions or works councils with strong participation rights, through moving work to companies, industries, regions, or countries where these institutions are weaker or nonexistent.

Research has shown that the factors associated with expanded exit have also contributed to the erosion of collective worker voice. However, the frames that researchers use to understand these developments have increasingly diverged—with a focus on either labor's declining collective voice at the national level, particularly in coalitional politics between employers, labor, and the state; or the situated politics of organizational restructuring and concession bargaining at company and industry levels.

In comparative political economy, researchers study the political dynamics associated with declining collective worker voice at the national level. Their focus has been on how developments associated with liberalization and financialization have changed the power and interests of labor, capital, employers, and the state that underpinned different varieties of capitalism. Early efforts to theorize institutional change in coordinated models like Germany came from insiders in these older debates. Hall, Thelen, Streeck, and others argued that employers were finding less broad and universal value to worker voice as an economic input, as financial incentives shifted toward short-term value extraction and as they found they could still get the benefits of coordination through selectively cooperating with their core workforce (Hall and Thelen 2009; Streeck and Thelen 2005; Thelen 2014).

Baccaro and Howell (2017) have developed these liberalization arguments most comprehensively. They find different mechanisms of institutional change across Europe, but with labor, business, and the state playing similar roles in these changes. Employers are more confident and politicized in seeking to undermine traditional industrial relations systems, unions are weakening, and states are acting as "midwives" to speed up labor market restructuring. Howell (2021, 742) argues along similar lines that recent state intervention has involved "efforts to transform and reconstruct employment relations systems" and that state action is thus central to understanding why employer discretion has increased so significantly vis-à-vis unions or workers.

Baccaro and Howell explain this common neoliberal trajectory as following from the collapse of Fordist growth models, which relied on domestic consumption and thus had enabled some degree of compromise between labor and capital. One might say this compromise rested on the redistributive effect of strong collective worker voice, as rising wages and conditions supported mutual gains on the demand side, expanding the domestic market for products and services. As new growth models required either expanding exports, profits, or debt (rather than domestic wages), the interests of capital and the state increasingly came to diverge from those of most workers (see also: Baccaro and Benassi 2017; Baccaro and Pontusson 2016).

The above analyses are grounded in a certain set of assumptions concerning the collective interests of business and the state. In particular, employer interests in compromising with labor through accommodating collective worker voice have declined. Nation-states no longer rely on unions for the "legitimation" of economic policy (Culpepper and Regan 2014); and the redistributive effects of collective voice are seen as conflicting with economic growth under different post-Fordist growth models. Certainly declining labor power is part of this; but it is also tightly bound up with broader changes in the global economy that are beyond the control of workers or their unions. The structural advantage of business in democratic capitalism comes to the fore, and this structural power is exercised in an increasingly activist way to weaken collective voice institutions due to declining employer interests in cooperating with those institutions.

A second vein of research, dominated by employment relations scholars and sociologists, has focused more directly on the micropolitics of these institutional changes; or how organizational strategies have contributed to weakening the power of workers and their unions to exercise collective voice. If comparative political economists focus on the national political coalitions shaping liberalization and financialization, these researchers focus more directly on the company and workplace-level politics of vertical disintegration. According to this literature, one of the central challenges to collective voice is an institutional mismatch between the increasingly networked and international structure of capital and labor's traditional approach to organizing workers within national, industry, and company boundaries (Anner, Fischer-Daly, and Maffie 2021). While this is a diverse and often empirical literature, several insights are worth highlighting.

First, research has documented the role of employer-led benchmarking, whipsawing, or "coercive comparisons" in weakening workers' ability to use formal collective voice institutions to improve conditions. This takes different forms. One occurs within multinationals—which have increasingly centralized their human resource decision-making, and so seek to roll out certain best practices across their subsidiaries (Almond et al. 2021). Management can threaten to disinvest, or to locate a new product in a subsidiary with more compliant worker representatives, to encourage labor cooperation (Edwards,

Marginson, and Ferner 2013; Greer and Hauptmeier 2008, 2016; Royle 2004). A second form of coercive comparison occurs across internal and externalized workers, as employers benchmark the pay and conditions of their own workforce with those of often cheaper subcontractors, service subsidiaries, or agency workers (Hermann and Flecker 2013; Holst 2014; Jaehrling et al. 2018; Mori 2017). Peter Berg and I argue that this kind of benchmarking is often used to undermine unions' agenda-setting power (following Lukes 1974), or their ability to influence the range of considered options or perceived legitimacy of certain practices (Doellgast and Berg 2018). The legitimacy of worker interests in high-quality jobs declines as employers start negotiations with a bottom-line demand that workers first agree to be as flexible and cheap as subcontractors or subsidiaries. These demands are often backed with the credible threat of collective layoffs or transfer to a subcontractor if they do not agree.

A second insight of this literature is that changing organizational structures and boundaries make it more difficult for different groups of worker representatives to coordinate with each other, both within a company and across a production or value chain. Independent collective voice requires institutions that establish procedures for representative democracy within a clearly defined workforce. As companies themselves restructure, they break up the old boundaries and introduce more competition (or disrupt coordination) between unions and other worker representatives (Benassi and Dorigatti 2020; Doellgast and Greer 2007; Marchington, Rubery, and Cooke 2005).

At root, both of these dynamics connect declining worker voice to expanding exit threats by employers. The possibility of exit from collective regulation and bargaining arrangements can undermine both formal institutional supports for collective voice, as well as workers' willingness and ability to use their rights as a source of countervailing power. They are also both at root a challenge to labor solidarity, as they break apart old solidaristic bargaining structures and introduce competition across a more diverse group of workers for jobs or investment. This is thus a good transition to the third factor in my framework: strategies of inclusive labor solidarity. These strategies represent possibilities for worker agency, as workers and their representatives respond to a secular shift from the democratic politics of collective voice to the discipline-based dynamics of employer exit.

Strategies of Inclusive Labor Solidarity

The discussion so far has focused on the ways in which institutions supporting collective worker voice or constraining employer exit are bound up with (and can influence) the interests and power of employment relations actors. However, collective agreements, labor market policy, and welfare states were built through social movements, and are continuously being reproduced or contested. They thus have strong ideational underpinnings, in that they rely on the collective capacity of workers and citizens to define shared interests and mobilize around common ideals. The term "solidarity" captures these intangible ties within a group or society that bind individuals together. It is also a central principle of collective action, involving some degree of self-sacrifice to achieve shared goals. Differences in the "strategies of solidarity" adopted by unions and other worker representatives, to define these goals and mobilize workers around them, are crucial to explaining different outcomes in terms of building more inclusive social regulation of markets.

The term "solidarity" has been defined in a range of ways, used to explain the cohesion of groups, the development of social policy and welfare states, the discourse underpinning certain political ideologies, or the goals and tactics of labor and social movements (Blais 2007; Van Hoyweghen, Pulignano, and Meyers 2020). In classic social theory, debates over the meaning and function of solidarity turned on different views concerning the relationship between individuals and society. Weber (1922) viewed solidarity as developing within groups stratified by social status, as they pursued shared interests based on gaining economic or social advantage. Thus, "the feeling of belonging together is always associated with the exclusion of others" (Stjernø 2009, 38). In contrast, Durkheim (1893) described solidarity as playing an integrating role, distinguishing between traditional forms of mechanical solidarity grounded in shared experience and consciousness and organic solidarity where the division of labor connects (and creates interdependence among) individuals. These express different perspectives on whether society is held together primarily by relations of competition between internally solidaristic classes or identity and interest groups, or by relations of cooperation across classes and among citizens, ideally grounded in a more integrative form of social solidarity.

The focus in this book is on labor solidarity, which can be seen as a form of political solidarity. Political solidarity is defined by Scholz (2008, 6) as political activism aimed at social change; or "a moral relation that marks a social movement wherein individuals have committed to positive duties in response to a perceived injustice." This notion of solidarity as activism is distinct from, but connected to, classic concepts of social solidarity as the ideational glue binding or ordering societies. The institutions that underpin ideal redistributive models of social solidarity—such as solidaristic welfare states—were built through past "political activism aimed at social change," led by labor movements and the political parties they sponsored. Baldwin (1990, 31) describes social solidarity as representing justice defined in terms of need, or a movement from redistribution based on charity to the institutionalization of positive social and political rights: "La justice d'aujourd'hui, c'est la charité d'hier." Put another way, solidarity in a more general sense pulls together social and political solidarity, as it "implies a readiness for collective action and a will to institutionalize that collective action through the establishment of rights and citizenship" (Stjernø 2009, 2).

A central component of solidarity is shared identification, underpinning a commitment to redistributive justice within the group or society. It thus involves an act of political and social imagination, to identify the boundaries of a group and the qualities or ideals that hold it together. This has been theorized in different ways, including Anderson's (1983) "imagined community," socially constructed by people who hold in their minds a mental image of their affinity; Taylor's (2004) "social imaginary," based on how a group of people imagine their collective social life; or Hall and Lamont's (2009, 12) "collective imaginary," as "sets of representations composed of symbols, myths and narratives that people use to portray their community or nation and their own relationship as well as that of others to it." If identities emerge from imaginaries, these also contain "specific conceptions of social justice," while imaginaries themselves are constructed by past political movements for social justice (Hall 2017).

Movements underpinned by political solidarity thus both rely on and help to construct the narratives that generate cohesive collective identities. However, as Hooker (2009, 19) observes, this capacity to envision a shared identity is often construed in a narrow and exclusive way: in her analysis, taking the form of racialized solidarity. Political solidarity therefore requires some amount of intention, in building and sustaining social movements based on a discursive language of rights grounded in collective identification that extends beyond narrowly defined interests. Bell hooks (1984, 62) describes this more radical or inclusive approach in her critique of feminist movements based on similar experiences of oppression. Because women are divided by racism and class privilege, we "must learn to accept responsibility for fighting oppressions that may not directly affect us as individuals. Feminist movements, like other radical movements in our society, suffer when individual concerns and priorities are the only reason for participation. When we show our concern for the collective, we strengthen our solidarity."

This book focuses on strategies of solidarity that center on defending and extending the collective regulation of work and employment, and that are organized by or through unions and worker representatives. I use the term "labor solidarity" to emphasize the focus on issues of work and employment. Labor solidarity has been defined as workers' willingness to support collective action around issues relating to work and the workplace (Heckscher and McCarthy 2014, 629). Building on the preceding discussion, union strategies to strengthen labor solidarity require defining shared interests and identities in a way that constructs an imagined community.

Levesque and Murray (2010, 336–338) describe internal solidarity as a central component of union power, which they argue has two interrelated features: First, cohesive collective identities, or a perception of shared status based on cognitive, moral, and emotional connections; and second, deliberative vitality, based on the extent and quality of member participation in and engagement with the union. Fantasia (1989, 11) similarly argues that solidarity comes out of a process of mutual association, so collective action itself not only expresses solidarity but also creates solidarity. Solidarity seen in this way is a main source of union power and leverage, as the basis of strikes and mobilization. But it is also generated by strategies concerning how to organize collective action: whom to involve, what targets to focus on, and the claims or demands that are presented to employers and the public at large.

A central distinguishing feature of labor solidarity concerns how broadly or narrowly a union defines its collective identity, including the scope of its constituency and purpose. Exclusive forms of solidarity rely on a kind of Weberian focus on the particularistic interests of groups of workers, based on their occupation, workplace, and status. This may take the form of "business unionism" strategies seen as typical of the US labor movement, with bargaining strategies that advance the (perceived or short-term) economic interests of a particular group of workers prioritized over strategies that pursue encompassing regulation and redistribution based on social movement or class-oriented mobilization (Durazzi, Fleckenstein, and Lee 2018; Hyman 2001). It can also center on defending or advancing the economic interests of groups of workers who share certain social identities, organized along the lines of sex, race, or native versus migrant status and excluding those who do not share those identities. An example is police unions in the United States, which, according to Thomas and Tufts (2020, 129), demonstrate exclusionary solidarity "by constructing the interests of police unions as distinct from those of external groups, and by seeking to undermine the interests of such groups."

In contrast, inclusive forms of labor solidarity take up bell hooks's call for the more powerful or privileged to mobilize around forms of oppression that do not directly affect them as individuals. Lillie, Pulignano, and I described solidarity as inclusive where it can be redefined to include new groups of workers, particularly those whose social rights and position in a production process or value chain put them in a disadvantaged position (Doellgast, Lillie, and Pulignano 2018). Extending the boundaries of solidarity typically requires deliberate work to establish "a community of interest with the oppressed and exploited" or between groups of workers with more or less structural power (Arendt 1963, 84). At the level of unions or worker organizations—which are often divided by ideologies or by national, industry, and company boundaries—it demands what Greer and Hauptmeier (2012) describe as "identity work," based on framing interests and problems, developing shared norms and goals, strengthening social ties, and building trust.

The above discussion establishes definitions and forms of solidarity, but also provides a common basis for comparing union strategies across and within countries. Under what conditions does labor solidarity take more inclusive forms? Comparative theory and research suggest that two interrelated sets of factors matter: first, the way in which institutions construct the interests of, and coalitions among, different groups; and second, historic differences in (and divides among) union identities.

First, arguments focusing on interest construction attribute more inclusive strategies of labor solidarity to more encompassing union structures. These allow unions to bring together groups of workers with more or less power, or "core" and "peripheral" workers, into coordinated (rather than competing) unions. As Rathgeb (2018, 22) explains, encompassing unions organize more outsiders, and so incorporate their demands in "interest formation"; and they also give voice to policy demands from workers who are most exposed to precarious employment. Scandinavian unions, for example, developed solidaristic bargaining within strongly centralized and coordinated union federations. Groups of workers with stronger labor market power reduced their own wage demands to bring up pay and conditions in sectors, companies, or occupations with lower profit margins or skills. This encouraged redistribution from more strongly organized industries or worker groups to weaker ones (Erixon 2008, 51). More recently, Scandinavian unions have extended collective bargaining to cover temporary and other non-standard workers (Benassi and Vlandas 2016), as well as subcontractors (Sørensen and Weinkopf 2009), which narrows differences in pay and conditions. This, in turn, makes it more difficult for employers to use these differences to demand concessions or to threaten to relocate jobs (Doellgast, Sarmiento-Mirwaldt, and Benassi 2016). Put in the terms of this book, institutions restricting employer exit also promote more inclusive strategies of labor solidarity.

Second, historic union identities or ideologies can also make a difference for labor strategies, particularly concerning how unions define the scope and target of their efforts to strengthen social regulation. Hauptmeier and Heery (2014) describe union identity as principled beliefs that provide a framework for understanding the world and for acting accordingly. According to Hyman (2001), union identities are grounded in a tension between market, class, and society, leading to three ideal types: business unionism, class unionism, and social partnership. These orientations are tightly bound up with the goals that unions pursue, and particularly how they perceive the constituency for campaigns and actions aimed at improving working conditions. Trade unions can variously, and often in combination, see themselves as labor market actors (defending members' economic interests), as "vehicles of anti-capitalist mobilization" (contributing to more militant movements for radical social democracy or communism), and as agents of social integration (advancing reform-oriented social democracy that prioritizes social cohesion and improvement in social welfare) (p. i).

This notion of identity is related to ideology, though the latter represents a more formal system of ideas and ideals; defined by Budd and Bhave (2008, 94) as "a theory that is used to advocate and justify behaviors, outcomes, and institutions." Kelly (1998, 29) argues that ideologies are central to explaining why different unions are more or less militant in pressing their claims; but also differences in their capacity to mobilize workers around these claims. Ideologies provide "emotionally loaded categories" for understanding the employment relationship (e.g., in terms of exploitation or social partnership); and for labeling group interests as "rights." Thus, "the abstract ideologies that circulate in the labour movement—varieties of Marxism, Christian socialism, social partnership, etc.—are consequently of fundamental importance in understanding the concrete day-to-day behaviours of workers."

More militant and politicized bargaining aimed at bringing in or representing new, precarious groups is more often associated with class unionism, most prominent in southern European countries like Italy and France. Strategies focused on defending the economic interests of already organized or privileged workers are seen more often under business unionism, typical of the United States. At the same time, internal differences in union ideologies, within an employer, industry, and country, can divide labor movements and render the more solidaristic class orientation of some unions less effective when these conflict with a more narrowly construed business unionist or social partnership orientation of others (Benassi, Dorigatti, and Pannini 2019).

The preceding discussion suggests that identity, ideology, and construction of interests often are interdependent. Dorigatti (2017, 921) shows that union strategies in response to vertical disintegration in the German chemical and metal sectors were influenced by not only member interests but also their identities, with internal worker representatives more likely to support external or contingent workers where they understood their role more broadly as representatives of all workers. Another way to theorize this interdependence is through cause and effect: the encompassing collective bargaining institutions that incorporate outsiders' demands in "interest formation" were established through past social struggles strongly grounded in ideology or ideas about solidarity and its boundaries. The Scandinavian example again can be seen as a positive one where the combination of a broadly held social partnership orientation by the unions, underpinned by some degree of class consciousness, promoted more inclusive strategies of solidarity (Stjernø 2009).

For example, Berman (2006) traces the different policy approaches taken by the German and Swedish social democratic parties between World War I and World War II to long-held differences in ideas and the policy legacies those ideas helped to create. Many comparative scholars have attributed Sweden's solidaristic welfare state to interest-based, cross-class coalitions between, e.g., labor and farmers (Baldwin 1990; Esping-Andersen and Korpi 1984). However, Berman argues that these coalitions were possible due to the social democrats' flexible interpretation of socialist ideas, such as the compatibility between socialism and capitalism and the nature of class struggle. Jansson (2020, 14) further argues that the Swedish labor movement itself was central to this outcome, with union leaders constructing "a collective identity based on the reformist ideology" or downplaying class struggle in favor of consensus, and then disseminating these ideas to members through popular education.

Similar implications can be drawn for the labor movement in other countries. Leaders, officials, and activists decide whom to include in their coalitions, and how best to pursue a set of shared goals oriented around both members' economic interests and broader concerns with social justice. In Scandinavian countries, social democratic parties' ideas were articulated in close cooperation with labor unions, and in turn influenced unions' strong identification with social partnership. In a more general sense, cooperation among unions and other worker organizations, and developing structures to support that cooperation, ultimately rest on some moderation of self-interest for the common good. Put in terms of intersectional theory, more radical solidarity involves centering on the struggles of the most oppressed workers to pursue broader goals of equity and justice (Lee and Tapia 2021). This has traditionally been easier where the two other factors in my framework were present: constraints on exit and supports for voice. But solidarity itself, as a set of ideas or collective imaginary, is an essential component to building these institutions and sustaining them over time.

Challenges to Inclusive Solidarity: Divisions in Society and in the Labor Movement

The preceding discussion described the ideal institutional and ideational conditions that underpin more broadly inclusive forms of labor solidarity. However, as with constraints on exit and supports for voice, inclusive solidarity has become (even) more difficult to build and sustain—under pressure from liberalization, financialization, and vertical disintegration. These challenges mirror the factors discussed above that have promoted inclusive forms of labor solidarity in the past: the erosion of encompassing union structures and challenges to past identities in the labor movement that emphasized class mobilization or a broadly solidaristic social partnership orientation.

A first set of challenges concerns the relationship between union and employer structures and the construction of worker interests. As national labor movements become less centralized and coordinated, unions and workers that once cooperated increasingly compete. The competitive dynamics that vertical disintegration or fissuring introduces between groups or workers and their unions have already been discussed. Through disrupting traditionally coordinated union structures and dividing workers across production chains, these changes create new groups of precarious outsiders not covered by collective agreements and labor market protections. They also undermine the kinds of strategic and altruistic trade-offs that underpin solidaristic bargaining.

The literature on the dualization of formerly coordinated European economies has sought to model new forms of partisan coalitions or alliances. One set of arguments holds that trade unions representing manufacturing workers, in coalition with their employers, promote policies or collective agreements that advance their members' short-term interests in preserving their status at the expense of more peripheral groups: service workers, those on temporary or nonstandard contracts, and the unemployed (Palier and Thelen 2010; Thelen 2014). Hassel (2014) describes "producer coalitions" of export-oriented firms and core workers' representatives in Germany. Both groups cooperate on plant-level restructuring and social policy change in a way that drives up inequality through accepting the expansion of lower wage, more insecure jobs. A related argument from Rueda (2007) focuses on decisions by social democrats to liberalize certain parts of the economy while protecting the status and rights of workers in others. Fiscal crises and the need to attract increasingly mobile capital necessitate choices by once egalitarian and solidaristic parties and governments concerning which workers should be exposed to market-based risks. Thus, unions are complicit in driving up precarity, as they seek to protect their members in already privileged occupations or sectors (Eichhorst and Marx 2021; Emmenegger 2014; Rueda 2007).

This focus on insider-outsider divides assumes a certain sustained trajectory, based on deepening dualism between workers with more or less structural power. However, research has shown that short-term decisions by unions to prioritize the interests of core over peripheral workers typically lead to a long-term shift of jobs to lower paid, insecure contracts. In their analysis of the German metal industry, Benassi and Dorigatti (2015) show that unions facing deepening dualism often recognize this as a threat, and can change their bargaining approach over time. Liberalization policies in Germany made it easier and cheaper for employers to replace core manufacturing workers with temporary workers, while also putting pressure on unions and works councils to agree to concessions. The result was erosion in everyone's conditions, or expanding precarity from the periphery into the core. The metalworkers' union IG Metall recognized this conflict of interest and adopted new, more broadly solidaristic campaigning and bargaining strategies that both reduced the use of temporary contracts and improved conditions for workers on those contracts. Vlandas (2013) makes a related argument to explain why French unions sought stronger regulation of temporary contracts. Permanent workers were increasingly replaceable via these contracts, and so unions were acting in the interests of their own core constituency by restricting their use.

These analyses agree that changes in the structure of bargaining—moving from more to less encompassing—can divide workers and unions via perceived conflicts of interest. However, they show that in the longer term these divisions undermine union power, and so can be a kind of way station to more far-reaching liberalization of employment relations. Unions sometimes do shift from exclusion to inclusion "before it's too late." However, their success in building back coordination and cooperation is likely to be uneven, depending on the formal framework of labor market and industrial relations institutions. It is certainly easier to sustain or rebuild solidarity where bargaining coverage and union density are high (as in the German metal sector), and where subcontracted and service workers are already organized (as in Sweden), than to organize new groups of workers and collective agreements.

The globalization of companies and their value chains presents related but distinctive challenges to inclusive labor solidarity. A large literature evaluates these challenges, as well as union strategies to overcome them (Anner 2011; Brookes 2019; Givan and Eaton 2021; Lillie 2006; McCallum 2013). Reviewing this literature is beyond the scope of this chapter. However, findings are broadly similar to those in research on labor responses to restructuring within countries. Competition over investment and jobs and the way this is used by employers to gain concessions from unions or governments throw up difficult obstacles to inclusive solidarity. Unions that have retained some institutional power, in companies headquartered in the Global North that are more often at the center of value chains, may be reluctant to use their power to help workers in distant countries. While these are not impossible challenges to overcome, they do require a degree of inter-union cooperation that rests on an uneasy combination of recognizing mutual interests and committing political and organizational resources to campaigns tying together global labor movements. Thus, the challenges that unions and other worker organizations face in building solidarity within countries are amplified within multinationals and along their value chains.

The above discussion focuses on the intersection between strategies of solidarity, institutional structure, and worker or union (perceived) interests. A second set of challenges to inclusive labor solidarity is broadly associated with changes in ideas and identities, both within the workforce and in the labor movement. Two kinds of changes are particularly important to organized labor's capacity to mobilize workers around goals grounded in inclusive solidarity. The first concerns the growing importance of individualistic and entrepreneurial norms under neoliberalism; and the second relates to the increasing role of social identity as an organizing axis for social and political movements.

Foucault (1979, 226) described neoliberalism as resting on a theory of *homo œconomicus* as an "entrepreneur of himself [sic]" rather than a partner of exchange, "being for himself his own capital, being for himself his own producer, being for himself the source of his earnings." Dardot and Laval (2014) build on Foucault to theorize the ideational, ideological, and discursive underpinnings of neoliberalism. They describe the shift to neoliberal society as involving the shift from a plural character of the person to a unitary figure, the entrepreneurial or "neoliberal subject" (p. 259):

> Individuals should work for enterprises as if they were working for themselves, thereby abolishing any sense of alienation and even any *distance* between individuals and the enterprises employing them. The individual must work at his [sic] own efficiency, at intensifying his own effort, as if this self-conduct derived from him, as if it was commanded from within by the imperious order of his own desire, which there is no question of resisting. (p. 260)

Dardot and Laval argue that this dynamic renders power illegible and destroys social bonds via the ideology of individual success (pp. 290–291). Put another way, neoliberal subjects are likely to reject the collective identity and shared ideas of social justice that are the basis for labor solidarity. Again, competition plays a central role, as managerial or entrepreneurial states are subject to meta-laws of competition, while citizens shift from political subjects to consumer-citizens focused on self-interested outcomes (p. 254).

Central to these developments are changes in the individual's relationship to work and employment. In Germany, Voß and Pongratz (1998) described a transformation in the character of labor from employees (*Arbeitnehmer*) to labor entrepreneurs or "entremployees" (*Arbeitskraftunternehmer*) responsible for marketing their own labor as service contractors. They argued that this was associated with a new logic of corporate labor control, where employees come to view their own skills or capacities as a commodity, and then to see themselves as responsible for marketing these capacities. The result is a breakdown in the separation between work and non-work.

This theorization of broad changes in norms, rationality, or ideology associated with neoliberalism is relevant for understanding the challenges unions face in organizing around more collectivist norms that underpin strategies of inclusive solidarity. The ideas that workers have collective social rights, that labor is more than an input bought and sold on free markets, and that precarious (short-term and insecure) contracts are unfair, all are central to union campaigns to extend encompassing labor market regulation and collective bargaining. These can seem old-fashioned when set against ideas that celebrate the employee as entrepreneur—and are certainly presented in this way by companies and politicians resisting these campaigns. The recent struggles over the classification of gig or platform workers as independent contractors are a case in point. Platform companies contest efforts to reclassify their contractors as employees, based on arguments that new regulations will undermine these workers' freedom (Collier, Dubal, and Carter 2018). Meanwhile, organizations' own practices to manage gig workers as "enterprise-units" can produce consent among the workforce for precarious and non-standard working arrangements (Moisander, Groß, and Eräranta 2018). Other analyses emphasize the rise of financial, shareholder value, or globalization discourses within a wide range of companies and workplaces, which frame restructuring as the inevitable result of competitive pressures or shareholder demands, rather than a management choice that can be influenced through worker mobilization (Ikeler 2016; Rothstein 2022).

Another set of changes concerns the identities around which labor, social, and political movements organize. While most labor movements in the past viewed class, trade, or occupation as key organizing axes for solidarity, contemporary movements place a stronger emphasis on social or status identities—variously described as "identity politics" or new social movements (Bernstein 2005). One analysis in this vein is by Piore and Safford (2006), who argue that in the United States, the replacement of the old New Deal industrial relations system by an "employment rights regime" can be attributed to shifting axes of mobilization from economic to social identities and personal characteristics, particularly those associated with social stigma or discrimination. They put an optimistic spin on these changes, arguing that traditional collective employment rights are not collapsing, but rather changing their form and substance. On the other hand, Fraser articulates a common critique of these movements' more symbolic efforts to promote diversity and empowerment, which she terms "progressive neoliberalism," arguing that they obstruct more inclusive forms of solidarity resting on redistributive social justice (Brenner and Fraser 2017, 131).

This debate has at its heart the question discussed earlier in this section: How do labor and social movements overcome divides based on a narrow construction of interests? Historically, their success relied on the willingness of more powerful groups of workers and citizens to mobilize in support of the demands of less powerful groups. Researchers have studied efforts of worker organizations in the United States and Europe to advance racial justice and immigrant rights (Alimahomed-Wilson and Reese 2021; Pannini 2021; Tapia and Turner 2013). Many successful campaigns have used an explicitly intersectional lens that centers on the overlapping forms of discrimination faced by precarious workers who face amplified oppression due to their race, sex, sexual orientation, disability, and migration status (Alberti, Holgate, and Tapia 2013; Tapia, Lee, and Filipovitch 2017). The Black Lives Matter movement and mobilizations against police violence and for racial justice have been supported by labor unions and have been joined by union members in a number of countries. While this support has often been more symbolic than substantive, it provides a starting point for coalitions grounded in shared goals of social and economic justice.

The case studies in this book include attention to race, gender, and migration status only indirectly—in that call center workers are largely female, technicians are largely male, and in some cases racial minorities and migrants are concentrated in externalized jobs. These divides are most evident in union campaigns against the offshoring of call center work, which have raised difficult questions concerning how to both protect member jobs and act in solidarity with workers in, e.g., India or the Philippines who are employed by offshore subcontractors. However, it is important to acknowledge the role of social and status identities in the inclusive strategies of labor past and present—particularly the salience of race and "racialized solidarity" in dividing workers (within and across countries). The rise of far-right nationalist populist movements and politicians—seen from the election of Donald Trump as US president to the United Kingdom's "Brexit" from the European Union and the success of the National Rally party in France or the Law and Justice Party in Poland—can be seen as both challenges in their own right to more inclusive labor movements and evidence of continued deep divisions within the countries discussed in this book (e.g., Hofmann et al. 2019; Ost 2018).

The preceding discussion points to the interrelated challenges to labor solidarity associated with both the changing structures of unions and companies, and the shifting identities and ideologies that unions mobilize around. Traditional organizing axes appear to be shifting away from—or perhaps more accurately, diversifying beyond—class, industry, and occupation. While individualistic, particularistic, or entrepreneurial identities can produce consent, it is an unstable consent when not bolstered by concessions to workers' economic interests. The extension of precarious working conditions into groups within the workforce who were traditionally more secure can also change how core workers and their unions see their interests. This creates the possibility for new coalitions. These coalitions promise to be strongest where they are based on inclusive strategies of solidarity that recognize that "an injury to one is an injury to all."

Re-embedding Markets in Society

The above discussion has focused on the intersecting dynamics of constraints on employer exit, support for collective worker voice, and strategies of labor solidarity. In their more inclusive and encompassing forms, all three have been important and mutually reinforcing factors underpinning the social regulation of markets. Employment has most often been seen as a matter of negotiated rights resting on the socialization of risks where these three factors have developed in tandem. Together, they provide complementary tools for workers to challenge market-based employment and restructuring decisions through establishing a democratic balance of power within employers and industries, as well as at a broader societal level.

At the same time, labor movements seeking to strengthen social regulation face steep challenges, due to changes in the economy and society associated with liberalization, financialization, and vertical disintegration. In the chapters that follow, I show that these have had similar broad effects across the ten case study companies in driving up worker precarity and making it more difficult for unions both to sustain past gains for their core members and to organize new groups of peripheral or precarious workers.

A central task of the comparative analysis in this book, however, is to explain national differences, within similar occupations, companies, and industries. Under what conditions can labor market and industrial relations institutions be sustained or strengthened, to constrain employer exit, encourage worker voice, and promote inclusive solidarity? The answer is developed across the chapters in this book. However, the above discussion leads to some broad observations, which are central to the argument I develop here.

First, as argued by Hirschman, exit and voice can be viewed as alternatives. Thus, where countries have both strong constraints on exit and support for voice, outcomes will likely most closely approach the social regulation of work, containing precarity and promoting broad access to high-quality jobs. Second, these institutions both shape and are sustained by or built through labor solidarity. As described above, union structure and access to institutional resources can shape both their interest in and capacity to reduce precarity among their own members and to represent (potentially) precarious worker groups. Where these institutions are weaker, or labor movements more divided, the role of union identity comes to the fore; particularly, how unions perceive the appropriate scope of action, and how they seek to build coordinated and inclusive campaigns to overcome divides.

All three factors—constraints on exit, support for voice, and strategies of solidarity—thus complement one another and strengthen unions' countervailing power in contests over restructuring. The analytical task in this book is to compare union success in encouraging more social over market-oriented management choices in response to similar pressures.

2
Mapping Exit, Voice, and Solidarity in the Case Studies

In Chapter 1, I discussed past theory and research on three factors central to the social regulation of work: constraints on employer exit, support for collective worker voice, and strategies of inclusive labor solidarity. In this chapter,[1] I compare each factor across my ten case study companies, focusing on the laws, collective agreements, and representation structures that shape them. This requires both a historical and a multilevel analysis. Institutions and actor strategies change over time, and they are articulated differently at national, industry, company, and workplace levels. My aim is not only to present a series of facts on the resources and constraints that unions face in each country, but also to begin to compare the form and impact of these differences.

Constraints on exit take the form of legal or negotiated job security protections and encompassing minimum standards, via equal pay rules, sectoral bargaining, and transfer of undertakings protections. Encompassing regulation has been maintained or strengthened in some countries, with collective bargaining institutions extended to new companies and their subcontractors. In others, these institutions cover a shrinking core of workers, with new entrants and subcontractors or temporary agencies remaining non-union or following weaker collective agreements.

Institutional supports for voice, via unions and participation rights and structures, are closely connected with constraints on employer exit. However, countries also differ in the strength of participation rights and thus the capacity of worker representatives to participate substantively in management decisions. In addition, differences in union membership density and rules concerning industrial action or strikes influence unions' capacity to mobilize workers to assert these participation rights, to both negotiate strong agreements and hold management to these agreements. Democracy at work requires countervailing worker power, most basically grounded in a well-organized membership base.

---

[1] This chapter and Chapter 3 contain material previously published in a final project report coauthored with Katja Sarmiento-Mirwaldt and Chiara Benassi (Doellgast, Sarmiento-Mirwaldt, and Benassi 2013).

Exit, Voice, and Solidarity. Virginia Doellgast, Oxford University Press. © Oxford University Press 2022.
DOI: 10.1093/oso/9780197659779.003.0003

My comparison of labor solidarity focuses on national differences in two areas. One difference concerns the structures and rules supporting cooperation among worker representatives—or alternatively, encouraging union and works council competition. The second concerns the identity or ideology of union confederations or labor organizations. Each of these is important for understanding the institutional framework supporting or undermining inclusive solidarity, as well as the most salient divides in the labor movement. I then examine the role of these various structures and identities in the development of union cooperation or competition in the telecom industry. I describe four general patterns across the cases: structural inclusive solidarity (Austria and Sweden), representation domain divides (Denmark and Germany), ideological divides (France, Italy, and Poland), and structural exclusive solidarity (United Kingdom, United States, Czech Republic, and Poland).

The final section develops a model that summarizes how these three factors intersect across the ten cases. This model is the basis for comparing responses to organizational restructuring strategies in the following chapters.

Constraints on Employer Exit

National Differences

The ten countries in this study were chosen based on a matched pair research design, with two countries each from five different models. However, while each pair shares similar institutions, they also differ in important ways that influence the scope and coverage of employment standards or exit options available to employers.

Denmark and Sweden are considered Nordic, Scandinavian, or social democratic countries. They share traditions of universal welfare provision, established by strong social democratic parties pursuing "a welfare state that would promote an equality of the highest standards, not an equality of minimal needs" (Esping-Andersen 1990, 27). Social insurance is based on principles of social citizenship, with comprehensive public services financed through general taxes (Pontusson 2011). Both countries also have voluntarist bargaining systems, in which most labor market regulation occurs through collective agreements negotiated between employer associations and unions, rather than through legislation. For example, there is no statutory minimum wage in either country—with wages assumed to be regulated through collective bargaining. Collective agreements cover a majority of the workforce (82% in Denmark and 88% in Sweden as of 2018; OECD and AIAS 2021). However, as there is no formal extension of collective agreements by the state, the decision to follow and negotiate agreements is voluntary on the employer's side.

At the same time, the two countries differ in some fundamental ways. First, there is special legislation in Denmark establishing legal minimum terms and conditions for white-collar workers—the Act on Salaried Employees—which collective agreements often refer to. This includes a minimum wage, termination periods, sick pay, and a range of other minimum terms and conditions of employment. Second, a historic agreement stipulates that the service union HK must prove that at least 50% of an employer's white-collar workforce are union members before applying a collective agreement. The union is thus not able to strike or picket service employers who are members of the major employer associations until they pass this threshold.

The system of wage bargaining also differs. At the sectoral level, Ibsen (2016) finds higher rates of defection from pattern bargaining in Sweden than Denmark. At the same time, Denmark has experienced more bargaining decentralization and wage flexibility. In 2014, 81% of Danish employees were covered by company-level wage negotiations and close to a quarter were working under "figureless" agreements, in which contracts do not specify any wage increase (Ibsen and Thelen 2017, 419–420). In Sweden, agreements set stricter limits on wage flexibility, and were more likely to be centralized, with only 8% under figureless agreements.

Germany and Austria are often grouped together as Germanic, Center European, or neo-corporatist countries. They share conservative or Bismarkian welfare states, with social insurance connected to class and status via earnings-based benefits (Esping-Andersen 1990). Employment protections also follow a typical corporatist welfare state pattern, with strong protections for permanent workers and weaker rules for temporary workers. Different categories of temporary contracts, including temporary agency work, were significantly deregulated in both countries in the 2000s. Germany and Austria also both have social partnership traditions, with major unions playing a role in sectoral bargaining and corporatist policymaking. Similar to Denmark and Sweden, sectoral bargaining is based on the principle of *Tarifautonomie*, meaning that collective agreements between employer associations and unions should be free from state interference.

One significant difference between the two is that collective bargaining is more centralized and coordinated in Austria. Workers are required by law to join the Chamber of Labor (*Bundesarbeitskammer*, AK) and employers must join the Austrian Federal Economic Chamber (*Wirtschaftskammer Österreich*, WKÖ). The WKÖ and its sectoral chambers are responsible for negotiating sectoral agreements—and because membership is mandatory, these agreements cover close to the entire workforce. German employers are also traditionally organized in associations that negotiate sectoral and company-level agreements with unions. However, there is no equivalent mechanism for extending collective agreements to more poorly organized companies and workplaces. According to the Collective Agreement Act of 1949, the Ministry of Labor can only extend agreements when the extension is applied by at least one bargaining party; bargaining coverage is at least 50% of the workers in the sector concerned; and the extension is in the public interest and is supported by a special collective bargaining committee. As a result, establishing and maintaining sectoral bargaining has been much more difficult in Germany (Hermann and Flecker 2013; Shire et al. 2009), where bargaining coverage was 54% in 2018 compared to 98% in Austria (OECD and AIAS 2021).

France and Italy are typically described as having Southern, Mediterranean, or state-led models. They are often grouped together with Germany and Austria as conservative welfare states. However, state intervention in industrial relations and labor market regulation is stronger, and unions are organized along ideological lines. In both countries, multiple union confederations are involved in negotiations within a given sector, via parallel industry federations. They also are known for having relatively strong employment protections, though these are combined with multiple formal or informal opportunities to bypass the protections through non-standard contracts.

An important difference between the two countries is the method for extending agreements. In France, sectoral agreements are binding on all members of the employer association signing the agreement, as well as (typically) those who are not members. This is because the government, via the Ministry of Labor, usually extends the agreement to a defined group of companies falling within the sector. This has led to 98% bargaining coverage in France. In contrast, in Italy there is no state extension of collective agreements. As Italy's constitution provides rights to fair pay, and these agreements are used as a benchmark, the unions can bring individual cases to court to challenge employers who are not following the sectoral agreement. This may explain why the Organisation for Economic Co-operation and Development (OECD) reports 100% bargaining coverage in Italy in 2019, compared to 78.3% employer organization density (OECD and AIAS 2021). At the same time, Italian employers have broad discretion to "choose" the sectoral agreement they will apply—which can be a means of undercutting pay and conditions through joining a cheaper agreement.

The United States and the United Kingdom are often grouped together as Anglo-Saxon, Anglo-American, or liberal countries. Hall and Soskice (2001) coined, or at least popularized, the term "liberal market economies" to describe how multiple market-based institutions—in finance, inter-firm relations, industrial relations, and training—support corporate strategies relying on markets to coordinate economic activity. Their welfare states are characterized by targeted, mean-tested assistance and a heavier reliance on privatized or employer-provided insurance. Collective bargaining is decentralized and primarily occurs at the company or workplace level. However, the United Kingdom has held on to higher bargaining coverage, at 27% in 2019 compared to 12% in the United States (OECD and AIAS 2021).

Employment protections in both countries are among the weakest in the OECD, while both have below average statutory minimum wages. At the same time, the United States stands out for the prevalence of at-will employment contracts, allowing most non-union employers to fire their workers for a good reason, a bad reason, or no reason at all. The National Health Service in the United Kingdom provides universal, publicly funded healthcare services, which in the United States are typically employer-provided via an expensive private insurance system. A number of EU directives were transcribed into United Kingdom laws, extending certain universal labor market protections not present in the United States. These included a working time directive requiring twenty days of annual paid vacation and limits on the number of continuous and weekly working hours; and a directive requiring equal pay for part-time work. In the United States, workers have no guaranteed paid vacation or formal working time limits in salaried positions; and part-time workers often are paid less than their full-time counterparts and are denied equivalent benefits. Unemployment insurance and welfare support for those out of work are more difficult to compare, and both are probably becoming more similar in generosity (or lack thereof) following over a decade of austerity in the United Kingdom. However, the United Kingdom has a process in place to regularly review and update national minimum wages, while the United States has not adjusted its national minimum for over a decade (as of mid-2022); contributing to significant state-level variation.

Finally, the Czech Republic and Poland share a number of historical and institutional similarities, as former state socialist, Central and Eastern European (CEE) countries within the "Visegrád Group" alliance (together with Hungary and Slovakia). These countries had experimented with market-based economic reforms under communism, and preserved their more encompassing welfare states to some extent in the following period (Bernaciak 2015). Unemployment and health insurance provide a stronger safety net compared to the United States. Minimum wages are lower even than the federal minimum in the United States (based on purchasing power parity) (Adema et al. 2019). But both countries do have institutions supporting organized tripartite social dialogue at the national level. In Poland a tripartite commission was replaced by the Social Dialogue Council in 2015. At the same time, Bohle and Greskovits (2007, 445) describe the Czech Republic and Poland as having "embedded neoliberal" regimes, in which "social protection has increasingly lost its former purpose and institutional underpinnings."

The two CEE countries also have some important differences. The Czech Republic has maintained higher bargaining coverage, at around 35% by 2019—compared to 13% in Poland (OECD and AIAS 2021). This is due to stronger mechanisms for extending industry-level collective agreements to all employers in a sector, which has been applied, for example, in the construction, agriculture, and transport industries. Poland has some mechanisms for negotiating "multi-workplace" agreements, but these are relatively rare, with most agreements at the company level. Moreover, Poland has a particular loophole where employers in financial difficulties are able to suspend collective agreements and other terms of employment contracts for up to three years. Poland also significantly deregulated labor market protections in 2002–2003, including removing restrictions on fixed-term contracts, leading to an increase in flexible and non-standard employment. In contrast, reforms in the Czech Republic were more modest, maintaining stronger protections for collective dismissals and establishing two-year limits on fixed-term contracts (Sil 2017, 425–426).

The above summary describes some broad differences between national models that affect the strength and form of constraints on employer exit. The Nordic social democracies are typically thought to have the most encompassing institutions and the Germanic neo-corporatists to produce more dualistic bargaining structures based on industry divides. The Mediterranean state-led economies restrict exit from basic legal minimum standards for standard contracts, through strong employment protections and extension of collective agreements, while allowing significant deviation through non-standard contracts. The Anglo-American liberals represent the opposite model: weak collective institutions, heavy reliance on markets, and readily available exit options. Meanwhile, the embedded neoliberal CEE Visegrád countries fall somewhere in between, deregulating their labor markets while retaining some vestiges of their former encompassing welfare states and employment regulations.

At the same time, the comparison above also shows differences within each group. Sweden, Austria, and France have higher bargaining coverage, due to either effective maintenance of coordinated bargaining or formal extension mechanisms; while employers in Denmark, Germany, and to some extent Italy find it easier to exit or avoid collective agreements—particularly in newer service industries. EU directives, combined with traditions of more encompassing welfare states, have led to stronger labor market protections and a higher social wage across the European countries, including the United Kingdom and the CEE countries, compared to the United States. And even within the two CEE countries, we can see differences in rules affecting flexible employment contracts and extension of sectoral collective agreements, with stronger limits on employer exit in the Czech Republic.

56 EXIT, VOICE, AND SOLIDARITY

The comparison below will show that these broad characteristics of national institutions apply to some extent in the telecom case studies, helping to explain patterns in the nature and extent of exit options. Differences in bargaining structures and institutional loopholes have been particularly important for the development of sectoral institutions in a "new" industry. At the company level, unions have often been able to strengthen constraints on exit through negotiating employment protections for their members; but these are often at the expense of concessions where bargaining coverage is low in the telecom industry or across in-house and outsourced or temporary agency employers.

Comparing the Cases

Constraints on employer exit from institutional protections take two main forms. First, job security provisions, in collective agreements or national laws or policies, can make it more or less difficult for employers to downsize their internal workforce. Second, encompassing collective agreements or laws extending negotiated minimum standards to different categories of workers can make it difficult for employers to exit strong social standards when they externalize work through outsourcing or contracting with temporary agencies.

Table 2.1 compares constraints on exit in these two categories across the cases. Chapters 3–5 give more detail on the specific institutions and collective agreements referred to in the table.

Table 2.1 Comparison of Constraints on Exit (2010–2012)

Company	Constraints on Exit from Internal Employment Relationships	Constraints on Exit from Inclusive Minimum Standards
TDC—Denmark **Moderate**	MODERATE/WEAK – Weak legislated employment protections – Negotiated employment protections increased costs associated with downsizing; stronger protections covered former civil servants (35% of workforce)	MODERATE – Equal pay rules for temporary agency workers allowed lower pay if covered by collective agreement – 85% bargaining coverage, multiple telecom sector- and company-level agreements – Decentralized bargaining allowed wage differentiation in call center and other subsidiaries – Minority of subcontractors covered by a sectoral or company-level collective agreement – Moderate transfer of undertakings protections

Table 2.1 Continued

Company	Constraints on Exit from Internal Employment Relationships	Constraints on Exit from Inclusive Minimum Standards
Telia—Sweden **Strong**	STRONG – Moderately strong legislated employment protections, but can be bypassed by collective agreements – Strong negotiated employment protections (backed by threat of reversion to legal rules)	STRONG – Equal pay rules and high bargaining coverage for temporary agencies – 88% bargaining coverage, telecom sector agreement – Majority of subcontractors covered by a sectoral agreement establishing minimum pay and working conditions – Moderate/strong transfer of undertakings protections
A1—Austria **Strong**	STRONG – Moderate legislated employment protections and job security in collective agreements – High proportion of civil servants with very strong protections (60% of workforce) – Works councils have consultation rights over dismissal decisions	STRONG – Equal pay rules and collective bargaining for temporary agency workers – 100% bargaining coverage, telecom sector agreement – All subcontractors covered by a sectoral agreement establishing minimum pay and conditions – Moderate/strong transfer of undertakings protections
Deutsche Telekom (DT)—Germany **Moderate**	STRONG – Strong legislated employment protections and job security in collective agreements – Some civil servants with very strong protections (35% of workforce) – Works councils have co-determination rights over dismissal decisions	WEAK – Equal pay rules and collective bargaining for temporary agencies – 80% bargaining coverage, multiple company-level agreements – Decentralized bargaining at DT allowed wage differentiation in subsidiaries – Very low bargaining coverage for subcontractors, with no national minimum wage (before 2015) – Moderate/weak transfer of undertakings protections (Employer can switch to weaker agreement with same union)

(*continued*)

58 EXIT, VOICE, AND SOLIDARITY

Table 2.1 Continued

Company	Constraints on Exit from Internal Employment Relationships	Constraints on Exit from Inclusive Minimum Standards
France Telecom (FT)— France **Strong**	STRONG – Strong legislated employment protections – Strong job security in collective agreements – High proportion of civil servants with very strong protections (70%)	MODERATE – Equal pay rules and collective bargaining for temporary agencies – 100% bargaining coverage, telecom sector agreement – Majority of subcontractors covered by a sectoral agreement establishing minimum pay and working conditions at national minimum wage – Availability of offshore subcontractors with very low labor costs – Moderate transfer of undertakings protections
Telecom Italia (TI)—Italy **Moderate**	MODERATE/STRONG – Strong legislated employment protections – Moderate job security in collective agreements	MODERATE – Equal pay rules for temporary agencies, but based only on sectoral agreement (not higher-paid company agreement) – 95% bargaining coverage, telecom sector agreement – High bargaining coverage for domestic subcontractors, but they could choose lower-cost agreements and use cheaper freelance contracts – Decentralized bargaining at TI allowed wage differentiation in subsidiaries – Moderate transfer of undertakings protections
BT—UK **Weak**	MODERATE/WEAK – Moderate/weak legislated employment protections – Moderate job security in collective agreements	WEAK – Equal pay rules for temporary agencies introduced in 2011 but could be bypassed using pay between assignment contracts – Under 50% bargaining coverage, company-level agreements – Subcontractors not covered by collective agreements – Availability of offshore subcontractors with very low labor costs – Moderate/weak transfer of undertakings protections

Table 2.1 Continued

Company	Constraints on Exit from Internal Employment Relationships	Constraints on Exit from Inclusive Minimum Standards
AT&T—US **Weak**	WEAK – Very weak legislated employment protections – Moderate job security in collective agreements	VERY WEAK – No equal pay rules for temporary agencies or collective agreements for subcontractors – 17% bargaining coverage, company-level agreements – Decentralized bargaining at AT&T allowed wage differentiation in call centers with lower-tier agreements – Availability of offshore subcontractors with very low labor costs – No transfer of undertakings protections
O2 Czech Republic (O2 CR)— Czech Republic **Weak**	WEAK – Moderate legislated employment protections – Weak negotiated employment protections	WEAK – Equal pay rules for temporary agencies – Sectoral collective agreement— but low coverage (most subcontractors not covered) – Decentralized bargaining at O2 CR allowed wage differentiation in subsidiaries – Moderate/weak transfer of undertakings protections
Orange Polska (OP)— Poland **Weak**	WEAK – Moderate/weak legislated employment protections – Negotiated employment protections improved over time	WEAK – Equal pay rules for temporary agencies – No sectoral collective agreement; very low bargaining coverage of telecom operators and subcontractors – Decentralized bargaining at OP allowed wage differentiation in subsidiaries – Moderate/weak transfer of undertakings protections

First, *constraints on exit from internal employment relationships* are influenced most directly by legislated and negotiated employment protections. Employment protection laws in Denmark, Poland, the United Kingdom, and the United States were relatively weak at the time of my research, meaning that employers faced few restrictions on laying off or dismissing employees. At the same time, unions in all these countries negotiated agreements that include stronger protections for incumbents' employees (see Chapter 3). In Sweden, the Employment Protection Act included more strict provisions on notification periods and priority rules ("last in, first out"). However, unions and employer organizations at the central level could negotiate or approve deviations; and central unions were able to delegate the power to negotiate deviations to local union representatives—giving employers a strong incentive to negotiate these plans with unions.

In Austria, Germany, France, Italy, and the Czech Republic, formal employment protections for employees on permanent contracts were moderate to strong. Employees with regular contracts were difficult (and costly) to dismiss, due to notification procedures, limits on the grounds for dismissals, and high severance payments. The incumbents in each country differed, however, in the extent to which collective agreements enhanced these national protections. Several continued to employ civil servants, who enjoyed special protections. TDC, Telia, A1, Deutsche Telekom, and France Telecom all had a large proportion of civil servants in their workforce at the time of privatization, with distinctive rights and pay structures—typically including lifetime job security and more generous pensions. These companies negotiated different arrangements for transitioning civil servants to private contracts or allowing them to retain their status (see details in Table 2.2 and in Chapter 3).

Table 2.2 Civil Servants at Incumbent Firms

Company	% Civil Servants 2010	Changes in Civil Servant Status with Privatization
TDC	[36%]*	Civil servants lost their status, but kept pension (10%–15% higher) and right to 3 years salary if made redundant.
Telia	0	At time of privatization, employees had to give up civil servant status if they remained at Telia.
A1	60%	Civil servants kept their status across the corporate group.
Deutsche Telekom	35%	Civil servants could keep their status, but had to give it up if transferred to subsidiaries (with right of return).
France Telecom	70%	Civil servants kept their status across the corporate group.

* Percentage refers to former civil servants

Second, *constraints on exit from encompassing minimum standards* differed significantly. One important factor here was the structure and coverage of collective agreements. Across the ten countries, there was no sectoral bargaining structure in telecommunications before market liberalization because there was only one major employer. These institutions were set up between the mid-1990s and early 2000s in six countries. In Denmark, Sweden, Austria, France, Italy, and the Czech Republic, employer associations negotiated sectoral collective agreements with peak union confederations that covered almost all of the telecom workforce. In contrast, Germany, Poland, the United Kingdom, and the United States did not establish sectoral bargaining in telecommunications. This is particularly striking in Germany, which has a tradition of sectoral bargaining but lacks these institutions in many newer sectors, for reasons connected with both weak extension mechanisms and union divides (explored later in this chapter).

In Denmark and Sweden, the incumbents voluntarily joined employer associations in the mid-1990s, and applied agreements that were followed by a majority of telecom companies. In Austria, France, and Italy, all employers were formally covered by agreements—in Austria, due to mandatory membership in employer associations, and in France and Italy due to different mechanisms to extend agreements. However, across these countries, telecom agreements typically did not include subcontractors, which often followed separate industry or company-level agreements. In the Czech Republic, the sectoral framework agreement established certain broad parameters for pay and conditions, but detailed agreements were then negotiated at the company level.

In the United Kingdom, the United States, and Poland, agreements primarily covered the incumbents. Companies negotiating collective agreements, like AT&T and BT, had stronger employment protections, but were still able to fire workers for failure to meet performance goals. Subcontractors and temporary staffing agencies in these countries are typically non-union, with no collective regulation of pay and conditions. In addition, US, UK, and French telecom companies have broad access to offshored business services. All three countries rely heavily on their former colonies: India, the Philippines, and Morocco have developed particularly large BPO industries in call centers and information technology (IT) services, which gave incumbents ample lower cost (and non-union) options for relocating service work.

Union membership density and bargaining coverage in the telecom sector also differed. Figures provided by unions and other stakeholders in 2011–2012 suggest three different patterns: in the Nordic countries, the industry had both high union density (50% Denmark, 73% Sweden) and high bargaining coverage (85% Denmark, 88% Sweden); the Germanic and Mediterranean countries had low density (20% Germany, 30% Italy) but moderate to high coverage (100% Austria, 80% Germany, 95% Italy, 100% France); and the Anglo-American and

CEE countries had low coverage with low density (~15% United States, 10% Czech Republic, 20% Poland).[2]

Equal treatment rules and bargaining arrangements for agency workers could further affect ease of exit from minimum standards. The United States had no framework of equal treatment legislation, which distinguished it from all nine EU countries. EU Directive 2008/104 required equal treatment of temporary agency workers with respect to "basic working and employment conditions." However, it gave governments the ability to implement exceptions; and the "Swedish derogation" allowed agency workers employed under open-ended contracts who were paid between assignments to be exempted from equal pay rules. In most countries the principle of equal treatment could also be derogated based on a collective agreement.

Thus, the strength of negotiated and legal protections varied across the European countries based on how the directive was transcribed into national law, and on the bargaining arrangements in place for agency workers. In Sweden and Denmark, collective bargaining provided relatively encompassing protection of agency workers due to both high coverage and high union membership rates (Benassi and Vlandas 2016). The more fragmented bargaining system in Germany opened more possibilities for deviation via exemptions through "agency-specific" collective agreements—which were negotiated with the German Trade Union Confederation (DGB). In Austria, the sectoral agreement for temporary agencies was encompassing and was negotiated with the Union of Private Sector Employees, Printing, Journalism, and Paper (GPA-djp—from 2020 *Gewerkschaft GPA*). In Italy, the three major union confederations established unions for atypical workers, which signed a collective agreement for temporary agency workers; while in France, the unions relied on stronger legal protections and incorporation of agency workers under established agreements.

The United Kingdom represents an interesting case, in which agency workers had relatively weak protections prior to the Agency Workers Regulations 2010. This legislation included the "Swedish Derogation" discussed above, which allowed an opt out of equal pay rules if workers are given a permanent contract and are paid between assignments. As I will discuss in Chapter 5, this constituted a significant loophole that allowed agency workers at BT to be paid at a lower rate than permanent workers. From April 2020, workers employed on a "pay between assignments" contract were entitled to pay parity with directly hired employees, but only after 12 weeks on the job.

---

[2] Sources: European countries: estimates by union representatives (2011–2012); United States: 2012 data from the Current Population survey, "Wired telecommunications carriers" and "Other telecommunications services," Hirsch & MacPherson (2013). Union density figures were not available for Austria, France, and the United Kingdom; bargaining coverage figures were not available for the United Kingdom, Czech Republic, or Poland.

In addition, across Europe, the EU Acquired Rights Directive required member states to pass laws safeguarding employee rights during transfers of undertakings, businesses, or parts of businesses, including rules that collective agreements continue to apply for at least a year. The strength and scope of legal requirements differed, with weaker rules in the United Kingdom and CEE countries, and stronger employee rights to consult over the transfer, or contest "equivalence" of conditions, in Sweden, Denmark, Germany, Austria, France, and Italy. Each country also had its own loopholes. For example, in Germany, employers could bypass the requirement to retain employees' former collective agreement terms for one year where they were being transferred to a different agreement negotiated by the same union. This was particularly important for the Deutsche Telekom case, as the service union ver.di had a separate call center agreement, with lower pay and conditions, than its telecom agreements. US employers are not subject to these kinds of transfer of undertakings rules, and thus any protections came out of collective agreements and bargaining strength.

Summary

In sum, legal and negotiated *constraints on employer exit* varied along different dimensions, which are relevant for different restructuring strategies analyzed in this book. Table 2.2 presents a summary and rough classification of the overall strength of constraints on exit across the case study companies, ranging from strong at Telia, A1, and France Telecom; to moderate at TDC, Deutsche Telekom, and Telecom Italia; and weak at AT&T, BT, O2 Czech Republic, and Orange Polska. In general, we can say that where constraints on exit are moderate or low, employers are more likely to either take advantage of these exit options, through downsizing and/or moving work to cheaper subcontractors and agency contracts; or to use benchmarking to win concessions from their unions. At the same time, their willingness and ability to do so will also be affected by institutions supporting worker voice—which is the focus of the next section.

Support for Collective Worker Voice

As discussed in Chapter 1, democracy at work is most directly enabled by laws providing workers with legal bargaining and participation rights, supported by strong structures of workplace representation and union organization. At the same time, worker representatives are better able to use these rights and structures where they are backed by a well-organized and educated membership.

Put another way, legal rights encouraging collective worker voice are more effective where workers are willing and able to exercise these rights. Below I discuss differences in these two forms of support for voice across the countries and case study companies.

Participation Rights and Structures

Participation rights and structures differ most significantly at the national level—because they are rooted in laws establishing the organizational structure of collective bargaining and rights to information, consultation, and participation in decision-making.

First, the ten countries differ in their *structure of workplace representation*, for example, through works councils, local union representatives, and shop stewards; and the consultation or co-determination rights attached to these bodies. Denmark and Sweden both have a "single channel" system of workplace representation, in contrast to Germany's "dual channel" system—meaning workplace representatives are typically not independent from the unions. Sweden's Co-determination Act (*Medbestämmandelagen*, MBL) of 1976 "obliges employers bound by collective agreements to consult with the trade unions on all important changes in their organizations or in the labour relations of their workers" (Diedrich and Bergström 2006, 5). However, Sweden does not have a system of statutory works councils, with workplace representation carried out by unions on the basis of these legal rights.

In Denmark, in contrast, there is a system of parity-based works councils or "cooperation committees" (*Samarbejdsudvalg*) whose representatives are elected by the workforce. These secure local representation for the unions, ensure a link between central and local levels, and give shop stewards a role in management decision-making during peace periods between collective agreement negotiations. However, works councils' participation rights are limited to "information and consultation" rather than co-determination. The establishment of a works council is only required if the employer or employees request it, in companies with more than thirty-five employees that are covered by a collective agreement.

In both Sweden and Denmark, unions have primary responsibility for formal negotiations with employers at the company level, within a framework established at sectoral and national levels. National agreements define the framework of roles and responsibilities for unions and employers or the "social partners." At the sectoral level, general agreements establish rules on working time and minimum levels or minimum percentage increases in pay, which then set parameters for local collective agreements. Collective bargaining addresses a range of topics, including flexible working hours and vocational or further training—two issues that are particularly important in the telecom case studies. Pensions, vacation, and sick leave are governed by regulations and collective agreements.

Austria and Germany both have dual systems, with unions that are involved in sectoral and company bargaining, as well as independent company- and workplace-level works councils (*Betriebsräte*). Works councils are formally independent from unions; however, in practice works councilors often are union members and coordinate closely with labor unions, recruiting union members and playing an active role in union campaigns.

In both countries, works councils are elected by the workforce in workplaces with over five employees, and have responsibility for consulting over certain management decisions as well as for negotiating formal works agreements (*Betriebsvereinbarungen*). One important difference is that in Germany, there are often parallel union structures at company and workplace levels, with *Vertrauensleute* playing a role that is something like shop stewards in other countries. In Austria, it is more unusual to have a separate union structure, due to the greater importance of coordinated sectoral bargaining. In addition, Austria has separate works councils for blue- and white-collar workers, while Germany does not. Works councils in both countries have strong co-determination and veto rights, particularly over the introduction of monitoring, discipline, firing decisions, variable pay, and scheduling practices.

France and Italy have more significant differences in the structure of workplace representation. In France, local negotiations or consultations traditionally occurred through union delegates appointed by unions; and elected employee delegates responsible for grievances (*délégué du personnel*, DP), works councils responsible for information and consultation (*comité d'entreprise*, CE), and health and safety committees (*comité d'hygiène, de sécurité et des conditions de travail*, CHSCT). From 2017, new legislation required these bodies to merge into a social and economic committee (*comité social et économique*, CSE).

Different combinations of these workplace representatives were nearly universally present in large French employers at the time of my research. In 2010–2011, 59% of private-sector workplaces with fifty or more employees had both elected representatives and trade union delegates, 40% had just elected representatives, and 70% had a health and safety committee (Pignoni and Raynaud 2013). One important role of these local bodies is to determine the level of employee support for different unions, as union membership itself is very low in France. Company-level union agreements could only be signed by a representative trade union with at least 10% employee support in elections for workplace representatives.[3]

---

[3] From 2010 it was possible for a company with less than 200 employees with no union delegate to negotiate agreements with its employee representatives or employees chosen by the union (modified in 2015 to give precedence to union-mandated employees).

French employers are required not only to fund meetings and contribute to works councils' cultural or social budgets, with often considerable organizational resources devoted to staff time and salaries, but also to hire consultants to carry out research demanded by worker representatives. While works councils have weak formal bargaining rights, with most playing predominantly a consultation role, this can vary depending on union strength and the degree of employer resistance or cooperation. Béthoux and Mias (2021) found that social dialogue practices and outcomes varied significantly across the French companies they studied, due to differences in how local management and unions reacted to similar legal requirements.

In Italy, workplace representation is "single channel," with local representatives connected to the unions. This can either take the form of unitary workplace union structures (*Rappresentanza Sindacale Unitaria*, RSU), elected by workers based on union lists, or company workplace union structures (*Rappresentanza Sindacale Aziendale*, RSA), which are basically union bodies representing each union present in a workplace. Similar to France, elections for these bodies provide a measure of the support in the workforce for different union confederations and help to establish whether they are "representative" for purposes of signing agreements. However, their role is more simply and directly to act as representatives of the trade unions at the local level, and so they do have more formal rights to negotiate binding agreements covering their workplace. At the same time, most of their information and consultation rights depend on collective agreements—and so can differ across companies and industries.

In the United States and the United Kingdom, workplace representation is typically synonymous with collective bargaining. Local union representatives or shop stewards are responsible for negotiating and enforcing formal collective agreements at company and workplace levels. In the United States, collective bargaining traditionally has been organized through a more formal legal framework. Unions are recognized through a certification election overseen by the National Labor Relations Board (NLRB), and based on a bargaining unit determined by the NLRB. Legal bargaining rights are also limited: if a union is certified, the union and employer must bargain "in good faith" about a clearly defined, and quite limited, set of issues relating to wages, hours, and other terms and conditions of employment.

The United Kingdom has traditionally had a voluntarist system, with limited state involvement in bargaining; though legislation in 1999 introduced a statutory procedure for recognizing a union where a majority of employees in a bargaining unit are either union members or vote for the union in a ballot. Unions and workers have formal information and consultation rights on a wider range of topics than in the United States, including on redundancies and transfer of undertakings. These rights were strengthened by new laws or policies adopted in the 2000s to 2010s, to implement EU directives. There are also procedures for introducing joint consultative committees or works councils, but these are still relatively rare.

Finally, the Czech Republic and Poland have broadly similar workplace institutions. Collective bargaining with unions (where it exists) is the main form of local representation. Unions have broader consultation rights compared to those in the United States or even the United Kingdom; but these are strongest in the Czech Republic—covering, for example, work organization, pay and appraisal systems, and training. The Czech Republic also requires unions and employers to come to agreement on changes to work rules or regulations.

Works councils were introduced in the mid-2000s to comply with EU directives. These bodies became more common in Poland than in the Czech Republic, where rules for establishing them were complex, and they were not allowed in companies with union representation (Skorupińska 2018). In both countries, trade unions often saw works councils as competitors; this was exacerbated by legislation in Poland that allowed for some duplication of consultation roles between the two.

Second, the ten countries differ in worker rights to *representation on corporate boards*. These differences can be summarized more succinctly. Italy, the United Kingdom, and the United States have no legislation or formal arrangements enabling or requiring board-level representation. The Czech Republic and Poland limit board-level representation to mostly state-owned companies (though until 2014 these rights extended to private companies in the Czech Republic). The other countries have formal board-level participation rights, but they differ in thresholds and proportion of seats held by employee representatives. For example, in Sweden, companies must have at least twenty-five employees to trigger the election of employees to one-third of board seats; while in France (at the time of my research), the threshold was 1,000 employees for one-twelfth of seats. These differences are summarized in Table 2.4 later in the chapter. Of course, selection procedures, the form of board representation (single or two-tier), and their rights and responsibilities also differ. However, for purposes of this study, the most relevant difference is whether there is an institutionalized structure for worker representatives to participate in, or be systematically informed about, corporate decisions and strategies at this level.

National institutions translate directly into differences across the cases in *participation rights and structures*. The second column of Table 2.3 summarizes these differences.

Works councils at Deutsche Telekom and then at A1 had the strongest codetermination rights, giving them potentially significant influence over management decisions in areas such as the design of variable pay, working time rules, and the implementation of new technology. Board-level participation rights are

Table 2.3 Comparison of Support for Collective Worker Voice

Company	Participation Rights and Structures	Union Mobilization Resources
TDC— Denmark **Strong**	MODERATE-STRONG – *Samarbejdsudvalg* (cooperation committees) have consultation rights – Strong union bargaining rights and roles – Board level: one-third of seats where >35 employees—TDC: 4 elected employee representatives on 10-person board	STRONG – Solidarity strikes, blockades, boycotts allowed; peace obligation between negotiations; moderate/high strike rates – Union membership ~67% (national); 50% (telecom industry); 75% (TDC) – TDC: moderate use of strikes; wildcat strikes common—but at industry level strikes restricted by white-collar "50% rule"
Telia— Sweden **Strong**	MODERATE-STRONG – No works councils; shop stewards have consultation roles – Strong union bargaining rights and roles – Board level: 2–3 members or around one-third of seats where >25 employees—Telia: 3 employee/union representatives on 12-person board	STRONG – Solidarity strikes, blockades, boycotts allowed; peace obligation between negotiations; low strike rates – Union membership ~65% (national); 73% (telecom industry); 85% (Telia) – Telia: low use of strikes; no wildcat strikes—but strike threat more credible in telecom and subcontractor sectors compared to Denmark
A1— Austria **Strong**	STRONG – *Betriebsräte* (works councils) have strong consultation and co-determination rights – Strong union bargaining rights and roles – Board level: one-third of seats where >300 employees—A1: 4 members delegated by A1 works council; 1 member delegated by A1 trade unions on 15-person board	MODERATE-STRONG – Solidarity strikes usually illegal; civil servants not allowed to strike; warning strikes common; peace obligation between negotiations; low strike rates – Union membership ~28% (national); 65% (A1) – A1: low use of strikes
Deutsche Telekom— Germany **Strong**	STRONG – *Betriebsräte* (works councils) have very strong consultation and co-determination rights with veto across a wide range of management areas – Strong union bargaining rights and roles – Board level: one-third of seats where 500–2,000 employees; one-half (less 1 management Chairman) where >2,000—DT: 10 employee representatives on 20-person supervisory board	MODERATE-STRONG – Solidarity strikes usually illegal; strikes restricted to where employers covered by CBAs; civil servants not allowed to strike; warning strikes common; peace obligation between negotiations; moderate/low strike rates – Union membership ~18% (national); 20% (telecom industry); 55% (DT) – DT: increasing use of strikes (from 2007), high use of warning strikes

Table 2.3 Continued

Company	Participation Rights and Structures	Union Mobilization Resources
France Telecom— France **Moderate**	MODERATE – *Comités d'entreprise* (works councils), *délégués du personnel* (workforce delegates), and *comités d'hygiène, de sécurité et des conditions de travail* (health and safety councils) have information and consultation rights; social budget. *Délégués syndicaux* (union representatives) have bargaining rights through unions. – Moderate union bargaining rights and roles – Board level: One-twelfth seats where >1,000 employees, private companies; one-third seats in state-owned companies (at time of research)— FT: 3 elected employee representatives on 15-person board	STRONG – Solidarity strikes highly restricted; individual (not just union) right to strike; no peace obligation between negotiations; high strike rates – Union membership ~11% (national) – FT: high use of strikes, with intensifying conflict through 2010
Telecom Italia—Italy **Moderate**	MODERATE – *Rappresentanza Sindacale Unitaria* (RSU) are elected union representatives with information and consultation rights – Moderate union bargaining rights and roles – No board-level representation	MODERATE-STRONG – Solidarity strikes restricted; individual (not just union) right to strike; peace obligation between negotiations; moderate/high strike rates – Union membership ~33% (national); 30% (telecom industry); 26% (TI: CGIL) – TI: moderate use of strikes, though short and more ritualistic
BT—UK **Weak**	WEAK – Employee consultation rights over some restructuring areas; procedure for establishing works councils, but rare in practice; union shop stewards represent employees through contract enforcement (via grievances) – Weak union bargaining rights – No board-level representation	MODERATE – Solidarity strikes illegal; peace obligation between negotiations; low strike rates – Union membership ~24% (national); 90% (BT) – BT: low use of strikes; sustained labor-management partnership

(*continued*)

Table 2.3 Continued

Company	Participation Rights and Structures	Union Mobilization Resources
AT&T—US **Weak**	WEAK – Union shop stewards represent employees through contract enforcement (via grievances) – Weak union bargaining rights – No board-level representation	MODERATE – Solidarity strikes illegal (exceptions for some industries); peace obligation between negotiations; lockouts and hiring replacement workers permitted; agency shop in some states; low strike rates – Union membership ~10% (national); 15% (telecom industry); 88% (AT&T) – **AT&T**: moderate use of strikes, increasing in recent years; past partnership but deterioration over time
O2 Czech Republic—Czech Republic **Moderate**	MODERATE – *Závodní rada* (works councils) allowed but rare and not present at O2 CR; union shop stewards have local consultation rights and some veto rights – Weak/moderate union bargaining rights – Board level: one-third of seats in state-owned and "currently private" companies where >50 employees (at time of research)—**O2 CR**: 1 elected employee representative on 3-person supervisory board	WEAK-MODERATE – Solidarity strikes permitted; peace obligation between negotiations; low strike rates – Union membership ~11% (national); 10% (telecom industry); 38% (O2 CR) – **O2 CR**: low use of strikes, despite conflict
Orange Polska—Poland **Moderate**	WEAK-MODERATE – *Rady pracowników* (works councils) allowed and more common and present at OP; union shop stewards have some consultation rights – weak/moderate union bargaining rights – Board level: 40% to one-third seats on boards of state-owned companies (different % depending on whether state minority, majority, or sole shareholder)—**OP**: no employees on supervisory board	MODERATE – Solidarity strikes permitted (but only for half day); peace obligation between negotiations; low strike rates – Union membership ~13% (national); 20% (telecom industry); 25% (OP) – **OP**: moderate use of strikes, peaking in mid-2000s

particularly strong in large German companies like Deutsche Telekom, where half of supervisory board seats are held by worker representatives. At TDC and Telia, elected workplace representatives were more closely tied to the unions and had weaker formal negotiation rights, and so were more heavily dependent on union bargaining power and management's willingness to cooperate. Both companies also had several employee representatives on their corporate boards, giving them access to information and the opportunity to consult on decisions at the corporate level.

France and Italy diverge more significantly—though both can be described as having moderately strong formal participation rights and structures. At the time of my research, France Telecom had the full set of workplace representatives, listed in the second column of Table 2.3, as well as three employees on its fifteen-member Board of Directors. Telecom Italia had elected RSU bodies at company and workplace levels, but workers had no board-level representation. In both cases, workplace representatives played primarily a consultation role regarding management practices, with negotiation over substantive issues relating to pay, working time, and other more distributive issues occurring with unions at the company or industry level.

A similar pattern of divergence can be seen between the two CEE cases. O2 Czech Republic's union representatives enjoyed stronger bargaining rights compared to those at Orange Polska, and they had access to corporate decision-making via one employee representative on a three-person supervisory board (with no board-level representation at Orange Polska). Orange Polska did have works councils, but they played primarily a consultation role, meeting with management around three times a month. They were also dominated by activist union members. As one union official observed, "The question is who is on the works council. If they are, say, union members, then their knowledge will at least help the union with its activities, because . . . all the things that the firm does not have to consult with the union, it has to consult with the works councils, and this certainly facilitates the work of the union" (SKPT official, November 8, 2011).

Formal bargaining rights are weakest in the United Kingdom and the United States. This affected the areas in which employee representatives were able to influence management strategy, as well as their bargaining power in negotiations over restructuring. Both BT and AT&T had established agreements and a history of labor-management partnership with their unions, leaving a legacy of some partnership structures to consult on work reorganization and day-to-day management. However, this partnership had been sustained over time at BT, while it had largely broken down at AT&T, as discussed below.

Union Mobilization Resources

A second set of differences relevant for worker voice concerns the institutions that support unions in recruiting members and mobilizing those members. As described in Chapter 1, democracy at work requires not only legal rights, but also countervailing worker power backing those rights. Some degree of power comes from institutions such as sectoral bargaining or agreement extension described in the section above. However, here I am most concerned with factors supporting worker mobilization. These are summarized in the third column of Table 2.3 as *union mobilization resources*.

One important set of differences are again at national level, based on *legal and state support for unions*—through rights to strike and support for member recruitment. In both Sweden and Denmark, bargaining coverage is kept high in part through the legal right to take a wide range of sympathetic or solidaristic industrial actions, including strikes, blockades, and boycotts. Solidarity strikes are outlawed, for example, in the United Kingdom and in most US industries; and the use of blockades and boycotts is more significantly restricted (or at least not covered by enabling legislation) in all of the other countries in this study. Nordic unions face much tighter restrictions, however, if they already have a collective agreement with an employer, and they are not able to strike during the "settlement period" of negotiations (called the "peace obligation").

Union membership density is also high in both countries, at 65%–67% (OECD and AIAS 2021). This is widely attributed to the Ghent system, through which labor unions organize the major unemployment insurance funds, funded through a combination of payroll taxes and member fees. Government reforms have weakened this system and have led to the growth of "yellow unions" offering competing insurance funds at cheaper rates. However, the continued role of established unions in administering insurance and training, as well as strong union organization at workplace level, have kept membership high—particularly in large employers with a legacy of trade union representation.

In Germany and Austria, strikes face stronger legal restrictions. In Germany, strikes are only allowed where employers are covered by collective agreements or where employees' contracts mention the agreement. Civil servants in both countries are also not legally permitted to go on strike, which reduces the potential impact (particularly historically) of a strike at the telecom incumbents. German and Austrian unions can, however, organize short "warning strikes" to put pressure on employers during collective bargaining, which has become a common form of industrial action. Union membership is voluntary, as in Denmark and Sweden. However, there is no Ghent system tying social insurance to union membership, and membership has declined much more significantly, to below 18% in Germany and below 28% in Austria.

In France and Italy, the legal right to strike or participate in collective action is an individual right, rather than one held exclusively by trade unions (which is more common in Europe). France stands out, however, as also not having a "peace obligation" that prohibits collective action while a collective agreement is in force. France also has one of the lowest union membership rates in Europe, at below 11%. This is often attributed to the generally weak presence and role of unions at the workplace level, and their relatively greater importance at sector and national levels, as well as free-rider problems associated with state extension of collective agreements. However, French unions historically were able to mobilize large numbers of non-members in conflicts with employers or the state—thus reducing both the need to recruit members and the practical meaning of membership rates as a measure of union support. In Italy, union membership is closer to 34%.

The United States and the United Kingdom both have significant legal limits on secondary industrial action and rules concerning the timing and form of strikes. The United States stands out, however, as having broad and comprehensive rules allowing lockouts and hiring of replacement workers—actions that are prohibited or more restricted in most European countries. The United States also permits agency shop requirements that employees pay union or agency fees if covered by a collective agreement, though many states have passed "right to work" laws that outlaw these arrangements. In the United Kingdom, closed shop rules requiring union membership have been illegal since 1990, with no agency shop provisions. Despite these differences, the United States has suffered a steeper decline in bargaining coverage, leading to a union membership rate close to that in France at 10%, compared to 24% membership among UK employees.

Finally, the Czech Republic and Poland are again mixed cases. Secondary or solidarity strikes are permitted, though restricted to only half a working day in Poland, and employers are typically not allowed to replace strikers. In Poland, warning strikes are also permitted and used. Around 11%–13% of employees in both countries are union members.

Legal supports for union member organizing or rights to strike also influence company-level outcomes, but do not directly translate into union strength. An important point of comparison is thus union density within the telecom sector and in the incumbent companies. We were not able to get sector-level figures for all the cases; however, union representatives in seven countries estimated density based on their internal figures in 2010–2012. This ranged from (highest to lowest) 73% in Sweden, 50% in Denmark, 30% in Italy, 20% in Germany and in Poland, 15% in the United States,[4] and 10% in the Czech Republic. These are

---

[4] The US membership density figures are based on 2012 data from the Current Population survey, "Wired telecommunications carriers."

rough figures, based to some extent on union respondents' interpretation of the boundaries of the sector.

Union representatives were more confident in estimating membership rates at the incumbent companies. Figure 2.1 shows that most incumbents continued to have at least moderate union membership rates by 2005–2010—in all cases higher than the industry as a whole. BT and AT&T had maintained very high rates, close to or above 90%. While there is a general pattern of membership decline, this is not universal. While Telecom Italia appears to have low membership rates, the estimate provided is only from the largest two unions. Finally, O2 Czech Republic and Orange Polska show an interesting contrast, with membership rates declining significantly at the first, but from a much higher starting point, and remaining at 38%, compared to 25% at the Polish incumbent.

These density figures provide some indication of unions' bargaining power and mobilization potential. BT and AT&T's unions in particular have strong potential associational power within each incumbent. However, a further factor

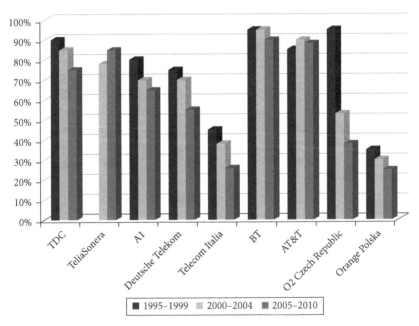

Figure 2.1. Average union membership density in incumbent telecommunications firms.

Source: Union and management estimates.

Notes: Historic membership density at AT&T is calculated based on percent of membership at AT&T, BellSouth, Ameritech, Southwestern Bell, and Pacific/Nevada Bell—which through M&As make up the current company AT&T. No data were available for France Telecom. Union density data for Telecom Italia only include SLC-CGIL and FISTEL-CISL, and thus underestimate total membership.

likely to be important is the culture of partnership or conflict, or the willingness of unions to organize strikes matched with the general attitude of cooperation (or opposition) from management. We asked union representatives to describe the relationship between the union and management at different time periods, based on a scale ranging from "very conflictual" (1) to "very cooperative" (7). Figure 2.2 shows a deterioration in four of the case studies: TDC, Telia, A1, Deutsche Telekom, and France Telecom. However, BT unionists report an improvement over time, while Telecom Italia, O2 Czech Republic, and Orange Polska all experienced a decline in the period 2000–2004, followed by an improvement in the 2005–2010 period.

The preceding discussion suggests that worker representatives across the cases have access to different combinations of resources to assert democratic worker voice. Unions' strength is often shown through their ability to mobilize workers in industrial conflicts or strikes. This is particularly important during a period of intensive restructuring. However, industrial conflict can also be a sign of institutional weakness, as traditions of social partnership break down.

The rate of industrial disputes has long been higher in Denmark than in Sweden—a gap that has significantly increased over the past decade (ETUI

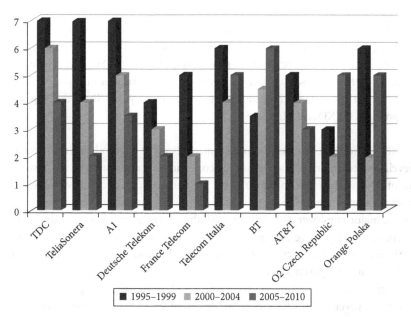

Figure 2.2. Level of labor-management cooperation: 1 = very conflictual, 7 = very cooperative.

Source: Survey of union representatives from each company. Answer to question: "How would you describe the relationship between the union and management at these different time periods? Please indicate on the scale below from [1] very conflictual to [7] very cooperative."

2020). This difference is also reflected in the recent history of the telecom industry. In both countries, unions are only legally permitted to organize strikes during the period when they are negotiating a contract. However, Dansk Metal has organized large strikes and protests at different points in TDC's history, for example, when mass redundancies were announced (see Chapter 3). In addition, unsanctioned or "wildcat" strikes have been more common.

In Sweden, labor relations in telecommunications and at Telia were relatively peaceful over several waves of liberalization, privatization, and restructuring. In the early 1980s, there was one large national strike; and then at the beginning of the 1990s there was a major industrial action associated with changing rules on employees' use of cars. However, there have not been wildcat strikes like those in Denmark at TDC, which Swedish union officials attributed to the cooperative relationship with management and (historically) generous agreements on downsizing and redeployment.

One union representative noted, however, that there was growing pressure from workers to organize a strike, given increasing conflict and willingness of management to not honor past agreements. "Members say, 'why don't we strike? Why do we have to work when it's so miserable?'" (Unionen rep Telia, 8/12/11). Another union official observed:

> You have to understand the Swedish mentality: the Swedish don't want to fight. [. . .] In Sweden, we have to get to work, if we really do want to get changes, we have to go out and have strikes. It is very difficult to get the Swedish people to agree to this, because they have a long time of friendly relationships—there has been workplace democracy in Sweden for too many years. That's the biggest problem. (SEKO rep Telia, June 27, 2012)

At the same time, as regards industrial relations at sectoral or cross-sectoral level, service unions in the Danish telecom and call center sectors have a significant disadvantage due to the 50% rule for clerical workers described above. To recap: unions are not able to strike or picket service employers who are members of the major employer associations, with the goal of securing a collective agreement, until they prove that at least 50% of the workforce are union members. This has limited the effectiveness of coordinated action outside of the incumbent in Denmark compared to Sweden.

Both Germany and Austria have traditions of social partnership and low strike rates. However, strikes have become relatively less common in Austria (ETUI 2020). Again, these patterns are reflected in telecommunications. Both Deutsche Telekom and A1 had a history of industrial peace, with virtually no strikes before liberalization. After liberalization, conflicts at A1, as well as at other telecom employers, continued to be resolved through largely peaceful negotiations.

However, as shown in Chapter 3, organized protests, demonstrations, and strike threats came to play an increasingly central role in union campaigns against unpopular downsizing measures.

Strikes did become more frequent at Deutsche Telekom. Short warning strikes, or *warnstreiks*, were, and continue to be, a common tool of the union during collective bargaining to show member support for their position. However, ver.di organized the first major strike at the company in 2007 in response to spin-off plans (see Chapter 5), and one union representative observed that threatening or organizing strikes was becoming more of a standard part of their strategy in negotiations:

> Strikes and other forms of industrial action [*Arbeitskämpfe*] are important means to distinguish oneself and to win members. [. . .] They fight, they risk something, and then they should also profit from this. (ver.di official, August 14, 2018)

Italy and France are known for high levels of industrial conflict (ETUI 2020). Strike rates have also been high in both countries' telecom sectors, particularly in the former monopolists. However, overall relations were more cooperative at Telecom Italia, particularly around the period of privatization and liberalization.

France Telecom experienced a number of mobilizations and national strikes around planned job cuts from the late 1990s: e.g., in 1999 against a major redundancy plan; in 2002 against a restructuring plan to reduce the company's debt; in 2004 in the wake of the French government's sale of its majority stake in France Telecom; and in 2007 based on a major redundancy announcement. More recent strike actions related to restructuring measures, and to protest management's response to a wave of employee suicides, are discussed in Chapter 3.

In Italy, union representatives reported that although strikes were common at Telecom Italia, member mobilization and their substantive impact were relatively low. One noted, "For every redundancy plan there is a sort of a fixed fee, which are the redundancies. Let's say that it is then automatic that we answer that way (*with a strike*)" (SLC-CGIL official, June 15, 2011). Another observed that they always went on strike, but usually in more of a ritualistic way:

> Always! It is part of the history of Italian unions. They (the management) present the redundancy plan, you bargain and organize a strike to support the negotiations [. . .]. In Italy there is an ideological culture. It seems that, if you bargain without striking, you haven't fought enough. [. . .] [At the same time] you can count our hours of striking on the fingers of one hand . . . when Telecom Italia announced 6,400 redundancies, we struck for four hours. It's not

much, because we immediately found a solution. Our sector is not conflictual. (FISTEL-CISL official, June 14, 2011)

As described above, the United States has much lower union density than the United Kingdom, and in many ways US unions face a political environment that is more hostile to unionization. Strike rates have declined significantly in both countries, but still remain higher in the United Kingdom. However, in the incumbent companies, the US union, the CWA, has been more willing to use strikes in conflict with management than the United Kingdom's CWU.

Both AT&T and BT have a tradition of partnership with their unions. At AT&T, the 1992 Workplace of the Future Agreement (WPOF) extended management neutrality to non-union subsidiaries in union organizing campaigns and elections, improved job security, and made it easier for redundant workers to be transferred to subsidiaries (Boroff and Keefe 1994). However, the partnership became increasingly irrelevant as the company cut close to 60,000 jobs, with little consultation. WPOF finally collapsed in 1999. From the mid-2000s, the unions increasingly used a combination of strikes, partnership over regulatory approval, and more local or ad hoc workplace and company partnership to achieve favorable agreements in bargaining (Katz, Batt, and Keefe 2003). The largest strikes were organized at Verizon, in 2000 and 2011, and more recently a forty-five-day strike in 2016. The CWA has also struck at AT&T, including a three-day strike in 2017 involving close to 40,000 employees and a 2019 strike involving around 20,000 employees in nine southern US states.

Labor conflict has been rarer at BT. The last company strike was in 1987, during a CWU action over pay that "ran for more than two weeks until BT agreed to a two-year pay rise worth 12.66%" (Wearden 2010). Both unions adopted a labor management partnership known as "New Dialogue" in 1992, which was sustained over time. The unions were able to take advantage of funding and support for partnership provided by the New Labour government in the 1990s, including the Union Learning Fund. Connect took industrial action during pay negotiations in 2008, and the CWU got very close to taking industrial action for similar reasons in 2010, but was advised by its lawyers that the balloting process had not fully complied with labor relations laws (Wearden 2010). Several CWU unionists described striking as a "nuclear option":

The culture—it still is in BT—is to try to avoid disputes. National strike in BT, it's like a nuclear button. [. . .] I think there's a maturity. It's a very old company and a very old union employer, and it's a very Anglo-Saxon approach as well. We don't have such a powerful network of employment legislation protecting people. It's much more flexi-bargaining. So you come up with your own traditions in a way. (former CWU official, December 1, 2011).

Finally, we can also see different levels of labor conflict between the Czech and Polish cases. Both have very low national strike rates. However, in the incumbent companies, the unions were more willing or able to organize strikes at Orange Polska. Although both companies experienced conflict with their unions in the mid-2000s over restructuring measures, at Orange Polska the unions fought back through a nationwide strike—with 92% of employees voting in favor of industrial action, and many participating in an organized hunger strike (see Chapter 3).

The above discussion suggests some systematic differences in patterns of conflict or mobilization across the companies. First, Telia, A1, and to some extent BT, Telecom Italia, and O2 Czech Republic all showed a partnership culture with (comparatively) low labor conflict. This can be traced in part to strong and encompassing institutions in Sweden and Austria, and at least a stable union presence and role at the other cases. Second, TDC, Deutsche Telekom, France Telecom, AT&T, and Orange Polska showed increasing use of strikes as tools in the context of a breakdown of social partnership traditions (TDC, Deutsche Telekom, France Telecom) or of past partnership agreements (AT&T, Orange Polska).

Summary

Together, the comparison in this section allows a rough ordering of the strength of *support for collective worker voice*, through a combination of participation rights and structures and mobilization resources. These are strongest at the incumbent companies based in the Nordic and Germanic countries (TDC, Telia, Deutsche Telekom, A1) due to worker representatives' access to more comprehensive institutional support for participation in decision-making at multiple levels, combined with moderate to strong resources to mobilize workers to back up those rights when companies attempt to bypass them. The Mediterranean and CEE countries have more moderate voice resources—due to somewhat weaker formal bargaining or participation rights, but with generally moderate to strong mobilization resources at the incumbents. Finally, the liberal United Kingdom and United States have the weakest institutional backing for collective voice, although in both countries unions enjoyed among the highest membership rates within the incumbent companies. This gave them strong mobilization potential, but it was used to different ends, backing sustained partnership at BT and increasing strikes at AT&T.

These differences are significant for both the extent to which and the means through which workers were able to shape management strategies in different areas, as will be seen in the following chapters. However, the success of mobilization and the scope of voice institutions depended on the capacity of worker representatives to work together within the incumbent companies and across their supply chains and industries. This cooperation depended most fundamentally on the structures and ideologies supporting solidarity.

Strategies of Inclusive Labor Solidarity

Solidarity within the labor movement is a dynamic factor that changes over time, and that is expressed through the strategies or actions of unions and other worker representatives. Consistent with the focus in this book, a particular concern is with inclusive campaigns or strategies aimed at organizing and representing precarious workers. However, labor solidarity across corporate groups, within and between industries, and along value chains also underpins efforts to sustain existing protections, with the goal of preventing more work from becoming precarious. The discussion of past theory and research in Chapter 1 suggests that two factors are most relevant for explaining different patterns of labor cooperation or competition: union and bargaining structures, and union ideology or identity.

First, labor cooperation is strongly influenced by *union and bargaining structures*—and particularly the degree of overlap between union representation domains. Consistent with the political economy literature, we would expect unions to represent a broader range of worker interests where collective bargaining is more encompassing of these different workers (Rathgeb 2018; Thelen 2014). Thus, the institutions that constrain employer exit can also encourage unions to act with more solidarity. Sectoral bargaining, with one agreement negotiated for all workers in an industry, and ideally also covering subcontractors and agency workers, not only prevents employers from exploiting exit options, but also facilitates labor cooperation. Even where multiple unions are involved, they operate within a structure that encourages them to work together to negotiate these agreements, while also facing less pressure to compete for members or to "poach" employers and their workers from another agreement through lowering their terms.

Union representation domains are related to bargaining structures, but they can take different forms even within more or less encompassing systems. If unions have clearly defined domains with minimal overlap—for example, by industry or occupation—they should find it easier to focus on establishing and maintaining collective agreements across a sector or value chain without being distracted by competition from other unions. In multi-union systems, clear domains make it more likely that unions will coordinate with each other in collective bargaining, without worrying about potential poaching of members.

A second factor that contributes to patterns of labor solidarity concerns *union identities or ideologies*. This has two dimensions, as discussed in Chapter 1. First, the dominant identity of a union can influence the willingness of leaders and members to organize and to represent precarious workers. Industrial relations scholars have argued that class unionism is more often associated with militant and politicized bargaining, including that aimed at representing precarious workers, while business unions see their primary role as defending their members' immediate economic interests (Benassi and Vlandas 2016; Hyman 2001). Social partnership unions are again a third type, which prioritize social welfare—and perhaps are more likely to compromise with management or the state to further broader social goals.

National labor movements may lean more strongly toward one (or fall between two) of these ideal-type identities. Second, however, conflicting union identities and ideologies within a country, sector, or company can be an important source of labor divides, making solidarity more difficult to build and maintain at different levels (Benassi, Dorigatti, and Pannini 2019). This conflict is particularly important in countries like France, Italy, and Poland, where multiple union confederations organized along ideological lines are present in the same industries and workplaces.

In the following sections, I first compare union and bargaining structures and union ideologies in each matched pair of countries. I then discuss four patterns at the sector level, based on the level of inclusiveness in union structures and the main form of labor divides.

National Differences

A comparison at the national level shows both similarities and differences within each country pair in the structures supporting union cooperation or coordination at different levels, as well as the role of identity and ideology as a general feature of a national labor movement or major source of division among unions.

Historically, unions in Denmark and Sweden shared both an ideology prioritizing social partnership and traditions of "solidaristic wage bargaining" typical of the Nordic model, in which workers in more productive or higher skilled jobs agreed to wage restraint (or below-market wages), while subsidizing higher wages for less productive or lower skilled jobs. This system was significantly eroded through a movement toward decentralized and flexibilized wage bargaining (Iversen 1996). However, pattern bargaining has been maintained, whereby a percentage wage increase is agreed in a "pattern-setting" industry (typically manufacturing)—and then other bargaining units follow with similar increases (Ibsen 2016). Bargaining coordination is thus high compared to the other countries in this study.

At the same time, the structure of unions and their confederations differs in ways that are particularly significant for union cooperation. Denmark has a strong legacy of craft-based unions, while the Swedish labor movement was earlier dominated by industrial unions (Emmenegger 2010). Danish unions came to be organized along a combination of craft/profession- and industry-based lines. At the time of my research, a significant majority of these unions and their members were organized in the Danish Confederation of Trade Unions (LO). There were three other major (though much smaller) confederations, organized more clearly along occupational lines: the Danish Confederation of Professionals (FTF)[5], the Danish Confederation of Professional Associations (AC), and the Danish Association of Managers and Executives (LH). In Sweden, union membership was more evenly distributed among three large confederations: the Swedish Trade Union Confederation (also called LO) organizes primarily blue-collar workers; the Swedish Confederation of Professional Employees (TCO) organizes white-collar or "salaried" employees; and the Swedish Confederation of Professional Associations (SACO) includes university graduates across a range of professions. While members of the Swedish LO are industry-based unions, TCO unions are a mix of occupational and industry-based; while SACO is occupation-based.

Employers are also organized differently. In Denmark, the largest employer organization at the national level is the Confederation of Danish Employers (DA), with eleven affiliates in manufacturing, services, retail, transport, and construction. DA and LO negotiate a basic agreement (*Hovedaftalen*) and a cooperation agreement (*Samarbejdsaftalen*) at the national level, which "build a framework for bargaining the sectoral agreements by defining fundamental procedural rules—including the right to organise, a peace obligation, cooperation at the workplace or the handling of unfair dismissals" (Jørgensen 2012, 6). In Sweden, the Confederation of Swedish Enterprise (SN) is the major national bargaining partner with the LO. Like in Denmark, an agreement at the national level (*Saltsjöbadsavtalet*) sets the framework for bargaining structure and roles.

At the sectoral level, Danish employer organizations are more concentrated than those in Sweden in manufacturing sectors, but are more fragmented in its service sectors. In Sweden, there are nine employer associations in manufacturing. In contrast, there is only one major service association, Almega, with 11,000 member companies organized across nine sub-associations. In Denmark,

---

[5] The FTF merged with the LO in 2019, and the LO became part of a new Danish Trade Union Confederation (FH).

nearly all manufacturing employers are organized in the Confederation of Danish Industries (*Dansk Industri*, DI). DI merged in 2008 with the third-largest employers' association, the Confederation of Danish Commercial Transportation and Service Industries (HTS), and so represents both manufacturing employers and a range of service-sector and public-sector employers. DI and CO-Industri (its counterpart association of labor unions) negotiate both blue-collar and white-collar agreements, which set "the standard for the rest of collective bargaining in Denmark" (Jørgensen 2012, 5). However, DI competes for members and influence in service industries with the Danish Chamber of Commerce (*Dansk Erhverv*, DE), which was formed in 2007 through a merger between the Danish Chamber of Commerce (HTS-I) and Danish Commerce and Services (DHS). The competition between these two associations is particularly important in the telecom sector, as described below.

In Austria and Germany, unions also have prioritized social partnership. However, this represents a more delicate balance between the particularistic economic interests of groups of workers at company and workplace levels in "dual systems" characterized by a formal separation between unions and works councils. This structure opens up greater possibility of *Betriebsegoismus*, roughly translated as company or workplace selfishness, where local worker representatives seek to defend local jobs through cutting special deals with management. Strong union leadership, coordinating bargaining within sectors, ideally helps to prevent this kind of competition. In Germany, this coordinating role has been more difficult to maintain due to sharply declining bargaining coverage, bargaining decentralization linked to "opening clauses" in sectoral agreements (Seifert and Massa-Wirth 2005), and the negative impact of vertical disintegration on works council coordination across corporate groups and supply chains (Doellgast and Greer 2007; Greer 2008). In addition, in Germany the large gap in organization rates and bargaining strength between sectors has led to a growing split between manufacturing unions (which continue to prioritize partnership) and service unions (which more often embrace labor militancy) (Behrens and Pekarek 2021; Dribbusch 2019).

In Austria, unions' social partnership orientations or identities were preserved to a greater extent. This was probably due in large part to their stronger institutional security, as their sectoral collective agreements continued to be extended via employers' mandatory membership in the WKÖ. At the same time, the degree of union and bargaining cohesion differs by industry. For example, research in Austria's waste (Sørensen, Kirov, and Holtgrewe 2018) and postal delivery (Benvegnú, Haidinger, and Sacchetto 2018) sectors found that employers made widespread use of labor arbitrage through shifting their membership to sectoral associations with cheaper collective agreements and using self-employed workers to reduce terms and conditions.

In both countries, most large unions are members of one major confederation: the DGB in Germany and the ÖGB in Austria. However, while the ÖGB is the only confederation, the DGB faces some competition from two smaller confederations: the German Civil Service Federation (DBB) and the Christian Trade Union Federation (CGB)—as well as autonomous occupation-based unions. In addition, while the ÖGB coordinates the political activities of its affiliate unions, German branch unions have more independence and pursue distinct political agendas (Heinisch 2000). Both major confederations are organized primarily on an industry basis, with formal agreements between the unions not to compete within industries. However, Holst (2008, 29–30) observes that the negotiation of sectoral agreements in Austria has traditionally been based on coordinated pattern bargaining focused on broader economic goals, compared to German unions' greater strategic focus on industry-specific worker mobilization and economic conditions. In Austria a major cross-sectoral union, the GPA, negotiates separate agreements for white-collar workers—though coordinating closely with other unions negotiating agreements for their blue-collar members (or in manufacturing, actually negotiating joint agreements). In contrast, Germany's large service union ver.di has multiple departments, or *Fachbereiche*, organized along industry lines, with separate agreements and weak coordination (Holtgrewe and Doellgast 2012).

In France and Italy, multiple union confederations are involved in negotiations within a given sector. In France, five major national union confederations are recognized as "representative." This means they are able to negotiate sectoral agreements with employer associations, which are then extended by the French state to employers in that sector. These include the General Confederation of Labor (CGT), the General Confederation of Labor—Workers' Force (CGT-FO), the French Democratic Confederation of Labor (CFDT), the French Confederation of Christian Workers (CFTC), and the French Confederation of Management—General Confederation of Executives (CFE-CGC). CGT is the most left-wing or militant of the confederations; while CFTC, CFDT, and CFE-CGC are known as more reformist or social partnership–oriented unions. Before 2008, these confederations had rights to negotiate collective agreements or to nominate candidates for company-level representatives without demonstrated employee support. Following 2008 reforms, unions were required to gain 10% of votes in elections for works councils or employee delegates at the workplace level and 8% at the sector level to be able to negotiate collective agreements.

There are also a number of smaller autonomous or independent unions in France—many of which focus on organizing professional members (Béthoux and Laroche 2021). An important organization in this space is *Union syndicale solidaires*, which in 2012 included forty-three unions and federations, representing around 100,000 members. *Solidaires unitaires démocratiques*

(SUD), a group of independent leftist unions which has high membership in telecommunications, is an important member of this organization.

In Italy, rival trade union confederations are also organized along ideological lines, although "the pattern is less complex" than in France (Gumbrell-McCormick and Hyman 2013, 23). The General Confederation of Labor (CGIL) is the largest union and closest to the French CGT, with a communist background and continued leftist political leanings. The Confederation of Workers' Trade Unions (CISL) is the second largest confederation, with a more conservative identity and politics rooted in its historic ties to the Christian Democratic Party; while the smaller Italian Labor Union (UIL) also takes more conservative positions, though it was traditionally allied with the Socialist Party. Italy also has a number of smaller confederations and autonomous unions, as well as the "cobas," which are groups of rank-and-file workers that have been at the forefront of recent industrial actions—for example, in the logistics industry (Benvegnú, Haidinger, and Sacchetto 2018; Curcio 2018).

In both countries, these rival confederations have parallel industry federations: for example, in metalworking, construction, and telecommunications. In Italy, the major industry federations typically agree on a common platform and then negotiate and sign sectoral agreements jointly. This system broke down in the metal industry from 2009, when CGIL refused to co-sign agreements due to conflicts over concessions regarding use of agency work, among other issues (Benassi, Dorigatti, and Pannini 2019). In France, coordination among the unions at sectoral level is weaker, and it is more common for some unions to refuse to sign agreements in protest. Sectoral agreements must be signed by unions that have shown they have support from at least 30% of that industry's workforce—based not on union membership, but on votes cast in elections for worker representatives—and must not be opposed by unions supported by more than 50% of the workforce.

Unions in the United States and the United Kingdom were traditionally organized along craft lines, and although unions began to organize at the industry level in both countries from the 1930s, this history continues to shape industrial relations in both countries. In the United States, the major confederation, the American Federation of Labor and Congress of Industrial Organizations (AFL-CIO), was formed in 1955 through a merger of the craft-based AFL unions (e.g., building trades, Teamsters, American Federation of Musicians) and the industry-based CIO unions (e.g., United Auto Workers, United Steel Workers). In the United Kingdom, the Trades Union Congress (TUC) is the major confederation, dating from the 1860s. While its members include smaller industry or occupational unions, mergers have created a smaller number of general unions that organize workers across sectors and occupations, including Unite, Unison, and GMB. This history in both countries means that despite being in the same confederations, jurisdictional disputes are common: unions frequently organize groups of workers from the same industry or occupation. While US labor law includes supervisory and managerial exclusion rules, UK managers can join unions. However, they often belong to separate unions from the employees they supervise. For example, the union Prospect organizes engineering, scientific, management, and professional staff across a wide range of sectors (including telecom).

The US labor movement also stands out among the ten country cases for its historic dominance by a business unionism identity. Past socialist or class-based unions such as the Industrial Workers of the World (IWW, or "Wobblies") were largely marginalized or actively suppressed, for example during the Red Scare after World War I and during the Cold War. Employers have long exploited racial and ethnic divisions among US workers, rooted in the country's history of slavery and systemic racism. This contributed to an inward focus on union members' immediate economic interests, rather than on broader goals of social partnership or class mobilization (Eidlin 2018). At the same time, US unions have historically supported or played a leading role in social movements fighting for, e.g., minimum wages, social security, and health and safety regulations (Katz and Colvin 2021). There has also been change over time, with a growing focus from the 1990s on social movement unionism, and recent campaigns connecting to broader concerns with social, racial, and economic justice—for example, through Bargaining for the Common Good and support for Black Lives Matter (Givan and Lang 2020).

In the United Kingdom, unions shared to some extent this identity of "unionism pure and simple." Despite the stronger presence (or at least persistence) of socialist ideologies within the UK labor movement, the TUC allied with the AFL-CIO during the Cold War in anti-communist political activism. Business unionism leanings were somewhat attenuated by the central role of the Labour Party in British politics, with around half of TUC unions members of the party, providing funding and serving on its executive committee. This was a vehicle for a greater social partnership orientation, particularly during Labour governments. At the same time, British unions have also been divided in their support for partnership versus organizing and mobilization (Johnstone and Dobbins 2021).

Czech and Polish unions differ most significantly in institutional support for cooperation at the sector level, with sectoral bargaining common in the Czech Republic and very rare in Poland. They also differ in the extent of competition among unions at the local level and political or ideological divides in the labor movement, with significant union rivalry and deeper, historically grounded political divides in Poland.

In Poland, unions are organized at the workplace (*zakład*) level, with more than one union in a workplace. The largest national confederations are the

Independent and Self-Governing Trade Union Solidarity (NSZZ Solidarność), the All-Poland Alliance of Trade Unions (OPZZ), and the Trade Unions Forum (FZZ). However, there are many smaller confederations, as well as unaffiliated national or workplace unions that are not associated with any of the higher-level structures. At the time of our research, the Labor Code required a trade union to have organized 10% of a plant's workforce (or 7% if it was an organization above the plant level) to be considered representative—and thus eligible to negotiate with the employer on behalf of employees. If no union fulfilled this criterion, the largest trade union at the plant level was recognized as representative. The major confederations were traditionally allied with different political parties—NSZZ Solidarność with conservatives, and OPZZ with social democrats. These ideological divisions contributed to what Trappmann (2012) calls a "dualistic" labor movement. This has weakened the unions' ability to articulate a shared position, both in national labor policy and in company-level bargaining (Sil 2017, 430). More recently, NSZZ Solidarność has cooperated closely with the right-wing populist Law and Justice (PiS) party, while OPZZ has moved to more informal cooperation with social democrats (Czarzasty and Mrozowicki 2021).

In the Czech Republic, in contrast, there is one major confederation, the Czech-Moravian Confederation of Trade Unions (ČMKOS), which has remained unallied to political parties. Several smaller confederations are organized around specific industry sectors (ASO ČR originally for the agricultural and food sector and KUK for the cultural sector) or political ideologies (the communist OS ČMS and the Christian KOK). However, this did not contribute to the kind of major split in the labor movement seen in Poland. Sil (2017, 431) writes, "while ASO did become the second largest federation, [. . .] at no point did it account for more than 15% of union members; more importantly, it encompassed diverse branch unions pursuing independent labor actions without much coordination." ČMKOS's member unions are also broadly organized on an industry basis; and while smaller unions may be present in the same workplace, there is nothing like the degree of rivalry in Polish companies.

In sum, at the national level, we can see both similarities and significant differences in union structure and ideology within each paired case. Broadly, Sweden and Austria have strong institutional support for labor cooperation, based on encompassing bargaining and clearly defined union representation domains. This support is present but weaker in Denmark, Germany, France, and Italy due to greater divisions across unions and/or a more fragmented landscape of collective agreements. Finally, the United States, the United Kingdom, the Czech Republic, and Poland all have the weakest formal institutional support for labor cooperation, with very low bargaining coverage, leaving the majority of workplaces and workers not covered by any union agreement. This leads to

88 EXIT, VOICE, AND SOLIDARITY

different dynamics of internal rivalry, based on defending an already small and shrinking core membership.

The countries group differently based on the form that labor divides take, connected to both union representation domains and identities or ideologies. In France, Italy, and Poland, the major divides are ideological, grounded in the different political orientations of their historically divided union confederations—in industrial relations systems characterized by multiple unions within workplaces, companies, and sectors. The other countries show greater potential for labor competition over which union will represent workers at the workplace or company level (Denmark, Sweden, Germany, United States, United Kingdom, Czech Republic); at the sector level (Austria, Germany, Czech Republic); or based on occupation or professional group (Sweden, United Kingdom).

These two sets of factors shape changing patterns of labor cooperation and conflict in the telecom sector, which is the focus of the next section.

Comparing the Cases

Table 2.4 summarizes the major labor unions present in the telecom sector of each country, the main form that labor divides have taken, and institutional factors relevant to labor cooperation. These broadly track national differences in the structure of industrial relations institutions, but show some patterns that are distinct to telecommunications (or at least more typical of services than manufacturing). Rather than summarize these differences by country pair, I divide my discussion below into four general patterns across the cases: structural inclusive solidarity (Austria and Sweden), representation domain divides (Denmark and Germany), ideological divides (France, Italy, Poland), and structural exclusive solidarity (United Kingdom, United States, Czech Republic, and Poland). For each, I compare differences in union structures and ideologies relevant to labor solidarity at sectoral and company case level.

Structural Inclusive Solidarity: Sweden and Austria

In Sweden and Austria, inclusive labor solidarity in the telecom industry is most directly grounded in encompassing bargaining structures and clear union representation domains. Thus, I group them together as examples of "structural inclusive solidarity." In both, formal bargaining and union structures make it easier for unions to cooperate at different levels to maintain or extend protections to different groups of workers.

In Sweden, industrial relations in the telecom industry developed in a centralized and coordinated way. The three major union confederations were present in both the incumbent and other telecom companies. The Union for

Table 2.4 Support for Labor Solidarity in the Telecommunications Industry (2010–2012)

	Major Labor Union(s)	Employer Associations (Involved in CBAs)	Sectoral Agreement	Form of Labor Divides	Level and Form of Union Representation Domain Overlap
Denmark *Representation domain divides*	Dansk Metal (TDC) HK Privat (services—telecom industry)	Dansk Industri and Dansk Erhverv	Yes—but competing agreements	Company/within-industry (same confederation)	MODERATE: division of responsibility between incumbent and other telecoms, but conflict associated with outsourcing, mergers & acquisitions (M&A)
Sweden *Structural inclusive solidarity*	UNIONEN-TCO (white-collar) SEKO-LO (blue-collar) SACO (graduate professionals)	Almega IT&Telecom	Yes	Occupational group and workplace (different confederations)	LOW: all unions present in incumbent and industry, coordinate bargaining
Austria *Structural inclusive solidarity*	GPF (A1) GPA (white-collar, services)	WKÖ, Wirtschaftsbereich Telekommunikation	Yes—coordinated with incumbent	Company/within-industry (same confederation)	LOW: division of responsibility for incumbent vs. telecom and service industry; unions coordinate bargaining
Germany *Representation domain divides*	ver.di (DT, telecom, call centers, services) IG Metal (some telecom firms) IG BCE (some telecom firms)	None with collective bargaining role	No	Company/within-industry (same confederation)	MODERATE: division of responsibility by employer; but conflict over outsourcing and M&A; no bargaining coordination between unions
France *Ideological divides*	CGT-PTT SUD-PTT F3C-CFDT CFTC CFE-CGC FO (all in FT and telecom industry)	UNETEL-RST	Yes	Ideology (different confederations)	HIGH: all unions present in incumbent and industry, compete in local representative elections and for members; unions coordinate bargaining, but some don't sign agreement

(*continued*)

Table 2.4 Continued

	Major Labor Union(s)	Employer Associations (Involved in CBAs)	Sectoral Agreement	Form of Labor Divides	Level and Form of Union Representation Domain Overlap
Italy *Ideological divides*	SLC-CGIL FISTEL-CISL UILCOM UGL-COM (all in TI and telecom industry)	ASSTEL (from 2002)	Yes	Ideology (different confederations)	HIGH: all unions present in incumbent and industry, compete in local representative elections and for members; unions coordinate bargaining
UK *Structural exclusive solidarity*	CWU (non-management grades at BT and other telecom firms) Prospect (managers)	None	No	Occupational group (same confederation)	LOW: clear division of responsibility by employee grade; unions coordinate bargaining
USA *Structural exclusive solidarity*	CWA (AT&T, other telecom firms) IBEW (AT&T, other telecom firms)	None	No	Company/ within-industry (same confederation)	LOW: clear division of responsibility by workplace; unions coordinate bargaining
Czech Republic *Structural exclusive solidarity*	OSZPTNS OOPR	Český svaz zaměstnavatelů pošt, telekomunikací a distribuce tisku	Yes—but low coverage	Industry (same confederation)	LOW: one main union in the industry and incumbent
Poland *Ideological divides + Structural exclusive solidarity*	SKPT-NSZZ, FZZPT-OPZZ are representative; other small unions non-representative (all in OP and telecom industry)	Konfederacja Pracodawców Polskich and PKPP Lewiatan	No	Ideology (different confederations)	HIGH: all unions present in incumbent and industry, compete in local representative elections and for members; unions coordinate bargaining, but some don't sign agreement

Service and Communications Employees (SEKO) is an LO (blue-collar) union, while Unionen is a TCO (white-collar) union. Telecom employees are also represented by SACO (academics and graduate professionals) unions, including CF (engineers), CE (managers), and JUSEK (lawyers, social scientists, and economists).

In the mid-1990s, the incumbent Televerket was a member of the employer association for state-owned companies. This disbanded in 1996, and its members moved to the Swedish Employers Association (SAF) associations for their industry sectors. At that time, SAF established a new industry association for telecom and IT, which later became Almega IT&Telecom—one of seven service industry associations in the Almega organization. According to union officials, the sectoral agreement had seventy-nine signatory companies in 2011, covering 86% of companies and 88% of employees in the industry. Moreover, telecom companies that were not members of the employer association typically applied the same basic terms and conditions from the collective agreement.

Union representatives noted that there was competition between the major unions for members: "We are competing with each other—there are not strict lines between what is a Unionen and what is a SEKO member" (SEKO official, May 10, 2012). Local agreements were negotiated by the union that had higher membership, but both unions were signatories for the telecom sectoral agreement, with close coordination across levels. Thus, both the incumbent and competitor companies were organized in one major association that negotiated one encompassing agreement, while the same unions worked together at both sector and company levels to coordinate bargaining in the industry.

In Austria, several different sections within the Austrian Federal Economic Chamber (WKÖ) were reorganized into a telecom section by the late 2000s. All companies offering telecom services in Austria (roughly 50–60) became members of this section. "The big five" companies, representing 90% of all telecom employment, had primary responsibility for negotiating the collective agreement. However, all companies were required to abide by the agreement. The section negotiated a sectoral agreement with the Trade Union of Postal and Telecommunications Workers (GPF) and the service union GPA. Unusual in Austria, this agreement did not cover Telekom Austria/A1, which continued to negotiate a separate agreement with the GPF under the terms of legislation that transformed the incumbent into a private-law company (Traxler 2002). Still, these two agreements were closely coordinated and established a nearly identical pay structure for similar job categories: "By and large, the collective agreement at Telekom Austria corresponds to ours [with the GPA]. [. . .] For the employees, the salary scales are almost identical" (works councilor T-Mobile Austria, July 25, 2011) This high degree of coordination was possible because of strong union cooperation based on a clear division of responsibility.

Representation Domain Divides: Denmark and Germany

The second pattern can be seen in Denmark and Germany, where past encompassing institutions—more broadly similar to those in Sweden and Austria—broke down as incumbent companies were privatized and as new competitors entered liberalized markets. This breakdown can be attributed to the different union structures that developed in each country, with more substantial overlap between union representation domains, as well as competing collective agreements with little coordination (Benassi, Doellgast, and Sarmiento-Mirwaldt 2016). Both represent a pattern of growing competition among unions through "representation domain divides," which undermined efforts to build inclusive labor solidarity.

In Denmark, the incumbent and new competitors came to be fragmented across multiple unions and employer associations. This contrasts with developments in Sweden described above. In 1996, Tele Danmark joined the employer association, the Confederation of Danish Industries (DI). In 1998, its union at the time, the Telecommunications Union (TKF), accepted a modified version of DI's white-collar agreement, with the commitment to make further adaptations over the years. TKF then joined the Central Organization of Industrial Employees (CO-Industri) (the union counterpart to DI), under special conditions. In 2003, TKF merged with Dansk Metal. A new secretariat was created for IT and telecom employees, headed up by the former president of TKF. Meanwhile, as new telecom companies entered the liberalized industry, they were typically represented by the Union of Commercial and Clerical Employees (HK)—the major LO union responsible for telecom employers outside of TDC. Other smaller unions from different union confederations also organized telecommunications and IT companies, such as PROSA—an FTF union.

All of these unions competed with each other for members, and in some cases undercut each other through negotiating lower cost agreements with employers. Because both Dansk Metal and HK are LO unions, they had agreements concerning which area of the industry each was responsible for organizing. All companies in which TDC had over 50% ownership were the responsibility of Dansk Metal; while other telecom and IT companies were the responsibility of HK. Despite this agreement, there were ongoing conflicts: "the main problem in Denmark for the unions is that we don't agree. [...] We don't work good [sic] enough together to get the maximum benefit for members because there's too many kings who want to keep their kingdoms" (Dansk Metal rep TDC, April 24, 2012).

The collective bargaining situation was further complicated by the absence of a single employer association in the telecom sector. At the time of my research, TDC was a member of the industry IT, Telecommunications, Electronics, and Communications (ITEK) in DI and applied the basic terms of its white-collar collective agreement. However, collective agreements were negotiated separately by Dansk Metal at the TDC corporate group level and across its subsidiaries, leading to widely divergent pay scales and terms and conditions for similar employee groups within TDC. Telia Denmark was a member of DI, as well, but was formally the responsibility of HK. Other large telecom companies were often members of both DI and DE—however, they were able to choose which agreement (if any) to apply.

Employers were also able to change agreements voluntarily, although they were not supposed to change agreements "just" to reduce the level of employment terms and conditions: "they can just write a letter saying, 'we want to get out of DI Dansk Industri and we're changing to Dansk DE,' and then the collective agreement will have to change. [. . .] It's really . . . it's kind of difficult when there's not just one law for things" (HK official, April 26, 2012). Union officials estimated that collective agreements covered around 80% of the telecommunications workforce. Still, many small companies did not negotiate agreements, and pay and terms and conditions differed widely at the company level due to differences in union organization and shop steward experience.

In contrast to both the Nordics and Austria, Germany lacked an encompassing sectoral collective agreement or effective mechanisms to extend the terms of company-level agreements. This meant that many competitors were able to avoid collective bargaining altogether—particularly small service resellers and internet service providers, but also some larger employers.

Bargaining disorganization both encouraged and was exacerbated by inter-union competition. As described above, Austrian unions had a clear division of labor and jointly established a coordinated bargaining structure. In contrast, in Germany several industry-based unions negotiated company-level agreements with Deutsche Telekom's newer competitors, with little or no coordination of terms and conditions. Many of these competitors were originally established as subsidiaries of larger companies based in the public, metalworking, chemical, and energy sectors—and thus historically had agreements with, e.g. Transnet, ötv, IG Metall, and IG BCE. The constant reorganization of these companies intensified conflict among unions seeking to defend or expand their membership.

The major unions negotiated a formal agreement in 2000 that divided up responsibility for telecom and IT companies; however, this did not prevent conflict. For example, ver.di had agreed that the mobile phone company D2 Mannesmann Mobilfunk fell under IG Metall's jurisdiction, as it was a subsidiary of a metal industry company. After the British company Vodafone took over Mannesmann, ver.di representatives initially argued that they should be responsible for the new company. In another example, Deutsche Telekom established a strategic partnership with Nokia Siemens Networks that led to the transfer of 1,600 technicians in 2008. In this case IG Metall had agreements with Nokia, leading to some uncertainty about which union should have responsibility for this group. More recently, in 2019, Vodafone purchased Liberty Global's cable networks—which had formerly been spun off from Deutsche Telekom, and so continued to have collective agreements with ver.di.

Ver.di can be compared to the GPA in Austria. Like the GPA, it represented workers across a range of service industries, including several connected through subcontracting relationships. However, unlike the GPA, ver.di included members and union representatives from the incumbent company, Deutsche Telekom, which in Austria remained in the union GPF. Ver.di experienced legitimacy problems as it sought to establish itself as broadly representative of telecom workers because most of its membership was at Deutsche Telekom. In addition, different service industries were represented by other departments that competed for resources within the union. In the period following the mergers that formed ver.di, the new union initiated several cross-department campaigns to organize across increasingly networked service industries. However, many of these were abandoned in the face of resource scarcity and intra-union competition (Holtgrewe and Doellgast 2012).

As a result, works councils became the central bargaining partners representing worker interests in many German telecom companies. However, unions found it difficult to organize or work closely with works councils outside of Deutsche Telekom. This lack of traditional "dual system" bargaining institutions had implications for works councils' independence from management, as well as for bargaining coordination within a company. Works councilors at individual locations often did not know each other. Membership in company-level councils changed frequently as divisions were spun off and former competitors merged. Moreover, works councils in different subsidiaries and business units of diversified corporate groups often viewed their interests as distinct or conflicting (Höpner and Jackson 2003; Sako and Jackson 2003).

Deutsche Telekom's subsidiaries had a younger workforce with a weaker connection to the union. This lack of coordination was exacerbated by the complexity of company- and subsidiary-level bargaining. One union representative estimated that in the mid-2000s there were 100 agreements across Deutsche Telekom. As new subsidiaries were established, management negotiated new collective agreements with diverging terms. While works councils were strong across the corporate group and most works councilors were ver.di members, they did not always communicate with their colleagues at other subsidiaries or with the union (Doellgast and Greer 2007).

Ideological Divides: France, Italy, and Poland

A third pattern can be seen in France, Italy, and Poland. These countries all have labor movements divided along ideological lines, with multiple unions involved in negotiations within the incumbent telecom companies and in the sector. France and Italy both have more encompassing sectoral bargaining structures, but, similar to Poland, their main base of membership and bargaining power is in the incumbent. The common challenge unions face in building more inclusive solidarity is thus overcoming these "ideological divides" to coordinate positions and campaigns to organize and represent precarious workers or to prevent growing precarity within the core workforce.

Sectoral bargaining in telecommunications developed in the late 1990s in both Italy and France. Before privatization, wages and working conditions at Telecom Italia were regulated by an in-house, company-level agreement. When the market was liberalized, similar to Germany, new companies typically adopted the agreement for the sector their parent company belonged to. For example, Omnitel applied the metalworking agreement, while Wind and Blu both had company-level agreements (Paparella 2000).

The first telecom agreement was signed in 2000 between the national employer federation Confindustria and a confederation of the major unions. It is unusual for Confindustria to negotiate agreements; however, the sectoral employer association, Federcomin, did not have an institutionalized bargaining position at the time. By 2003, the other big telecom companies such as Wind and Vodafone applied the telecom agreement.

In France, France Telecom and its major competitor Cegetel established an employer association, the National Union of Telecommunications Companies (UNETEL), in the late 1990s. UNETEL signed an agreement in 1998 with a consortium of five unions (Mias 2008). Non-civil servants at France Telecom were moved to the sectoral agreement, while other companies initially followed an existing agreement from the IT sector and established a separate branch of their employer association, the RST. Then in 1999 the French State extended the UNETEL agreement to all companies in the sector, defined to include telecom and internet providers, cable operators, television and radio broadcasting units, and call centers owned by companies in these industry segments. After this decision, RST merged with UNETEL. By 2010, its members represented 19% of companies employing 90% of the telecom workforce. Membership was not compulsory; however, any agreement signed by the employers' organization was extended to all telecom companies, including non-members.

In Poland, in contrast, there was no sectoral agreement, with low union membership and very few collective agreements outside of the incumbent Orange Polska and its subsidiaries. According to a works councilor, "many young people do not even know that there are unions, are not interested [. . .] and treat this as something from a bygone era" (SKPT works councilor, February 15, 2012).

While the three countries developed different sectoral institutions, they have a similar "multi-union" bargaining structure with strong ideological divides—which are most noticeable within the incumbent companies that represent the strongest, and most institutionalized, base of union membership.

The first collective agreement for private law employees at France Telecom and La Poste was negotiated in 1991. By the late 2010s, CGT, CFDT, and SUD had the highest membership at France Telecom and in the sector, followed by FO and CFE-CGC. Elections for worker representatives were an important measure of support for each union, and the most successful were CGT, SUD, and CFDT (in this order).

The three main unions in the Italian telecom sector (in order of membership) were the Union of Communication Workers (SLC), affiliated with the former communist CGIL confederation; the Trade Union Federation of Information, Entertainment, and Telecommunications (FISTEL), affiliated with the catholic confederation CISL; and UILCOM, a member of the socialist UIL. A further union, UGL-COM, is a member of the right-wing General Union of Labor (UGL), which does not usually bargain together with the other unions, but often signs the same collective agreement. Similar to France, the largest concentration of membership was in the incumbent. In addition, there were many small unions at Telecom Italia; but from the perspective of the larger unions, their focus was almost exclusively on bringing management to court. A Telecom Italia manager described them as "a legal studio surrounded by a void" (TI HR manager, May 14, 2012). According to a union representative, even this legal support was usually not successful, and many workers eventually ended up asking the main unions FISTEL and SLC for help (SLC-CGIL official, March 23, 2012).

Thus, in both France and Italy, multiple unions were competing over members and influence within the incumbents, often on the basis of the positions they took on different restructuring measures or management proposals. The left-wing unions more often opposed planned measures, or were less likely to sign agreements, while the more conservative or social partnership–oriented unions sought compromise.

The high degree of inter-union conflict was a particularly common theme in interviews in France—and so it is worth going into more detail on how these conflicts played out at France Telecom. One former manager who had been responsible for change management and restructuring described how the unions' different ideological positions influenced his own negotiating strategies:

In France you have two types of trade unions. Those who kind of find solutions—it's mostly the case with CFDT and in some way FO; but two others are CGT and SUD, they were against anything, they didn't really want to negotiate anything. . . . In France therefore, especially in the Paris region, SUD has the majority, so they were against all our projects and they didn't want to negotiate anything. So it was just a matter of procedure, a formal matter. [. . .] So actually there were two levels of negotiation: the formal level where you don't negotiate anything, not even kind of playing; [then] sometimes you negotiate separately with the trade unions, and everyone is playing their part. (former FT manager, June 28, 2010)

Union representatives also described the differences in approach between unions—with quotes from CFDT and CGT representatives showing how each saw their own and competitor unions:

> The CGT is . . . I don't know if you know something about the philosophy of the different unions. For me at France Telecom, the CGT is employment, the big industrial project [*les grands projets industriels*]. . . . I have the impression that the CGT is still influenced a little by visions that are a bit Stalinist: big projects organized by the state, but that stay at the same time in the capitalist system, which does not jeopardize the operation of this system even if they cry . . . while at CFDT or SUD, we are more likely to say that it is how something works that is important, not what we do. So globally it is the CFDT that makes proposals in negotiations. (CFDT rep FT, May 4, 2010)

> There are a few different strategies between unions, because there are some who are more or less likely to use the method of mobilizing employees. Unions that are called "reformist" [CFDT, CFTC, FO, and CFE-CGC] tend to say that they will find the solution together with the management, sitting around a table. We [CGT] think we need to sit at the negotiating table, but often to get things done, we need the direct support of employees and of the weight they represent. Therefore, we need to get them to get into the action and help us [. . .]. SUD actually is not very constructive in the negotiations; they do not come with constructive proposals, they often come to meetings just to tell the employers that they do not agree with them, but often they stop there; they do not necessarily say what should be done to make things go better. They are more about the protest itself; they stop at the protest. (CGT rep FT, May 12, 2010)

These quotes illustrate how ideological divisions were reflected in different approaches to bargaining and mobilization within France Telecom, with implications for management's own strategies in working with (or bypassing) different unions.

In Poland, a divided structure of union representation developed over time in the incumbent. In the past, Telekomunikacja Polska (later Orange Polska) was officially subdivided into twenty-three employers in different parts of the country. There was a management board and beneath it a company board (*dyrekcja spółki*) and then workplaces. Negotiations over wage increases or redundancy pay were conducted by the company board with the nationally representative unions. However, work or social rules, bonuses, and other details were negotiated at workplace level. Thus, employees' conditions and social benefits differed across locations depending on the negotiating skills of the union's director.

Telekomunikacja Polska then underwent a process of consolidation, moving to one employer in 2005. This meant that smaller plant unions became corporate organizations and the number of unions able to negotiate at national level increased. At the time of our research, around twenty unions were active at Orange Polska. The two with the most members and influence were the National Section of Telecommunications Workers (SKPT)[6] of the more conservative NSZZ Solidarność and the Federation of Unions for Telecommunications Workers (FZZPT) of the more leftist OPZZ. Both unions introduced interbranch organizations (*międzyzakładowe*) at the incumbent and its subsidiaries around the year 2000. Some smaller unions, such as the Forum's Union of Engineers and Technicians (ZZiT), represented specific professional groups. The very smallest unions had from tens to hundreds of members. Unions reported that in the 2005–2010 period, about 25% of all Orange Polska employees (excluding the subsidiaries) were members of the FZZPT, and about 30% were members of SKPT (including the subsidiaries).

All unions took part in negotiations over wages, restructuring, and the broad parameters of work organization. Delegates from the two representative unions were always present, as well as one or two representing the other unions. They had thirty days to reach a common position; and if they failed to do so, the two largest were required to agree in order to engage in dialogue with the employer. However, if these two unions did not agree, then the employer had the freedom to decide. Relations between the SKPT and the FZZPT were at times fairly conflictual, making agreement difficult and thus indirectly assisting the employer.

Structural Exclusive Solidarity: The United States, the United Kingdom, the Czech Republic (and Poland)

A fourth pattern can be found in the US, UK, and Czech telecom sectors—which I term "structural exclusive solidarity." Poland belongs in this group, as well; though unions were ideologically divided within the incumbent, they lacked the sectoral bargaining resources present in France and Italy. Although there was sectoral bargaining in the Czech telecom industry, agreements were not extended and coverage was low—and so the union's main area of influence was within the incumbent O2 Czech Republic. In both AT&T and BT, two unions were present, but they had relatively clear representation domains; and so union competition

---

[6] SKPT is an industry structure bringing together three NSZZ Solidarność union organizations: (1) OMPT (or inter-plant organization of NSZZ Solidarność telecommunications employees), which is active at employers such as TP, OCS, PTK Centertel, CC, OPCO; (2) EmiTel; and (3) TP Edukacja i Wypoczynek.

was minimal. The distinguishing features of this group are decentralized and primarily company-level bargaining with unions that have little reach or influence beyond their core employers. Across the four cases, unions had very weak institutional power resources to organize and represent workers at subcontractors or on more precarious contracts. Thus, the major dynamics of labor solidarity were inward focused, with the aim of preserving or re-internalizing jobs within the incumbent.

In the US telecom sector, there are two major unions, the Communications Workers of America (CWA) and the International Brotherhood of Electrical Workers (IBEW), with the CWA by far the largest. Both continued to have most of their telecom members in companies that have their origins in the AT&T and Bell System. The two unions had some conflicts in the past: "There are always tensions. We are the bigger union, so the danger is always that they will negotiate a separate contract, and it will be a situation where the tail is wagging the dog. It's been a struggle, but we have to build relationships to ensure that it will work" (CWA official, March 9, 2013). But their relationship is generally cooperative: they each agreed to jurisdictions based on the regions and workplaces where they have historically represented workers, and they worked closely on campaigns while bargaining some contracts jointly.

There are also two unions at BT and in the UK telecom sector: the Communication Workers Union (CWU) and Prospect. However, unlike the United States, these unions represent different professional groups: the CWU represented non-managerial grades in telecom companies, while Prospect organized first-, second-, and third-line managers and professionals in many industries. Prospect had a sector called "Connect," which was specifically devoted to telecommunications. By the 2010s, BT employees were divided into different grades (e.g., B2 for field technicians or C3 for network technicians). Most of these grades were eligible for membership in the CWU, while around 25,000 employees (at the time of our research) were employed in Prospect grades. Thus, the unions had clear and distinct representation domains. The CWU had around 90% union membership density across its eligible grades in most parts of BT, while Prospect had a little over 50% density in its grades. The two unions worked together closely, bargaining separately over wages but with joint union forums or "single table bargaining" on pensions, health and safety, and equality issues. Both also had recognition in several other telecom companies such as Vodafone and O2, but in those companies their collective agreements were separate.

The most important trade union in the Czech telecom sector is the Trade Union of Postal, Telecommunications, and Newspaper Services Employees (OSZPTNS), which was the only major union active at the incumbent at the time of our research. Some much smaller unions had members in smaller companies or business units, but these were not involved in collective bargaining.

In all three countries, collective bargaining coverage had declined from nationally encompassing, when the incumbent had a monopoly, to more fragmented and company-based. In the United States, a national bargaining structure was established by 1974 that covered AT&T and the Regional Bell Operating Companies (RBOCs, Regional Bells), with a national contract for wages, benefits, and employment security. Following divestiture, national bargaining was replaced by a two-tiered system, with company-level and local agreements on different issues. However, they maintained pattern bargaining, led by AT&T, until 1998, when expiration dates and terms of the various agreements started to diverge. By 2010, AT&T had reconsolidated through mergers orchestrated by the former Regional Bell SBC and had six regional contracts, with a number of special contracts for newer areas such as internet services. AT&T Mobility was covered by three major collective agreements in different union districts, organized by states, with a fourth contract in Puerto Rico.

As in the United States, there was no sectoral agreement in the UK telecom industry. As stated above, Vodafone and O2 did have agreements. However, these were not coordinated with BT, and many UK telecom employers remained non-union, including one of BT's largest competitors, Cable & Wireless. At the same time, BT's agreements were more centralized and coordinated across the corporate group compared to those at AT&T. Bargaining took place at company level and covered the entire company, including BT's subsidiaries, though union officials observed that local managers did not always follow these central agreements. In many lines of business, they might say, "We don't need this. We'll just do it our way. This is the Retail way" (Prospect official, November 1, 2011). Collective agreements were also negotiated at the Line of Business level, e.g., BT Retail, Openreach, BT Wholesale; however, these were closely coordinated with company-wide bargaining.

In the Czech Republic, similar to Poland, the incumbent was significantly decentralized and then re-centralized in the transition period after 1989. Between 1990 and 1998, Český Telecom was divided into 130–150 local organizations, with matching local union organizations that, for example, conducted wage bargaining or bargaining over working conditions. This local structure was only unified after 1998. A major motivation was provisions in the Labor Code stipulating that employees had to be treated equally in a company, requiring more centralized bargaining. As a result, the number of collective agreements at the company dropped from 120 to one.

There were four levels of union representation at the time of our research. Local organizations of unions negotiated or consulted at workplace level. Regional representatives were elected for four regions. A central-level enterprise coordination union committee was elected across the company. And finally, at the sectoral level, an agreement was negotiated between OSZPTNS and the

Czech Union of Postal, Telecommunications, and Press Distribution employers. This fixed certain broad parameters such as holidays, weekly working time, and formal rules for cooperation or consultation.

The company agreement negotiated between O2 Czech Republic and OSZPTNS was valid only for the main central business unit, not for the company's subsidiaries. Thus, when the mobile provider Eurotel was a subsidiary of Český Telecom, it was not covered. Eventually it was integrated into the company, and the collective agreement was extended to former Eurotel workers.

Thus, in the United Kingdom, the United States, the Czech Republic, and Poland (as an overlapping fourth case), union power in the telecom sector was concentrated in the incumbents. Bargaining was most centralized and coordinated within the incumbent at BT—though with some cooperation across the two unions required. AT&T had the largest variation across different collective agreements, by region and business unit. However, at all four, union representation outside of the incumbents was very low. They all did have some degree of division among or conflict between unions, with the most severe divisions at Orange Polska, as discussed in the previous section. However, the strongest divides were between the highly organized core workforce and the weakly or unorganized periphery.

Summary

The above comparison shows cross-cutting similarities and differences in union structures. In Denmark, Austria, and Germany, one major union was present in the incumbent and a different union or unions represented employees at most other major telecom companies. The Czech Republic is distinctive in having one main union both in the incumbent and for the industry. In Sweden, the United Kingdom, and the United States, multiple unions were present in the incumbent but represented clearly delineated groups, with no or minimal competition. In France, Italy, and Poland, multiple unions competed for members and influence within the incumbent—Poland being the most extreme case with about twenty unions present at Orange Polska.

There was also variation in bargaining structures within the incumbents' corporate groups. First, they differed in the degree of bargaining centralization. Agreements were most centralized at company level at Telia, A1, and BT. TDC, Deutsche Telekom, Orange Polska, and O2 Czech Republic had separate agreements and pay structures for subsidiaries, with some coordination between them. AT&T had a large number of collective agreements, with differing terms by region for similar employee groups. In contrast, Telecom Italia closely followed the pay and conditions outlined in the sectoral agreement, with small

102   EXIT, VOICE, AND SOLIDARITY

differences in bonuses and terms across its subsidiaries; while France Telecom had a standard model for pay and variable pay that applied across the corporate group.

All of these differences are significant in providing resources for or constraints on labor cooperation and bargaining coordination—central to influencing strategies of labor solidarity that are discussed in the chapters that follow. However, I have emphasized above the four broader patterns that distinguish groups of countries, based on the most significant structural and ideological factors promoting labor cooperation or divides: structural inclusive solidarity (Austria and Sweden), representation domain divides (Denmark and Germany), ideological divides (France, Italy, and Poland), and structural exclusive solidarity (United Kingdom, United States, Czech Republic, and Poland). These prove important in explaining both failures and successes of campaigns aimed at closing off exit options and applying or extending worker voice across the case studies.

Comparing Exit, Voice, and Solidarity

Figure 2.3 presents a summary model that brings together th ree factors discussed in this chapter: constraints on employer exit, support for collective worker voice, and strategies of inclusive labor solidarity.

The classification of cases based on each of these three factors has been developed in detail in this chapter. The figure illustrates how they relate to one another,

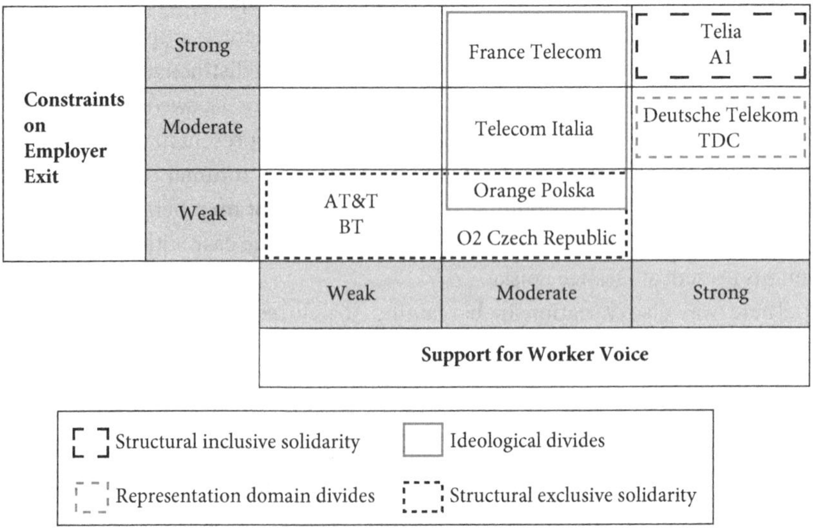

Constraints on Employer Exit	Strong		France Telecom	Telia / A1
	Moderate		Telecom Italia	Deutsche Telekom / TDC
	Weak	AT&T / BT	Orange Polska	
			O2 Czech Republic	
		Weak	Moderate	Strong
		Support for Worker Voice		

Legend:
- Structural inclusive solidarity
- Ideological divides
- Representation domain divides
- Structural exclusive solidarity

Figure 2.3. Framework for comparing the case studies.

helping to distinguish general patterns. The combination of strong constraints on exit and strong support for employee voice corresponds with *structural inclusive solidarity* in the Austrian (A1) and Swedish (Telia) cases. This does not mean that solidarity was easy to establish and maintain: in both cases, unions disagreed or faced divisions within their own organizations and across different groups of worker representatives. They also had to make choices to concentrate resources on organizing and representing peripheral groups. However, the structures of inclusive bargaining, few exit options, and strong participation rights and structures did make the challenges of maintaining a solidaristic front vis-à-vis employers much easier to overcome. Conflicts of interest and ideology were less salient within centralized and inclusive bargaining structures, and institutional resources to extend bargaining and union representation to precarious worker groups were more readily available.

On the other extreme, weak constraints on exit and weak or moderate support for employee voice underpin *structural exclusive solidarity* in the United States (AT&T), the United Kingdom (BT), the Czech Republic (O2 Czech Republic), and Poland (Orange Polska). Here again, the institutional structure of bargaining is the most important factor in understanding patterns of labor cooperation. There was coordinated bargaining within the incumbent companies, backed by organized membership, but unions faced constant threats that employers would exit internal employment relationships; for example, via downsizing, spin-offs, or outsourcing. At the same time, institutional resources to organize and extend bargaining to new companies or groups of workers were weak. Together, this influences the parameters of solidarity strategies: unions' main power resources are within their core employers, and so they focus on using these resources to fight the expansion of precarity—often leading to trade-offs when employers demanded concessions in return for job security. At the same time, the main institutional tools for improving conditions across the workforce are based on strengthening legal protections, in countries with overall weak legal minimum standards.

The middle two categories are situated in between these extremes, with most of the cases showing moderate to strong constraints on employer exit or support for collective worker voice. Across these cases, labor divides are often the most significant obstacle to be overcome in fights against precarity. The challenge in these countries is to organize coordinated campaigns aimed at closing institutional loopholes or strengthening participation rights and structures. Unions are best able to meet these challenges when they succeed in bridging divides to establish coalitions or agreements within sectors and across value chains. In Denmark and Germany, the main divides are at the company level, based on *representation domain divides* with multiple, competing unions seeking to organize different telecom companies and their subcontractors. In France and Italy (and to some degree also Poland), *ideological divides* are more central, with multiple unions present within the incumbents and in the sector. These divisions can be exploited by employers, leading to systematic undercutting of terms and conditions. At the same time, unions' success in mobilizing against precarious work depends on overcoming these divides—working together to bridge ideological differences or more clearly define and coordinate across representation domains.

In the chapters that follow, I use this model as a starting point for analyzing the politics of restructuring in the ten case study companies. Chapter 3 focuses on negotiations over downsizing, which are strongly shaped by differences in constraints on employer exit—particularly employment protections. Chapter 4 focuses on performance management in call centers and technician workplaces, where worker voice resources come to the fore—as worker representatives negotiate over alternative approaches to motivate and discipline workers. Chapter 5 compares externalization through subsidiary spin-offs, temporary agency work, and outsourcing, where strategies of labor solidarity play a central role in efforts to organize and represent workers across organizational boundaries. In each case, institutional structures and rules were important to outcomes; however, the choices unions made led to change over time, with sometimes surprising outcomes. Across the cases, employers have sought to assert market-based values in decisions to downsize employment, introduce new monitoring and variable pay practices, and shift jobs to contracts or workplaces covered by weaker legislated and negotiated protections. Unions' success in reasserting the legitimacy of social values and outcomes in the employment relationship depended on how they combined constraints on exit, support for voice, and strategies of solidarity. All three underpinned worker power and were central to fighting the expansion of precarious work.

3
Downsizing

Downsizing is the most publicly visible and contentious of restructuring measures. As employers cut employment, they can create severe stress for laid off workers and their co-workers. It is also an area where labor market and collective bargaining institutions can make a significant difference, affecting the strength of job security for different groups, the form and generosity of redundancy payments, and support for (or requirements concerning) retraining. Unions are often heavily involved in negotiating over, or seeking to block or contest, decisions that could cost their members their jobs.

From the perspective of incumbent telecom companies and their managers, downsizing has been seen as a necessary response to shrinking market share and technological change. More service providers are competing for customers across a growing number of market segments, with expanding menus of products and services: from mobile phones to TV, fixed-line phone service, and high-speed internet. Changes in the network (from copper to fiber—and from fixed-line to wireless) mean less required maintenance and thus fewer technicians.

At the same time, decisions concerning how much to downsize and in what ways are often highly politicized. Privatization and changing ownership structures have increased the pressure these companies are under to maximize shareholder value. Combined with financial distress, ballooning debt, or declining share price, concerns with investor interests can push employers to adopt radical plans to restructure employment—in part to convince credit rating agencies that managers are taking measures to cut costs. Downsizing is often accompanied by (or undertaken as an alternative to) the spin-offs or outsourcing measures that I discuss in Chapter 5. However, it is distinctive as a set of policies explicitly aimed at cutting jobs across the company and in certain areas of the business.

In this chapter, I compare restructuring measures aimed at reducing workforce numbers at the ten case study companies in response to these common trends. At all of the companies, downsizing decisions, and the collective negotiations surrounding them, involved contests over the social value of work. Labor unions were almost universally successful in negotiating generous voluntary redundancy and early retirement plans in the 1990s. However, during the following decade, management came under increased pressure to reduce the cost of these plans. Growing competition from companies with lower labor costs, more

Exit, Voice, and Solidarity. Virginia Doellgast, Oxford University Press. © Oxford University Press 2022.
DOI: 10.1093/oso/9780197659779.003.0004

activist shareholders, and often high debt ratios pushed employers to pursue more aggressive cost-cutting. This, in turn, encouraged a shift away from prioritizing social concerns with coordination and equity, toward a market-based focus on minimizing labor costs. The outcome was growing insecurity, shrinking employment, and, typically, increased conflict between management and worker representatives.

However, the cases differ significantly in the overall generosity of terms, the extent of their erosion, as well as the form and outcome of labor conflict associated with downsizing. I divide them into two broad groups, based on the strength of the institutional limits on exit that most directly affect downsizing decisions, such as employment protections in national legislation and collective agreements, and job security attached to civil servant status. This is based on the second column of Table 2.1 in Chapter 2: *Constraints on exit from internal employment relationships*. The first group, AT&T, BT, O2 Czech Republic, Orange Polska, and TDC, all show overall either more involuntary layoffs or less generous redundancy plans, in the context of easier "exit" from internal employment. In the second group, Telia, A1, Deutsche Telekom, Telecom Italia, and France Telecom, unions were able to negotiate largely voluntary layoffs and preserve more favorable redundancy terms, or to negotiate alternatives to layoffs with the support of state subsidies or programs. Within each group (and over time in each case), outcomes differed depending on union capacity to mobilize countervailing power through collective worker voice and labor solidarity.

In the following sections, I first give background on changing markets and ownership structures. I then compare negotiations over downsizing in each group of cases. I summarize major restructuring plans and agreements, and then examine one case study in more detail—TDC in Denmark for the cases with weaker exit constraints; and Telia in Sweden for the cases with stronger exit constraints.

Changing Markets and Ownership Structures

The telecom industry has transformed over the past two decades from one organized around national markets and dominated by state-owned public telecommunications operators (PTOs) or regulated monopolies to a highly competitive and international information services industry. This shift was partially due to technological advances, as costs of establishing competing networks fell and new market segments such as mobile, internet, and cable began to compete with fixed-line telephone services. It has also been driven by changes in regulation and ownership. National governments in Europe fully or partially privatized their PTOs—in the mid 1980s in the United Kingdom and in the 1990s in the rest of Europe—and passed laws aimed at curtailing their market power. In the United States, following an anti-trust lawsuit, the monopoly provider AT&T gave up control of its regional subsidiaries, which were established as seven Regional Bell Operating Companies (Regional Bells).

The liberalization of telecom markets occurred at different times and rates across countries. The United States and United Kingdom passed legislation in the mid-1980s promoting competition in certain segments, such as long distance; but incumbent companies continued to have protected markets in other areas. In the United States, full competition was introduced in the long-distance market in 1984, but the Regional Bells maintained their monopolies in regional and local markets until 1996. BT competed in a duopoly with Mercury Communications from 1982 until 1990, when licenses to operate fixed-line networks were opened up to a wider range of companies.

Elsewhere in the European Union, the timing of liberalization was influenced by a Council of Ministers directive in 1993 requiring all EU member states to end monopolies on telecommunications network infrastructure and voice telephony services by January 1, 1998. Denmark, Austria, Germany, France, and Italy all introduced similar legislation complying with this directive between 1996 and 1998 (see Table 3.1). Sweden was a distinctive case: the telecom market was largely unregulated, with the state-owned provider Televerket (later Telia) holding a de facto rather than a formal or regulated national monopoly. The government began to allow competitors to connect to Televerket's network in 1980, and its monopoly on phones and telephone exchanges ended between 1985 and 1989. Neither Poland nor the Czech Republic were EU members in 1998; however, market liberalization was required as part of both countries' EU accession negotiations and was carried out in early in the following decade.

The timing and pace of liberalization affected each incumbent's market power, as well as the intensity of pressure to restructure employment in different time periods. Most of the case study companies experienced a steep fall in market share for fixed-line calls between 1999 and 2005. For example, France Telecom's market share fell from 97% to 71% over this period, dropping further to 53% by 2010. In most countries, competition stabilized between 2005 and 2010. However, patterns differ by country. BT experienced the most dramatic decline between 2005 and 2010, falling from 60% to 39%, while TDC's market share increased somewhat from 66% to 69%.[1]

A second difference concerns ownership structures. Again, the Anglo-Americans are distinctive here: AT&T was a regulated monopoly with no state

---

[1] Sources: EU countries from European Commission (2012); US from Federal Communications Commission (2013 and 2007).

Table 3.1 Market Liberalization and Privatization of Incumbent Firms

	Year First Public Share Offering	Year Fully Privatized or (% State Ownership 2012)	Year Market Liberalized (Fixed-Line Segment)	Market Share (Fixed-Line Segment) 2010*
TDC	1994	1998	1996	67%
Telia	2000	(51%)	1993	59%
A1	2000	(28%)	1998	55%
Deutsche Telekom	1995	(32%)	1998	52%
France Telecom	1997	(27%)	1998	51%
Telecom Italia	1997	2003	1997	56%
BT	1984	1993	1990	39%
AT&T	1885	1885	1996	N/A
O2 Czech Republic	1995	2005	2001	60%
Orange Polska	1998	2010	2003	57%

* *Source:* European Commission (2010)

ownership, while BT was the first European operator to be privatized—with a majority of shares sold to the public in 1984 and the remaining government-held shares sold in 1993. The other European countries held on to state ownership for longer, but, again, differed in the timing and extent of privatization (see Table 3.1). Telia retained the highest percentage of state ownership, although it had fallen to 39.5% by 2021.

Privatization was accompanied by a growth in foreign ownership, or shareholdings by institutions or individuals based outside of the incumbent's home country. In all cases, there was some increase. However, again, patterns differ. France Telecom shares were still largely held by French investors before 2010, with only 15% foreign ownership; while TDC was over 75% foreign-owned (Thompson Financial 2012).

These ownership patterns are connected in part to differences in how shares were sold or acquired—and in particular the role of mergers and acquisitions (M&As). In some cases, major telecom operators based in other countries acquired majority ownership. Telekomunikacja Polska was acquired by France Telecom (France) and was rebranded as Orange Polska, and Český Telecom was acquired by O2 Telefónica (Spain). TDC was acquired by Ameritech (United States), which was taken over by SBC; and then in 2005 a consortium of five private equity funds acquired a majority stake in the company. Telia merged with the Finnish incumbent Sonera in 2002 and was rebranded as "TeliaSonera" until 2016. In other cases, acquisitions or takeovers occurred between domestic companies, such as the takeover of Telecom Italia by Olivetti in 1999—carried out through a system of "Chinese boxes" in which a chain of holding companies was created, with each company owning a (typically minority) share in the next company.

A final difference concerns sources of finance. Many companies took on debt in the early to mid-2000s to finance acquisitions and expansion. France Telecom doubled its debt ratio (the percentage of a company's assets provided via debt compared to equity) from 24% in 2000 to 48% in 2003 to finance a wave of international acquisitions—including its purchase of Orange plc from Vodafone for 43.2 billion euros. BT saw even larger increases in its debt ratio, from 14% in 2000 to nearly 60% in 2002. TDC more than quadrupled its debt ratio between 1995 and 2010, which in the later period is due to its ownership by private equity funds. In contrast, Telia, O2 Czech Republic, and Orange Polska either kept or returned their debt ratios to below 20% by 2010.

These different patterns of ownership and finance have had an impact on the pressures management faced to maximize cash flow and reduce costs during different time periods, as well as the goals and objectives pursued through restructuring. Traditionally, companies in continental European countries have relied on more long-term forms of finance or "patient capital," characterized by cross-shareholding between large companies and bank-based loans. This has been argued to reduce pressures for short-term growth and cost-cutting typical of the liberal and financialized Anglo-American countries (Gospel and Pendleton 2005; Vitols 2001). The state has been one of the most patient shareholders, with a longer-term view to infrastructure investment.

In the telecom industry, liberalization and privatization encouraged a similar (if differently timed) process of financialization across countries, increasing pressure on the incumbents to maximize shareholder value and secure short-term returns. For example, Curwen and Whalley (2004, 104) argue that the debt burden associated with the series of takeovers at Telecom Italia played a significant role in driving up cost-cutting pressures: "There was widespread concern that Olivetti was obliged to meet a stringent timetable to repay the €6.9 billion borrowed from banks at a time when telecom Italia's workforce was badly demoralised, and its victory was widely seen as bordering on the Pyrrhic."

At the most extreme end is TDC in Denmark, where ownership changed dramatically over a short period, from public to majority (foreign-based) private equity ownership. Union representatives observed that the focus of management strategy had shifted from a long-term orientation, characterized by investment and expansion, to a more short-term strategy focused on value extraction. "Everything that can be capitalized, they will do it. Their view is very short. They will look at how much money they can get out" (Dansk Metal rep TDC, April 24, 2012). This changing strategic focus was accompanied by a number of cash-generating measures that were opposed by the union, such as the sale of property owned by TDC and an attempt at accessing money from the pension funds. From management's perspective, the new owners were increasing efficiency in an unwieldy former public bureaucracy: "They had their targets, they showed us you have to generate this and that. And yeah, and put TDC on a strong diet, which TDC needed. [. . .] And strong goals, very strong goals; very, very strong" (TDC HR manager, April 23, 2012).

Even where shareholdings continued to be more concentrated and held by national investors and the state, major institutional investors were increasingly important in encouraging radical forms of restructuring. Although the private equity investor the Blackstone Group owned 4.4% of Deutsche Telekom shares in the mid-2000s, union and management representatives observed in interviews that it played a central role in advising management on downsizing, outsourcing, and subsidiary spin-offs during this period. At France Telecom, dividends increased by 460% between 2003 and 2009, while employees' share of earned revenue fell by 21.5% (Chabrak, Craig, and Daidj 2016, 507). Chabrak et al. (2016) describe the restructuring measures that France Telecom's management adopted during this period as "financialization policies" associated with both embracing an ideology of shareholder value and materially redistributing cash flow toward shareholders. Palpacuer and Seignour (2020, 425) cite a union representative who expressed incredulity that "*our* leaders would start acting like minions of Wall Street."

Finally, overall performance or profitability differed across the companies and over time. In most cases, incumbents experienced the largest drop in return on assets (ROA—net income in relation to average total assets) in the early 2000s—a time when most incumbents were adjusting to a large decline in domestic market share while financing a wave of domestic and international acquisitions. However, again, there was variation across companies, with TDC, Telia, and BT maintaining an overall high ROA of between 5% and 8%.

The preceding discussion suggests that the case study companies faced different pressures, from competitive markets, changing ownership structures, and their own structure of costs and debt, to restructure employment in the period after liberalization. At the same time, the scale and scope of these pressures were as a whole similar—and varied more as a function of time period, rather than systematically across companies. The remainder of this chapter examines how the ten companies downsized employment in response to intensifying competition and pressure from investors.

Downsizing under Weaker Exit Constraints

AT&T, BT, O2 Czech Republic, Orange Polska, and TDC are all cases that share weaker institutional constraints on exit from internal employment relationship (second column, Table 2.1).

O2 Czech Republic[2] shows among the worst agreements and outcomes overall, despite an improvement in terms over time. Downsizing was rare before 1997, due in part to the high rate of voluntary employee departures to other telecom companies in a growing industry. After 1997, downsizing occurred regularly. Around 19,000 domestic jobs, representing over 70% of the workforce, were cut between 1997 and 2010, with the largest reductions between 2000 and 2004. A majority were forced redundancies, with only about a quarter leaving through voluntary redundancies or early retirement.

A union representative described the downsizing process as fairly conflictual and argued that many conflicts arose "because management was not able to explain why the changes were introduced" (OSZPTNS rep O2 CR, June 8, 2012). He also described change over time, with conflict in 2002–2004 followed by growing cooperation after O2 Telefónica purchased Český Telecom.

At the same time, redundancy payments at O2 Czech Republic became more generous over time. Until 1995, employees were entitled only to the legal minimum amount of severance pay. In 1996, the union negotiated an increase based on age, years left until retirement, or years spent in the company:

> In the first period of the layoffs, we managed to negotiate better conditions for the people who were dismissed. We managed to increase the severance payment according to how long they had worked for the company. We also tried to ensure that the firm would provide some retraining. It was not very successful. This is why we tried to at least increase the severance payment so that people could use part of the severance payment for the increase or change of their education. The longer you worked in the company, the higher severance pay you would receive because you are harder to employ in another sector. (OSZPTNS rep O2 CR, June 8, 2012)

From the 1990s to the 2010s, severance pay gradually increased. However, this was rather a "catch-up" to terms in the other cases, as the level was low overall. The union also failed to negotiate alternatives to downsizing, including retraining.

At **Orange Polska**, unions were able to win stronger agreements compared to O2 Czech Republic, based in large part on successful mobilization. A massive

---

[2] The O2 Czech Republic, Orange Polska, BT, and A1 cases in this chapter are based on case write-ups by Katja Sarmiento-Mirwaldt, drawing on interviews she conducted.

downsizing process began after 1998 and accelerated in 2000. After a series of protests, the unions managed to negotiate a social package, which was available between 2000 and 2004. This guaranteed that there would be no forced redundancies, and granted severance pay above the level stipulated in the collective agreement. Employees who had worked for Orange Polska for twenty-five years or longer were entitled to fifteen times the individual average monthly salary of a staff member in the last three months of employment.

However, some unionists charged that employees were compelled to leave despite a formal policy of voluntary redundancies. There were many union protests over downsizing between 2001 and 2005. A 2001–2002 dispute ended with an agreement that extended the social package's provisions to the company's subsidiaries, guaranteed the voluntary participation of employees in a "Work for the Worker" program that bound subcontractors to employ former Orange Polska employees (see Chapter 5), and established a consultation process that strengthened union voice in organizational restructuring decisions.

Orange Polska then announced a new round of layoffs in 2005, and the unions held a strike referendum. Around 60% of employees participated, with 92% voting in favor of industrial action. This led to a nationwide strike (which management considered illegal) and a hunger strike in April 2005. After several weeks, the conflict ended with management modifying its original proposals by increasing the amount of severance pay. The agreement also prohibited management from coercing "voluntary" resignations. Then in July 2005, 1,500 employees of French-owned companies in Poland staged a protest at the French embassy in Warsaw. The trade unions involved—led by the SKPT—accused French employers of causing mass redundancies and lowering wages and conditions.

After this conflictual period, subsequent redundancies were negotiated up front between the unions and management. To show goodwill, the company offered mitigating policies that went well beyond legal requirements. These included so-called mini-internships, where employees could work temporarily in another job or department and decide whether they wanted to retrain or not.

An intensive retraining program was also developed (*Program Przemieszczeń Pracowniczych*) to help workers employed in shrinking areas, such as technical services, finance, or administration, transfer to jobs that were expanding, such as sales, customer service, marketing, and technical support. According to one unionist:

> Our customer service [. . .] was established on the basis of employees who have been largely transferred from other jobs that were abolished (because technology is changing) and who had to adapt to customer service. And those who have adapted to the customer service took with them their pay grades, which

were higher than those of people who were recruited from scratch. (OPZZ official, April 17, 2012)

These transfers often required workers to take a pay cut over time as they were transitioned into the new job categories. Some managers were also offered a downgrade, with a gradual reduction in salary. Still, a majority of employees in shrinking areas were willing to leave the company voluntarily. Union officials attributed this to their success in negotiating conditions and severance pay that were "among the best in Poland" (OPZZ officials, April 17, 2012).

At BT, downsizing occurred in the context of a strong partnership:

> We would normally sit down confidentially with the CWU. We had a higher level of trust with them than we did with the Post Office.[3] We would share with them very sensitive information, price-sensitive information. So if we thought that we were going to move from 120,000 full-time employees to 105,000, we would share that with them and say to them, "That's what we're going to do and here's why." (BT manager, November 22, 2011)

At the same time, that partnership was backed up by union power. Managers understood that the unions viewed maintaining voluntary redundancies as important to their members, and that they were likely to strike if this was breached. One manager at BT described the negotiations with the unions as based on avoiding a more heavy-handed conflict-based approach:

> Unions always said: "Compulsory—we'll die at the cross." We as the company always said: "We're not going to promise you this will last forever." But if I can get the volunteers, and then I can redeploy people and retrain them, and they want to stay, why would I want to be heavy-handed? [. . .] Secondly, if you want to be heavy-handed, as I have always told my boards, and make it compulsory and not wait for volunteers, get out of here. Why, if I can avoid legislation, tribunals, and strikes? "No compulsories" has been a constant CWU selling proposition to their members, so you are attacking their hard line. And why would you pick a fight if you don't have to?" (BT manager, November 22, 2011)

Thus, redundancy plans were based exclusively on voluntary leave and early retirement. Until 2001, BT offered a voluntary leavers' package that offered certain employees a maximum enhancement of their pensionable service of up to 6.7 additional years. And if any employee over the age of fifty retired, they could take their pension early with no adverse financial consequences.

---

[3] BT used to be part of the Post Office: it became independent in 1981.

In the early 2000s, BT began to notice the high costs of its earlier agreements. Management would joke that BT was a company servicing a pension scheme, because it had a huge pension deficit—based on a £39 billion commitment with a £9 billion hole. In 2011, the original, defined benefits pensions plan still applied to 60,000 current or former workers. However, employees who had joined after 2001 were on a less favorable defined contribution plan, based on a career average. The pensionable age was also raised from sixty to sixty-five.

In 2001, the company's redundancy package "NewStart" was introduced. Initially, NewStart included a full pension and very generous conditions: for each year of service, employees would get a month's salary, up to a maximum of twelve months, with the first £30,000 tax-free. This was often accompanied by additional incentives to encourage employees to leave voluntarily—for example, they would receive three months' extra salary if they decided to leave by a certain date. However, the terms of NewStart were reduced over time, and by 2013, they were capped at nine months' pay.

At the same time, the CWU negotiated a "commitment for commitment" agreement. This meant that the company would try to retain redundant employees, while the union would encourage these employees to accept retraining and redeployment into a new position. This work would normally be in or within a certain distance from their old location. Interviewees estimated that tens of thousands of employees were redeployed through this program.

A broad retraining strategy complemented BT's commitment to no compulsory redundancies. In 2008, a BT Transitions Centre (BTTC) was established to centralize redeployment and retraining. Initially, large groups of workers could be assisted at one time in the BTTC—for example, 200 engineers[4] would be moved from one function to another, receiving similar training and placement services. As surplus labor declined, the BTTC offered more individualized placement. The target was to redeploy an employee within three months, with a 70% skills match—meaning the retrainee must have 70% of the skills for an advertised role. In most cases, engineers were retrained for other engineering jobs or administrative and support positions. Redeployed employees kept their terms and conditions as well as their previous pay and pension entitlements.

However, it was not always possible to achieve a close skill match. Between 2009 and 2011, 1,500–2,000 engineers were moved into call centers, which caused particularly high resentment due to the very different cultures:

> We had union support for the redeployment and retraining. So we took engineers and retrained them into call centers. They hated it, but the union said, "If

---

[4] The group of telecom employees referred to as "technicians" in the United States are called "engineers" in the United Kingdom.

you want to stay part of the company, and the company is bending over backwards to not make you compulsorily redundant, you're going to have to do that." (BT manager, November 22, 2011)

Despite concerns, many preferred to accept the new position rather than leave BT. One reason was the proverbial loyalty of BT employees: "once you go to BT, you're BT for life" (BT manager, May 23, 2012). Another was the generous pension scheme for employees who started working for BT before 2000, which one interviewee described as a "golden handcuff" (Prospect official, November 1, 2011).

AT&T is a complicated case, because it was formed through mergers of several companies. Below I focus on AT&T's legacy agreements, covering employees who were with AT&T prior to the wave of mergers in the 2000–2005 period, and on agreements with the former SBC, which merged with AT&T in 2005.

At AT&T "legacy T," employment had shrunk from 120,000 post-divestiture to 5,400 in 2013. Management relied on a combination of involuntary layoffs and voluntary leave, with increased use of voluntary redundancy over time. The level of termination payments for employees who were involuntarily laid off was linked to seniority, with a maximum of 104 weeks' pay for those with over thirty years of service. Because of this, more junior employees were typically selected first for layoffs. Prior to the early 1990s, more senior employees could volunteer to take their place, but they would get only the level of termination pay that the junior employee was eligible for. This was replaced by "Voluntary Term Pay" (VTP), which allowed more senior employees to take their full termination pay. This was originally intended to be used only when a surplus was declared. However, an arbitration case in the early years of the following decade held that AT&T could offer VTP at any time.

Union representatives observed that management was using VTP to bypass terms in the collective agreement stating that work could not be outsourced if employees performing that work had been laid off (see Chapter 5):

(*Unionist A*) Originally when we bargained it, it was to replace a surplus. So if you said: "she's junior, I'm senior, I'll take her place," originally what you got was whatever her term pay was: it was called "Sip and Vip." That was the original. Then we moved to what was called VTP, voluntary term pay. [. . .] When we moved to that, it was to be for strictly surplus conditions. Then they moved to be at any time. So we arbitrate the issue, got a terrible arbitrator, and we lost. The arbitrator said: "they're free to do whatever they want."

(*Unionist B*) And actually it's worse than that. We have language in our contract that says we can't subcontract out in an area where there have been involuntary layoffs. So what the company could do, say they were going to lay off ten technicians—they couldn't outsource the work if those technicians had been laid off. But if the top ten senior technicians took it as a voluntary, what that arbitrator said was, since it was not an involuntary layoff, those technicians could be replaced by contractors. So that was the worst part of that decision: it was used to almost eliminate certain whole titles because they would keep offering VTP, keep offering VTP, keep offering VTP. (CWA officials, June 5, 2013)

At the same time, the plans at AT&T included a range of benefits. One was an education program called the "Alliance" providing money for further training for laid-off workers. "Extend-comp" allowed redundant employees who were close to pensionable age to stay on the payroll until they became "pension eligible," with rights to be called back to work for temporary assignments: "so say you have twenty-eight years' service, and you needed a year and a half to get your pension eligibility, you could do the extend-comp: you could stay on roll, you don't work, the company sends you a check, and when you get to your significant date you exit. You get to a pension that way. We have a lot of people who end up using that" (CWA official, June 5, 2013). Another requirement was called a "job offer guarantee (jog)" where management was required to offer workers a job they were qualified for somewhere else in the United States: "It could be another city near you or it could be across the country. We've had people use jog four and five times" (CWA official, June 5, 2013).

Thus, even though there were involuntary layoffs (unlike at BT), the CWA negotiated creative programs that cushioned workers or encouraged voluntary leaves:

> We bargained a lot of small stuff like that—every one of them reduces the amount of involuntary layoffs. We've lost tons of jobs, but in terms of people who have really been hurt by involuntary layoffs, the numbers last time were a couple of hundred, who actually lost their job. We have a lot of people who took other jobs, took retirement, we have a TLA thing that's a transition to retirement, we have all these things that. So we've managed to help a lot of people while at the same time losing half our workforce. (CWA official, June 5, 2013)

The two CWA officers cited above described a recent "surplus notice" announcing the closing of five centers as an example. The union bargained a "watermark" that prevented them from reducing employment below a certain number and another hard limit on the number of involuntary layoffs. However, they did not come close to the involuntary number, as employees took advantage of the different programs described above (like jogs).

The CWA also bargained no-layoff provisions. This included temporary provisions at "Legacy T"—for example, in 2009 (13 months) and in 2012 (1 year).

Other provisions affected particular groups of workers. Installers (technicians) hired before 2004 were covered by a no-layoff clause that protected their jobs until retirement, while Network Technical Specialists (a group of field technicians) had a no-layoff clause from 2009 and a watermark. "So if they've got a thousand technicians and 300 retire during the life of the agreement, they've got to hire another 100—because our watermark is 800 in the Legacy T Contract" (CWA official, June 5, 2013).

The case of Legacy T discussed above seems superficially similar to BT, with a history of partnership and some favorable agreements. However, there was often more conflict (e.g., with the arbitration case); and there appeared overall to be less trust, with a perception that management was taking advantage of some provisions in the agreement to move work.

SBC represented a somewhat different trajectory. Shortly before the 2005 AT&T/SBC merger, the CWA called a four-day strike against SBC in May 2004—with job security as a major concern; 100,000 workers went on strike in thirteen states. The CWA reached an agreement with management after the four-day strike that included 2.3% wage increases for five years, improved worker access to jobs in growing areas, improved pensions, protected health benefits, and job security guarantees. SBC agreed to a no-layoff clause while the contract was in force, and to rehire 600 workers who had been laid off prior to the agreement. They also agreed to a guaranteed job offer (within the same state or region) for workers whose jobs had been eliminated.

The no-layoff clause had ended by the time I was doing interviews in 2012–2013; however, the CWA had held on to the guaranteed job offer. I spoke with a union representative in a former SBC region of AT&T, who felt this was useful, but would be under threat due to the lack of jobs, combined with a shrinking pool of high seniority workers who were willing to take voluntary buy-outs:

> There's been maybe three to four surpluses a year. AT&T tends to do these surpluses on a quarterly basis, as the company is changing. [. . .] What has happened is there have been so many surpluses there are no more jobs to put people in, and we're faced with a situation now where there have been four or five surpluses, and these people—because the company had to keep them, because of the contract language—that are literally still sitting in their chairs, who are like ghost people, that aren't on the record as being employees anymore in that title but they literally are still sitting there. That's coming to a head. (CWA rep AT&T, March 14, 2012)

Another union official observed that this kind of protection in their contract also was an important deterrent to outsourcing, or incentive to find jobs for local workers, which could help protect jobs from further layoffs. When I asked her how they had gotten those provisions, she cited a long history of conflict and mobilization:

> Through years of negotiations; through strikes; through, you know, the contracting letter and the guaranteed job offer that's been in the contract for years, I mean, a lot longer than I've been doing this. It's just through years and years of negotiations, and going on strike and mobilization, and things like that. (CWA rep AT&T, June 13, 2012)

TDC in Denmark: From Social Partnership to More Unilateral Downsizing

The above four cases are in countries with weaker national employment protections and overall less encompassing industrial relations institutions. Union strategy and success do vary across the cases, but perhaps it is not surprising that overall, unions had weak recourse to national institutions, instead relying on mobilization within their core employers (or labor-management partnership backed by a fear of mobilization) to preserve some social conditions for workers in the midst of an overall trajectory of downsizing.

TDC is somewhat of an outlier in this group: it is based in Denmark, which is often held up as one of the last bastions of social democracy—or at least as representing a kinder, gentler approach to liberalization via "embedded flexibilization" (Thelen 2014). Certainly, Denmark has higher union density and bargaining coverage at the national level than the other four cases; and, unlike those cases, most large telecom employers negotiate or follow collective agreements. However, Denmark's telecom industry has become significantly market-oriented over the past two decades. The Danish government pursued quite radical liberalizing reforms of telecommunications in the 1990s, including selling off its former state provider to Ameritech in the United States—eventually leading to ownership by Private Equity funds from the 2010s. There are multiple agreements with different terms and conditions, and competition across unions. At the national level, Denmark also has among the weakest employment protections in Europe: known as the poster child for "flexicurity"—the combination of flexible labor markets (with ease of layoffs) combined with a strong social safety net.

It is thus worth taking a closer look at the politics of downsizing at TDC, to examine how unions have influenced these decisions over time, within a country that shows both strong residual union organization and bargaining power, but also weaker institutional constraints on employer exit. The trajectory of TDC shows some early wins for the union as a result of worker mobilization against downsizing—and public support for that mobilization—but then gradual expansion of mandatory layoffs and declining terms and conditions attached to voluntary redundancies.

In 1996, Tele Danmark brought together six regional companies into a more centralized structure, divided by geographic area. This was accompanied by an efficiency drive, which included planned workforce reductions of around 2,500 employees during 1997–1998, to prepare Tele Danmark for privatization. The union TKF (which later merged with Dansk Metal) initially cooperated with management plans to downsize the workforce, but negotiations turned sour when the company increased the target number for layoffs (Colclough, Nordestgaard, and Andersen 2003).

One of the union officials who was involved in the negotiations over the restructuring plan described the conflict and resulting strikes:

> I think we, in negotiations in the works councils, accepted that there were 1,000, 1,200 too many. And that was confirmed. The CEO confirmed that was the number that was also their target. But suddenly they changed and put more than 300 in. And that's when we had strikes and demonstrations in Aarhus, and it was tough. [. . .] And then we had a demonstration when the Board meeting took place in Aarhus, the second town of Denmark. And then we had a demonstration in front of the Board meeting here in Copenhagen. . . . It was at least 70% [employee participation in the strike]. It was successful and the media was supporting us. They said it was a scandal that such a company with so much revenue would start sacking so many people. (Dansk Metal official, April 19, 2012)

In the end, management negotiated a generous redundancy package with Dansk Metal, which ensured that nearly all redundancies were voluntary and gave employees one year's salary and up to three months of training. Redundancy agreements were tailored by groups: they had an initial round where everyone over age fifty-nine could apply for voluntary retirement, which added up to around 400 employees. Then they had a second round where the limit was reduced to fifty-five or fifty-six years old, which brought an extra 300 or so employees. "And then the rest was direct discussion with the person, and give them an offer" (Dansk Metal official, April 19, 2012).

> One thousand we accepted for voluntary, and they wanted nearly 2,500. We got very good conditions, I can tell you. We were smiling when they left [. . .]. It was up to one year's payment [. . .] and so much extra for education. And lots of people took it and they took a job in competing companies, and got one-year payments and then they got higher wages in a new company at the same time.

That was what I would call a successful agreement. (Dansk Metal official, April 19, 2012)

The decision concerning which employees should be approached to request redundancy was debated with management: while the company preferred to select employees based on performance, the union sought to protect weaker employees and ensure that the process was as "voluntary" as possible:

> We were, of course, very cautious about, that they didn't take the weak and disabled, and all that. They had a list and we went through it, and we ... well, I know some of them, we could not accept. [...] We said: "not that one, not that one," for social reasons. So we had to find some new ones, because the numbers were fixed. I mean, they go [sic] out to all their local managers and said: "Who do you want to get rid of, how many can you get in to fulfill this number, 1,200?" And then we asked our shop stewards, "Local, this is a list we've got from the company, what do you say?" And they said, "This person will never get a chance to find a similar job outside," or "it's too early," or something like that; "he's too young, he's too old," or whatever. But we ... I'd been negotiating for two weeks, I think, and we had a whole weekend when we sat and we went through the numbers. And only one was sacked. There was pressure from the media, we could go out saying, "Well, we didn't sack them actually, we gave them voluntary redundancy." (Dansk Metal official, April 19, 2012)

In its annual report, Tele Danmark reported that of 2,176 employees covered by the redundancy plan, 1,418 employees left through voluntary retirement agreements, 552 employees left through "voluntary or compulsory redundancy"; and 206 employees were covered by "separate arrangements with Tele Danmark" (Tele Danmark 1997).

Colclough et al. (2003, 41) observe that 1998 "was a bad year for Tele Denmark": employee satisfaction was low, customer service was criticized from all sides, and the lack of communication from the new owner to employees created "turmoil and uncertainty about the group's future." Then a new director, Dyremose, was appointed at the end of 1998, who managed to change the management style and develop a constructive relationship with the unions, seeking their input for the restructuring process (Colclough et al. 2003).

One important change that occurred at this time was the shift in ownership from public to private, which also brought the question of what to do with workers on civil servant contracts. It was decided when Tele Danmark was privatized that civil servants could not work for a private company—only for public companies. So, unlike in Germany and France (discussed below), it was necessary for employees to give up their special rights. The changes in collective bargaining described in Chapter 2, in which the company adopted the Dansk Industri (DI) collective agreement, involved transforming a civil service agreement to a private-sector agreement. At this time, the company stopped hiring civil servants, and around half of the employees who had civil service status lost this status. At the same time, the union was able to negotiate exceptions that allowed these employees to keep their civil service pension, as well as the right to three years' salary "in the event of dismissal due to insufficient workload" (TDC 2010). The civil-service pension was around 30% higher than private industry pensions at the time of privatization (based on "defined benefits"). Over the years, private-sector pensions have become more generous, as unions agreed to wage moderation in exchange for pension rises. However, these continued to be around 10%–15% lower than civil service pensions.

This change was accomplished with little direct conflict, due to an overall cooperative relationship at the time between the union and management. In addition, management had a strong incentive to negotiate a favorable agreement that the union would accept, as this was necessary for convincing civil servants to transfer to private contracts:

> We grew up with the management, we changed the company together from a public company to a private company. They couldn't do that if we didn't agree with them: we had all the civil servants organized.... At that time there were around 10,000 civil servants in TDC. So they had to have agreements, both from the political side and from the management side, from the unions that we would support this change. Because civil servants cannot be forced to accept a change in their payments. So it was built on understanding between political power, management, and the unions that we make that change together. [...] We went out to the members and said they should change their status—we were positive, we were selling it also to the members that they should do that. (Dansk Metal official, August 19, 2911)

An HR director at TDC estimated that in 2012 around 25% of the call center workforce and 60% of the technician workforce were former civil servants.

The second major wave of planned redundancies occurred between 2003 and 2004, involving 1,626 employees (TDC 2004). TDC justified the cuts in its annual report as part of a strategy "to adapt to a market in which self-services and do-it-yourself installation products are gaining ground" (TDC 2003, 15). The union (Dansk Metal from 2003) was more critical of the process through which dismissals were handled and represented several cases of unfair dismissal in the labor courts, arguing that management forced employees to volunteer to leave (Colclough et al. 2003).

These two waves of redundancies directly preceded a change in ownership: "Because the big one in the '90s was connected to privatization, and the one in 2005 was connected to the funds coming. So it made it fit for sale each time, so the new owners don't have the dirty work [laugh]. Yeah, that's the philosophy" (Dansk Metal official, April 19, 2012).

After 2005, when the capital funds acquired TDC, management adopted a policy of cutting 5%–6% of the workforce a year, which some years rose to 8%–10% or 600–800 positions annually (TDC 2005, 2006, 2008, 2010). Over the same period, a number of IT and mobile technician positions were outsourced (see Chapter 5). By the end of 2010, these measures resulted in 4,999 fewer employees compared to 2005.

TDC had negotiated an agreement in 2005 with rules concerning how layoffs were handled, giving the union the right to be involved in the process and decisions. One union official observed that, "it's not just a raw sacking where they have to leave" (Dansk Metal official, August 19, 2011), instead providing some protection of salary and investment in training. There were three different employee groups, who left with different terms. State civil servants had a right to three years of full pay—paid for jointly by TDC and the pension fund. Other civil servants could have up to three years paid, but not at full pay. All other employees could get a minimum of three months of paid leave (after one year tenure), up to six months (after eight years' tenure), with some better terms for those with higher seniority who did not have civil servant status.

Managers described the downsizing process as one of setting targets for job cuts, and then trying to figure out how to manage with these cuts:

> First we downsize and then we make it possible. We don't make it possible before, because then we'll never succeed. But that's true, we cut and then we make it work. [. . .] We have it every year. We have . . . every single unit has to cut X per cent. And it's a part of our forecasting process that we know that 2012 is 10%, for example. And then we try to find out where could that be, these 10%, in this area, in this area, in this area; are we going to outsource anything; are we going to . . . or are we going to do the salami way, you know, just a little bit there, a little bit there; or how will we do it? But it's always a matter of getting more and more efficient. (TDC HR manager, April 23, 2012)

Management viewed these downsizing policies as generous—particularly given weak employment protections in Denmark:

> Denmark is very liberal. You can lay off people easily, I mean, compared to Italy or France or Germany, and it's so easy. Sweden is difficult as well. So, I mean, we can, without any problem, fire people in a very short time. . . . We've done

a lot to make sure that we give them good ... a very good way of getting out of the Company. When I started in TDC, I thought, my God, they are really, really putting gold on the wings of these people who are getting fired. (TDC HR manager, April 23, 2012)

We prolong what we have been doing for the past years, and every time it gets a little better. That's the way we are doing it because it's better to do that and have understanding with the unions. ... And of course it's very, very expensive, but I think it's a better way of doing it. (TDC labor relations manager, April 24, 2012)

Managers and union representatives acknowledged that the process of deciding which employees would be made redundant was typically based on performance considerations—so redundancies were used in practice to cut the bottom 5%–10% of performers in the organization (see Chapter 4). At the same time, management needed to take into account social considerations in managing the redundancies; and shop stewards and union officials played a central role in ensuring that "correct procedures" were followed for evaluating the impact on employees:

Even though you don't say it directly, it will always be the ones performing the worst... at the same time, we have a lot of protected employees. [...] Extremely many resources ... are dedicated to managing the redundancy process. First of all, you have to identify, together with the manager. Typically the HR partner, that will be one of my HR partners who would sit with a [local] manager. [...] When you have a meeting with the one who has been fired, you have to do a list a week or ten days before, I mean, a deadline, because the unions have to check it all over: have we done it right, is it okay that it's him and not her? And they are going through it all with all the protections and not protections, and all these kind of things. (TDC HR manager, April 23, 2012)

An HR director described the difficulty in moving employees across different jobs—which is the preferred strategy of unions for reallocating employees within TDC: "We have just had a round of layoffs in our shops, and we did succeed in getting about 50% of the ones we laid off into other positions, and 50% that's a lot" (TDC HR manager, April 23, 2012).

Union officials and shop stewards observed that it had become more difficult to get generous terms for employees affected by downsizing: "I think it's just getting worse and worse. I mean, poorer and poorer agreements. Nothing like what we did in the '90s. [...] So it's about profit, very much" (Dansk Metal official, April 19, 2012). "The company is trying to cut down everything ... the prices, the people. [. . .] And they come, every day to say, 'Now we have to fire more people.' And that is what I'm fighting against" (Dansk Metal rep TDC, May 7, 2012).

One area of conflict concerned an attempt by management to move from a practice of allowing employees paid leave—meaning, as soon as they were made redundant, they were able to go home or switch employers while continuing to receive their salary from TDC for three to six months—toward a policy of treating those three to six months as a notice period, with employees continuing to work in their jobs while they were collecting their TDC salary: "That's one of our best things. And perhaps it's about to melt away from us, because TDC doesn't want that" (Dansk Metal rep TDC, April 24, 2012).

Despite considerable frustration expressed by union officials and shop stewards concerning the ongoing downsizing and attempt by management to reduce the level of benefits, managers observed that the level of conflict over downsizing had declined over time, as unions became more accustomed to ongoing redundancies:

> To some extent, [unions are] getting weaker. To some extent they're getting weaker because . . . and I must say, to be honest, I mean, doing what we do with so many layoffs each year, we have—well, you can say, not to be superstitious—but, you know, we have very little conflict about it. They protest, they think we're horrible, and they think, oh . . . and of course they do, that's their role, that's what they should do. But I think they're quite patient with us, to be honest [. . .]. They are very used to—and that's always a little scary—they're used to in TDC that we have these layoffs. (TDC HR manager, April 23, 2012)

This one case of TDC illustrates the changing political and power dynamics associated with downsizing policies. There were early conflicts over downsizing, with a strike that was resolved in favor of the workers—with very generous redundancy plans and union success in limiting the number of redundancies. Over time, however, layoffs became increasingly accepted as the normal course of business, with declining conflict. The union still played a role in making sure they were organized in a social way but had declining influence over these decisions and associated terms and conditions.

Summary

Table 3.2 summarizes the redundancy policies negotiated at these five cases. We distinguish between the late 1990s to the early 2000s; and the mid-2000s to the early 2010s.

Table 3.2 Redundancy Policies at Firms with Weaker Constraints on Exit from Internal Employment

	Redundancy Policies (late 1990s–early 2000s)	Change in Terms (mid-2000s–2010s)
O2 Czech Republic	– Partly voluntary redundancies and early retirement; but majority compulsory redundancies – Severance pay above the level required by law: based on age, tenure	– Partly voluntary redundancies and early retirement; but majority compulsory redundancies [maintained] – Further increases in levels of severance pay
Orange Polska	– Voluntary redundancy and early retirement – [2000] social package: additional severance pay; >25-year tenure entitled to 15 times average monthly salary in last 3 months of employment [2002] extended social package provisions to subsidiaries	– Voluntary redundancy maintained – Social package maintained, with extra resources for retraining
BT	– Voluntary redundancy and early retirement – Pre-2001: employees taking voluntary leave received a redundancy payment and up to 6.7 years enhancement of their pensionable service. – [2001] "NewStart": for each year of service employees received a month's salary, up to a maximum of 12 months. The first £30,000 was tax-free.	– Voluntary redundancy maintained – NewStart terms were reduced over time: from a 12-month to a 3–9 month payment; and the pension option was withdrawn [by 2013].
AT&T	– Compulsory redundancy, voluntary redundancy, and early retirement – Severance pay based on years spent in the company: maximum 104 weeks pay for over 30 years of service – "Voluntary Term Pay" (VTP) allowed a more senior employee to take their full termination pay if they volunteered to take redundancy.	– Compulsory redundancy declined – Increased use of VTP in "non-surplus" conditions – Extend-comp allowing redundant employees to stay on the payroll until pension eligible – Guaranteed job offer (former SBC)
TDC	– Voluntary redundancy – Non-civil servants: 1 year paid leave; up to 3 months paid training – Former civil servants: up to 3 years paid leave	– Compulsory redundancy introduced – Non-civil servants: between 3 and 6 months paid leave – Social considerations included in layoff decisions, with union oversight

The cases differed in the extent of decline in terms and conditions, as well as overall level. TDC and BT saw a gradual erosion in the generosity of redundancy policies, while these policies became more generous at AT&T and O2 Czech Republic (though from a lower level). O2 Czech Republic continued to use largely compulsory redundancies, while BT and Orange Polska primarily used voluntary redundancies across the two time periods. However, TDC experienced a shift from exclusively voluntary to compulsory redundancies, while AT&T experienced a decline in the use of compulsory redundancy.

Across the cases, improved terms of these downsizing policies, or sustaining decent terms, resulted from management awareness of unions' potential associational power (and interest in averting a strike), as in the BT case; or actual labor conflict and strikes that showcased that associational power, as at AT&T (former SBC) and Orange Polska. BT and AT&T are interesting cases to compare, as both companies were privatized (and their markets liberalized) earlier than those in in continental Europe. BT relied on voluntary departures and retraining, with very little union conflict but with general erosion in terms over time. AT&T showed a combination of partnership and conflict, with some significant gains won through member mobilization and strikes—particularly in regions in which the union could rely on a strong and militant membership.

While the unions in all five cases had weaker institutional power, here in the form of strong national employment protection legislation or state support for alternatives to downsizing, they were able to somewhat compensate by mobilizing their membership to assert their rights to collective voice and to negotiate more favorable agreements. Success was based on giving workers choices and cushioning the insecurity typically associated with downsizing. These programs were costly and were based on successfully inserting social concerns into accounting of the economic costs and benefits of layoffs.

Strong Institutional Constraints on Exit

The second group, A1, Deutsche Telekom, Telecom Italia, France Telecom, and Telia, are all cases where institutional constraints on exit from internal employment are stronger—through a combination of national and negotiated employment protections (and requirements concerning redundancy payments and timing) and special employment rights for civil servants.

At **Deutsche Telekom**, the DPG and then ver.di had negotiated strong job security protections. Private law employees had guaranteed employment security at the age of forty with fifteen years of service; and civil servants had "iron-clad" job security. Other employees were protected from *betriebsbedingte Kündigung*, or business-related layoffs. The DPG extended contract provisions after privatization to employees in both West and East Germany.

Between 1995 and 2004, Deutsche Telekom cut 110,000 positions in its core operations. Network services experienced the most severe job losses, as the telephone network was digitalized and many technicians became redundant. Because the collective agreement prohibited business-related layoffs, management used early retirement, voluntary buy-outs, and natural turnover. Around 90,000 employees left through these programs between 1995 and 2000, and a further 24,000 transferred voluntarily into other divisions (Sako and Jackson 2003, 17).

A large number of employees decided to remain with the company after their jobs were made redundant. In 2002, ver.di and Deutsche Telekom negotiated an agreement that allowed the company to move these employees into a new subsidiary called Vivento Personal Service Agentur (PSA). They were then placed in different divisions for short-term projects or were recruited to fill new job openings. Vivento was set up as a temporary agency that would also offer services on the private market, but demand was insufficient to provide regular employment for thousands of redundant workers. Deutsche Telekom also used Vivento PSA to transfer civil servants to other areas of the public sector—representing 9,000 employees in the 2008–2010 period.

Another challenge at this time was to decide who would be moved into Vivento PSA. This was a form of involuntary layoffs. Even if employees could stay within Deutsche Telekom, they would have to move out of their former jobs. Ver.di was concerned that management would use this to just cut the worst performers. To resolve this, a system was set up to decide who would go based on ranking every employee's performance along 20 points (1–20). Then the workforce was divided in half, based on those who had more than 10 points or less than 10 points. As jobs were cut, they took first a "good" performer, then a "bad" performer, alternating between the two groups—"So that there was a mixture of high performers and low performers, because they wanted to be able to place the employees [at Vivento] in external jobs" (works councilor DT, September 13, 2011).

This "Clearing" process created a lot of stress among the workforce:

> At the time, that was very destructive, particularly in terms of motivation and the feeling of belonging among employees. A lot of people felt like they were abandoned, because they saw, "my colleague, with whom I have been working, has to go and isn't needed anymore." Then when she was needed later, she wasn't brought back, but instead was hired from an external firm." (works councilor DT, September 13, 2011)

In 2004, around 20% of employees were protected from layoffs through a collective agreement, while the rest were either civil servants with lifetime job security or fell under rules that prevented layoffs if employees were forty years old or had fifteen years of service. While the final two categories of protections were pretty much impossible to change, the collective agreement was up for renegotiation in 2004, and any changes to job security overwhelmingly would affect the East German workforce.

Deutsche Telekom negotiated an employment pact in 2004 with ver.di that reduced working time from 38 to 34 hours, with only partial wage compensation—meaning employees would be paid for the equivalent of a 35.5-hour work week. Civil servants also had their weekly working time cut but retained their full pay. In return, management extended job security protections until the end of 2008. As part of the 2004 pact, Vivento PSA employees retained their full salary when placed in a job, but pay was cut to 85% of their former salary when they were not working. The employment pact was estimated to have saved the company around €300 million (Dribbusch 2004). It also clearly involved a trade-off of job retention for pay concessions.

Then in 2005, management announced plans for 32,000 redundancies, only 7,000 of which would be moved to Vivento. At the same time, 6,000 new staff would be recruited to work on the roll-out of the fiber-optic network. The union called on the company to renounce the job cuts and rule out forced redundancies beyond 2008. Meanwhile, ver.di asked the German government to extend funding for civil servants' pensions to include early retirement, to cushion the impact on the workforce. Around 25,000 employees protested against the cuts, and ver.di said it would "escalate" opposition to the layoffs if no satisfactory package was agreed.

In February 2006, a compromise agreement between management and the union collapsed, with ver.di claiming that the company's plans for offering retraining, severance pay and other conditions were unacceptable. In April 2006, they reached an agreement to cut 27,000 jobs by the end of 2008 across the group, but with no forced redundancies. Around 1,100 employees accepted compensation for voluntary departure; and others were transferred within Deutsche Telekom. An agreement on partial retirement allowed workers close to retirement age to reduce their hours for up to eight years (starting at age 55 and up to age 63). In 2015, a new agreement extended partial retirement to employees over age 63.

The union succeed over time in keeping the prohibition against forced redundancies, which was extended until 2012, and then until the end of 2014:

> We are not yet laying off any employees because we have an agreement prohibiting forced redundancies. [. . .] At the same time, we also offer our

people incentives to leave the company. Of course, we also try to encourage employees to take these incentives who have a problem with their skills and cannot or do not want to develop further. (DT HR manager, September 24, 2010)

A1 had a similarly high number of civil servants and strong job security at the company and national levels. Over time, the number of civil servants dropped from 85% in 1995–1999 to around 60%–65% in 2011—most of these through retirements, voluntary transfer to other civil service positions, and transfer to other jobs within A1.

Initially, downsizing was exclusively voluntary and was organized through early retirement, with generous terms, as well as severance pay negotiated with the union. Management announced the first major redundancies in 1996, to prepare for liberalization in 1998. Employees over the age of fifty-five were given the option to take early retirement with 80% of their salary and no reduction in pension payments. Around 3,000 took this, with a further 1,500 taking voluntary redundancy.

A second major downsizing plan was announced in 2000, in the leadup to Telekom Austria's IPO—with an announced goal of 5,000 job cuts by 2005. As part of this, all Telekom Austria's employees were transferred into "Telekom Austria Personalmanagement GmbH," which was charged with managing restructuring, including workforce development, retraining, outsourcing, and downsizing. The union, GPF, negotiated a favorable social plan, and around 900 employees accepted early retirement. The remainder took voluntary redundancy, reduced their working hours, or transferred to other departments where employment was growing.

Similar to Deutsche Telekom, Telekom Austria also began to move workers into a leasing firm, or internal employment agency, which then placed these workers in short-term positions within the incumbent or at other companies. A manager at A1 described the move of the civil servants to this leasing firm:

> The fact is because these civil servants have been assigned to Telekom Austria to work, those civil servants must be employed. The CEO cannot say, as with the employees, "They are being terminated," [. . .] but a civil servant has a very special status, a very special protection, but also has a lot of duties. But one of the rights is that he needs to be employed. And if not, you can only let him sit at home, move him into a so-called pool, today it's called "ServiceCom." This will of course cost the employer, but he can save himself a little of the extra fees and allowances, if that employee carries out any work. (A1 manager, May 12, 2011)

Initially this was organized in cooperation with the union. However, conflict increased after 2008. McKinsey drew up a savings plan called "Target09" to save 160 million euros in 2008 and 2009, 60% of which was anticipated to be from personnel cuts. The most controversial recommendation was to transfer 2,500 civil servants to the internal employment agency. In one version, all 9,800 of Telekom Austria's employees would be transferred to this personnel pool, and the company would then lease back 6,900 of those workers.

Austria's Social Democratic Party joined the GPF union and the company's works council in opposing this plan. Union representatives derisively described it as an attempt to create a *Beamtenparkplatz* (parking lot for civil servants). Employees in the fixed-line division held a general meeting attended by nearly half the workforce in which they rejected the transfer, and the union threatened strikes. In the end, the president of the Federation of Austrian Industry intervened and came up with a compromise to make transfer to the leasing pool voluntary, with incentives including wage security, the right to take up one's previous employment, and support for further training. In June 2008, the federal chancellor of Austria stated that no employees would be contracted out without union agreement.

The A1 manager cited above also reflected on this conflict:

In 2008, with this Target09, it was the case that the worker representatives had absolutely no sympathy for it, because, unfortunately, one of the members of the Board of Directors stated at the annual press conference: [...] "I don't know if there will be 3,000 or 4,000 fewer, but there have to be fewer." This statement was so harsh for the worker representatives that they threatened strikes. It was such an arbitrary act from the outset: "We definitely want to cut staff, regardless. We have to reduce the headcount."

[Interviewer: And were there then strikes?]

There were big company meetings. There were really big rallies in front of the headquarters, in front of the Ministry of Finance, in front of the various ÖAG-Branch Offices. This has, of course, already partly led to corporate managers coming under pressure here, and also from politics. (A1 manager, May 12, 2011)

Then between November and December 2008, more conflict occurred after a new plan was announced to cut up to 2,500 jobs by 2011, including a social plan with a lump sum payment for employees taking voluntary redundancy. At that time, around 90% of the workforce participated in a protest, and the works council warned it would strike during Christmas if the company did not withdraw its plans and negotiate an alternative plan with the union. It demanded new measures to create jobs and that the company end the practice of leasing temporary employees from its internal employment agency. After a long negotiation, management agreed to a no-layoff guarantee, to further investments in retraining, and to continue to employ downsized workers until they retired. A1 also increasingly made use of a new form of early retirement. In total, about 2,500 civil servants whose jobs had become redundant were given pre-retirement leave in return for a reduced salary.

At **France Telecom**, employees with civil servant status were protected by the "France Telecom Law" (1996) which limited the company's obligation to a defined annual contribution, giving them no liability for shortfalls in pension plans for this group (France Telecom 2001). Civil servants' defined benefit pension plans were administered by the French state. This provided some additional state support for early retirement, cushioning the cost of general plans applying to both civil servants and "private law" employees.

The law itself came out of a compromise between France Telecom and Force Ouvrière (FO), which was the only union willing to sign an agreement with management on a social plan for layoffs—but with the conditions that it last ten years and be written into law. Pascal Courtin, an FO leader, stated: "We thought that if we didn't negotiate to get the best deal possible then, we'd end up with mass layoffs being forced on us later" (Abboud 2006).

Under the terms of the 1996 agreement, employees were able to take early retirement when they were age fifty-five with 70% of their salary and a bonus worth 60% of one year's salary. Around a third of the workforce took advantage of these terms between 1996 and 2006 (when the agreement was terminated).

> Everyone left at 55, with bonuses of between 2–20 *briques*—roughly between 20,000 and 200,000 francs [~3,000€ to 31,000€] [. . .]. For the technicians, the bonuses would usually be between 80,000 and 140,000. They had never seen so much money in all of their life. So that motivated people to leave between 1996 and 2006 [. . .] and so there wasn't any noise at that time, because everyone was happy to leave. The drinks [*arrosages*] were over from 2003. Before it was a party. Between 1996 and 2003 it was one big leaving party. From 2003 to 2006, it was a funeral, leaving for retirement [. . .]. People were fleeing, there is no other way to say it. And in 2006, there were plenty of people who thought we would maintain that. In one blow, the maximum age that was 55 years at France Telecom [. . .] in 2007 it was 56, in 2008 it was 57, etc. And now we have people who are 62 years old. (works councilor FT, May 18, 2012)

In addition, a large number of civil servants were transferred to the public sector over this period: for example, over 1,600 transfers were made between 2003 and 2004.

Civil servants at France Telecom had also long been moved from areas with shrinking employment (such as technician units) to those with expanding jobs (such as call centers and shops). These measures were associated with a reported 10,000–12,000 job changes a year by 2000, up to 13,800 in 2001—or almost 10% of the workforce annually. Job changes were facilitated by civil servant mobility rules.

However, the use of transfers was accelerated under France Telecom's controversial NExT plan, announced in 2006, which included a three-year goal of 22,000 redundancies and 14,000 job changes.[5] It included a policy called "Time to Move," which made it a requirement that employees change their job every three years—often combined with mandatory physical relocation. One manager described the motivation as:

> To create chaos—to create movement. To encourage people to move, that can be necessary, but that is not how it was done [. . .]. Managers had quantified objectives to move people out of the company. For example, a manager of a team would have 20–25 people, he could have the goal over the year to get rid of 3 people [. . .]. Regardless of how you do that, to push out people who are civil servants through making them want to leave. When you start to give people goals, telling them they have to push out two in a year, etc. that ends in a catastrophe. (FT manager, June 30, 2010)

Managers were given special training on how to meet these objectives, often based on ethically questionable methods (Diehl and Doublet 2010, 89–90). In some cases, employees were required to relocate on short notice, to force them into retirement or to quit their job.

The unions organized protests against the plan, but initially had little impact. Over the next few years, they jointly organized several creative initiatives to study and publicize problems of stress in the workplace. SUD-PTT (representing mostly blue-collar workers and civil servants) and CFE-CGC (representing managers and engineers) organized an "Observatory for Stress and Harassment at Work" that studied the impact of restructuring on the workforce and then communicated its findings across France Telecom, with unions and employees at other firms, and with journalists and the public. The two large leftist unions SUD and the CGT organized a theater project that dramatized problems of worker stress at the company in front of large groups of employees and worker representatives. Each initiative brought together coalitions of unions that traditionally had been reluctant to cooperate with each other. They also shared

---

[5] I draw on material here that was previously published in an article co-authored with Maxime Bellego and Elisa Pannini, which also contains more detail on the France Telecom case: (Doellgast, Bellego, and Pannini 2021).

information and resources; for example, the theater project drew on research from the Observatory and performed at its meetings.

In 2008-2009, as described in the Introduction, France Telecom experienced a "social crisis" in which a wave of close to forty employee suicides were associated with aggressive restructuring policies—and were covered widely in the press, which referred to data and quotes provided by the unions' Observatory. In September 2009, management opened up negotiations on a series of social accords aimed at addressing the problems that had contributed to the social crisis. One union representative explained that mobilization had brought management to the table:

> In the month of September, when the first suicides happened, I think that I've never seen anything like that since I've been at France Telecom—in many locations, at the same time, thousands of employees left. That is to say that the employees walked out, and the unions were often all together ... and it was then that France Telecom said: we are opening negotiations in five areas. (CGT rep FT, May 19, 2010)

The accords included agreements that mobility should be voluntary, with no systematic closing of locations; a commitment to survey employees every two to three years on stress, with committees established to prevent stress at the group and subsidiary level; a consolidation of employee committees with new coordination structures; an agreement on work organization with provisions for improving policies around breaks and holidays; and an agreement on work life balance. A plan for senior employees allowed them to work 50% of their regular hours while being paid 80% of a full-time salary. The plan was adjustable, so part-time could be accumulated to allow an employee to leave earlier.

The unions also directly appealed for state intervention through the courts. The union SUD filed a formal complaint to the Paris prosecutor's office concerning the company's abusive practices, which was eventually joined by the other unions. In response, the office opened an inquiry in 2010 to examine France Telecom's human resource policies. A representative of SUD explained that this is not the "traditional" kind of union activity, but one that is gaining importance:

> We filed a complaint against the company and against its managers for their responsibility for the development of the ACT Plan and 22,000 job cuts and all the consequences, including the death of our colleagues. [...] it seems to us complementary to the creation of a balance of power in favor of employees to use the law through judges to remind employers of their responsibilities not only to the stock market and shareholders but also for the health of employees.

That practice is extremely important and relatively new for our union, because this legal activity is done fairly regularly when we judge that there is likely to be litigation—but now we are attacking on a theme that was quite innovative, which is the responsibility of employers to the health of workers. (SUD rep FT, June 28, 2010)

The inquiry concluded in 2016, with the Paris prosecutor recommending that former France Telecom executives be put on trial for "destabilizing" employees and "workplace harassment." Management policies at the time were accused of creating a "professional climate that provoked anxiety" at the time of a "delicate restructuring" of the company (BBC 2016). The trial then took place over the summer of 2019, leading to further press coverage and extensive public debate. The prosecution asked for a 75,000 euro fine and one year in prison for the former CEO, deputy CEO, and head of human resources. In December 2019, the criminal court found Orange/France Telecom and its top managers guilty of "moral harassment" connected to thirty-five suicides. The former management team, including the former CEO, faced jail time and fines, while the company was ordered to pay 3 million euros in damages to the victims. This was a landmark decision, which was seen to have broader potential repercussions—holding managers legally responsible for the well-being of their workers (Bellego 2021).

Unions' response to the social crisis at France Telecom required bridging ideological divides between the unions, to develop a shared critique of restructuring as a form of moral harassment and to communicate this broadly among the workforce and then with the wider public (Doellgast, Bellego, and Pannini 2021). This case thus shows most vividly the role of inclusive solidarity as a key tool in restricting employer exit and asserting collective worker voice. France Telecom changed its own policies as a result, both ending forced mobility and setting up structures that strengthened union and worker voice in future restructuring policies. But these campaigns also had a broader impact on institutional support for worker voice in France. They led to a new precedent for prosecuting management based on moral harassment and a legal requirement that employers evaluate psychosocial risks, in consultation with workers.

Telecom Italia[6] and its unions also negotiated no-dismissals policies, instead making use of early retirements and retraining. The Italian government provided a form of unemployment insurance that gave employees a minimum replacement income for their salary for two years in northern Italy, and three years in southern Italy. Employees were encouraged to take voluntary redundancy when they were two to three years from retirement age, with an added incentive

---

[6] The Telecom Italia case in this chapter is based on a case write-up by Chiara Benassi, drawing on interviews she conducted.

that Telecom Italia topped up retirement pay to 90% of their salary. This policy was first implemented in 1995 and had not changed by 2010: "From 1999 until today almost 50,000 people left Telecom Italia.... But I want to point out: No dismissals! Everyone left voluntarily and with the parachute of retirement and with economic incentives. At the end of the day, no one lost anything" (FISTEL-CISL official, June 14, 2011).

In 1995, management announced a plan for 12,000 redundancies by 1998. The agreement negotiated with the unions encouraged transfers of workers from areas and regions with staff surpluses to understaffed areas. Telecom Italia paid moving expenses, gave financial support for buying a new house, and offered salary increases and a part-time position for family members.

In 2000, a plan was announced to cut employment by 13,500, including 9,000 redundancies and 4,500 early retirements. The unions organized an eight-hour strike in February and two four-hour strikes in June and October. Negotiations were conducted at the Ministry of Labor, and the resulting agreement included a plan for several categories of redundancies, all of which were voluntary. First, 3,636 redundancies would be managed through the transfer of workers between companies and retraining, which was paid for by a national unemployment compensation plan. Second, 3,065 voluntary early retirements were organized through a system called *mobilita volontaria*, in which workers could decide to participate in a two- to three-year mobility scheme, with 800 euros/month of their salary paid directly by the state. Then the unions and management negotiated additional funds to cover the gap between this amount and 90% of a worker's previous salary. This was extended in further redundancy plans in 2002–2003 and 2005–2007, which involved around 6,000 workers leaving under the same programs. The unions managed to keep the same generous terms through a series of strikes and further agreement at the Ministry of Labor.

Similar to Deutsche Telekom, Telecom Italia also negotiated agreements to reduce working hours in lieu of layoffs. This was supported by solidarity contracts (*Cassa integrazione*, CI) or short-time work arrangements, through which workers received the equivalent of 80% of their monthly salary from the Italian state. Solidarity contracts could be used up to a maximum of 24 months, and then renewed twice for 12 months each time. This procedure was bargained between management, unions, and representatives of the local or state administration. They discussed the reasons for using CI and negotiated over the extent and nature of the restructuring measures, as well as the selection procedure. The Italian Ministry of Labor had to approve the resulting agreements.

In 2010, 6,822 redundancies were announced, and the unions organized a one-day strike. Telecom Italia then signed an agreement with the unions that created the "solidarity contracts" described above. The plan covered 29,200 workers and allowed the company to retain 1,100 workers whose positions would have been cut under the original redundancy plan. The workers affected had reduced working time (around 47%) with partial pay compensation—meaning they had to take a pay cut but with higher hourly pay. The agreement also stipulated the organization of specific courses for the professional retraining and re-employment of affected workers. If they attended a retraining class, they received up to their full pay.

> This agreement signed on August 4 is important not only for the arrangements used, which are more or less the same, but because we [CGIL] had a dispute with FIAT [auto manufacturer] at the same time. Let's say, we in Telecom wanted to think of a different model. That is: You have these redundancies, if we manage to retrain them and to find a new job for them, we can deal with redundancies in a different way. . . . If we succeed, this is a challenge, a bet on the way to face redundancies. I don't know whether we will succeed, but the attempt is noble. (SLC-CGIL official, June 15, 2011).

Union representatives pointed out that it was difficult to convince workers to accept a working time reduction when this resulted in a direct loss of pay with more distributed (or solidaristic) benefits that helped colleagues in other business units. However, the unions agreed to this option because early retirement was no longer a viable way to downsize, as the workforce had become too young, with fewer eligible employees.

Telia: Institutional Power Lost and Regained

Telia is particularly interesting to compare to the TDC case discussed in the earlier section. Both companies are in Nordic countries with a history of strong social democratic governments, high union density and bargaining coverage, and encompassing welfare states. However, Sweden differs markedly from Denmark in the strength of national employment protections, which provide an important "institutional resource" for unions to draw on when management seeks to pursue more unilateral approaches to restructuring. The case of Telia shows the role of mobilization and coordinated, solidaristic union action in successfully turning these legal protections into a resource for negotiating good terms for the internal workforce.

Major downsizing at Televerket occurred in the 1990s. Over 9,000 employees left between 1991 and 1993, through a combination of early retirement, natural attrition, spin-offs, and employee development and training projects (Geary et al. 2010). Prior to privatization, employees had civil servant status with lifetime employment. When the company was privatized, they had the choice to keep their civil servant rights or stay at the incumbent and lose the status. In 2003, these employees continued to receive a pension of 73% of final salary at a retirement age of sixty-five (Murhem 2003).

Telia initiated a three-year reorganization and downsizing process in 1995. Management negotiated an agreement with the company's three unions guaranteeing no compulsory redundancies during 1995–1998. A "staff support division" was created, where employees were given training and assistance moving to a new job within or outside of Telia, while being paid their regular salary. At the beginning of this process, all employees (around 20,000) were moved to the division and had to apply for jobs in the new organization. Only 6,500 employees stayed to retrain and were given three years to prepare for another job. Within this group, 35% got new jobs at Telia, 21% found new jobs outside Telia, and 34% retired (Eurofound 2002). All decisions on recruitment and redundancy had to be made together with local union representatives.

Managers agreed to this structure in part because it gave them more flexibility. A collective agreement with the unions allowed Telia to bypass more rigid requirements in Sweden's Security of Employment Act (1974), which required dismissals to be made according to a "Last In, First Out" order of priority; as well as priority rights for employees who had been dismissed to be re-employed in cases of new recruitment. The collective agreement allowed Telia to suspend these rules, meaning management could keep employees who had the desired or required skills, and could concentrate downsizing and retraining on those in shrinking areas (Eurofound 2002).

By 1998–1999, only 195 employees were left in the division, and it was disbanded and replaced by a new agreement in which responsibility for redundancies was decentralized to the business unit level. In 2000–2001— around the time Telia's subsidiary businesses were being reorganized and sold (see Chapter 5)—a new "Telia Re-Adjustment" unit was established to support employees and managers affected by restructuring (Geary et al. 2010). Throughout this period, employees could take early retirement at age fifty-seven (SEKO rep Telia, May 28, 2012).

This cooperative model for managing redundancies appears to have survived until 2008, when union representatives noted a marked change in labor relations: "the company and local trade unions couldn't work together—the company didn't want to work with the old model any longer. Local trade unions say that management thinks they can make all the decisions: 'We, the Company, we must take all the decisions'" (SEKO rep Telia, May 28, 2012). "It's a new culture. [. . .] I would say that the climate between the unions and the group leading this company gets worse and worse each day. They don't want to have us, they don't want to meet us, and they try to drive over us, I should say" (SEKO rep Telia, June 27, 2012).

The new 2008 agreement provided employees with two rather than three years of salary when they were downsized, with the option of taking the money or a pension through early retirement, and no additional funds for further training or redeployment within Telia.

> We have had the best agreements regarding downsizing, but this agreement was, Telia didn't want to keep it, so they ended the agreement: this was made in 2008. We have had a lot of discussions, we couldn't get it back, it was canceled. To make a very long story short, they made a decision and ended the contract, the collective agreement. It was very, very good, but it turned out to be something else after this. (Unionen rep Telia, August 12, 2011)

These changes had an impact on how past collective agreements are interpreted:

> If you are a subsidiary, you need to adapt to the central agreement (CA), even if you are brought into the company. It's not as easy as it sounds, as everyone is reading the CA with different eyes. [. . .] Now when there are other managers coming into the company, they read it and say: "what is this, we can't do it like this—we'll do it like this instead." We have been at the central level several times to say, they do not behave as they should. And then it's very, very tricky, because there is an understanding when the parties sign the agreement, why was the collective agreement signed, the intention was something. (Unionen rep Telia, August 12, 2011).

Then in 2010, management announced redundancies without negotiations or consultation. "Last year (2010), they started to make the personnel redundant— even though they had this promise and the collective agreement, but they said, oh, but it doesn't say . . . [. . .]. It was very, very tough for our members" (Unionen rep Telia, August 12, 2011).

Because Telia had exited the agreement with the unions, the company then had to follow Swedish employment protection rules, which put much stronger restrictions on which categories of workers management could downsize. The Swedish Employment Protection Act (*Lagen om anställningsskydd*, LAS) requires employers to try to prevent redundancies and to explain the economic and financial circumstances that make them necessary. LAS also has provisions on notification periods, priority rules, and judicial remedies (Diedrich and Bergström 2006). However, unions and employer associations at the "central" level can negotiate or approve deviations from the LAS, and central unions are able to delegate the power to negotiate deviations to local union representatives.

Thus, when Telia management tried to make these decisions unilaterally, the union was able to refer to the stronger provisions in Swedish law to challenge their policies through the labor courts: "They try to downsize based on performance, we try to stop them. The company wants the freedom. We have to negotiate and we have to agree" (SEKO rep Telia, June 27, 2012).

> They [management] terminated that agreement in 2008 that was very good for the members in times of redundancy. Then the new management tried to do redundancies only following the Swedish laws. And they discovered that it was not so good, there were big problems—we, in the unions of course, we took a lot of fights for individual members who were dismissed unlawfully. It took a lot of time from their lawyers in the company to work on those issues, it took over two years to solve all of those issues. (Unionen rep Telia, October 27, 2014)

By 2011, managers realized it was in their interest to cooperate with the unions in negotiating a new plan.

> The management didn't want that trouble that they had in 2008–9 with those negotiations, and all that time the lawyers had to work with those disputes. So we got an agreement: that of course, the management also profits, but our members also profit. They get more money in redundancy pay than they should have gotten elsewhere. (Unionen rep Telia, October 27, 2014)

In the new agreement, employees received double the past redundancy payments, with additional payments for those employed more than twenty years. Redundancy remained primarily voluntary: although workers could be involuntarily laid off if other measures were exhausted, this rarely happened.

Comparison

Table 3.3 summarizes the redundancy policies at the above five cases, distinguishing again between the late 1990s and early 2000s; and changes in terms of redundancy packages between the mid-2000s and the early 2010s.

These policies were overall more favorable to workers, with almost universal use of voluntary redundancy and early retirement, and quite generous redundancy packages. In all of the cases, employers relied on retraining and job-transfer programs to move workers from shrinking to growing divisions and jobs. Strong job security from national legislation and collective agreements, and a high proportion of civil servants at Deutsche Telekom, A1, and France Telecom, encouraged creative policies to organize redundancies in a way that allowed them to retain workers who did not leave voluntarily. Both Deutsche Telekom and A1 made use of leasing firms that received transfers of large numbers of civil

Table 3.3 Redundancy Policies at Firms with Moderate-Strong Constraints on Exit from Internal Employment

	Redundancy Policies (late 1990s–early 2000s)	Change in Terms (mid-2000s–2010s)
Deutsche Telekom	– Voluntary redundancy and early retirement – [2002] some compulsory redundancies from positions, but moved to "Vivento PSA" internal employment agency	– Voluntary redundancy maintained – Increased transfer of civil servants to public sector – [2004] working time reduced to avoid redundancies; with partial pay compensation. – Reduced pay for Vivento PSA – [2006] management plan to introduce compulsory redundancies successfully stopped; introduction of partial retirement (extended in 2015)
A1	– Voluntary redundancy and early retirement – Some shift of workers into "ServiceCom" internal employment agency	– Voluntary redundancy maintained – [2008] management plan to introduce compulsory redundancies successfully stopped – Growing use of internal employment agency – Increasing emphasis on early retirement
France Telecom	– Early retirement at 55; employees received 70% of their salary and a bonus of 60% of one year's salary – Transfer of civil servants to public sector	– Voluntary redundancy maintained – [2006] generous early retirement plan ended – [2009] senior employees could work 50% of their regular hours while being paid 80% of a full-time salary
Telecom Italia	– Voluntary redundancy and early retirement; employees received up to 90% of their salary	– Voluntary redundancy maintained – [2010] "solidarity contracts" introduced; working time reduced for many employees to avoid redundancies
Telia	– Voluntary redundancy and early retirement at 57 – 3-year preparation period for another job, while being employed by Telia	– (Primarily) voluntary redundancy – [2008] 2-year prep period for another job, while being employed by Telia; can take money or early retirement – [2011] double redundancy payments; up to 29 months paid prep for another job; additional payments if >20-year tenure

servants (and other employees) and could hire them out for short-term positions within the incumbent and at other companies. Telecom Italia and Deutsche Telekom both negotiated agreements to reduce working hours. Telia retained workers for up to three years after cutting their jobs, while they retrained for another position inside or outside of the company.

These policies were supported by or encouraged within institutional settings that put stronger constraints on employer exit from internal employment contracts. If employers wanted to adjust employment, they had to cooperate with their unions and works councils to develop an acceptable set of social conditions. In addition, national governments helped to finance or encourage these social plans, supporting early retirement via state pensions at France Telecom and a voluntary mobility scheme and solidarity contracts to reduce working time in Italy.

At the same time, terms and conditions did decline over time, and employers sought to introduce more unilateral plans to save costs. Unions responded by using collective worker voice to maintain or strengthen agreements. At all of the cases, restructuring plans announced by management were often met by strikes, demonstrations, and protests. In some cases, national governments or courts intervened directly to help resolve labor conflicts and encourage companies to adopt more social approaches to downsizing—for example, at A1 and France Telecom. At Telia, an initial turn toward union marginalization, with management pulling out of previous agreements, was turned around when managers realized it was more costly and inefficient to follow national employment protection rules.

The above cases also show the importance of labor solidarity in supporting these mobilization efforts. At Telia, the unions worked together to coordinate their response to unilateral downsizing policies. France Telecom's unions drew on both internal and public campaigns to strengthen supports for collective voice in the wake of a wave of suicides at the company. Central to these campaigns were union coalitions, which overcame ideological divides to organize jointly against precarity. Unions succeeded through building associational power via inclusive solidarity and then using this to strengthen institutional resources for collective worker voice and institutional constraints on employer exit at company and national levels.

Conclusions

This chapter has shown most centrally that the strength of institutional constraints on employer exit—through legal or negotiated job security protections—made a difference for worker precarity associated with downsizing.

These institutions were a source of countervailing power for workers and their unions, as they sought to assert social over market values in negotiations over restructuring measures. At the same time, collective worker voice, supported by legal participation rights, member mobilization, and partnerships with management, could help to either compensate for weak formal constraints on exit or to enforce and strengthen those constraints through collective bargaining. Together, constraints on exit and support for voice encouraged employers to negotiate compromises that retrained and redeployed workers, increased the generosity of redundancy plans, or attached social conditions to the process of managing layoffs.

Because downsizing most directly involved internal workers, strategies of labor solidarity played a less prominent role in explaining different outcomes between the cases or over time. Union cooperation was most important within those incumbents that negotiated with multiple unions with some representation domain overlap (see Table 2.4, Chapter 2): France Telecom, Telecom Italia, and Orange Polska. In each of those cases, union coordination in mobilization and bargaining over downsizing decisions was viewed by representatives as crucial to their successes. Thus, even where the boundary of solidarity was within the organization, overcoming divides within the labor movement could be an important challenge and resource for inserting social values in restructuring decisions.

4
Performance Management

In the previous chapter, I compared company-level downsizing policies across the ten case studies. In this chapter,[1] I compare negotiations over business unit or workplace-level performance management policies. "Performance management" is a general term used to describe the range of practices that companies adopt to motivate and compensate workers. These include goal-setting and quotas, performance monitoring and feedback, coaching and training, rewards (such as bonuses and promotions), and sanctions (such as progressive discipline, pay at risk, and dismissals).

Downsizing policies are often directly linked to worker precarity, through their impact on either the experience or fear of job and income loss. Performance management practices can have similar effects, but on an ongoing basis—so they affect workers' day-to-day experience of precarity. Jobs feel more insecure when managers adopt a discipline-focused performance management system that relies on constantly changing targets and quotas, variable pay that varies from month to month based on meeting these targets, limited opportunities to be promoted or move up to a better paying job, and the possibility of being fired for not meeting certain performance benchmarks. Alternatively, management can motivate workers through high involvement performance management practices, which rely on training and promotions, typically backed up by more job discretion, control, and some degree of job security.

Because performance management policies are so central to workers' job quality, security, and well-being, they are often a focus of collective bargaining. Unions and works councils seek to negotiate fair procedures for evaluating performance, job security provisions limiting or prohibiting discipline based on poor performance, and commitments by management to focus on training and development rather than progressive discipline and sanctions (O'Brady and Doellgast 2021). Worker representatives also often are involved in daily oversight of these practices, through serving on joint committees to hear employee complaints on targets that are unreasonable or arbitrary; ensuring that management adheres to agreements limiting the intensity, form, and use of monitoring;

---

[1] This chapter includes material previously published in an article coauthored with David Marsden (Doellgast and Marsden 2019). Katja Sarmiento-Mirwaldt carried out many of the interviews at BT, and the summary of that case draws on her case study write-up.

Exit, Voice, and Solidarity. Virginia Doellgast, Oxford University Press. © Oxford University Press 2022.
DOI: 10.1093/oso/9780197659779.003.0005

and representing employees who are unfairly disciplined or dismissed—through grievance procedures or in labor courts. These agreements or actions strengthen the social regulation of performance management and reduce precarity associated with more market- or exit-based and discipline-focused practices.

This chapter compares union and works council efforts to improve the social regulation of performance management in four of the case study companies: BT (United Kingdom), France Telecom (France), TDC (Denmark), and Deutsche Telekom (Germany). I focus on call center employees and technicians—two groups that represent a large share of service employment in incumbent telecom companies but differ in terms of skills, autonomy, and tasks. Technicians work alone or in teams and visit customers in their homes or businesses at a designated time, usually with a specific task, such as telephone and broadband line installation or equipment repair and maintenance. Call center employees work in large, typically open-plan offices and are responsible for customer service, technical support, and inbound and outbound sales—with target times for inbound calls typically ranging from 5 to 10 minutes per call. Technicians tend to have a higher level of technical skill and autonomy in their work, while call center work can be more tightly controlled and monitored. However, both jobs require considerable knowledge of different products and services, with increasing responsibility for sales in each.

In the following sections, I discuss in detail the performance management model in each case and across the two employee groups, focusing on the role of worker representatives in negotiating constraints on, or trying to fight against, practices associated with increased precarity. I then compare the cases and discuss the reasons for differences, based on the three factors underpinning the social regulation of work: constraints on employer exit, support for collective worker voice, and strategies of inclusive labor solidarity.

Collective worker voice comes to the fore in this chapter, as a central tool for worker representatives to challenge more precarious, discipline-focused practices and to propose or co-design alternative models prioritizing worker well-being. At the same time, formal institutional supports for voice, via bargaining, co-determination, or consultation rights and structures, were not enough. Constraints on employer exit, particularly those that made it difficult for employers to dismiss workers based on their performance, helped workers to effectively use these rights in negotiations. While all four cases moved toward more competitive and market-based performance management, unions and works councils were most successful at maintaining or re-establishing some degree of social protection where they could draw on a combination of constraints on exit and supports for voice. Precarity was lowest where collective agreements both closed off the option of discipline and dismissals and improved the fairness of evaluation and rewards.

Inclusive labor solidarity meanwhile underpinned efforts to establish more equitable pay rules and improve conditions for the most insecure or low-paid groups of workers. While cooperation between worker representatives was a source of labor power and unity across the cases, it played a particularly important role at France Telecom due to the presence of multiple unions within the incumbent.

The Social Regulation of Performance Management: The Case Studies

BT: Weakest Supports for Voice and Constraints on Exit

The BT case shows a move to a discipline-focused performance management model that increased precarity, in the context of both fewer formal rights for worker representatives to participate in the design of practices and overall weak job security. BT had long tracked performance, communicating results to employees and supervisors. But before the early 2000s, there were few consequences associated with poor performance. According to one manager, "People were able to underperform for a long time before anything was done about it. That changed heavily within a short space of time because the management realized that it's not feasible to carry on that way" (BT manager, May 23, 2012).

A new performance management model was then implemented in 2003, which required benchmarking employees on a bell curve: "I want to see a normal distribution of performance. I want to see 4% performance exits. [. . .] Because, if I've got 50 people, 5 are superlative, 40 are in the middle, and 5 are poor, the biggest efficiency I can get, besides moving those 40 a bit, is to get those 5 up" (BT manager, November 22, 2011). This was a major culture shift. Employees agreed on their target at the beginning of each quarterly or six-month period with their supervisor. The company wanted to use industry benchmarks, but the unions encouraged their members to insist that targets were "specific, measurable, achievable, realistic, timely" (SMART). If any worker struggled to meet targets, they were put on progressive discipline and given additional coaching. If after several attempts they still did not improve, they could be dismissed.

Starting around 2008, the unions began accusing the company of "managing people out the door" on performance grounds to reduce headcount. Managers would grade individuals down to encourage them to take redundancy. This led to conflict with the unions and an explosion in grievance cases. In response, BT and both the CWU and Prospect negotiated an agreement on performance management called the "two-way deal" in 2010, stipulating that the company would state very clearly its expectations, employees would perform accordingly, and there would be no surprises after a performance review. At the same time, some union representatives felt that managers were violating the terms of the new agreement—for example, through redefining appraisal categories from "generally satisfactory" to "development needed."

According to one union official, this developmental approach only lasted six months. After that brief honeymoon, BT returned to the aggressive, punitive, and "bell curve"–driven approach to performance management, even though this was not supposed to be used under the agreement. While central management blamed the backtracking on "rogue and mis-guided managers who are acting alone," union representatives felt that this was not true—as supervisors were often told to grade their team members on a bell-shaped curve (email, Prospect official, February 15, 2013). Managers also used so-called compromise agreements (car park deals) where an employee would be graded as having unacceptable performance and given 3 months' severance pay as an "unregretted leaver," rather than being put through the two-year performance process.

Another union representative described these as implementation and management problems:

> The agreement we have got is absolutely fine: at the end of the year, you see if you have achieved the standards agreed at the start of the year and if you do, then you are at least an "achieves standards" which is rank 3 in the company performance management structure. And this should get you a pay rise. If your performance is not meeting targets, it should be clearly advertised to you and you should get performance plans to get you back on track where necessary. But because of the requirement for quarterly levelling, you often find that there are targets for a certain distribution of marks, though the company absolutely denies this. A certain percentage needs to go to the bottom, the Jack Welch model." (Prospect official, November 1, 2011)

Call Centers

At BT, the consumer call centers were located in the business unit "BT Retail."[2] In 2012, BT Retail employed 10,000 call center employees in 38 UK-based locations. BT's in-house call centers recruited into both specialized and multi-skilled positions. The call center we visited in 2012 handled billing, business sales, residential service and sales, and technical support.

---

[2] The case study companies frequently reorganize their business units and subsidiaries. My description of organizational structure refers to that at the time of my research, unless otherwise specified.

In residential service and sales, employees were organized into teams of 10–15, with one coach per team. Every agent was coached at least once a week, for half an hour to an hour depending on their needs. Individuals who did not meet their targets were placed on coaching plans, or later on performance plans, where they received a minimum of two coaching sessions per week, one from the manager, one from the coach. Coaching was ongoing and happened every day in different forms. Ninety percent of all inbound and outbound calls were recorded using a system called Viewer, and coaches could book a one-to-one session to listen to calls that had been recorded. As part of these sessions, the advisors evaluated their own calls. Calls could also be listened to remotely, and the coaches gave advisors feedback directly after. Finally, the coach could sit by the advisor and give them "on the spot" coaching. If there were any points that the advisors missed, they were given further advice. Finally, coaches also monitored "compliance," i.e., whether an operator used the systems properly or added notes correctly. If agents did not do this, they automatically scored zero, regardless of how well they dealt with the customer.

Across BT's call centers, targets typically included sales, hourly calls, financial reporting, repeat calls, contact resolution, transfers, complaints, customer satisfaction, and call handling time. There were team targets and individual targets, which every agent was supposed to be able to fulfill. These targets varied between segments. For example, in sales, meeting sales goals were more important, while agents responsible for "faults" were expected to minimize call handling times. Each target had a weighting that changed monthly and factored into an overall performance indicator. A traffic light system, based on a program called Merlin, measured adherence to targets, as well as sign-on, shrinkage, and sick days. Each individual was either "green" (adhering to targets), "amber" (needs improvement), or "red" (not meeting targets).

Being in red for three weeks would lead to an advisor being placed on an informal coaching plan. If the agent did not improve, a performance case was raised. In the call center we visited, almost every agent had been on a performance plan at least once. The initial warning took four weeks; the next warning came after three weeks; and the final warning came after two weeks, followed by the decision stage. The agent could leave or appeal at every stage of this ten-week process, and the union was also involved at every stage to provide support.

If an employee "misbehaved"—for example, had a cigarette or watched TV instead of working—a discipline case would be raised. HR managers were responsible for deciding if an incident would be classed as "misconduct" or "gross misconduct"—or to just issue an oral or written warning. The process for discipline cases to move to dismissal took about four weeks.

Another performance management tool was the quarterly performance review. Supervisors would sit down with agents and highlight the areas where improvements were needed and ways to achieve them. However, bonuses were only attached to meeting targets in the sales area. Management observed that this was due to the CWU's long-standing resistance to performance-related pay. The union agreed to commissions for sales jobs because targets were easy to measure and employees wanted them. Bonuses were paid based on sales targets, which averaged 35% of agents' salary. Top performers could make £45,000–£50,000 a year including bonuses, while employees who met 85% of their targets would receive around £20,000 a year. Only 3–5 people consistently did not achieve 85%, in which case they would receive additional coaching and feedback under a performance plan. Again, if they did not improve, they would eventually be dismissed. High performers across the different call types could enter a national competition for a prize, and would get recognition from their manager through, e.g., a £25 voucher or a prize.

Generally, union representatives and managers considered the performance management process to be very cumbersome. The CWU negotiated an agreement with BT Retail called "Together we will make a difference" that identified standards of best practice. These included, for example, clarity about expected standards and behaviors; provision of timely and effective training and ongoing development; commitments not to use targets or quotas for "managing people out of BT on performance" or for "forced distribution of performance ratings"; and a commitment to use individual performance information "in a positive and constructive manner to support improvement or recognize and celebrate individual or team achievement and success."[3] While the agreement laid out best practices, union representatives felt it was most useful as a reference document. It established principles of transparency and fairness that they ultimately had to enforce via filing grievances and representing employees undergoing progressive discipline for poor performance.

Technicians

Technicians at BT were employed in two main business units: Operate, in charge of the network before the exchanges, and Openreach, dealing with the "last mile" after the exchanges. I focus here on Openreach, which employed around 20,000 technicians—referred to within BT as engineers. Around 8,000 were responsible for network delivery, building the fiber optic network and maintaining the copper network; and 12,000 were responsible for service delivery (i.e., as field technicians or field engineers).

---

[3] CWU, "Together we will make a difference," available at https://www.cwu.org/wp-content/uploads/2018/03/Together-We-Will-Make-A-Difference-document-signed-2.pdf (accessed January 2013), p. 4.

Openreach engineers only saw their managers about once a week or once a fortnight, depending on the part of the country. However, they were constantly directed, monitored, and tracked by an online system or "machine." Engineers started to work from their homes in their BT vans. These vans were equipped with a tracking device, which sent data to the central system to efficiently plan their routes. Each job was allocated based on a skills analysis that matched jobs to engineers with the required training. The system also calculated the average time it should take to clear that task, so it predicted when each engineer would be available, and then calculated the distance to the next job for all the engineers in the vicinity. If an engineer had not finished a job on time, the system would send them an alert.

When GPS was first put in the vans, engineers and union representatives were concerned about what the company would do with the information. Management explained that it was about managing work effectively, not having Big Brother watching them. According to one manager:

> We've got a really good relationship with unions. For example, by the efficiencies that Openreach has been able to generate in terms of having the new work planner, work allocation system GPS in the van, has meant that we have been able to bizarrely grow that business because the price points have come down. (BT manager, January 12, 2012)

The union remained skeptical. An ongoing concern was how management used supplementary information that the GPS provided, for example, on engineers' location and unauthorized stops, which could be a resource in disciplinary cases.

As described above, performance management only began to be pushed at BT in the mid-2000s. Its introduction was a particularly stark culture shock for BT's engineers, who were used to having a lot of autonomy. According to one manager, its purpose could have been explained better because "... in parts of the business, and certainly in parts of Openreach, we have created a worry around performance management that people are about to get sacked" (BT manager, June 12, 2012). Field engineers were assessed on four criteria: the number of jobs they performed, repeat faults, health and safety, and customer satisfaction. On the first, the system split the types of jobs into different categories and calculated how long each job should take based on two-year averages. If an engineer took much longer than the average allocated time, they were required to explain this in their daily report.

If an engineer consistently did not meet targets, the supervisor was sent a request to act. The manager first tried to find out if the engineer had a personal problem. The data also permitted managers to identify types of work at which their engineers struggled, and they could then allocate a coach who would go out with them on their route. Engineers had a six-week period to improve, and if they did not, they could be dismissed. However, this happened very rarely. In 2010, dismissals through performance amounted to less than 0.1% of the Openreach workforce. Even if there were no particular problems, operations managers (OMs) were expected to draw up coaching plans for all of their teams to identify technical, training, and support needs, and other forms of assistance such as job shadowing, a course, or mentoring.

According to one senior manager:

> So we've got 33,000 people frightened [of performance management], but only ten people, if you like, need to be frightened. And what we're doing now is we're trying to reposition performance management and we've flipped over and started calling it "improvement performance," about the power of coaching, about making sure it's about helping. (BT HR manager, February 6, 2012)

In the opinion of several unionists, performance management had harmed quality: "We've seen it in the last couple of years. They've had to form a complete new unit in Openreach to look at the quality of the network because they drove the performance up but the quality down, and then they ended up having repeat reports" (Prospect official, June 12, 2012). Repeat reports, where a fault occurs again within twenty-eight days, were not supposed to be higher than 4% nationally, but often exceeded this target. Another unionist criticized the use of work allocation systems for monitoring the engineers, arguing that it had contributed to a more discipline-focused culture:

> The company has a difficult position because it has endless metrics.... I mean an engineer can't breathe unless they're telling him how many times he breathes in a day. It's got to an absolutely ridiculous level. And that has come to an end, where certainly from the engineering point of view there was going to be industrial unrest, and even to the extent of strikes and non-cooperation over the way in which that was utilized. Because it's always used as a hammer to beat people over the head with. It's never used in a constructive way. Openreach has come to a crossroads and it has publicly stated that it will use the information in a different way and will have a different culture of performance management. (Prospect official, January 9, 2012)

Summary
BT adopted an increasingly discipline-based performance management system in both its call centers and technician units. This system motivated workers through a combination of centrally developed targets and intensive monitoring,

with failure to meet performance objectives potentially resulting in dismissal. BT's unions played an important role in moderating the impact of these policies on workers, using collective bargaining, grievances, and partnership to improve fairness and protect against precarity. Collective agreements built some predictability into coaching, feedback, and "progressive discipline"—ensuring that this was carried out in a standardized way that gave employees opportunities to improve through intensive coaching. In addition, performance-based pay was limited to sales roles, where targets were more easily measured. However, these negotiated rules were relatively blunt instruments in influencing the actual design of the performance management system—which had become more punitive over time. There was quite a lot of measurement, monitoring, and individual-based control focused on performance. In addition, labor relations around implementation of these rules were relatively conflictual, in an organization that otherwise had a tradition of strong labor management partnership.

France Telecom: Strengthening Support for Voice, Strong Constraints on Exit

France Telecom is an interesting case where worker voice in performance management decisions was strengthened over time, through solidaristic worker mobilization (Chapter 3). One important overarching difference from BT was France Telecom's much stronger dismissal protections. As a result, and in sharp contrast to BT, France Telecom did not rely on progressive discipline. Local managers explained this as due to both the high number of civil servants in the workforce, as well as restrictive employment protection rules in France:

> France Telecom is an old public company with civil servants. So in general, people who are older than thirty-eight are civil servants ... in 80% of cases, so they have protected employment, and even if they make serious mistakes or they are not at the right level, you can't do much. On the other hand, we have employees who are on the *droit privé* [private law] contract [...]. In France it is necessary to have several warnings, a reprimand, etc., to be able to build a case for dismissal. But France Telecom doesn't go into this area. Instead, we try with managers, with human resources, to help them to progress, to put them in a new position. (FT manager, April 8, 2010)

This meant that sanctions or the threat of dismissals could not be widely used to motivate the workforce. Instead, managers used a range of tools based more on incentives, through variable pay and promotions, as well as training and development.

152 EXIT, VOICE, AND SOLIDARITY

Of course, as discussed in Chapter 3, France Telecom managers had sought to get rid of their difficult-to-dismiss workers in more problematic ways before the social crisis of 2009, through forced relocation and "management by stress." By the time of my interviews, unions and managers referred to these past practices as an example of the company's culture of often top-down and unilateral management decision-making. Put in the terms of this book, workers' formal collective voice resources, through union agreements, works councils, and a range of workplace-level consultation bodies, had a marginal impact on day-to-day management. A representative of a labor consultancy who had worked with the works councils at France Telecom to prepare reports for their "information and consultation" meetings with management explained:

> Management says: "okay, it's a good report. But we decide. Okay, maybe the expert is right, but that doesn't do anything, it's we who decide...." In France, there is a very important right to information. You can know a lot, a lot of things, but you can't oppose what they do. Right to information, but not a right to opposition, there isn't even the right to negotiation. So the French law says that we could have all the information, but if you don't agree, that's too bad, and that's kind of the problem. We informed you, we did what the law says we have to do. Now, if you aren't happy, that's not a problem. (consultant, March 12, 2010)

However, a number of policy changes had been negotiated in the post-2009 social accords, including an end to forced relocations and a joint labor–management commission to monitor the impact of management practices on workers' psychosocial health. These limited the use of disciplinary practices, with management continuing to use or strengthen more traditional tools based on intensive coaching and incentives such as promotions, as well as (particularly among technicians) expanded discretion and skill. The practices in place at the time of my research could thus be traced to a combination of institutional constraints on exit and the successful use of (newly strengthened) collective worker voice to improve the social regulation of performance management in the period after the social crisis. As described in Chapter 3, solidarity between traditionally ideologically divided unions was important for mobilizing workers around a common critique of "management by stress," which strengthened the focus on worker well-being as a legitimate outcome to be pursued in performance management decisions.

Call Centers

France Telecom's consumer or residential call centers were based in two major units, with separate centers dedicated either to fixed-line and internet customers or to mobile customers. However, at headquarters level, they were under one manager and were organized in an identical way: "the same way of operating, the same principles of fixed and variable pay, the same principles of representativeness, the staff representative bodies are the same" (FT manager, March 8, 2010). There was also an attempt to gradually bring these areas together, and at three of FT's call centers, employees could service all three segments. One manager noted that this required an "extremely intense and extremely long" training course to enable employees to answer calls relating to a wide range of products and services.

In 2010, France Telecom's residential call centers employed around 14,000 agents. Employees were organized in two "levels," with multiple specializations within each. Level 1 received 80% of the calls and included a matrix of three employee groups (sales and termination, customer service and account management, billings and collections) with a further three customer segments: gold (high value), standard (low value), and new customers. Level 2 received the remaining 20% of calls, and included five groups handling complicated collections, customer retention, technical assistance, after-sales service, and e-delivery tracking. Both levels were closely integrated, with distinct "flows" for collections, sales, and service.

In the call center I visited, there was one team leader for teams of 12–15 advisors and one trainer for every 18 advisors. The team leader listened to calls, side by side or remotely, carrying out a "debriefing" and re-listening to past calls to identify areas of improvement. Customer complaints were also escalated to the team leader. The trainer organized individual training and support for each advisor. The team leader met with the trainer regularly to develop a work plan to help the customer advisor progress: "So, there is a tacit agreement between the manager, the trainer, and the customer advisor, saying, in this area, you are not at the expected level, so we are going to put in place help or a personalized course, we'll put in place everything you can imagine, to be able to help you improve" (FT manager, April 8, 2010).

Another important performance management tool was pay increases or "promotions" linked to formal performance evaluations. Team leaders and department heads carried out performance reviews twice a year for all employees. Based on these reviews, managers identified high-performing employees and recommended them for pay increases: "The manager decides, based on the development of the sales employee or other employee, regardless of the status of the person . . . his [sic] manager decides, based on his skills and performance, and the way he conducts his work, if he deserves a large increase or no increase" (FT training manager, May 26, 2010). Civil servants were eligible, but also had automatic seniority-based pay increases. One works councilor observed that in the past year, 70 employees in his region received these discretionary promotions in a workforce of 800–850 (8%–9%) (CGT works councilor FT, December 8, 2011).

This system meant that pay was effectively individualized for private law employees, despite the presence of formal pay scales. Union representatives were critical of this system of performance-based pay increases (called *augmentation managériale*):

> Today, for example, in my service center, where there are private law employees [. . .] they are all doing the same work, but there are none of them who are on the same salary . . . because there is this *augmentation managériale*, which makes it so that there are some who get higher pay increases than others. (CGT rep FT, May 19, 2010)

The union representatives cited above said that the CGT was working on improving pay equity, with a focus on equity between men and women. They found that on average a man who had started at the same time as a woman was making 400–500 euros more per month.

From management's perspective, performance evaluations and promotions were important tools for motivating employees in the absence of the ability to sanction poor performance:

> Good, there is necessarily the individual and his/her progression, but also we have team meetings, briefings, and what I ask is for the team to at least reach the KPI targets. But good, there is nothing, there aren't any sanctions, we have to try to make them improve as much as possible anyway. Of course, we have annual meetings—and there we evaluate the level [of performance], that could be insufficient, that could be an obstacle if someone wants to do another job or to get a promotion. So there are consequences [for poor performance]. (FT manager, April 8, 2010)

One concern was reducing high levels of absenteeism, which could be between 6% and 10%. Local managers described several strategies, including offering more flexible working time, or encouraging "team spirit" "because results are individually motivating but also motivating for the team" (FT manager, April 8, 2010). It was striking, in comparison to the BT case, that considerable effort was placed on developing a combination of intrinsic or team-based forms of motivation:

> There are preventative methods, but also "curative" methods: the idea is to create around the employee a good working environment that makes him [*sic*] want to go there, or that shows him that he is important to the team . . . so that

he notices that if he doesn't come, he gives his team problems—there is that game. (FT manager, April 8, 2010).

At the same time, there was also intensive monitoring: calls were recorded, and individual performance was measured along a number of different metrics. "We have a lot of controls ... everywhere, not only in call centers [...]. Everything is monitored: you arrive in the morning, you log on to your computer and you are monitored until the evening" (CGT rep FT, May 19, 2010).

Monitoring practices had changed over time. In the early 2000s, as part of a broader post-liberalization change in management culture (Giry 2014), monitoring was significantly intensified, based on a range of new metrics and up to seventeen different monitoring tools. Then, in the mid-2000s, France Telecom experienced a social crisis associated with a wave of employee suicides (see Chapter 3), as well as growing concern with declining customer service quality. At the time of my research, managers were working with union representatives to implement different initiatives to reduce stress, as well as to organize work in a more learning-oriented way—what one union representative described as a form of "ameliorated lean." He went on to describe union initiatives to try to improve working conditions in the call centers:

> What we've done in terms of work organization, there are very concrete things—we worked on a certain number of things. We are trying to identify the causes of stress. There are monitoring tools, and monitoring is increasing. We call it coaching, side-by-side listening, a number of things like that. [...] So we managed to make a number of things like that optional, especially with regard to the double listening and coaching. Not everywhere, but in a number of places. We succeeded in technical assistance, to get rid of the "wrap-up"— which was the incompressible time between two calls. So now the customer advisors are the ones who decide when they will be available to take the next call. So we try to extend that to all of customer relations, which [management] is stubbornly defending. (CGT works councilor FT, December 8, 2011)

A further tool for motivating improved performance was through competitions and variable pay. Agents could win 30 euros, a mobile phone, or other small prizes in national or local challenges. In addition, there were variable sales-based incentives. Under the earlier model, fixed-line and internet call centers had small incentives that were around 5% of salary, based on meeting individual goals, while mobile call centers had individual variable pay that averaged 15%–17% of salary and team-based variable pay that averaged 5% of salary.

By 2010, the system was standardized, and variable pay was restricted only to agents in sales positions—similar to BT. One manager estimated that across the call centers, 40% of employees were in these jobs. For this group, variable pay was linked to sales in relation to sales objectives, multiplied by a coefficient based on service quality, multiplied by a coefficient based on efficiency metrics (e.g., number of calls handled per hour). Sales were divided into ten families of products. In order to get variable pay, it was necessary to reach at least 70% of the objectives in each of the ten families. However, if customer satisfaction was low—for example, if employees sold customers products that they didn't ask for—then sales would be multiplied by zero.

> This variable system is sophisticated enough to try to avoid a situation where the customer advisors aren't focusing on one objective to the detriment of others. On the other hand, it's true that whatever isn't in the variable pay system can be a little forgotten, and often that which isn't in the variable pay system contributes to quality. (FT manager, March 8, 2010)

The average variable pay for a sales employee was between 200 and 300 euros/month—which averaged 10%–15% of pay. However, these sales incentives could be as high as 1,000 euros/month, paid on top of base pay.

A CGT union representative who worked in a call center observed that the CGT had long fought against introducing variable pay. Once it was introduced, employees wanted to keep it, due to the high level of extra pay they could get. However, its level had fallen by close to 60% over five years, as management sought to cut costs in response to declining operating margins. This was encouraging these employees to organize around improvements to their base pay: "When they see that this *part variable* goes down, they realize that their base pay is not high enough, so we start to discuss a little more about base pay and what is needed to live and claim a salary . . ." (CGT rep FT, May 19, 2010).

Another CGT representative on the works council observed that the model of calculating the level and composition of pay had moved from being almost exclusively based on individual sales performance measures to experiments with more team-based and service quality–focused measures. This was in part due to cases of mis-selling and fraud to gain a bonus:

> We [the CGT] always said that variable pay led to abuses, especially in the commercial field. The company is realizing today that we were right. Meaning that people profit from the system, there are a lot of mis-selling cases in the call centers or shops—meaning that employees sell customers things that they don't need. [. . .] This collective part, that is going to make up around 30%–40% of variable pay—so replacing the purely individual quantitative objectives that we had before. At the same time, there is a change in the level of [variable pay],

which ultimately is a way for the company to control its payroll costs. The big problem that we are going to have, is that for the employees who arrived these last years, they were recruited with promises about the high level of variable pay, and [. . .] tomorrow they are going to ask them to focus on loyalty. (CGT works councilor FT, December 8, 2011)

Technicians

At France Telecom, most technicians were located in two administrative units at the time of my research: the Network Control Units (UPR), responsible for network construction and "performance optimization"; and the Response Units (UI), which included all activities related to customer installation and repairs, network structure and local loop, and management of the existing network.[4] I focus here on the UI units, as they employed the majority of service or field technicians. All UI units, from 500 to 2,000 people each, included technicians with four main specializations: *répartiteurs* (repaired lines); *boucle locale* (worked on the network outside the customer's home); *intervention client* (installed telephone and internet service at the customer's home); and *réseau structurant* (managed the network structure). Technicians could also be specialized in *entreprise* (installation work in large companies). The work of each group overlapped: for example, *boucle locale* technicians were responsible for building and maintaining the network for both consumer and business groups.

Similar to BT, field technicians worked out of their vans, and their work was controlled through a centralized, AI-based dispatching tool: "OPTime." A director in the UI observed that there was a lot of union and technician resistance to the tool when it was first introduced, based on fears it would "destroy their jobs." Management responded by reorienting the tool and emphasizing the benefits: that it would improve the match between skills and demands and allow more follow-up with customers. Union representatives felt it had broadly undermined worker autonomy, "Thanks to OPTime, it is the machine that determines which technician has to go to a certain place depending on the distance. That's a machine and it does not worry about any other issue. The technician is completely dispossessed of any kind of leeway" (CFDT rep FT, May 18, 2010).

At the same time, as one works council representative observed, "in the end, they are happy because they still have their car, they are always free, even if they

---

[4] My discussion of technicians at France Telecom draws on collaboration with Maxime Bellego in our coauthored article: (Doellgast, Bellego, and Pannini 2021). His research findings on the work and professional experience of technicians during and after the social crisis are included in more detail in his PhD dissertation: (Bellego 2013).

are bugged with GPS, the system bothers them all the time etc. . . . They have remained artisans" (works councilor FT, May 18, 2012).

> This population [technicians] has for the most part retained a collective spirit [*esprit collectif*], which they still have. This is impressive. . . . A technician, he [*sic*] is proud of his profession and above all, he is proud to succeed in solving a customer's problem. And he puts that above everything, to the point that he won't obey his superiors, he will find ways to not strictly follow orders. (CFDT rep FT, June 30, 2010)

Monitoring and control over the length and timing of work had increased over time. Field technicians were given tight goals for how long they could spend with each customer: "The technicians were going back four times to a customer because they had 30 minutes and not 35 to complete their meeting. So at the end of 30 minutes, if he hadn't fixed the fault, he had to go to the next meeting. . . . That's a caricature, but it was really like that" (CGT works councilor FT, December 8, 2011).

In addition, after restructuring in 2006, management shifted monitoring of technician performance and targets from the team to the individual level:

> Instead of telling the team, "you have to do this (repair this thing by this date)," you choose a technician in the team and say: "you are going to do this on this day, at this time." They [management] began to decide on the work schedules for all individuals [. . .]. [In the past] they said: "there is this to do, but you manage yourself, we just want to know when it is done" [. . .]. The idea was to strengthen control. (CFDT rep FT, May 12, 2010)

The union representative quoted above felt that the motivation for this tightening of control traced back to the history of the technicians at France Telecom: there was a massive recruitment of technicians in the 1970s, when the French government invested in developing the national telecommunications infrastructure. They were specialists in complicated machines and technology, and developed an *esprit de corps* in which they had strong control over their professional duties and the content of their work:

> And that is something that management took very badly and always wanted to break. They tried several times, but without success. They always tried to find out what was happening in the technician units, to know how much work they were doing, how they could . . . at that time it wasn't Taylorized, but . . . to quantify the number of tasks, to know how long it lasted, etc. . . . And in most other

métiers [professions, jobs] this is done, but not among technicians—and that has never been forgiven. (CFDT rep FT, May 12, 2010)

Another union representative discussed the combined effects of narrower specialization and tightening control:

Pretty much the same thing happened that happened on the customer side of the business: namely they tried at the highest level of management to organize everything and to organize everything mathematically, saying: here is the region, I have this many technicians, I divide that by that, by that, by that—and hop! Normally, they should work like that. And so they began to manage more and more tightly, without necessarily always understanding what is done at the level of work organization for the people and how they did their work in practice. (CFDT rep FT, June 30, 2010)

These conditions were accompanied by increasing stress among the technicians in the UI associated with the growing fragmentation and de-skilling of work, loss of control over the content and pace of work, and the negative customer response to declining customer service (Bellego 2013).

Following the social crisis of 2009, a range of initiatives across France Telecom aimed at reducing stress. From 2010, any organizational change had to pass a psychosocial risks analysis at the regional level. Unions were involved in deciding on the methodology for the analysis, based on INRS methods (directed by the Minister of Health). Then unions or works councils were involved in local consultation on the results. This provided an opportunity for union representatives to be involved in the implementation of broader changes in work organization.

Two major changes occurred in the late 2000s. First, technicians were linked to call centers, to improve coordination between sales and installation. Second, within some of the UIs a new department was established based on multi-skilled teams, or *équipes multi-compétentes*, that included technicians from each of the four major specializations.

I interviewed a director who described the goals of this initiative:

We are in charge of all the customers and all the activities in a geographic area, and we try to develop multi-skills so that we can answer the demands of all kinds of customers and operations on networks. One of our big challenges is to develop these multi-skills aspects so that we can improve efficiency, and also it is also something that is asked for by technical people. They prefer to work on different activities and for different customers rather than to be specialized in one field of operation. (FT manager, February 24, 2012)

He observed that the initiative had pay-offs for the company. Variation in productivity had declined, and "global productivity" had increased. However, it was also part of an effort to improve the working environment within France Telecom:

> We are really in the process of changing the social contract, the business model. We were following a very prescriptive model, very top down; and then there is the model we are building now . . . where we want to improve things, develop versatility, etc.—and at the same time give a little more room for the human side, the room for *manœuvre* and at the same time accountability. (FT manager, February 24, 2012)

Workers and worker representatives had more mixed responses. They felt that the multi-skilled teams represented a broadly positive development, as it moved away from a trend toward an ever narrower division of labor. A field technician described the changes that occurred after his unit adopted the multi-skilled team model in 2014 as leading to more effective team work and better resolution of customer calls (e.g., for customer connections or repairs):

> It's true, it's good. It's good because that [to be divided, in different teams and buildings] does not create good relations between people. Above all, when you are specialized in an area, you have a tendency when something isn't as much your area or skill set to leave the work to others. What is good [with the multi-skilled teams] is that it breaks down partitions, and you are going to communicate with each other about problems that are essentially the same—that are in another area. (FT technician, July 27, 2016)

Local union representatives were consulted over the decision to adopt the teams in different regions, and then were involved in their implementation. Union representatives (particularly from CFDT) observed that technicians valued improvements in discretion, communication, and problem-solving. But they were still fighting to make sure workers were paid for extra skill and time; and that the changes did not drive up work intensity and stress. By 2017, technicians had secured a small wage increase associated with participation in the teams. In addition, all new technicians were recruited under a single job title, without a specialization, allowing them to move on to other skills. The unions were evaluating this for possible risks, for example, to future pay and promotion opportunities.

These changes in work organization and skills were a particularly important part of the "performance management system" among field technicians, because so much of workers' motivation in these jobs is connected to their professional discretion and ability to use and develop their skills. More directly, management sought to motivate workers in a similar way to in the call centers: through promotions, training, and performance reviews linked to targets.

At the local or team level, management sought to motivate employees based on work redesign and encouraging learning within teams, based on regular meetings. Team challenges or competitions also allowed the best performers or individual performers to receive an extra bonus. Two major targets for performance improvement were to identify and resolve the source of technical faults more quickly and to improve customer satisfaction. Satisfaction was measured through surveys and calculated as a net promotor score (NPS). An HR director observed that the field technicians were motivated to provide a good service to customers, rooted in a strong civil service culture, and so took the NPS very seriously. It was measured at the level of teams and the region: "In fact, the teams know very well where they are vis-à-vis their customers, and whether customer satisfaction is improving. And that is a real motivation" (FT HR manager, March 8, 2012).

There were also company-wide performance measures that different groups of technicians had direct responsibility for. For example, the service quality over different networks was publicly evaluated and ranked by the regulatory agency, based on sixty-one different metrics, such as sound quality of voice conversations, download time, and how long it took texts to be sent: "This is measured and then communicated. That's also a motivation for the employees" (FT HR manager, March 8, 2012).

One France Telecom–wide performance improvement program called "the learning company" (*l'entreprise apprenante*) focused on organizing support for employees who encountered problems in the course of performing their jobs. This was started in 2010 and was intensified in 2011 and 2012. The UIs were a pilot for this program—which an HR director felt was due to the characteristics of the workforce: "technicians who have problems with complicated subjects or areas of their work don't keep these problems to themselves" (FT HR manager, March 8, 2012). Another program was called "*Conquête* 2015," which included some broad goals around improving customer service and sales, encouraging mutual learning to raise productivity, and investing in the network.

In the UIs, technicians met with their supervisors for regular performance reviews—but again, as in the call centers, there were no direct consequences associated with the results of these reviews. Instead, results would be used for determining promotions or salary increases. At the same time, union representatives were critical of the way in which coaching and performance evaluations were conducted:

> If you do not meet these productivity goals, first they are going to ask you: how is it that you are less productive than the others? What happened? Do you need

training? Voilà: do you need this, do you need that, what do you need? Or they are going to say, listen, you have an attitude that isn't the norm. So the employee is going to be blamed because in effect, if I am below the others [in performance], I'm not good [...]. The management evaluation is always done with the intention to improve productivity. So the employee always has the impression that they are not doing enough for the company, that they don't deserve their salary in general, and so they should reduce their demands. He's going to be less likely to ask for a promotion or salary increase because his boss tells him: "but listen, you are not good." (CGT works councilor FT, June 30, 2010)

In contrast to France Telecom's call centers, there was no variable pay or pay for performance for field technicians. Union opposition was one reason, but management was also hesitant to interfere with the strong collective professional identity of the workforce:

The unions are very resistant and very opposed to all this [discussions about introducing variable pay], because they fear an opening up of competition between people. . . . And it is true that in the profession of technicians, in the sociological sense of the term, there is a real community of technicians, this is a real common culture, and the fear of the unions is that they will lose some influence vis-à-vis technicians. And more crucially, it is also harming this profession, in the sense of losing this collective thing. So I am extremely attentive to that which keeps the professional side collective, mutual; and at the same time, we need to get to a point where we can individually encourage those who want to go faster, farther, etc. (FT manager, February 24, 2012)

Summary

France Telecom managers faced strong constraints on the performance management practices they could adopt. Job security protections and rules restricting variable pay to certain groups of employees encouraged a different approach from that at BT. It was impossible for managers to use progressive discipline to improve performance, which essentially ruled out a competitive "bell curve" style of benchmarking. Instead, they adopted other practices to motivate employees—mostly through frequent coaching and development, as well as performance evaluation and sales incentives.

Unions and works councils historically had some direct, collective voice-based influence on these practices through opposing intensified monitoring or certain forms of variable pay and consulting over changes in management practices. Their power to substantively shape performance management practices had increased, however, following the social crisis. As described in

Chapter 3, unions had mobilized around the negative impact of top-down, punitive downsizing policies on workers' psychosocial health prior to the crisis. As a result, they won a more direct role in negotiations over measures to reduce stress and burnout, backed by the threat that they could "re-mediatize" stress. Many of the initiatives on work reorganization described above, which focused on increasing discretion and investing in worker skills, built on social accords negotiated by the unions, and were implemented in consultation with local union and works council representatives. This involved a significant culture shift from past practice, and allowed workers—particularly technicians—to reassert collective worker voice in management decision-making.

The following two cases—TDC in Denmark and Deutsche Telekom in Germany—show different patterns, based on stronger formal support for collective voice in both cases, but with significant differences in constraints on exit.

TDC: Weakening Supports for Voice Due to Weaker Constraints on Exit

TDC is based in Denmark, where formal support for collective worker voice is stronger than in the United Kingdom or France, but employment protections are weaker than in France or Germany. The ongoing process of downsizing through regular layoffs was described in Chapter 3. This downsizing process was used to dismiss employees based on performance—but with union involvement to make sure the company adhered to certain social conditions (TDC HR manager, April 23, 2012). Weaker job security thus enabled discipline-focused practices, similar to at BT, although with union oversight to protect more vulnerable employees.

The TDC case is particularly interesting as one where the greater ability of employers to exit internal employment relationships also weakened worker representatives' ability to use strong formal voice resources to limit precarity. Collective agreements and consultation with works councils (or "cooperation committees") did encourage more developmental approaches to performance management, including a focus on training investments and teamwork. Joint committees helped to oversee the fairness of targets and variable pay. However, managers increasingly relied on pressure from fear of being dismissed to motivate improved performance.

Call Centers

At the time of my research, TDC's call centers serving the consumer market segment were based in two main organizational units: the Consumer business unit (with 700 employees) and the subsidiary Call Center Europe (with 285 employees—over 200 of whom were primarily handling TDC calls). Although both received similar calls, they had some differences in performance management practices due to their history: Call Center Europe had been covered by a weaker collective agreement with another union, HK, prior to being purchased by TDC, and had broadly maintained the terms of this agreement (see Chapter 5 for details). Both units were the responsibility of TDC's union Dansk Metal, the Danish Metalworkers Union.

The Consumer call centers were organized into four groups: inbound service and sales; inbound technical support; outbound sales and telemarketing; and inbound and outbound billing. Consumer had recently moved from a structure where there were separate teams for fixed-line and mobile customer service to one with mixed inbound teams handling both kinds of calls. Call Center Europe had groups handling inbound service and sales, technical support, and billing; as well as two special departments dedicated to "employee deals" on mobile phone or computer services through large employers, and a "dealer service" to TDC employees in retail stores.

Employees in both the Consumer unit and Call Center Europe were organized in teams of 15–30 agents, with a team leader. All calls were recorded, and team leaders did side-by-side coaching daily. Employees had a 30–60-minute performance meeting with their team leader every three weeks to discuss performance, well-being, and any incidences of absenteeism or sick leave.

Compared to BT and France Telecom, TDC placed a stronger emphasis on prizes and team-building activities to motivate employees. Team leaders in the inbound groups in the Consumer business unit described a range of different tools they used to motivate employees, including small competitions, diplomas, happy hours, and celebrations for success: "Every time they make a sale they are clinging on a clock, and then we'll all clap and there'll be a celebration" (TDC team leader, April 27, 2012). Another team leader described the tools she used:

> I do a lot of talking with all of them, asking them why, what is it that is working for you right now? Making them share their success stories with each other. Also, to make it visible, we use . . . all of the things we have to perform on are bound together in a star, the "Performance Star." And I made a system where you can fill out the star according to how you perform. So each thing that you do well, will fill out the star. And we actually have it visible in the team, hung up for every month. And they also get it personally for themselves, every week. And it's in colors, and it's a very, very simple thing, but instead of, like, the dry numbers, that I look on every day, they will not find that very motivating! I try to make it a little bit fun and more easy [sic] to take in, also if it's not good. And I let them have some responsibility, the ones that do good, and the ones that

can handle it of course, they have some sort of responsibility in the team. (TDC team leader, April 27, 2012).

A shop steward from Call Center Europe noted that team work was important, with organized "support groups," a team-building week every three months, and a social event at the end of the week—with some teams planning regular excursions (Dansk Metal rep TDC, May 15, 2012).

Employees were also given a number of hard targets that they were expected to meet, including talk times, compliance with schedule, sales, and customer service. A shop steward from TDC's in-house call centers observed that there had been a shift in focus toward emphasizing sales—a common theme across the case study companies: "They're just . . . okay, sales, sales, sales . . . it's the most important thing for them" (Dansk Metal rep TDC, April 24, 2012). However, there had also been a growing focus on customer service, which had declined in the mid-2000s and then became the target of an initiative called TAC: "Take Aim to the Customer." One manager noted that increased focus on service in training, coaching, and targets helped to reduce customer complaints from 13% to 7% (TDC labor relations manager, April 24, 2012).

At the same time, managers used the threat of dismissal to encourage adherence to targets. The result was a system of performance management that combined a focus on coaching and team building with progressive discipline. For example, absenteeism rates were 10%–12% in the mid-2000s across the call centers. Management implemented so-called targeted measures which drastically reduced absenteeism by 2012 to 3.5%–4% in the Consumer unit call centers and to under 6% in Call Center Europe. Several managers described this success as the result of education, as well as having "a very strict procedure of how many times can you be sick in a period, before [you are dismissed]" (TDC HR manager, April 23, 2012). Another manager explained:

> We are talking to people, okay what's wrong. We don't let them just lie there and be sick; we talk to them. We have the policy to say, "okay, we'll talk to you if we are a little worried." So then we'll talk to you and say, "okay what can we do?" It's not hospital or whatever. If you can't do anything, out you go. (TDC labor relations manager, April 24, 2012)

Team leaders observed that a lot of time and effort was put into managing these cases, to try to decide on the right "decision" for each employee. However, they also stated that they had quite a lot of discretion over these kinds of dismissals, with the union intervening only in exceptional cases.

Call Center Europe also contracted with a health company that provided personal nursing services as a resource for sick employees. The company posted regular statistics on sick leave broken down by team and individual, so that employees could track their absences (and compare themselves to colleagues). These were viewed as particularly effective because they were linked to other aspects of performance management emphasizing team-based competition and commitment (Dansk Metal rep TDC, May 15, 2012).

Unlike both BT and France Telecom, variable pay was used for all employee groups (both sales and service) and was based on a range of performance metrics measured at the team level. Call center employees in the Consumer unit received around 10% performance-based pay, on top of base pay, while Call Center Europe employees received around 7% variable pay. The largest component of variable pay for most groups in the call centers was individual-based sales commission. However, the union had successfully argued for aggregating non-sales-based performance metrics at the team level, which was tied to a team-based bonus (Dansk Metal rep TDC, April 24, 2012).

Managers estimated that 60% of variable pay was based on individual performance and 40% on team performance. Call Center Europe had recently introduced a new initiative called "celebrate our successes," in which each team leader nominated the best employee in each team every quarter to receive an additional 2,000 Kroner ($290) bonus cheque.

In addition to encouraging team-based variable pay, union representatives had sought to improve the fairness and transparency of the sales commission system. Joint committees helped to develop and manage the bonus system in both Consumer centers and at Call Center Europe. Shop stewards from each described the procedure for setting goals:

> We work well together, yes. And we have made ... an agreement on this amount, or how much it is, and how much they are going to sell, and so on. And every month we have a meeting, and we see if things are as they should be, or if we could change something. [...] And sometimes, oh they try, "No, no no. . . ." There's a little agreement, and ... I feel that we have influence, and that's very good. (Dansk Metal rep TDC, April 24, 2012)

> We have meetings every month, where we discuss any changes to the parameters, and if they have changed, we discuss if they're fair. We have an agreement where everything about our bonus, how, if changes come along, what do we do. We have all kinds of details written down in this agreement, how to handle all this. Also define—this agreement defines how this bonus should be managed. You cannot make any changes that you just like, it should be a fair and meaningful change to the employee and for the company here, and also to the customer. [...] We have had a lot of work defining

this agreement with the bonus; and how it's describing the parameters; and when the parameters change, how quickly can they change; and what's important for the development of the bonus system. (Dansk Metal rep TDC, May 15, 2012)

The shop steward at Call Center Europe also described one example in which she and a colleague from Dansk Metal had been able to successfully argue for a change that provided additional compensation for employees who did coaching and training:

> The last case we argued for was that our instructors—the colleagues who coach us or instruct us when we get trained or get the education that's necessary when new products come—they had to meet exactly the same targets. But they didn't have the same amount of hours with the customers. They were unsatisfied, and they thought it was not fair and it was stressful and it made them unhappy, basically. [. . .] But we agreed that they be compensated, and then they were happy and motivated. (Dansk Metal rep TDC, May 15, 2012)

Technicians

The largest group of TDC technicians was in Operations and Wholesale. An HR manager estimated in 2012 that there were 1,700 employees in field and operations and 900 in network and capacity. Field and operations technicians were responsible for installing phone and broadband in private homes, as well as some repair or maintenance. Employees were organized in regions, as they needed to drive to customers. In every big city there was a central office with around thirty staff. One shop steward described a typical day on the job, which looked similar to the other case studies: field technicians logged onto an electronic system, and drove to customers' homes based on "orders" given to them:

> Press the button once, 29 minutes . . . and through the day . . . and when I've finished, maybe before the day is over, I call the center, and say, "Do we have more for me?" If I get a difficult customer so I cannot finish all the orders in my intranet screen, I call at one o'clock and say, "You will have to take something from me because I can't get finished with all of this." (Dansk Metal rep TDC, May 7, 2012)

Employees were organized in teams of around 20–25 employees, and would meet once a week to discuss union business, performance, and training. The performance management model instead involved a strong focus on performance reviews, with the threat of dismissal if employees did not meet targets or improve their performance in line with expectations.

All TDC technicians had an annual "development conversation" with their supervisor or line manager, focused on identifying training needs and discussing strategies to improve performance. They also were supposed to have an individual review once a month. If employees did not improve their performance within three to four months, they were placed in a "disciplinary process." If they did still not show improvement, they would be a likely candidate for redundancy:

> I always ask them to show me: how many do we have in a disciplinary process right now, and what is happening to them, how many are getting better, how many do we have to lay off? [. . .] Because in a company where you all the time lay off around 10%, between 8% and 10%, it's much easier sometimes for the management to think: "okay, I know in October, I have to do this and that, then I take him." (TDC HR manager, April 23, 2012)

As with call center employees, low performers were typically encouraged to take voluntary redundancy, but could be dismissed if they refused. Management was also implementing a "lean" model of continuous improvement that involved frequent meetings in the network operations area. "In TDC it's called TDC 2.0. [. . .]. We are measured on how much we are supposed to do, and what have we done, and why haven't we done what we're supposed to do, stuff like that" (Dansk Metal rep TDC, April 24, 2012). This was part of a larger push to improve productivity in network operations, in which management set increasingly difficult targets for the time required for different tasks. This had increased pressure on technicians, together with ongoing reductions of 10 percent a year in the amount of time they were given to do different tasks or jobs. These new targets were backed by the threat that if technicians did not meet the strict goals, they could lose their jobs:

> I think performance has gone up, but it's not because it's a good system, it's because people are frightened. If you have a company where you will fire . . . in my area, it's like we have a cut in employees by 12 to 15 percent each year, so people know if they don't perform then they will be fired. (Dansk Metal rep TDC, April 24, 2012)

TDC management was also trying to plan a way to extend the lean tools to field technicians, which was met with some skepticism by employees: "they are getting it together, so it fits to our work. But it's insane. You can't say to people, 'You have to work faster and faster, faster,' and then to the same people, 'You have to come to a meeting every morning'" (Dansk Metal rep TDC, May 7, 2012). The shop steward also observed that employees were increasingly afraid that they would be fired if their performance was not sufficient or if they were critical of management:

> It's all ... if you go to a meeting, and talk badly about the way that things are or so, then they come and they stop you. I, as a union guy can talk more freely because I am protected, but the employees – if they go to their chief and say, "This is bad, I don't want to do this, I don't want to do that," it's out.... If you don't, what is it, be flexible, if you don't do overtime or do that and do that, they will come after you ... we have a system where there is a talking warning, and there is a writing, and then it's out ... if they can't sack you because of this, and you are negative to a meeting or something, they find another way to do it, that you are too slow to do your job or ... there is not enough work ... so you have to go. (Dansk Metal rep TDC, May 7, 2012)

This shop steward estimated that 10–20 technicians out of the 450 he represented had been fired based on performance in the past several years, and 8–9 technicians had taken "vacations" due to stress-related illnesses.

> People are ... when I meet some of my colleagues, they feel they are ... if you look them in the eyes they are blank. It's ... there is no time to relax here. And then if you don't follow up on all this, then you're going to your manager, and he tells you, "You are not good at this, you are not good at this, you are not good at this.... You have forty days to make it up, or you are out." And we have more and more cases where sickness occurs with stress. (Dansk Metal rep TDC, May 7, 2012)

In the field technician area, targets for the number of customers per day had increased from four calls to five, with the target due to go up to six in 2013. Management also had introduced new guidelines and training with the goal of encouraging employees to focus more on customer satisfaction and service. A shop steward noted that the company required them to follow a certain procedure for talking with the customer when installing equipment, and conducted follow-up using customer satisfaction surveys: "Always put the customer first, they say, but they don't want to pay for it!" (Dansk Metal rep TDC, May 7, 2012).

At the same time, there was no pay for performance for technicians. Management had attempted to introduce this in the past, but had difficulty identifying the appropriate outcomes to measure and compensate (TDC HR manager, April 23, 2012). Shop stewards argued that management did not view variable pay as necessary to motivate the workforce. Employees were so concerned that they would lose their jobs, due to the high rate of downsizing, that they were very focused on monitoring their own performance:

TDC say there's no need for that [performance pay] because they can pressure people and get the work done, the performance is going up anyway because of all the fires [*sic*: firing workers] and there's no need for them to give money for us to work harder, because we'll do that anyway. So it's a kind of problem. [. . .] It's very funny, they won't give us performance pay, but they will have performance interviews. (Dansk Metal rep TDC, April 24, 2012)

Another shop steward from the field technician area said that there had been an attempt by management to introduce a variable pay scheme, and the union tried to negotiate a structure that would give additional pay to the team. This eventually fell through because the system was viewed as too complicated (Dansk Metal rep TDC, May 7, 2012).

GPS monitoring had been in place since 2007. Initially, it was used to track technicians in their cars; however, they experienced this as a form of direct control over their work. The union then negotiated an agreement that management could gather GPS data and use it to analyze patterns and improve overall efficiency, but would not be able to track or punish individuals:

We implemented GPS in autumn 2007, and it was causing strikes, and a lot of fuss and a lot of angry technicians because they found that they were being controlled and it was negative. [. . .] So they made an agreement of doing the GPS, but without possibility of using the data to follow up on an individual. You can only make patterns. You can make patterns and bigger conclusions on what you see and the data material from the GPS, and nothing else. (Dansk Metal rep TDC, April 24, 2012)

Together, this suggests that there had been work intensification in the technician area, enforced through regular performance reviews and the threat of dismissal. The union was able to negotiate some agreements protecting employees in the context of specific performance management tools—for example, on monitoring by GPS. Union representatives also noted that local cooperation could still be used to solve shop-floor problems or conflicts. However, at the level of formal policies, union representatives felt they had increasingly limited influence over management policies:

If there's a problem, maybe due to the setup of time or something like that, then we will go to the cooperation committee, [. . .] and lift it up there and say, "these and these conditions are not fair" or "what can we do to make this better?" And in most parts, we are getting okay results. The closer to the problems, you talk about the problems, you go like this, then you will get a more concrete talk about it, not like, "our principles are this and that." It's more concrete solutions we are doing, down at the lowest level of the committees. [...] It's getting more difficult to cooperate with the management because their goals they get are very, very strict. Not like before, when they have a broad goal and what they had to do on that, and they had put aside themselves. It's not like that now. (Dansk Metal rep TDC, April 24, 2012)

Summary

The performance management model at TDC combined a focus on team building, team-based competitions, intensive training and coaching, and individual- and team-based variable pay with progressive discipline and the threat of dismissal. There were weaker negotiated constraints on management's use of progressive discipline compared to France Telecom, and it was much easier to dismiss employees for poor performance. Variable pay in the call centers was permitted for a wider range of jobs and metrics than at both BT and France Telecom (where it was limited to sales roles). One reason for this is stronger traditions of and support for collective worker voice in this area via works councils or cooperation committees. Union representatives were able to influence the design and transparency of variable pay, as well as to ensure that the process for evaluating performance and implementing discipline was viewed as fair. This created a workplace environment in which the union facilitated or supported management's work, helping to create a cooperative culture in which there was some perception that practices balanced market with social concerns.

At the same time, the ability of the union and works councils to make substantive improvements had declined over time. Works councils had consultation rather than co-determination rights, and so relied heavily on a past culture of cooperation, backed by union strength. This had declined over time, weakening their impact on management decisions. Meanwhile, the lack of the hard constraint of job security opened the possibility for discipline-based practices – which were often, as at BT, connected with downsizing. This meant performance was often strongly motivated by fear of job loss, particularly for technicians.

Deutsche Telekom: Strongest Supports for Voice and Stronger Constraints on Exit

Among the four cases, collective worker voice was strongest at Deutsche Telekom. There were multiple layers of formal bargaining, including subsidiary-level and company-wide collective agreements with the conglomerate service union, ver.di, and works agreements negotiated with works councils at the workplace, subsidiary and corporate group levels. As discussed in Chapter 2, Germany's works councils enjoy the world's strongest legal co-determination rights, giving them a say in health and safety, the design of pay for performance, scheduling practices, and the use of electronic monitoring (among other areas). Deutsche Telekom's works councils had considerable experience using and enforcing these legal rights, when necessary, in the German labor courts.

In contrast to TDC and BT, and similar to France Telecom, Deutsche Telekom employees also enjoyed strong job security. National employment protections in Germany are more comprehensive than those in Denmark and the United Kingdom, making it difficult to dismiss employees for performance reasons. A high proportion of civil servants enjoyed iron-clad job security, and collective agreements guaranteed private law employees strong protection from involuntary layoffs or dismissals. In addition, works councils in Germany have the right to oversee decisions to dismiss an employee, and at Deutsche Telekom they used this to oppose dismissals on any performance ground other than gross misconduct.

Another feature distinguishing Deutsche Telekom was its strongly institutionalized apprenticeship programs, based in Germany's dual system of occupational or vocational training. New employees in both call centers and technician units were typically recruited and trained through apprenticeships, which involved 3–4 days on the job and 1–2 days of classes at Telekom Training centers, based in a subsidiary that placed apprentices in different areas of the company. One HR manager observed in 2010 that about 4,000 apprentices, or *Azubis*, started their training at the company every year. Since 2007, call center employees were brought in through two different vocational courses, *Beruf Kauffrau/-mann für Dialogmarketing* and a shorter two-year path, *Servicekraft für Dialogmarketing*. In 2012, there were 562 apprentices, or *Azubis*, in the call center subsidiary Deutsche Telekom Kundenservice (DTKS), and 400 were hired at DTKS that year, with around 150 finding jobs in other parts of Deutsche Telekom. Technicians were brought in through vocational courses in technician trades, the most common being *Systemelektroniker/in*. There was a commitment in the company's collective agreement with ver.di to hire a proportion of these apprentices in permanent positions every year, but at a much lower rate: representing around 80 new hires annually in the technician subsidiary DTTS in 2012.

Thus, of the four case studies discussed here, Deutsche Telekom had both the strongest support for worker collective voice in the design of performance management practices and the strongest restrictions on employers' use of performance-based dismissals. While these did not close off intensified monitoring or precarious, at-risk forms of variable pay, they did provide significant resources for worker representatives to challenge or reverse some of these practices and to negotiate social provisions that improved their fairness.

Call Centers

Deutsche Telekom's call centers went through a number of organizational changes, which were also associated with significant work reorganization and changes in performance management. In 2007, call centers from the T-Com (fixed-line and internet) and T-Mobile (mobile) business units were moved into a new subsidiary, Deutsche Telekom Kundenservice (DTKS) (see Chapter 5). This brought together around 22,000 call center employees from over 70 locations, which were later consolidated to 33 larger centers.

By 2012, DTKS was divided into five regions, with 12,000 in-house employees. These were further broken up into groups servicing seven different customer segments, based on low- to high-value products and designation as individuals or small businesses, and then were split into groups handling, for example, billing, specialized products, and outbound sales. DTKS also created teams of generalists at some locations—which were differentiated from the specialists. One works councilor described how former front-office and back-office groups were brought together in his region into a group called Homegold: "They now do everything—we always say that these are our egg-laying woolly-milk pigs [*eierlegende Wollmilchsäue*]. They have to be able to do everything, from billing to T-Mobile products, singleplay, doubleplay, everything" (works councilor DT, September 14, 2011). These employees had to use around thirty-nine systems, with different IT applications.

There was also a nationwide system of routing, in which every employee was identified in a very detailed way based on their skills and abilities; so when a call came in, it was first given to an employee who was ranked highly for that particular call area or skill—and then if the top-ranked employee was busy, it went to employee 2, then to employee 3, and so on.

In the past, Deutsche Telekom's works councils had used their co-determination rights to negotiate strong agreements on performance management in the company's call centers. These required all performance results to be aggregated to the team level and prohibited electronic monitoring, with all quality monitoring happening through side-by-side coaching and mystery calls. Variable pay was restricted to the team level and was not "at risk," meaning it was paid on top of base pay rather than as an assumed variable part of base pay (Doellgast 2012, 62–74). The works agreements and union agreements negotiated with the new DTKS subsidiary between 2007 and 2012 had allowed a number of changes in these practices, leading to increased monitoring, with more individualized and increasingly insecure pay. However, the works councils and union were able to strengthen these agreements over time, to improve predictability and reduce the at-risk component of pay.

First, a new monitoring system had been adopted that allowed calls to be recorded for the first time, called the Intelligent Routing and Reporting Platform

(IRRP). Three times each week, team leaders would look at a sample of calls and screen shots recorded in certain intervals. Employees' names were not attached to this information, but team leaders could identify employees based on their voice or other information and would go over the calls together with them to jointly develop training plans.

Works councils viewed the new system critically, observing that "[m]any employees see this as a monitoring and control system (*Überwachungssystem*): 'The system sees everything that I do'" (works councilor DT, June 21, 2012). Another works councilor observed that team leaders could abuse the tool to put additional pressure on individual employees to meet increasingly strict targets:

> I can now see for every employee, every step in their workflow, every keyboard click. They are only supposed to use this for training purposes. Most team leaders do this, too: conversations can be recorded, and then the employee and team leader listen to the conversation and training needs are identified. For example, how you can better organize a conversation with the customer. But there are also team leaders who abuse this. We are often working on this problem. (works councilor DT, September 14, 2011)

Coaching through sitting next to the employee and listening to calls had become increasingly rare. Instead, on some days, everything an employee did was recorded and the team leader gave feedback on this basis. Management also contracted with a third-party firm to carry out "mystery calls," but results were only evaluated at the team or department level.

If an employee did not improve after training, then there would sometimes be a discussion with the employee (at some locations), "whether they really think that this is the right job for them." The works council opposed this practice, which they viewed as pressuring under-performing employees to quit. This was prohibited in the central works agreement, which specified that the monitoring system could only be used for coaching and development, not for monitoring and control or discipline and dismissals (*arbeitsrechtliche Konsequenzen*) (works councilor DT, June 21, 2012).

A second change was the introduction of "pay at risk" with a smaller share of secure base pay. When DTKS was established in 2007, the new collective agreement introduced a variable pay system for the majority of former Deutsche Telekom employees, with 80% fixed salary and 20% of pay dependent on meeting goals in different areas. By 2012, in the sales and customer service area, 13% was based on team or group performance and 7% on company or subsidiary performance. Team goals were divided into five areas with different weights, including customer satisfaction, call handling time, products, sales, and product bundling.

These goals were agreed at the team level. If two-thirds of the team objected to goals, the case would be brought to a local joint labor-management committee, which would review the objection and make a decision on whether the goals should be revised. Employees could also contest the calculation of goals after the second or fourth quarter. One works councilor observed that in his region, 70%–75% of teams met their goals. Company (DTKS or Deutsche Telekom–wide) goals were set by the advisory board, and employees got this portion of their variable pay only if they were met.

Sales goals were an important point of conflict. Works councilors felt that these tended to be raised (or that management attempted to raise them) every quarter:

> We look carefully at this, there are certain developments. When a new product is introduced, I have an entry phase, then if the product is successful, there is a steep climb in sales, and then it flattens out when market saturation is reached again. That's logical. These are normal sales curves, when a product is successful.... And for this reason we always look carefully to see, what is possible in our view? And then we just try to influence it [the goals] in this direction. (works councilor DT, June 21, 2012)

The time spent on the phone per call also had become increasingly important. Management had put in place goals for each type of call, typically from 240 to 520 seconds:

> It's all broken down, and the people know it. And also they know that if I have a conversation where the customer is a bit harder to understand or a little slower, then I need maybe 10 minutes, which is 600 seconds, but I have only 300. So I have to resolve the next call more quickly. This puts pressure on people. The stringent time constraints are stressful. We talk about this over and over. But the number fetishists cannot be dissuaded from this. (works councilor DT, June 21, 2012)

This uncertainty was exacerbated by the pay structure. Employees in sales and customer retention had a higher variable percentage of 30%, almost entirely based on individual performance. This created some degree of pay precarity. For example, if a sales employee was in the lowest pay group, she would be making 24,000 euros/year, but 7,200 euros of this would be dependent on meeting her goals. Some employees were making only 30%–50% of their goals, particularly during times of the year when sales were low or if they were out sick for a period of time, which could have a substantial impact on their salaries.

As this was a new system, the works council was initially able to get agreement for protections. A major way this was accomplished was through the joint committee and appeals process. One works councilor noted that 52 appeals (at the team level) were made to the committee in her region in one quarter, out of around 300 teams (works councilor DT, September 28, 2010).

Following 2012 negotiations, a new agreement secured a larger proportion of fixed pay. The 70/30 variable pay split for sales employees was eliminated, and 80% fixed salary was secured for all employees. This was an important issue for the union and works councils, and a focus in negotiations over the collective agreement: "We succeeded in getting agreement after several days of strikes. So we also struck, we had conflict over this" (works councilor DT, June 21, 2012). The lowest pay group was also able to get a 3% pay increase, and other pay groups won a 2.3% pay increase:

> We said: without a result for this lowest pay group there is no result. We fought hard and there was great solidarity. Even by those who earn more, they said: that is exactly the right demand to make. So thank God we were able to get this adopted. We're still not at our demand of 100% [fixed], but 80% is already pretty good. (works councilor DT, June 21, 2012)

Another works councilor observed that the old model of setting and reviewing variable pay continued to operate in the sales area after the 2012 agreement, but the works council had succeeded in modifying the system of setting goals for non-sales employees across Deutsche Telekom. From 2013, this group would be evaluated based on the "six most important goals" or the "Big Six." This was in response to concerns that employees were not able to influence all of the different goals they were given, which was creating too much stress. The new model was overseen by and approved by the advisory board at the beginning and end of the year. Sales employees continued to have quarterly goals. In addition, the new agreement assured employees that they would get above 90%–96% of their base pay (depending on the function of the teams).

In 2012, all teams with the "Big Six" goals got 108% of pay. In a 2013 interview, a works councilor stated that only 4%–6% of variable pay was actually insecure—and in the next bargaining round they would try to reduce this further (works councilor DT, August 27, 2013). However, the works council also negotiated a new agreement at this time allowing management to monitor individual results, or KPIs (key performance indicators) for the first time (from 2013). This was a concession in exchange for expanding the in-house workforce (see Chapter 5).

A further pay equity topic in 2012 negotiations concerned differences in pay between apprentices in the technical occupations compared to those in sales occupations, who received around 80 euros less per month. The union argued that because there were more women employed in the sales areas, this difference was discriminatory. They succeeded in getting agreement to equal pay from 2013, with sales apprentices brought up to the technical apprentice pay level.

In addition to variable pay, management had long used team competitions with prizes, like a trip or an iPod. A DTKS works councilor observed that this was an area where they were fighting with management over an increased move toward centralization:

> We have a central works agreement about that, that this [local competitions] should be exclusively a subject of local co-determination, but the employer tried to regulate that centrally from the beginning. We didn't want that, because we say: at the local level it can be better determined whether people are now overloaded with work or can still do more, can handle this competition on top of everything else, etc. So there was a wide range of arguments, and in the end we as the works council are coordinating these competitions, when they are running nation-wide, and also we give a recommendation—so co-determination is clearly taking place at the local level. And the employer constantly is seeking to change that. (works councilor DT, June 21, 2012)

As at the other case study companies, reducing absenteeism was a major target of performance management. The absenteeism rate was 8%–10% across DTKS, but one works councilor observed that in some areas, depending on the time of year, it could be up to 40% (works councilor DT, September 14, 2011). The health insurance funds put out a report every year on reported sick rates in different areas, and this showed that over three years the rate of employees suffering from "psychosomatic illnesses" in the telecom sector had doubled. DTKS was responding by putting out baskets of fruit or giving special recognition to employees who had low absenteeism. However, the works agreement did not allow management to hold special meetings with employees about why they were absent after coming back to work—a common practice in other German companies. For long-term illness, the company agreement required a thorough investigation, followed by an invitation to a voluntary conversation with management. The agreement determined the exact process to follow, who could participate, and the role of the works council. Dismissal due to frequent absences was possible, but it did not happen very often because cases had to be extremely well documented to withstand scrutiny in the German labor courts.

The DTKS works council organized a project on health management, with support from university researchers, looking at different stressors and strains in the workplace: the workplace environment, temperature, and psychosocial stressors—including the degree of employee discretion and control. A works councilor involved in this project observed that they sat down with management with a list of recommendations based on their findings, and then management said: "we can do this, but not that." For many "action fields," the works council proposed or even tested alternatives. For example, in a pilot project, team leaders and team members were given broad discretion to allocate their own work—something like an experiment in "self-managed teams." Results showed that employees were far happier and that performance improved. But management refused to extend this pilot because it conflicted with their centralized model of workforce management.

At the same time, some changes were made based on the recommendations. Employees were given more targeted training on factors associated with psychosocial stress, with a focus on improving team leaders' awareness of occupational health and safety. These leaders met to discuss best practices in small groups and were given direct coaching on how to define targets and better support employees.

One works councilor observed that there had been a change over time in employee attitudes at DTKS toward issues of increasing pressure and declining working conditions. Negative feelings and conflict peaked during 2006–2009 and then declined in 2010–2012—as employees began to have some more "air to breathe" and were starting to enjoy their jobs again. He thought the works councils' efforts were one factor in this: "something like trust has returned. [. . .] if I have a problem, I can go there [to the works council] and something happens'" (works councilor DT, June 21, 2012).

One team leader observed that cooperation with the works council, including the agreements and initiatives discussed above, helped generally to improve fairness:

> I think it is important that cooperation works well, and also for the company. We benefit from each other, and I think that's the main thing. And I can go and get some advice, for example when I say "Did I really turn off my emotional side or was it still there?" Because you have some employees with whom you get along very well and others with whom you do not gel personally at all. Of course, I want to avoid treating or grading the employee with whom I get along less well, worse than somebody who I am close to. That is something that one can sort out with the works council. [. . .] It works when you cooperate well with the works council. (DT team leader, September 28, 2010)

Technicians

In 2007, similar to the call centers, most technician jobs had been moved from the business units into two new T-Service subsidiaries (see Chapter 5). DT

Technischer Service (DTTS) handled everything to do with the customer, including residential and small-business markets, while DT Netzproduktion (later DT Technik) handled construction and maintenance of the network. I focus here on DTTS, as this is where the field technicians (*Außendienst*) who were responsible for installing lines and fixing problems for customers were based. This area was further divided into groups responsible for service and faults or new orders; with technicians having different combinations of around fifty different skills (*Tätigkeiten*).

There were four main job categories. *Monteur* handled simple connections and product assembly: "They install lines and switches. Simple work, maybe lay the line at the customer's house and screw the box into the wall. Maybe even plug it into a modem. But he doesn't program the router" (works councilor DT, September 13, 2011). *Service Monteur* and *Service Techniker* were responsible for maintenance and repair. And *Service Techniker Spezial* built and maintained large business networks. A works councilor estimated that over 50% of the DTTS employees in his region were in the *Service Monteur* and *Techniker* categories. Almost all of these employees had completed apprenticeship training in the *Systemelektroniker/in* trade, and most received their training at Deutsche Telekom.

Before DTTS was set up, T-Com technicians had already been through a major work reorganization. Similar to France Telecom in the "pre-social crisis" period, management had decided that certain areas of job content should be divided up to increase efficiencies and reduce costs. When a customer ordered a telephone, a *Monteur* would lay and switch on the line; and then a *Servicetechniker* would attach the router. Management calculated how many employees they needed for each job, and then divided up the work. This meant that two different groups of employees were going to the customer, based on the logic that this would save money because of salary differences.

However, the savings were less than anticipated. In 2003, after a reorganization, the works council brought a formal complaint charging that over 600 employees were getting paid under their official skill level, in what was described as *unterwertig Beschäftigt*. In three years, the works council succeeded in getting 50% of these employees moved to a higher grade. They also prevented management from reducing the number of pay grades and got some skills valued at a higher pay level (works councilor DT, August 2, 2007). "So *Monteur* were standing there earning the same as a *Servicetechniker*. Because of this they weren't really able to make savings. Only imaginary" (works councilor DT, September 13, 2011).

In 2008, DTTS tried again to reduce pay through moving *Service Techniker* from the pay grade T5 to T4. However, to do this, management had to set up a central commission with ver.di, and get agreement on the decision to move the jobs. This was held up by several conflicting legal findings in Germany concerning management's right to reclassify jobs.

By 2013, there was an agreement with ver.di to reclassify employees upward who had been moved into the simpler *Monteur* job category but were doing more than 50% *Techniker* work in their jobs:

> They had said in the past: only the *Monteur* can do the simple work, and the *Techniker* do the higher value work. But then they figured out, that when you install a connection, the work is mixed. You cannot just do the connection, then the *Monteur* goes home, then the *Techniker* comes and installs the Modem. [. . .] This theory of the employer, that you can divide the work up, didn't work—that you can say: we send people out who just do installations, and they don't do anything else. They do only support work, and the higher value work is done only by people who get more money. You can't divide these jobs from each other. (works councilor DT, September 20, 2013)

Ver.di was still negotiating over which employees would be moved to the higher *Techniker* job category—but over 1,000 technicians had appealed or applied for this reclassification.

Thus, similar to France Telecom, management sought to break apart field technicians' tasks and responsibilities. However, the combination of employees' multi-skilled background through apprenticeship training and works council and union oversight on how skills were evaluated and compensated made a narrow division of labor difficult.

Similar to the other case study companies, technicians' job assignments were allocated through personal laptops, on the basis of calculations involving distances to customers and individual skills or product knowledge. In 2010, employees met with their virtual teams of 17–22 technicians at least once a month for two hours to discuss team goals and to receive training on new products. There was a works agreement mandating this minimum meeting time and frequency, but impromptu meetings were also held.

The trajectory of change in performance management practices was broadly similar to DTKS, but with some differences. As at the other case studies, Deutsche Telekom's technicians were long a privileged and relatively autonomous group. Works councils had resisted the introduction of pay at risk and had protected employees from electronic monitoring. Technicians thus traditionally enjoyed considerable autonomy, with few substantive consequences or incentives attached to meeting performance goals.

Management used the restructuring process after the creation of DTTS as an opportunity to renegotiate works agreements on a range of topics. In sharp contrast to the other cases, and even to DTKS, the works councils succeeded in preventing pervasive electronic monitoring. Deutsche Telekom was introducing GPS tracking systems in 2007 and began to discuss with its works councils the possibility of using this technology to monitor the movements of individual technicians, resulting in a limited pilot project. By 2012, however, DTTS still did not have this technology, because the unions and works councils resisted it. Similarly, there were discussions over an electronic drivers' logbook. One DTTS manager observed that this would not take place through GPS but at most would require the engineers to write down the routes that they drove and to distinguish between work and private routes (DT HR manager, September 24, 2010).

At the same time, job content had been standardized, with goals concerning how long it should take at each customer and a centrally planned set of guidelines for how technicians should carry out each job. This was regulated through an ISO9001 certification explaining that each connection should take twelve minutes, and technicians should try to sell additional products to the customer. A works councilor observed: "that is being massively pushed, there is real pressure behind this" (works councilor DT, September 13, 2011). The automated work distribution system also gave the team leader greater oversight over what individual employees were doing at different times, increasing monitoring and control to some degree.

In addition, similar to DTKS, the new DTTS collective agreement introduced pay at risk tied to performance. Variable pay was negotiated in 2007, allowing 15% variable and 85% fixed salary. This was broken down into 5% corporate group-wide goals, 5% DTTS goals, and 5% individual or team goals. To achieve one's full salary, it was thus necessary to hit goals in each area. By 2008, there were some works agreements on how this was implemented—particularly the individual and team component.

Management secured limited exceptions to works agreements that allowed supervisors to look at individual performance metrics. At the same time, performance measures and individual goals had to be agreed at the local level. One major objective in the performance evaluation was that after the first visit to the customer, there should be only 7%–8% "call-back" to return and fix problems. Individual goals could be moved or changed to team goals if there was local agreement, and the balance depended on the structure of jobs. In the *Außendienst*, almost all goals were team-based.

In 2011, a works councilor described how the system had developed. Team goals continued to be the focus of the 5% individual/team performance goals. Technicians usually got 3–5 goals worth 20%–40% of the total goal, including, for example, 80%–85% of appointments attended on time, generating a certain amount of sales, and percent of call-backs. For each target a range was defined, between 0% or 100% target fulfilment, with the maximum defined at 150%.

Typically, team leaders would try to negotiate with their team how they would meet these goals.

> They are still adjusting the screws [on this system]. You negotiate the goal with your team leader. You have to be able to influence the goals. If you haven't reached your goal for reasons that you don't have any responsibility for, then you can say that you can't do anything about that. Then they can adjust that from the top. And usually it is done in this way. (works councilor DT, September 13, 2011)

There were several forms of oversight by worker representatives, to make sure the system was broadly viewed as fair. First, the works council helped to define and agree on the targets. For example, management had wanted to implement a new performance measure, based on calling customers to ask them how satisfied they were with the technician's service. The works council opposed this, on the basis that it was performance and behavior control (*Leistungs- und Verhaltenskontrolle*). In the end, management decided not to push for this.

Second, as in the call center area, there was a parity commission with worker and management representatives that reviewed complaints or objections. If employees did not agree with goals, they first would try to negotiate this with the team leader; and if they could not resolve the disagreement, they would bring it to the commission. However, this process was very rarely used: "We have done this for 3–4 years, and it hasn't yet happened that someone got too little money" (works councilor DT, September 13, 2011). One regional manager observed, "We only have very few, maybe three teams out of 300, who did not achieve their goal. I think that's a good proportion" (DT manager, September 24, 2010).

The works councilor cited above observed that if you were in the top third based on goals, you were fine; if you were in the bottom third you had problems:

> Then you have to explain why you aren't achieving the goals. "Why are you so bad?" When you can explain it, it's fine. You can't meet all the goals all the time, they are too far-ranging. If I'm really good at meeting new orders and am punctual, then probably my *Entstörprozess* (fixing of faults) will be a bit worse, because we are now understaffed nationwide. There are no regions that can really do all of their work anymore. So holes are always being plugged. (works councilor DT, September 13, 2011)

Civil servants were not included under the variable pay system, and so managers had to find other ways to motivate them to try to reach the same goals. In 2008, the works council was trying to argue for a model where civil servants could move to the variable pay system, but with certain protections to their salary in a collective agreement.

In addition, while technicians had formal job security, as at DTKS, employees were worried that jobs would be reduced due to lost customers and downsizing if they did not improve performance:

> Through this cost and performance pressure, the ability and willingness to perform is greater; but for many employees, the fear of job loss is behind this. Employers repeatedly exploited downsizing: "When we are not able to do this, the customers will leave us." To some extent this is true. It is starting to be the case that employees are less convinced by this. When they are not convinced in whatever position, then they are threatened with a stick. And at some point he is sitting on the street. (works councilor DT, September 13, 2011)

This system was changed again in 2012/2013, after the collective agreement described above, which did away with individual goals and established "Big Six" goals at the subsidiary level (e.g., DTTS or DTKS level). In addition, ver.di secured 98% of pay—so that even if performance falls, employees can lose at most 2% of their "fixed" pay.

> In the end, it's difficult for individuals to have influence over this—but for every individual it is of course important to reach these goals. It has also changed, so that one is ensured that 98% will be paid regardless. You can at most lose 2%. That was different before. And you can also get additional pay if the goals are exceeded. In the end, it is more relaxed for individuals, who don't have so much individual or personal pressure. (works councilor DT, September 20, 2013)

This works councilor also observed that both employees and management were happy about the change, as the old system involved a lot of extra work without necessarily improving performance.

Summary

Like the three other case study companies, Deutsche Telekom had experimented with a range of new performance management tools intended to more closely measure and incentivize performance. Also similar to the other cases, these were part of broader strategies to restructure service jobs, based on attempts to cut costs through more closely matching worker skills with tasks. Initially, management used the creation of the DTKS (call center) and DTTS (technician) subsidiaries to negotiate changes in work organization, pay, and monitoring practices that sought to rationalize some jobs and establish variable performance-based pay.

However, the Deutsche Telekom case stands out for having sustained or re-established a set of "high-involvement" practices that relied on high skills, broad autonomy, and team-based incentives rather than threat of discipline to improve performance. Similar to TDC, consultation with worker representatives could serve as a resource for gaining agreement on potentially controversial measures, such as the introduction of variable pay, through improving its fairness. However, collective worker voice was backed up by formal, legally protected co-determination rights. These provided the strongest support across the cases for collective worker voice in the design of performance management practices, allowing works councils and the union to limit how performance information was collected and used and to participate directly in decisions concerning targets and compensation structure. In contrast to TDC and BT, and similar to France Telecom, Deutsche Telekom also faced constraints on employer exit, which closed off the option of motivating workers based on the fear of discipline. This meant that management needed to find compromises that met performance goals while also taking into account the impact on worker well-being.

Clearly worker representatives' power to introduce and maintain negotiated constraints had declined over time, but they were seeking to rebuild that power through creative compromises under more challenging conditions. Most notably, collective agreements had improved pay security and pay equity across different groups of call center workers and technicians. This was a particularly important goal, based on building solidarity among internal workers who were in more and less precarious jobs.

Comparison

Tables 4.1 and 4.2 summarize the differences in performance management practices for call centers and field technicians, circa 2010–2012. The case studies above show that some of these practices changed over time. At Deutsche Telekom, both DTKS and DTTS negotiated a reduction in the proportion of variable pay or pay at risk more recently, with additional protections for employees to avoid "pay precarity." However, these tables provide a snapshot of differences during my field research at the four companies.

BT and France Telecom were both cases with weak to moderate support for employee voice, due to the weak formal participation rights of worker representatives (second column, Table 2.3 in Chapter 2). At BT, unions had a strong company-level partnership with management, and union density was high; but they lacked institutionalized structures for worker participation in decision-making at the local level. At France Telecom, worker representatives' ability to

Table 4.1 Performance Management in Call Centers (2010–2012)

	Performance Monitoring and Coaching	Most Important Consequences or Incentives for Performance	Performance-Based Pay Structure and % of Total Pay Represented by Variable Pay
BT Retail	Constant remote monitoring and metrics tracking linked to individuals Coaching once a week with team leader	Progressive discipline leading to dismissal Variable pay for sales agents, over base pay	**Sales only:** Individual sales = 25% of total pay (sales staff only)
France Telecom AVSC (fixed/internet) and CCOR (mobile) units	Constant remote monitoring and metrics tracking linked to individuals Coaching three times a week with team leader; once a week with trainer	Promotion or pay increase based on performance evaluation Variable pay for sales agents, over base pay	**Sales only:** Sales (individual) × service quality (individual) × number of calls/hour (team) = 10%–15% of total pay
TDC Consumer and Call Center Europe	Constant remote monitoring and metrics tracking linked to individuals Daily side-by-side coaching with team leader	Progressive discipline leading to dismissal Variable pay for all agents, over base pay Team-based competitions	**Consumer:** Individual (60%) + team (40%) = 8%–12% of total pay **Call Center Europe:** Individual (63-77%); team (23-37%) = 7.5%–12% of total pay
Deutsche Telekom Kundenservice (DTKS)	Remote monitoring limited; but increasing Coaching three times a week with team leader	Variable "at risk" pay; with negotiated protections Skill-based promotion	**Service and sales:** Individual/team (67%) + company (33%) = 20% of total pay **Sales only:** Individual/team (100%) = 30% of total pay

participate substantively in the design of new practices was undermined by the presence of multiple, divided unions; low union density; and a history of conflictual labor relations. However, there were many forums for workplace consultation, with formal consultation rights; and the unions' role in overseeing the psychosocial impact of management practices on workers had recently been strengthened by the social crisis and subsequent social accords.

186 EXIT, VOICE, AND SOLIDARITY

Table 4.2 Performance Management in Field Technician Workplaces (2010–2012)

	Performance Monitoring and Coaching	Most Important Consequences or Incentives for Performance	Performance-Based Pay Structure and % of Total Pay Represented by Variable Pay
BT Openreach	Individual GPS monitoring Team meetings every 1–2 weeks	Progressive discipline leading to dismissal	No variable pay
France Telecom Response Units	Individual GPS monitoring Team meetings every 1–4 weeks	Promotion or pay increase based on performance evaluation Team challenges and competitions	No variable pay
TDC Field and Operations	GPS monitoring—but data not used to track individuals Team meetings every week	Progressive discipline leading to dismissal	No variable pay
Deutsche Telekom Technischer Service (DTTS)	No GPS monitoring Team meetings at least every month	Variable "at risk" pay; with negotiated protections Skill-based promotion	Individual/team (33%) + company (33%) + subsidiary (33%) = 15% of total pay

The two cases differed even more significantly in the strength of constraints on employer exit from internal employment relationships (second column, Table 2.2 in Chapter 2). France Telecom had strong employment protections, through the combination of employment protection legislation, collective agreements, and a high proportion of civil servants, which made it difficult to act unilaterally to downsize employment or sanction workers through performance-based dismissals. These constraints were more moderate at BT, due to weaker employment protections and fewer legal or negotiated provisions limiting the use of performance criteria for dismissing workers.

At BT, collective agreements built some predictability into coaching, feedback, and progressive discipline—ensuring that this was carried out in a standardized way that gave employees opportunities to improve through intensive coaching. In addition, performance-based incentives were limited to sales roles in call centers, where performance was easily measured. However, these rules were relatively blunt instruments in influencing the actual design of the performance management system, which had become more punitive over time. Performance evaluations were superficially linked to incentives, but also had a strong disciplinary focus—connected with weak job security and the broader system of sanctions. Labor relations concerning implementation of these rules were conflictual and relied heavily on grievances.

France Telecom's practices superficially were similar to those at BT. Performance incentives were also restricted to sales roles in call centers, although they encompassed measures of service quality. There was a strong emphasis on performance evaluation and promotion to motivate improved performance. However, stronger job security, connected with national legislation and the large number of civil servants, meant these evaluations could not lead to dismissals. It was impossible for France Telecom managers to use progressive discipline, which ruled out a competitive "bell curve" style of benchmarking performance. Instead, managers adopted other practices to motivate employees—primarily through coaching and development, as well as performance evaluation linked to promotion and pay increases. In addition, the aftermath of the social crisis had increased workers' countervailing power within formal consultation structures, strengthening their collective voice in decisions concerning work design, skills, and performance incentives. Intensified monitoring or control-oriented forms of performance management could increasingly be opposed on the basis of their negative impact on employee stress and psychosocial health, encouraging alternative strategies.

In contrast to the first two cases, Deutsche Telekom and TDC shared (historically) stronger formal institutional support for collective worker voice. In both companies, works councils and unions worked closely together to coordinate bargaining and consultation with each other and at different levels of the companies. They had traditions of labor-management cooperation combined with high union density and strong, democratic worker involvement in the design of management practices. These voice resources were strongest at Deutsche Telekom, where works councils' comprehensive co-determination rights, backed by collective agreements with the union ver.di, gave them additional tools to limit monitoring and influence the criteria for sanctions and dismissals (second column, Table 2.3).

These two cases also differed in constraints on exit from internal employment (second column, Table 2.2). As at France Telecom, Deutsche Telekom's managers had to comply with much stronger legislated and negotiated employment protection rules. This shaped the form that "negotiated flexibility" took—again with a major difference concerning the emphasis on sanctions or incentives.

The performance management model at TDC combined a focus on team building, team-based competitions, intensive training and coaching, and (in the call centers) individual- and team-based variable pay. However, this was backed up with progressive discipline and the threat of dismissal. Compared to BT and France Telecom, variable pay at TDC's call centers was permitted for a wider range of metrics and across different call center roles. Union representatives had some influence over the design and transparency of variable pay, and helped to ensure that the process for evaluating performance and implementing sanctions was viewed as fair. At the same time, the lack of the hard constraint of job security also allowed sanction-based practices. The constant threat of job loss was used as a tool to motivate both technicians and call center agents. As management had some discretion over which employees were chosen for downsizing, employees had a general sense that if they were lower performers they might be selected for involuntary redundancy. This dynamic was distinctive to TDC—and contributed to a more widespread perception of growing precarity, linking downsizing with performance management. Management's increased willingness and ability to discipline workers through exit thus also weakened historically strong collective voice structures.

Finally, Deutsche Telekom's performance management model was distinguished by strong collective worker voice in the design of performance monitoring, evaluation, and rewards, backed up by constraints on employer exit from internal employment relationships. Management sought to motivate workers primarily through training and development, team-based coaching and incentives, and performance-based pay. Works agreements had long prohibited recording individual performance data, requiring that this information be aggregated to the team level. In the technician units, this extended to the use of GPS data. Employees could not be put on progressive discipline or dismissed based on their failure to meet targets. As a result, performance management practices most closely approached the ideal "high-involvement" model, balancing market demands with concerns for equity and worker well-being.

Conclusions

This chapter has shown that both institutional support for collective worker voice and constraints on employer exit encouraged different approaches to performance management in four of the case study companies. The performance management models adopted, in turn, had important implications for worker precarity. Employers were able to adopt more discipline-based practices, motivating workers through fear of sanctions, where they faced few constraints on their own exit via performance-based dismissal and where workers' collective input into the design of these practices was weakest. Where constraints on employer exit and collective worker voice were strongest, as at Deutsche Telekom, management adopted alternative approaches to motivate workers through training and development, as well as through incentives that were attainable and fair. These built social concerns into an otherwise increasingly market-oriented set of objectives focused on increased sales and individual productivity, combined with (often unsuccessful) attempts at narrowing skills and intensifying monitoring.

The third dimension of strategies of inclusive labor solidarity continued to be in the background in these internal negotiations. Solidarity among unions at France Telecom during the social crisis was the basis for strengthening collective worker voice. Union strategies to improve conditions for the most precarious groups of internal workers also required building solidarity, to win pay equity for women or formally "lower skilled" tasks and occupations. In Chapter 5, labor solidarity comes more to the fore, as a central factor in worker representatives' response to the restructuring of jobs across organizational boundaries.

5
Externalization
Outsourcing, Agency Work, and Subsidiaries

Chapter 3 compared organization-level approaches to downsizing in the incumbent companies. Chapter 4 moved the focus down to the workplace level, to the performance management strategies these companies adopted for their call center and technician workforce. This chapter[1] keeps the focus on those call center and technician jobs, but considers how workers' experience of precarity is impacted by a third category of restructuring: measures to externalize work through outsourcing, use of temporary staffing agencies, and establishment of service subsidiaries.

The ten case studies all adopted different combinations of these externalization or "workplace fissuring" (Weil 2014) strategies in their call center and technician units. A strong motivation is often cost savings: either through moving work to a new organization with cheaper labor costs, or gaining concessions that reduce pay and conditions as a quid pro quo for keeping more jobs in-house. They thus typically increase precarity and inequality within the incumbent and across employees performing similar jobs for the incumbent's subcontractors, temporary agencies, and subsidiaries. At the same time, as with the other restructuring measures discussed in this book, these impacts are moderated by labor's power to contest market-oriented restructuring—to either stop or reverse the externalization of jobs in the first place, or to extend or protect encompassing employment standards across employers' vertically disintegrated networks of suppliers and contractors.

Consistent with the framework in this book, differences in both union strategies and worker outcomes across the case studies can be traced to a combination of constraints on employer exit, support for collective worker voice, and strategies of inclusive labor solidarity. The previous two chapters focused on constraints on exit and support for voice. In this chapter, strategies of inclusive labor solidarity come more to the fore. I organize my discussion of the cases

---

[1] This chapter includes case study material and data from research and case write-ups by Katja Sarmiento-Mirwaldt and Chiara Benassi; and findings published previously in three articles (Benassi, Doellgast, and Sarmiento-Mirwaldt 2016; Doellgast and Berg 2018; Doellgast, Sarmiento-Mirwaldt, and Benassi 2016) and one book chapter (Doellgast, Sarmiento-Mirwaldt, and Benassi 2015).

Exit, Voice, and Solidarity. Virginia Doellgast, Oxford University Press. © Oxford University Press 2022.
DOI: 10.1093/oso/9780197659779.003.0006

based on four patterns representing supports for or constraints on labor strategies of solidarity, discussed in Chapter 2 (Figure 2.3): (1) *structural exclusive solidarity*—represented by AT&T (United States), BT (United Kingdom), O2 Czech Republic (Czech Republic); and Orange Polska (Poland); (2) *representation domain divides*—at TDC (Denmark) and Deutsche Telekom (Germany); (3) *ideological divides*—at France Telecom (France) and Telecom Italia (Italy); and (4) *structural inclusive solidarity*—represented by the Telia (Sweden) and A1 (Austria) cases.

I first discuss employer strategies and union responses in each group of cases. I then compare outcomes, based on the extent of externalization, patterns of inequality, and downward pressure on pay and conditions. Unions had most success in reducing or reversing precarity in the "structural inclusive solidarity" cases of Telia and A1, where they were able to draw on inclusive institutions that both limited employer exit from encompassing bargaining and minimized divides or conflict between workers and their representatives. But unions also could respond creatively with new approaches that mobilized collective voice to bridge labor divides, encourage legal or negotiated extension of minimum terms and conditions, and organize externalized workers. Worker representatives were most successful in building or maintaining institutions that constrained employer exit from encompassing minimum standards where they worked together to strengthen supports for collective voice among diverse groups of workers through strategies grounded in inclusive solidarity.

Structural Exclusive Solidarity: United States, United Kingdom, Czech Republic, and Poland

Unions at AT&T, BT, O2 Czech Republic, and Orange Polska faced the most difficult conditions for exercising collective power in response to employers' externalization strategies. All four faced both weak constraints on employer exit and weak to moderate support for employee voice. These cases also share conditions I have termed "structural exclusive solidarity," characterized by decentralized and primarily company-level bargaining with unions that had little reach or influence beyond their core employers. Because unions faced seemingly impossible obstacles to organizing and representing workers in externalized workplaces— most notably at subcontractors—the major dynamics of labor solidarity focused on preserving or re-internalizing jobs within the telecom incumbents. This was particularly challenging because of the large cost differences between the in-house and external workforce. With limited leverage to improve conditions in the broader market, unions were more often in the position of agreeing to concessions to accommodate an increasingly market-based wage or trying to help preserve their members' pay and conditions as they were spun off to subsidiaries or subcontractors.

United States (AT&T)

AT&T had strong incentives to externalize work through outsourcing, as cost differences were high. The pay at US-based call center subcontractors was up to $13/hour lower than at AT&T's in-house call centers. Work could also be offshored to destinations such as India or the Philippines, with even larger savings. There were similar cost differences in technician units, although most of this work was performed on local networks and so was not offshored. Technicians employed by subcontractors typically were paid around half as much as AT&T's in-house technicians. Both call center and technician subcontractors also had lower benefit costs (including, most notably, health insurance).

AT&T moved over time from carrying out the majority of its technician work in-house to increased reliance on subcontractors for a range of specialized network construction and maintenance tasks, as well as field technician services. In 2020, the Communications Workers of America (CWA, 2020) reported that AT&T was working with more than 700 subcontractors in these areas, and a majority of surveyed members had experienced an increased workload as a result of having to fix or redo work by technicians working for these contract firms (CWA 2020).

AT&T's collective agreements with the CWA included some restrictions on subcontracting, including provisions committing the company to not contracting out work if it would result in layoffs, and limits on moving work outside of a state or region. Most call center agreements also had limits on the percentage of calls that could be sent to vendors. Several agreements (e.g., AT&T Legacy, Midwest, West) established a procedure for labor and management representatives to meet and review information on current work contracted out, and to establish joint committees at business unit or local levels, with a focus on suggesting ways in which AT&T could use bargaining unit members to perform the work at a competitive cost and within "the same completion time requirements."

However, AT&T was able to sidestep many of these provisions by using loopholes in the agreements and by adopting complicated restructuring measures that made it difficult to verify whether management was complying with their terms. The presence of multiple bargaining units across AT&T exacerbated this problem, particularly for call center workers—because calls could be moved to regions with collective agreements that had different provisions regarding outsourcing. As described in Chapter 3, generous redundancy plans allowed management "to eliminate certain whole titles" and shift the work to subcontractors (CWA official, June 5, 2013).

CWA had little chance of organizing externalized workers, due to the lack of collective agreements with call center subcontractors, very low union presence in technician subcontractors, and low union density overall in the United States. Instead, the union sought to both make it more difficult for management to outsource and to convince AT&T to bring work back in-house. "Our contract actually says, when you're going to do any contracting you're supposed to notify the union the intents of that. But the intent was for me to come up with alternatives, maybe the union can come up with ideas on how to help them meet that need [in terms of finding cost savings in-house]" (CWA rep AT&T, March 14, 2012).

In one example, the union formed a joint committee with management between 2001 and 2004 to try to narrow the cost differential between in-house and offshored call center work.[2] This resulted in proposals to create a new job title for employees handling lower-revenue work and to allow temporary work. In addition, a pilot project was proposed that reduced absenteeism and improved productivity through job rotation and flexible scheduling. However, as Goldman (2021, 250–251), CWA's former Research Director, observes:

> While the pilots showed some improvements, and the frontline account reps especially liked the job redesign, the results were not sufficient to overcome AT&T management's laser focus on cost as call volumes continued to drop at a rapid clip. The results of the trials did not convince AT&T to insource more work.

In 2002, one of AT&T's major BPO vendors offered the company even more significant cost savings through moving calls to its offshore locations; and by 2005, Goldman (2021, 251) notes, AT&T was offshoring 42% of its calls to India, Canada, Mexico, the Philippines, and Panama.

In 2004 contract negotiations, the CWA sought an agreement to insource 3,000 digital subscriber line (DSL) help-desk jobs that had been offshored to Accenture in India. Management agreed to bring this work back to the United States, in CWA-represented call centers, when the contract with Accenture expired in 2007—but only if the union negotiated "a competitive set of conditions." The help-desk jobs were internalized to five new call centers under a new job title in AT&T's Internet Services Agreement, with starting pay of close to $10/hour. One union rep observed: "The companies deliberately went to places

---

[2] Debbie Goldman (2021, 245–251) gives a detailed account of the various efforts and projects of this Subcontracting Committee, to bring down costs and improve quality at AT&T's consumer sales and service centers.

that had high unemployment. . . . A lot of places where there was [sic] low-income people, a lot of dropping out of school . . . that kind of thing, low education" (CWA rep AT&T, March 31, 2017). By 2013, 15 of these Internet Services call centers had been set up, employing 3,600 workers, and average pay had increased to $14/hour. Subsequent agreements applied a 2%–3% annual pay increase, but starting pay for customer assistants was still $12/hour in 2020.

At the same time, AT&T continued to close call centers and outsource these jobs. Between 2011 and 2018, the company closed forty-four call centers. In some cases, employees were "re-badged" or asked to move to subcontractors like Accenture, where they were expected to train their replacements—often on short-term H1B visa contracts from India.

In the technician area, the union also agreed to lower "second-tier" wage rates to reverse or stop outsourcing of jobs. One CWA representative described how this evolved over time:

We have a subcontract within our contract that has the new technicians and the new work at a lower rate of pay. We have had a hard time with the employer— we [. . .] were going to lose to contract labor if we didn't bargain an entry level. We're now bargaining our third contract for that work group. The pay is $13 to $23, which is less than an average of $36 for our regular technicians. They [management] wanted a competitive installer for a new video product, which we agreed to do with them in 2007. Then in 2009 we tried to make some improvements; we did fair on that but not good. [. . .] But if we hadn't agreed on the lower pay rate, they would have subcontracted it or have non-bargained employees do the work. For example, in Florida they had the same kind of video launch, but they were unable to come to an agreement, and it became non-bargained. (CWA rep AT&T, June 28, 2012)

Beyond concessions, the CWA organized public campaigns and political action to pressure AT&T and other employers to reduce outsourcing. Between 2017 and 2018, the union organized a series of actions, including rallies and pickets outside AT&T retail stores and call centers and at AT&T's annual shareholder meeting. In 2018, the CWA filed an unfair labor practice claim against AT&T with the National Labor Relations Board, arguing that the company had violated the AT&T Southwest bargaining agreement by laying off workers while using contract employees to do work union members were qualified for. Mobilization against job cuts continued through 2020, and in 2021 the CWA secured a job security agreement for technician titles. At the same time, AT&T committed to hiring 6,000 customer service employees.

The CWA also organized legislative campaigns at the state level, supporting bills that claw back state grants, loans, and tax breaks from companies that offshore a certain percentage of call center jobs, with provisions disadvantaging them in future bids for state call center work. Different versions of this legislation were passed in Louisiana and Alabama in 2018; in Colorado, Maine, and Nevada in 2019; and in New York in 2020. While the actual impact on jobs was difficult to measure, CWA's organizing around these bills became an important part of their strategy to mobilize members and put public pressure on their employers (CWA officials, August 13, 2019). In 2019, twenty-four state legislatures had introduced bills on call center offshoring. The US Call Center Worker and Consumer Protection Act was introduced at the federal level in 2017, 2019, and 2021—which would make companies that offshore call center work ineligible for federal grants and loans; require call center work on federal contracts to remain in the United States; and require offshore agents to disclose their location.

At the same time, the union sought to organize joint international projects through the global union UNI-ICTS and in partnership with unions organizing international call center subcontractors or "vendors" in the business process outsourcing (BPO) industry. In 2018, the CWA supported employees in the Dominican Republic in a successful campaign to organize a union at one of AT&T's BPO vendors, Teleperformance. The union also has worked with the BPO Industry Employees Network (BIEN) union in the Philippines, sending delegations to meet with workers and union activists, and participating in global actions protesting the arrest of BIEN activists in 2020 (CWA 2019; Galant 2020). These were part of a broader strategy of global solidarity, focused on improving worker voice and conditions across countries.

The CWA has traditionally used its influence over regulatory decisions and public infrastructure investments as a key source of bargaining leverage at incumbent companies, as well as a tool to improve employment standards in the telecom industry more broadly (Katz, Batt, and Keefe 2003). For example, the union has supported actions by the Federal Communications Commission (FCC) and state public utility commissions to mandate minimum investment levels, tied to transaction approval or service quality investigations. More recently, the CWA supported provisions in federal legislation on broadband infrastructure investment that would have prevented outsourcing of this work for the purpose of circumventing collective agreements. The 2021 Infrastructure Investment and Jobs Act passed by Congress included some (albeit weaker) worker protections sought by the CWA and other unions, including a preference for companies that have a track record of compliance with labor law and mechanisms to support future compliance. Given the challenges to organizing new workplaces or negotiating more encompassing collective agreements in the United States, these represent alternative strategies to raise wages and conditions across the sector.

United Kingdom (BT)

At BT, employers externalized a range of jobs through shifting work to temporary agencies and domestic and international subcontractors.[3] While all employee groups were affected, the union was most active in negotiating or campaigning around the externalization of call center work. At the time of our research, there had been less outsourcing of network or field technician services—referred to as engineers at BT. According to one interviewee, "the company would have had enormous problems with the CWU had it moved to outsource engineering functions. There would have been a dispute, because the heartland of the CWU industrial strength is there, the core of the CWU's political strength sits in engineering" (Prospect officials, March 22, 2012).

Still, subcontractors did make up about 10% of BT Openreach's engineering workforce in the early 2010s. Management argued that they were needed to increase flexibility, especially during certain times of the year when bad weather increases the likelihood of faults. CWU unionists noted that they were in ongoing discussions with management about bringing more of these jobs in-house—using the argument that the quality of subcontractors' work was inferior.

The "Commitment for Commitment" agreement that had been negotiated with the unions in the early 2000s (see Chapter 3) placed some limits on the number of jobs BT was able to outsource. At the same time, several hundred BT employees were transferred to other companies, as part of the shift of, e.g., finance functions to Xansa (later Steria); property functions to Telereal and Monterey; and IT support to Hewlett Packard, Computacenter, and Tech Mahindra. The employees involved were transferred under TUPE (Transfer of Undertakings, Protection of Employment) rules in UK law. This meant they retained their terms and conditions—typically including BT's voluntary redundancy package. However, interviewees observed that in the longer-term, BT forced its subcontractors to lower pay to comply with draconian targets, including a demand at one point that they cut costs by 15% across the board.

BT also offshored thousands of call center jobs, primarily technical support, to BPO vendors in India and, to a lesser extent, the Philippines, including First Source, HCL, and Whitpro. In 2003, BT announced plans to offshore 2,000 call center jobs to India. The CWU organized a protest, which involved—controversially—a large inflatable pink elephant. A Prospect official commented: "I thought it got dangerously close to looking like a little England, or worse, campaign, and the elephant in particular, I thought: no, no, no" (Prospect official, March 22, 2012). According to one unionist: "To stand up as a union

---

[3] The summaries of the UK, Poland, Czech Republic, and Austria cases are based on research and case study write-ups by Katja Sarmiento-Mirwaldt.

and say, 'They're outsourcing work to India, that's dreadful,' is very difficult to do because it implies you're potentially discriminating [. . .]. So running a campaign against outsourcing work to India was very difficult" (former CWU official, December 1, 2011).

Despite union resistance, BT went ahead with its offshoring plan. Management agreed to not make workers redundant in the United Kingdom while recruiting abroad, to provide training and development opportunities within BT, and to abide by ethical investment principles when employing people overseas.

In the early 1990s, BT also began to increase its use of temporary agency workers for many jobs traditionally performed by permanent employees. At one point in the late 1990s and early 2000s, around 10,000 employees were on temporary contracts across the company, representing 7% of the national workforce and almost half of the call center workforce in BT's retail business unit.

The terms and conditions for agency workers were poor. Many were paid considerably lower rates than their permanent colleagues, despite carrying out similar work. They received no company sick pay, no paid maternity leave, only statutory annual leave, and no job security. They also had a much more flexible shift pattern, meaning that in some areas they worked more during unsocial hours and weekends. Conversions from agency to permanent positions were rare. Unionists observed that some agency workers had been employed continuously at BT for more than ten years.

The CWU had long criticized the growing use of agency workers and their poor conditions. Around 2000, the union began to more actively seek to organize and represent them:

> It was a big internal debate about whether we recruited these people or whether we stood up and fought against the strategy of the company, and I think that it came to a point where we had vociferously tried to oppose the use of agency and it wasn't getting us anywhere. It was becoming so that they were moving so quickly bringing agency people in, and some of these agency people wanted to join the union, that we had to, I suppose, adopt a two-pronged strategy which was to recruit and organize amongst the agency, but to also still deal with BT so as to get these people permanent contracts of employment. So we were not endorsing the use of agency. We were actually going to the company and saying that we wanted these people to be given proper contracts. (CWU official, May 15, 2012)

The union started a campaign, "Justice for Agency Workers," to organize these workers and to work with the agencies to improve conditions. This campaign increased membership density among BT's agency workers to around 50%—a high rate for this group, though lower than the union's 90% membership density among the permanent workforce. The CWU also won union recognition agreements at several agencies, but these did not cover pay.

In response to union campaigning against both offshoring and agency work, the CWU and BT reached an agreement in 2006 called the Retail Sourcing Strategy. This allowed no more than 10% of the workforce to be composed of contractors, fixed-term workers, and agency workers from 2007. In the same agreement, management committed to a cap of 2,200 jobs in offshored locations. As part of this drive, well-performing agency workers in some call centers were given permanent BT contracts, with a salary increase of a few thousand pounds, although on a new lower pay grade in the collective agreement. New hires also started at this new grade, with on average 19,000 pounds less pay, higher working hours (40 rather than 36), less sick pay, and requirements to work nights and weekends. By 2013, around 35% of BT's call center workforce were on these new grades and over 1,000 new positions had been created. According to an HR manager:

> The existing national agreement would have made it too costly and too restrictive to place the work in the UK, but they [the CWU] recognize there are particular needs for this particular set of activities and work and we have negotiated a special set of terms and conditions that enable us to do that and we will create, certainly initially, hundreds and potentially more jobs. (BT HR manager, May 25, 2012)

Also in the mid-2000s, the CWU started to campaign for legislation guaranteeing equal pay and conditions for agency workers in the House of Commons, as well as at EU level. In 2008, the UK government reached a tripartite agreement with employer and worker representatives stipulating that agency workers would be entitled to the same pay as colleagues in equivalent permanent positions after twelve weeks on the job. The government also agreed to support the EU Temporary and Agency Work Directive on equal treatment of agency workers, which was passed in 2008 and transposed into UK law in 2011.

The new regulations ensured that workers on traditional agency contracts were entitled to terms equal to those of permanent workers concerning pay, annual leave entitlement, breaks, and the use of facilities. At the time, 4,000 BT agency employees and 3,000 CWU agency members (across BT and other companies) qualified for equal treatment. Union officials observed that most of these employees saw their pay increase, in some cases by as much as 20%.

However, the legislation included a clause known as the "Swedish Derogation," which exempted employers from equal treatment requirements if they employed an agency worker under a permanent contract of employment and paid the worker between assignments or jobs. Agencies immediately began to exploit this loophole. In February 2011, prior to the implementation of the new equal pay regulations in October, Manpower advised the CWU that they would be trialing "pay between assignments" (PBA) contracts for agency employees at BT. By 2013, these had become the default contract for this group of workers. Union officials observed that agency workers were required to sign these contracts without being advised that they were "contractually and legally signing away their rights to equal treatment on pay" (presentation, CWU official, November 21, 2013). As a result, pay gaps began to increase again, with agency workers in call centers paid between £2–4 less per hour than similar permanent workers at the same locations. In addition, the proportion of agency workers in the call centers began to increase again. In 2013, BT employed 3,050 agency workers in its UK call centers, compared to around 8,000 permanent employees (CWU official, October 17, 2013).

The CWU then initiated a new campaign called "Closing the Loopholes: Justice for Agency Workers." It had several objectives, including: securing amendments to the UK Agency Regulations ending the Swedish derogation and other loopholes; raising the profile of agency issues among CWU members and encouraging agency members to become active in the campaign; raising political awareness and support; engaging and working with the TUC and the global union UNI; and giving "consideration to challenging the UK Agency Regulations within the European Commission" (presentation, CWU official, November 21, 2013). In January 2013, the CWU organized an "Agency Action Day," in which agency workers at a number of BT call centers demonstrated against low pay and inequality of treatment.

In September 2013, the TUC made a formal complaint to the European Commission that the UK government had failed to properly implement the Directive, citing evidence—provided in part by the CWU—that tens of thousands of agency workers were being paid less than permanent staff doing the same job. After close to a decade of union organizing and campaigning efforts, the UK government finally amended the law in 2020 to remove the Swedish derogation provisions.

Czech Republic (O2 Czech Republic)

In contrast to BT, where the focus of externalization was call centers, the main outsourcing event at O2 Czech Republic was the decision to outsource most of the company's network and field technician services between 2005 and 2011, involving about 2,000 jobs. All field technicians were outsourced, as well as maintenance of the network and 50% of underground cable maintenance. Though the union opposed the decision, worker representatives did not organize strikes or protests, but instead sought to engage in a dialogue with management to help affected workers. According to one management representative:

The biggest part of the trade union's involvement on this overall process was during the preparation phase. There was a very intensive communication between the trade union and company representatives all the time that ensured the overall process as well as timing is suitable for both sides. The trade union had the chance to review and comment on the communication to people, redundancy rules and conditions, etc. And they were also heavily involved in the communication and "change management" that helped affected people to perceive this as a controlled and well managed process. (O2CR HR manager, June 8, 2012)

O2 Czech Republic dismissed most workers in affected positions—only about 500 technicians were transferred under Czech "acquired rights" rules, allowing them to stay on their former employment contracts until the end of 2013. However, according to one interviewee, a lot of the dismissed workers subsequently were rehired at these subcontractors (25% overall, but up to 80% in some areas)—at lower pay and typically without a union contract (OSZPTNS rep O2CR, June 7, 2012).

O2 Czech Republic also outsourced call center work to third-party subcontractors and used agency workers, although this developed organically, as call centers were relatively new and call volume was increasing. In 2012, the company employed 1,323 in-house employees and 1,236 agency workers, with 219 working for subcontractors. Inbound customer service calls were largely handled by agency staff, whereas outbound sales calls, customer retention, and technical support were more often handled by in-house staff. These agencies and call center subcontractors had low union presence and were not covered by collective agreements.

In line with the EU equal treatment directive, Czech law required comparable (though not identical) pay and conditions between agency workers and permanent employees. O2 Czech Republic also recruited high-performing agency workers into permanent call center positions. In 2011, around 700 new agency workers were hired, and 200 existing agency workers were moved to permanent contracts. A union representative noted, "Unions have no power to influence the ratio between core and agency workers. However, we express interest in employing core employees" (OSZPTNS rep O2 CR, June 7, 2012).

A quote from a manager illustrates this view that unions mostly played a consultation role in outsourcing decisions:

The trade unions, according to the Czech Labor Code and according to the collective agreement we have in place, they have the right to know and actually to negotiate about larger organizational changes [. . .] meaning either changes where it's a higher volume of people leaving the company for redundancy reasons or changes where we are outsourcing part of the company, that actually people are not effectively leaving or losing their job, they are just moving to the third party provider. [. . .] it's not really negotiation in terms of that the unions would have the right to say: "Okay we don't agree with that," it's much more about consulting, so actually saying: "Okay, we plan to implement this change, what's your opinion, what's your feeling, what would be your suggestions?" So actually there are not so many things where actually they have the veto. (O2CR HR manager, June 8, 2012)

Poland (Orange Polska)

Outsourcing at Orange Polska was typically carried out through spin-offs, in which locations and their employees were transferred to subcontractors. Transfer of Undertakings rules stipulated that pay and benefits under an employee's former collective agreement must remain in place for at least twelve months. After this period, however, transferred employees typically would be shifted to different—often less favorable—terms and conditions.

The first spin-off in 1997 involved building administration and cleaning services, with subsequent ones affecting drivers, couriers, security services, accounting, and remote computer maintenance. Then in 2002, 6,000 network and service technicians were transferred to subcontractors. The unions negotiated a program called "Work for the Worker": in return for standing orders from Orange Polska, the subcontractors agreed to employ its former employees on indefinite contracts and to guarantee them work for 1.5–3 years, depending on the region. The new employment contracts were individually negotiated by workers, who took a 15% average wage cut, compensated by one-time incentive payments (on average 20,000 złoty—around US$5,000). The decision to move was voluntary, but if technicians decided not to move, they would be laid off. Most affected employees took redundancy because the terms offered went far beyond what was required by Polish law.

Some unionists expressed pride in this agreement: "The conditions for the workers I think we managed to negotiate well, as far as Polish conditions go" (OPZZ official, April 17, 2012). However, these measures were only temporary. According to one unionist, "After the employment guarantees expired, there were further wage cuts and redundancies in many companies that took over workers" (email communication, SKPT official, October 11, 2012). According to another, the transitional period "was a camouflage, window-dressing. Because the employer survives these eighteen months and then he can do as he pleases, so it was only for a while" (OPZZ official, April 17, 2012).

In 2010, the customer service call centers for both mobile and fixed-line business units were spun off to the subsidiary Orange Customer Service (OCS). Unlike the situation with technician services, OCS remained fully owned by Orange Polska. Several waves of tough negotiations were associated with this spin-off, and the union SKPT led a collective dispute. In the end, the unions succeeded in extending the terms of the collective agreement for Orange Polska to the new subsidiary. Transferred employees received a two-year employment guarantee and no reduction in their salary. A similar pension scheme was also introduced, which constituted a gain for the former Centertel employees. A works councilor described the negotiations:

> When the new company [OCS] was founded, it did not offer workers anything except for the things that are by law offered to employees that move to another company, e.g., it sets a period of employment. . . . This new company initially did not offer anything. Only these negotiations that the unions undertook have led to these successes that [union official] mentioned. (SKPT works councilor OP, February 15, 2012)

Orange Polska managers stressed that these provisions went far beyond what is required by law: "This is important for us, a rather large group of people. We would like to carry this out in social peace, we want to be fair, we offer this, this and this, and that we will keep" (OP manager, July 10, 2012). Union representatives attributed this success to high membership density and union strength in the call center area:

> Technicians are a very fragmented group who are not all located in the same place. Especially since the network services were spun off in 2002, there have been fewer technicians who would put up a resistance to the company's restructuring plans. [. . .] Conversely, there was definitely concern about the call center employees, because there any walkout would be very noticeable for the company, because customers could not be served completely. It is the customer's only contact with the company. So there was a concern, so perhaps these protests, which took place then [when OCS was spun off in 2010] led to the company [. . .] fulfilling all these demands. And it fulfilled them, all of them were fulfilled. (SKPT official, April 19, 2012)

Summary

Across these four cases, management used a range of externalization strategies to move work outside of more highly unionized and protected workplaces, putting downward pressure on pay and conditions. Unions had limited ability to organize subcontractors or extend collective agreements to them, because there were no existing bargaining structures and very low possibility of success in trying to set them up. One key difference concerns whether unions sought to re-internalize jobs. Unions at AT&T and BT fought to keep or bring work in-house through provisions in agreements that increased the expense or difficulty of outsourcing, legislative campaigns to strengthen legal protections against outsourcing or require equal pay for temporary workers, and concessionary collective agreements to insource jobs at lower pay and conditions. At O2 Czech Republic and Orange Polska, unions seemed more resigned to management's outsourcing strategies, placing their focus on protecting conditions for transferred or downsized workers. These campaigns were most successful at Orange Polska, where workers were transferred under much better conditions. In the case of the call center subsidiary, this followed the unions' successful and solidaristic mobilization of workers to demand extension of past agreements.

Representation Domain Divides: Germany and Denmark

In contrast to the cases discussed above, the industrial relations systems in Germany and Denmark give unions more resources for extending agreements to new groups of externalized workers. Company or sectoral collective agreements covered at least a few of the major call center and technician services subcontractors. These provided some constraints on employer exit from encompassing minimum standards, as well as a resource for extending collective worker voice to these workplaces. At the same time, the coverage of these agreements was low, and terms and conditions were substantially worse than those for in-house workers in the same positions. Similar to AT&T and BT, managers at TDC and Deutsche Telekom were able to exploit exit options to gain concessions in exchange for keeping work in-house or re-internalizing jobs, effectively weakening union capacity to use collective voice to improve conditions for internal workers. These patterns were both produced and exacerbated by competition between unions based on "representation domain divides," which inhibited them from cooperating to build more encompassing, coordinated collective bargaining institutions.

Germany (Deutsche Telekom)

In Germany, similar to the "structural exclusive solidarity" cases, the telecom and related subcontracting industries were not covered by sectoral collective agreements (see Chapter 2, Table 2.1). Only one major call center subcontractor, Walter Services, had negotiated a company-level agreement with ver.di at the time of my research. However, starting pay in this agreement was close to half the level for call center workers at Deutsche Telekom. Technician services firms were either covered by agreements with different unions (for example, IG Metall) or had no agreement. Competing collective agreements with different industry-based unions, as well as fragmentation across departments within ver.di (Holtgrewe and Doellgast 2012), opened up large differences in pay and conditions between Deutsche Telekom employees and those performing similar jobs at its competitors and subcontractors. This encouraged the expansion of subcontracting, often through transfer to subsidiaries that were later spun off to third-party firms.

In the call center area, Deutsche Telekom had established the subsidiary Vivento Customer Services (VCS) in 2004. VCS took over employees who had been downsized in different areas of the company and moved into the temporary services subsidiary, Vivento PSA (see Chapter 3). A 2004 employment pact reduced the pay of these employees by 8.75%. Then, between 2006 and 2008, Deutsche Telekom transferred 12 of its 19 VCS call center locations, representing around 1,800 employees, to the subcontractors Walter Services and Arvato. Walter Services had a collective agreement with ver.di, but it was negotiated by a different department responsible for "miscellaneous services" and pay and conditions were lower. When Walter purchased the new locations, employees were automatically transferred to this existing agreement, based on a provision in German law that provides an exception to transfer of undertakings rules when both companies are covered by agreements with the same union. Employees who had formerly earned an average annual salary of 33,000–36,000 euros saw their pay cut by around a third.

Arvato had no collective agreement, so their existing agreement and terms were secured through 2009. However, in 2009 managers informed employees that they were required to sign individual contracts at a lower level. Pay would initially average 25,000 euros a year—with 1,224 euros/month paid by Arvato (the amount written into the individual contracts) and 800 euros/month paid as a temporary "top-up" by Deutsche Telekom. Ver.di initially encouraged employees transferred to Arvato not to sign these contracts, and instead sought to pressure Arvato to negotiate a collective agreement. However, management informally threatened to move work to other locations if employees refused to sign. This appeared to be a credible threat when Arvato announced that it would close former VCS centers in Potsdam and Freiburg by the end of 2009:

> We have an Arvato location in Potsdam. The colleagues got a *Gehaltssicherung* [protection of their pay], and Arvato got a certain sum of money from Telekom,

a contract guarantee. Arvato came at some point and put new employment contracts in front of employees; and the location was closed on 31 December last year—only four employees had signed the contracts. So the location was just closed. (works councilor DT, September 14, 2011)

In technician services, Deutsche Telekom increased its use of subcontractors to handle more unpredictable peaks in demand, as it was responsible for servicing the network and connecting customers who purchased services from their competitors. Subcontractors tended to do the simpler connection or wiring work for private or "mass market" customers, particularly for competitors selling services over Deutsche Telekom's network. Faults and repairs had been outsourced, but then brought back in-house due to high rates of customer call-backs.

In the mid-2000s, field technician work also was sent to the subsidiary Vivento Technical Services (VTS), which acted like an internal subcontractor while also selling technician services to external clients—similar to VCS on the call center side. At the end of 2004, VTS employed 1,400 individuals, and by 2007 its starting monthly salary was 1,900 euros compared to 2,300 euros for in-house technicians. Deutsche Telekom then established a strategic partnership agreement with Nokia Siemens Networks, and in 2008 transferred 1,600 VTS employees to Nokia. Employees were protected against redundancy for one year after the transfer, and contracts were secured for three years. This contributed to ongoing conflicts between ver.di and IG Metall, which had existing collective agreements with Nokia.

In 2007, in the middle of the developments described above, Deutsche Telekom announced that it planned to shift 50,000 of its technical service, technical infrastructure, and call center jobs to three new subsidiaries, under the name T-Service, and demanded that ver.di renegotiate pay and working conditions. Ver.di responded by leading a six-week strike. However, management threatened to spin off the subsidiaries to subcontractors, and the union was forced to accept a number of concessions to prevent this. These included reductions in wage levels for employees moved to T-Service and increased weekly working time without pay compensation, adding up to a pay cut of more than 10%. New employees' starting pay was 30% below the former level, variable pay increased, and call center workers were required to work on Saturdays. Management agreed to extend layoff protections until 2012, to refrain from selling the new subsidiaries until 2010, and to offer 4,150 jobs at T-Service to apprentices.

A works councilor from the technician subsidiary DTTS gave more detail about how the shift from being part of an internal business unit to a service subsidiary had intensified cost-based pressures:

> We are actually only a contractor for Deutsche Telekom AG as DTTS. We do not automatically get our money, but only as much as we bring in through orders. When we hook up a new connection, we get 50 euros for that—regardless of how often we drive there or how long we need. [. . .] Accordingly, we are productive or not productive, and in the red or in the black. But the catch is that Deutsche Telekom decides how much money we will get from them. At the beginning, when the GmbHs [subsidiaries] were established, we got on average 100 euros per order. At some point they said, "that is too much: you should only get half of that." There is no way that we are going to get more now. These are very difficult negotiations. (works councilor DT, September 13, 2011)

There were similar observations from works councilors in the call center subsidiary DTKS:

> Before we had a system of workforce planning . . . previously it was action-based [*Maßnahmenbezogene*] planning: that means, I knew that I had to implement a certain measure or strategy, and I needed so many employees for that. Now it's budget-oriented workforce planning. That is, each GmbH [subsidiary] gets a budget, and they have to work with that. That leads to a situation where they are interested in getting rid of the expensive employees and buying in cheap employees. This is often solved through using outsourcing partners. (works councilor DT, September 14, 2011)

At the same time, the proportion of jobs outsourced continued to increase for both call center and technician work. In 2010–2011, DTKS had 15,000 internal employees and 9,000 employees working for subcontractors (ver.di rep, September 20, 2010); while DTTS had 20,000 internal employees and around 8,500 working for subcontractors (works councilor DT, September 13, 2011).

> We are always under pressure, especially since we are a separate GmbH [subsidiary]. They say to us: "You have to earn money, otherwise we do not need DTTS." Of course, shareholders are behind this, profitability must be at a certain level: "If they don't get their 8%, then it isn't worth it to them. Then more work will always be outsourced." Through this process they have created a situation where the employee and the team leader see their team as a "Mini-AG" [small company], and the employee feels he is obligated to earn money. Unfortunately this is correct. If we do not make a profit, they will decide what to do with us. (works councilor DT, September 13, 2011)

A manager in DTTS observed that outsourcing could be a motivation tool (see Chapter 4), and technicians were working harder to bring up their own performance to justify in-sourcing work: "because we say that we can also do this work very well with our own employees. As you may know from the US, employees have to go a little faster if they want this" (DT HR manager, September 24, 2010).

Works councils in both subsidiaries objected to this trend. However, it became a central focus at DTKS, as declining call volume was also leading to internal job cuts. There was an agreement in 2010–2011, named *Zukunftsperspektive*, that sought to reduce the number of employees at subcontractors while stabilizing the internal workforce—as call volume was falling overall. The language in the agreement committed management to bringing back as many jobs as they could.

In exchange, the works council agreed to some changes in two areas: monitoring of individual performance indicators (see Chapter 4) and working time. The new working-time model aimed to give management more flexibility to hire workers during times that subcontractors were used in the past. The works council agreed to expand late and weekend hours, and that employees could be hired who would take on these shifts, such as students and younger employees. As a result, all new employees (with the exception of apprentices) were hired as part-time employees with 20–30 hours/week. This doubled the proportion of part-time employees, from a past level of 20% up to 40% by 2014. These new employees were usually hired to work shifts between 12 p.m. and midnight. In addition, the works council launched a new pilot project that gave employees three different options of alternative working-time models—each with different degrees of choice and flexibility (Doellgast and Berg 2018). This pilot led to a formal works agreement in 2013, which was then implemented in 2014.

This new working-time model allowed employees to select schedules that fit their individual needs, while meeting Deutsche Telekom's demands for better matching employee availability with customer demand and changing staffing at short notice. An additional component of this agreement was to give more discretion to local managers and works councilors to oversee employee schedules, via a system of joint committees. The number of employees needed would continue to be centrally planned, but regional committees decided which individuals were placed in the different working-time models. Regional and local works councils thus had the ability to help employees solve problems with their work schedules, while management was required to negotiate solutions to more systematic problems with the regional works council. This was viewed as a major win by the works council, as it had consistently contested and sought to reverse the centralization of schedules.

Management meanwhile committed to stabilizing internal employment and reducing the use of subcontractors and temporary agency workers. DTKS did not use a lot of temporary agency employees, and typically only to staff call centers during special sales campaigns. Around 2010, 500–600 agency workers were employed in DTKS call centers, but by 2013, there were only around 20–40. A works councilor observed that reducing the use of agency work was a goal of the same agreement aimed at reducing subcontracting: "Employee representatives spent a long time in discussions with the employer, how the *Zukunftsbündnis* from 2010 was going to be implemented. One of the themes was that employee representatives didn't want any temporary agency work" (works councilor DT, September 3, 2013).

Between 2011 and 2013, the number of subcontracted call center employees declined from 11,000 to 6,000. These numbers remained stable through 2015, when works councils faced a new set of challenges associated with the AI-enabled automation of a growing number of back- and front-office tasks (Bormann and Brandl 2019, 227–228). A works agreement in 2015 committed management to use the savings to reduce subcontracted work, essentially protecting internal workers from job cuts associated with automation. By 2021, this had resulted in a dramatic reduction in outsourcing, to just "a handful of jobs" in some areas (works councilor DT, December 13, 2021).

Denmark (TDC)

Unlike Germany, Denmark developed sectoral bargaining institutions in the telecom and related subcontractor industries. These collective agreements were not automatically extended, however, relying instead on voluntary compliance by employers. As described in Chapter 2, despite strong national industrial relations institutions in Denmark, employers enjoyed distinctive exit options in the Danish telecom industry and the incumbent TDC, due to multiple sectoral and company-level collective agreements and low bargaining coverage in the subcontractor sectors. Overlapping representation domains between Dansk Metal (in TDC), HK (in other telecom companies and call centers), and the electricians' union Dansk EL-Forbund (in small technician contract firms) meant that unions were competing with each other—and, as in Germany, they could gain members from other unions when employers outsourced or spun off jobs.

An additional challenge in Denmark was a historic agreement stating that when employers were members of an association negotiating white-collar agreements with the service union HK, it was necessary for the union to document that 50% of the workforce were union members before applying the collective agreement to that employer (see Chapter 2). Unions could not strike or picket service employers who were members of the association. This posed particular challenges for unions seeking to organize newer service employers with low union density. An HK organizer gave the example of Go Excellent, a call center subcontractor he had been trying (unsuccessfully) to organize for years:

> Go Excellent [. . .] are a member of DE [employer association], so they are protected from getting a collective agreement, unless half of the people join HK. When a company like that exchanges all their workers at least eight times during one year, it's almost impossible to get 50% at one time, also because it's very young people. They've just left school, they have no idea what working is all about. But we're trying, and we're close, but they [Go Excellent] get protected because they joined DE. (HK official, April 26, 2012)

TDC was able to exploit these exit options to introduce a widely varying structure of pay and conditions across similar groups of employees. TDC diversified within Denmark by acquiring flexible start-up companies in different segments and continuing to operate them as independent subsidiaries. While responsibility for their workforce shifted to Dansk Metal, the subsidiaries often maintained lower pay and conditions than those in core business units. For example, TDC purchased the subcontractor Call Center Europe in the early 2000s. By 2012, Call Center Europe had 285 employees, around 200 of whom worked primarily on TDC contracts. The company originally followed a separate collective agreement and were represented by the service union HK. Employees were transferred to Dansk Metal after 2002, but the subsidiary continued to follow its previous agreement. The typical salary of a call center agent was almost 10% lower than at TDC and the wage structure was more compressed. In addition, in-house TDC employees enjoyed a paid lunch break and a range of other perks, such as more favorable pensions and holidays that were not extended to Call Center Europe: "Later we came under Dansk Metal, but we still have a different agreement. We work under a lone agreement down here but we do the same job [. . .]. We have to be more flexible, and we are" (Dansk Metal rep TDC, May 15, 2012).

In 2004, TDC acquired NetDesign, a provider of IP/LAN infrastructure for business customers. It also maintained a separate collective agreement and terms and conditions. TDC transferred 200 of its own technicians to NetDesign, which almost doubled the number of employees. This meant integrating a group of older technicians, who were Dansk Metal members and often former civil servants, with the younger "flexible" (mostly non-union) workforce of a smaller former start-up IT company.

TDC also acquired a number of smaller service providers, which it operated as "no-frills" brands. These competed to some extent with the TDC brand, but with a focus on lower price market segments. Most did not have collective agreements prior to being purchased by TDC and continued to have low union membership and little Dansk Metal involvement. An HR director described this strategy of keeping the "no frills" brands separate from TDC:

> In the Consumer, we have the no frills brands; we call them, like on the phone it's called Telmore, FullRate, M1. And they all have their own call centers but, you know, small call centers. . . . I don't think they have that much kind of negotiations with the unions at all, the daughter companies, but they have their separate [overall collective agreement that covers them]. [. . .] we bought them in order to fill out the whole palette of telecom products. I mean, if we didn't have the low-end products, low-end companies, somebody else would. (TDC HR manager, April 23, 2012)

Large differences in collective agreements generated conflicts between unions as TDC outsourced work. For example, between 2003 and 2008, TDC outsourced around 1,000 IT employees to Computer Sciences Corporation (CSC), a US-based subcontractor specializing in IT and BPO. Transferred employees remained under Dansk Metal agreements for two years, but were then moved to the "lower value" white-collar agreement negotiated by HK. A Dansk Metal official observed that this had contributed to tensions between the unions:

> We tried to negotiate with the union [HK] who should take them over, and ask them if they would allow us to renew their agreement, because that would be a stronger position for the workers. But they were so interested in getting those 1,000 members, so it didn't work to the benefit of the workers in my opinion. We tried everything, but they were not interested. (Dansk Metal official, August 19, 2011)

The origin of this lower value agreement lies in the linked challenges presented by competing agreements and a high degree of inter-union competition. CSC had earlier decided to shift employees from a collective agreement with the small IT union PROSA to a less favorable agreement for the IT industry negotiated with HK (Ilsøe 2012). PROSA challenged this in the labor courts and organized a series of strikes. However, because PROSA was not a member of the LO union confederation, it was not able to get support from other LO unions for solidarity strikes or actions. In addition, HK's sectoral agreement had legal priority over PROSA's company-level agreement. In the end, CSC moved to the sectoral agreement, allowing it to reduce pay and conditions for its workforce, which came to include TDC's outsourced IT services.

In the 2010s, TDC shifted some of its remaining IT work to the Indian subcontractor Tata—again, moving this work to the HK-negotiated IT agreement. An HK representative reflected on the Tata case, noting, "I think [. . .] Dansk Metal would like to tell the story that we just offer employers discount agreements; that's not entirely true, but then again it's not exactly a lie" (HK official, April 26, 2012).

TDC also announced plans to outsource the operation and development of its fixed-line network in 2008, which would have involved the transfer of 1,800 employees. If this had gone through, all of TDC's network and field technician services would have been performed by subcontractors. Ericsson, Nokia-Siemens, and Alcatel-Lucent all bid on the deal, but TDC decided that they would not be able to make sufficient cost savings (TDC HR manager, April 23, 2012).

At the same time, there had been a gradual shift toward increased outsourcing of small areas of technician services. Maintenance of the fiber network was outsourced to a consortium of small companies, with 157 technicians transferred in 2011. A portion of order management, in which employees get the orders for work and decide how to distribute them among technicians, was offshored to the Philippines. One shop steward estimated that 120 employees from subcontractors were working for TDC in the field technician area, alongside 800 TDC employees. These employees were paid an hourly wage, and so (unlike TDC's technicians) they were not paid for lunch; and field technicians were paid from the first customer rather than from when they left their house.

Dansk Metal had targeted outsourcing as a campaign issue, and sought to organize technician subcontractors. However, as one union official noted, "it is very difficult because these companies [TDC is] outsourcing to are very small, a boss and two to three employees. [. . .] We tried to negotiate with TDC on outsourcing, but we get this thing from the boss: they want to focus on their core business. So there has been no progress" (Dansk Metal official, May 13, 2011).

An HR manager described how TDC approached the union to ask for concessions in exchange for keeping technician work in-house:

> In Operations, we have had a lot of outsourcing going on during the last year. And we had four outsourcing projects and we had decided that we should outsource. But at the same time, in one of the areas, the chairman of the technicians [union], he said, "but listen, I think you should stay here, we can do it as cheap as you could have it outsourced." And we said, "fine with us, as long as you can guarantee us we are saving this amount of money, and you make today expenses 30% less, for example." [. . .] They tried and they had a working group, and they tried all kinds of things in order to see if they could do it. But when it came into the end of it, if we should do it 30% cheaper, we had to . . . they had to change the agreements we have about, they have free lunch, they have all these kind of things. And these agreements, they wouldn't even touch these agreements. (TDC HR manager, April 23, 2012)

Where technician subcontractors were unionized, they often followed a collective agreement negotiated by the electricians' union Dansk EL-Forbund (DEF), further exacerbating union conflicts:

> We also have a fight with them [electricians union, DEF], because we think it's problematic that you can simply shift between collective bargaining agreements. They have their agreement with TEKNIQ, that's the electricians' and plumbers' employer association. (Dansk Metal official, June 17, 2015)

TDC was not using call center subcontractors at the time of my earlier fieldwork (2011–2012). Instead, it had the subsidiary Call Center Europe, which served as a kind of internal subcontractor; and around 20% of the in-house call center workforce worked for temporary agencies. The hourly wage for this temporary agency staff was typically 106 kroner; employees at Call Center Europe had a starting hourly wage of 108 kroner, which increased to 120 kroner after fifteen months, while in-house call center employees were typically paid around 126 kroner per hour. In addition, in-house TDC employees enjoyed a paid lunch break, which was not given to the other two groups, and a range of other perks such as more favorable pensions and holidays.

Similar to negotiations in the technician area, management used these cost differences to demand the renegotiation of terms and conditions for in-house employees. Dansk Metal was concerned about the growing use of temporary agencies, which were covered by separate collective agreements. In addition, managers began to more actively benchmark labor costs and performance across internal and external call center workers. In 2011, union representatives negotiated an agreement that committed the company to converting temporary employees to permanent contracts after three months, in exchange for a concession that new employees would not have paid lunches until they had been working for eleven months.

The background of this agreement was a change in EU law requiring equal treatment of temporary workers, which was expected to reduce their cost advantage. Meanwhile, the union felt it was worthwhile to convert temporary into permanent contracts, as these employees were then eligible to be Dansk Metal members. Union representatives also were motivated by the need to reduce their in-house costs, in order to remain competitive. A shop steward observed:

> We have just been in a case in call centers, where we were presented some results from Call Center Europe. They are faster, they don't sell more than us, but in every other thing they are cheaper. The salary is cheaper too. It's about 15 kroner every hour less than us.... And they don't have so many breaks, and so everything is made up in money. So we were presented this and were asked if we could match that. And we can't. We can't match it, but when we were in this

dialogue, we told them that we're in-house, we are loyal and we made an agreement that when we get new [employees] in, at us, in the call center, they don't get paid for their lunch break. [...] This agreement is a test, and if it doesn't give TDC the money that they have expected, then I'm afraid that ... another thing could also be that they outsource our work to other countries, or other places here in Denmark. That was one of the threats. That's why we made this agreement! (Dansk Metal rep TDC, April 24, 2012)

In 2012, Dansk Metal agreed to a more flexible working-time model and reduced terms for new workers in exchange for a two-year commitment not to outsource these jobs. Then, in 2014, management demanded further concessions—and when the union did not agree, the company transferred half of its call center workforce to the multinational BPO vendor Sitel, which negotiated a company-level agreement with HK. This resulted in a substantial reduction in pay and conditions for former TDC workers. They retained their former agreement during a transition period, due to transfer of undertakings rules, but then were shifted onto HK's agreement in 2016.

After management had shown its willingness to make good on its threat, union representatives and shop stewards were much more inclined in the 2015 bargaining round to agree to concessions. In exchange for a commitment to secure jobs through 2018, both groups gave up paid lunches, effectively extending their workday by a half hour, compensated by a one-time payment of 50,000 krone (roughly US$7,500) to technicians and 15,000 krone (US$2,200) to call center employees. In addition, they agreed to give up overtime premiums during the first hour (technicians) or fifteen minutes (call centers) of overtime, which would be integrated into a more flexible system of working-time accounts. Employees would be obligated to finish work with their final customer within that time window; and managers would be able to use "plus time" in the working-time account to send employees home early when demand was lower. In the call centers, new employees also had reduced holidays, holiday allowances, and pensions under the agreement.

This agreement not only ended further outsourcing, but also brought down costs for the in-house workforce closer to the level at subcontractors. By 2020, TDC had ended its contract with Sitel and had re-internalized its call center jobs.

Summary

The above cases show similar strategies at Deutsche Telekom and TDC to externalize call center and technician jobs (among others) through a combination of outsourcing, service subsidiaries, and temporary agency work. This resulted in growing precarity and inequality across increasingly fissured workplaces. Workers transferred to subsidiaries and subcontractors experienced downgrading of pay and conditions, while large differences in labor costs between the in-house and subcontracted or agency workforce were used by management to demand concessions in exchange for keeping work in-house. Union competition based on "representation domain divides," combined with low union density in externalized workplaces, made it difficult to organize solidaristic strategies to mobilize and represent externalized workers.

Union strategies at the incumbents focused on preventing externalization or re-internalizing jobs, similar to the US and UK cases. Where they succeeded, worker outcomes were mixed. More jobs returned to or remained in companies with overall stronger unions and less precarious conditions. Worker representatives were able to use collective voice in creative ways to balance employer demands for flexibility with improved conditions for in-house workers. This could be seen most clearly at Deutsche Telekom, where works councils used their co-determination rights to negotiate a new set of working-time models in the call centers that gave workers some choice and control (Doellgast and Berg 2018). At the same time, the overall trend was to bring internal conditions closer to those in externalized firms.

Ideological Divides: France and Italy

Compared to the above cases, France and Italy both have sectoral bargaining institutions that broadly include telecom companies and their subcontractors, reducing exit from encompassing minimum standards. At the same time, employers were able to exploit legal loopholes, allowing them to either move to a lower value agreement or to hire workers on more poorly protected nonstandard contracts. Unions' capacity to respond in a coordinated way was influenced by the multi-union bargaining structure, where multiple union confederations sign collective agreements at company and sector levels, and directly compete for members based on their different ideologies (from militant and leftist to more cooperative and conservative). At both France Telecom and Telecom Italia, leftist confederations had the highest membership or support among the workforce. This contributed to a stronger "class-based" focus on organizing externalized workers, or at least a reluctance to compromise through concessions to bring jobs back in-house.

France (France Telecom)

France Telecom relied heavily on outsourcing in both call center and technician areas. In 2010, the company operated around twenty internal call centers (14,000 workers) and subcontracted with twenty external call centers (6,000 workers), around half of which were located in Morocco and Senegal. Call center subcontractors in France are covered by a sectoral agreement that sets the minimum salary at the national minimum wage. This was only 12% lower than the starting salaries at France Telecom's call centers in the early 2010s, but the overall labor costs were lower because of higher turnover (and thus a larger percentage of workers at the starting salary level), a large proportion of part-time workers, and less generous pensions and other benefits. A much larger gap existed between in-house and offshored workers. Management estimated that labor costs in the offshore call centers were on average 75% lower than those in the in-house call centers (FT manager, August 3, 2010), with typically no union representation. A works council representative estimated that generally when a France Telecom call center employee cost 200 euros, an employee in a subcontractor cost 100 euros, and an employee in Maghreb cost 50 euros (CGT works councilor FT, December 8, 2011).

A manager observed that the organization was identical between the internal and external or subcontracted call centers, with standardization of how calls were handled across specializations and levels: "The external center is solely focused on the management of its resources and not at all on the way of doing the work. The way of doing the work is determined here [centrally at FT]. [...] The IT is our IT, and the subcontractors just have to buy the necessary PCs. [...] So the subcontractor actually has very little room for manœuvre" (FT manager, March 8, 2010).

In the *Unités d'intervention* (UI), handling most residential field and network technician services, there were around 25,000 in-house technicians and 10,000 working for subcontractors. Subcontractors in the technician area were mostly small companies and were typically under the construction industry collective agreement, rather than the telecom agreement. A director in the UI estimated that subcontractors cost the company between 0% and 30% less than internal technicians, with the largest difference in rural areas and for simpler tasks (FT manager, February 24, 2012).

One union representative described the expansion of subcontracting technician work in the line construction area from the 1970s:

> Already at that time, everything that involved putting up telephone poles and laying of cables began to be outsourced. At the beginning it was local subcontracting—a family company of a few people. It was almost craft workers [*l'artisanat*] but it became rooted in the region in an important way. Quickly enough, almost all production operations were outsourced. (CFDT rep FT, May 4, 2010)

By 2010, more complicated work typically was kept in-house and simpler technical work or new construction and maintenance were subcontracted, such as on the 4G mobile or fiber optic networks. However, subcontractors also performed some of the same jobs as the in-house workforce—for example, filling in when employees went away for summer vacation or during unexpected increases in the volume of work. An HR manager observed that the management of this group of employees was kept completely separate from the in-house workforce. However, they would meet at the same restaurants for lunch and in the company (FT HR manager, March 8, 2012).

Unions formed a committee within France Telecom's "economic commission," with the aim of gaining commitments to reduce outsourcing. One union representative described a long process of trying to get information on the volume of work outsourced and associated costs:

> At first, it was necessary to gain their [management's] trust, and that was at the level of the economic commission, and we met with the human resource department. At first, she gave us a figure for the level of outsourcing that was . . . that clearly didn't correspond with the costs. [. . .] It changed from one day to another to a calculation from 10,000 subcontracted employees to 26,000—that's to say they had doubled the number of possible subcontracted employees in the company. (CGT works councilor FT, June 30, 2010)

They succeeded in getting access to outsourcing data by convincing management they were committed to working with them to internalize jobs under good conditions:

> This is really something that we won. It took time, it took a lot of confidence. We had to say to them: no, we will not use this to embarrass you in front of your competitors or create difficulties in the press. We want to use it because we think that employees [. . .] are treated better when they are employees of the Group than when they are subcontracted outside of the group. That is the reality. (CGT works councilor FT, June 30, 2010)

France Telecom did reduce the volume of call center work outsourced in the mid-2010s; however, managers and union representatives attributed this in part to declining call volumes. Cutting outsourcing was the easiest adjustment strategy because of the high costs associated with downsizing.

Although the above examples show that France Telecom's unions sought to reduce outsourcing, they did not place a high priority on this in negotiations. Unlike many of the cases described above, unions did not seek to make concessions to reverse outsourcing, nor did management use the benchmarking of costs between internal and externalized workers to argue for changes in pay and working conditions. There are two reasons for this. First, extension of sectoral agreements combined with a high minimum wage meant the labor cost difference between subcontractors and in-house staff was not as high, at least for domestic outsourcing. Second, the large number of civil servants combined with strong employment protection laws made it difficult to spin off departments in a way that undermined workers' pay and conditions.

The unions also faced difficulties in developing a coherent approach to organizing or mobilizing workers around improving conditions across networked workplaces. A CFE-CGC representative—from the union representing managers—highlighted some differences in union approaches to outsourcing:

> If you want to get rid of subcontracting, you must get organized and we need to organize the work in a different way. We cannot both say no to outsourcing and no to opening call centers on Sundays and after eight o'clock in the evening. We cannot say at the same the time, we do not want to serve the customer and we do not want the company to find other ways to serve the customer. (CFE-CGC rep FT, July 1, 2010)

However, the presence (and high membership density) of more militant union confederations like the CGT and SUD within France Telecom meant that there was little chance of developing a union strategy of concession bargaining to bring work back in-house. The unions held the line on keeping their high social conditions and were not willing to increase flexibility in ways management demanded to make the workforce more "competitive" with the subcontractor sector. At the same time, the unions had very low membership density in subcontractors, and so their best chance of raising conditions for these external workers was in general efforts to strengthen legal protections at national level.

Italy (Telecom Italia)

Telecom Italia externalized work through a range of outsourcing, subsidiary, and agency contract strategies.[4] In Italy, similar to France, subcontractors were covered by sectoral agreements. However, bargaining coverage was lower (as the Italian state does not extend agreements in the same way as in France), and employers could typically choose which agreement to apply. For example, call centers could apply either the telecom, retail, or insurance agreements, with varying terms and conditions.

Between 2000 and 2004, Telecom Italia spun off a range of services to third-party subcontractors, including IT work, payroll services, car maintenance,

---

[4] The summary of the Italy case is based on research and a case study write-up by Chiara Benassi.

logistics, cleaning, and building maintenance. At the beginning, unions did not contest these decisions. One union representative observed:

> At the first externalization, there was not much alarm, neither among unions nor among the workers themselves. It was our fault, we didn't inform them enough, I don't know. At the beginning we were lukewarm. In 2001, we signed an industrial plan defining the core activities in order to set a limit to externalizations. At the time, we were accused of abandoning the workers outside the borders of the core. They were right, but it was a defensive strategy. It was not meant like "OK, all the others can go!" but it was just an attempt to protect the majority. (SLC-CGIL rep TI, March 23, 2012)

Other unionists argued that they were more consistently opposed to outsourcing. For example, an SLC representative claimed that the CGIL never signed an agreement to externalize business units—they only signed agreements for improving the working conditions of externalized workers (SLC-CGIL official, March 23, 2012). A FISTEL representative stated: "In most of the cases, at the beginning we did not bargain any agreement because we were politically against the externalizations" (FISTEL-CISL official, June 14, 2011).

One form of union support for externalized workers was to help them go to court to argue that the company had externalized units that were not functionally and economically independent from Telecom Italia—thus violating Italian legislation on outsourcing. If these companies did not survive after a few months or years, this meant that the company only wanted to get rid of failing business units. "You cannot pretend that the externalized company unit is autonomous if the workers do exactly the same job, with the same instruments or tools, in the same offices and work stations in the same position in the network hierarchy in terms of responsibilities, information, data" (SLC-CGIL official, March 23, 2012).

While many workers succeeded in winning their cases in court, the decision could take eight years, and workers needed to win yet again at the Court of Appeals to return to their jobs at Telecom Italia. Sometimes, when the company lost, management paid the salaries but did not let the workers come back to work. Sometimes lawyers had to start a new legal procedure every six months to make the company pay, because the money transfers would always stop. At the time of our research, there had been no cases where workers had been successfully rehired. "In these eight years these people have been reduced in terms of employment but, most of all, they have been devastated in their soul. The union rep [. . .] who spoke at the meeting . . . well, I'm not saying that he was crying, but I could actually say it" (SLC-CGIL official, March 23, 2012).

In one example, thirty workers in Rome won their case, complaining that Telecom Italia had sold a call center back office to a subcontractor, but the workers had kept doing the same job and even remained in the same offices. The company announced thirty redundancies in the call center a few days later—"in revenge," according to unionists.

These legal wins only applied to those individuals who brought their cases to court. However, they did encourage some companies to be more cautious about outsourcing—for instance, the telecom company Wind decided not to externalize its technicians' unit in Bologna following court decisions favoring re-integration of workers, fearing that the well-unionized technicians would immediately go to court.

Telecom Italia also had started outsourcing call center work in the 1990s. Its collective agreement prescribed a fixed working time between 8 a.m. and 5 p.m., so to increase flexibility, management started using the subcontractor Atesia. Like most call center subcontractors at the time, Atesia initially hired most of its workers on freelance or "co.co.pro," project-based contracts that were introduced by law (*Pacchetto Treu*) in 1997 and were regulated by the Biagi law from 2003 until 2015. The definition of a "project" was broad and unclear, allowing abuse.[5] When workers were employed under a co.co.pro contract, employers had no obligations at the end of the "project," and social contributions (e.g., to cover health and other insurance benefits) were around half of those for standard work contracts. A representative from NIDIL, the CGIL union for atypical workers, observed:

> In call centers there is a legal fiction which allows the company to do it [use co.co.pros]. I (as the company) can say that you are formally—in reality, you are dependent and come every day for six hours in order to earn your monthly wage—but formally the call center can say that you are a co.co.pro who organizes her time autonomously and makes a certain amount of hours available for providing certain services. Thus, there is a completely different situation between law and reality, between what really happens and what's written in the contract that should happen. (NIDIL-CGIL official, June 14, 2011)

At Atesia, co.co.pro contracts had low pay—mainly based on performance—and social contributions were well below levels in the sectoral collective agreement. According to the Atesia workers' blog, the monthly compensation was up to 40% lower than the salaries for Telecom Italia's in-house call center agents.

---

[5] A labor market reform—the Jobs Act—defined more precisely the characteristics of project-based work to reduce the number of co.co.pros by January 2016.

In the early 2000s, Atesia workers started mobilizing against this practice with union support, organizing a series of demonstrations that were widely covered in the media. In 2005, in the wake of these protests, union representatives and Telecom Italia management negotiated an agreement aimed at improving Atesia workers' precarious conditions. Telecom Italia purchased 20% of Atesia, and then integrated the workers into its subsidiary Telecontact under permanent contracts. The agreement also required Atesia to convert around 4,000 freelancer (co.co.pro) contracts for its remaining workers into standard contracts—which were then covered by the telecom industry's sectoral agreement. At the same time, Atesia continued to employ many workers on project-based contracts who were not covered by this agreement.

The unions also mobilized around the high use of co.co.pros in call centers, with the aim of bringing this to the attention of the public and building support for legal reform. These campaigns encouraged the government to include provisions in its 2007 Financial Act that improved co.co.pros' social security benefits, increasing employers' pension contributions and introducing the right to maternity and sick leave. In addition, two legal ordinances came into force in 2006 and in 2008 that were intended to limit the use of these contracts—the Damiano Ordinances (*Circolari Damiano*). The first ordinance required inbound call center agents to be offered permanent contracts, because the work did not have the characteristics of an autonomous project. When the first Damiano ordinance was passed, Atesia asked the union confederations to bargain an agreement covering only those co.co.pros working on inbound contracts (excluding, for example, outbound agents). However, they refused this compromise. Atesia subsequently agreed to transition the freelance contracts of inbound call center agents to permanent part-time contracts at a lower pay grade (Panici 2013).

The unions then pushed for a second ordinance covering outbound call center agents. They argued that this was necessary, not only because it was difficult to distinguish between the two, but also because this ambiguity was being exploited, with some outbound agents assigned inbound activities so that the company could continue using the project-based contracts. The second ordinance did not require outbound co.co.pros to be placed on permanent contracts but did require evidence of autonomous work. Call center and telecom companies were given one year to bargain the transition from atypical contracts with unions.

Atesia initially responded by moving all its co.co.pros (around 6,000) to permanent contracts, though mainly with part-time or apprenticeship status. But then it backtracked and started hiring co.co.pros again. The unions responded with a series of strikes and by helping individual workers bring their cases to court (Atesia 2008); and, again, Atesia was forced to transition the majority of its workforce onto permanent contracts. This presented some challenges in terms of staffing up or down. However, unions worked with management to find alternative ways to be flexible: for example, in October 2012, they signed an agreement on short-time work arrangements to avoid redundancies.

While the different Italian union confederations worked together to reduce precarity for this group of workers, interviewees also pointed out that there were ongoing conflicts between the more radical CGIL and social partnership-oriented CISL on how to approach negotiations over co.co.pros. In general, CGIL unions did not want to sign agreements for improving co.co.pros' working conditions where they judged the use of this kind of contract to be illegitimate or illegal. A representative of CGIL's union for atypical workers, NIDIL, explained:

> In a call center where you answer and make phone calls, there is no autonomy so we are not going to make any agreement for regulating the labor costs. The only agreement we do is the transition to a standard contract, because there is the risk to legitimate the co.co.pro contracts otherwise. Therefore, exchanging "working conditions for legitimation" is unthinkable for us. We do not bargain for increasing the salaries by one euro and then remain trapped in that contract typology. At this point, the advice I'm giving to you from a personal, political, and union perspective is: You will get the money back including the interest rates. [. . .] Where there are bandits, I do not bargain with bandits, I'll send them to the police; and after the police, there is the labor inspector; and if it's not the labor inspector it is INPS [National Institute for Social Insurance and Welfare] which is going to fine them! (NIDIL-CGIL official, June 14, 2011)

In 2004, there was an agreement for call center agents on project-based contracts, negotiated by the three confederal unions for atypical workers and the employer association Assocallcenter, which set minimum pay levels at around 8.50 euros per hour. Unfortunately, as observed by a representative of ALAI, CISL's union for atypical workers:

> It's not been enforced, it's not been applied, workers cannot get upset because they do not get the contracts renewed. And if you have the choice between remaining at home or standing up for your rights. . . . (ALAI-CISL official, June 13, 2011)

While the ALAI unionist attributed the failure of this agreement to a lack of bargaining power among these freelance workers, FISTEL-CISL unionists felt that the "ideological" approach of CGIL prevented unions from working together to enforce the contract. According to them, the CGIL feared these contracts because they could contradict or call into question the application of sectoral collective agreements. This marked a real split, as CGIL refused to sign any agreement that opted out from the sectoral collective agreement, while CISL had been in favor of the decentralization of industrial relations. Thus, FISTEL-CISL signed a few company-level agreements separately from SLC-CGIL to improve the working conditions of co.co.pros in call centers. As a FISTEL unionist explained:

> We are for giving rights to those who do not have them, because while she waits for the collective labor agreement (CLA), she might never be able to get it. Then we go step by step, thinking that in the future the sales activity of the company will consolidate, and we will be able to bargain a national agreement. But at the moment, we have at least improved the conditions of 150 workers. (FISTEL-CISL official, June 14, 2011)

The unions worked together more consistently within Telecom Italia, including on a campaign to reduce the use of agency work within Telecom Italia's call center subsidiary, Telecontact. Telecontact was set up in 2001, with an explicit goal to reduce labor costs for internal call center workers. Its call centers were located in greenfield sites in southern Italy (Napoli, Caltanissetta, and Catanzaro) to get tax discounts from the government. It also had lower wage rates, as it followed only the sectoral telecom agreement. A company agreement was negotiated after a few years, but it only added variable pay linked to company profitability. The workforce was also younger than was typical at Telecom Italia, which allowed workers to be assigned to lower salary levels (SLC-CGIL official, June 15, 2011). An HR manager at Telecom Italia described the strategy:

> The idea was to try to be more competitive and at the same time to maintain call center jobs within the perimeters of the Telecom Italia group. [. . .] We hired a young workforce and all part-time, an ideal condition in terms of stress management of call center jobs and of distribution of working time according to traffic peaks. (TI HR manager, May 14, 2012)

Similar to other incumbents, these lower costs were used to put pressure on the in-house workforce. An SLC unionist observed: "Obviously Telecom Italia uses Telecontact for telling its call center workers 'Look at that! You'll end up there too!'" (SLC-CGIL official, June 15, 2011).

Telecontact also initially hired workers on fixed-term training and agency contracts to increase flexibility. Its 2001 collective agreement permitted 30% of the workforce to be employed on agency contracts. This was much higher than in other areas of the company. As in the other European cases, Italy has legislation requiring equal pay and treatment of agency workers. However, in contrast to the United Kingdom—which, as described above, allowed exceptions for "pay between assignments" contracts—these regulations were more encompassing and consistently applied, with national equal treatment legislation in place since the 1990s. The collective agreement also established a special fund for unemployment benefits and training. When agency workers had a permanent contract with their agency, they were entitled to receive 800 euros/month and to attend vocational training classes while they waited for their next contract. At the same time, equal pay referred to the wage levels set in sectoral collective agreements; thus, agency workers were not eligible for social benefits and variable pay in company-level agreements.

In 2008, the unions negotiated a new agreement to shift 300 of the company's agency workers onto permanent contracts. By 2012, there were no agency workers in the call center subsidiary. This was the result, according to unionists, of a concerted campaign that benefited from high union density (40%–50%) and strong worker support.

The different campaigns described above had the combined effect of raising pay and improving working conditions in the call center subcontractor sector and, in particular, at a major Telecom Italia subcontractor and subsidiary. They were also associated with some internalization of call center work, with only minor initial concessions for internalized workers that were later mitigated by the union. Thus, Italy represents an unusual case where worker representatives succeeded in extending negotiated and legal protections to externalized workers, effectively shrinking the cost differential between internal and external labor.

In the field and network technician area, Telecom Italia had long used subcontractors for network construction, installation, and maintenance. According to a Telecom Italia HR manager: "The installation you do only once, it's more self-evident and requires some machines and tools . . . for instance, Telecom Italia does not do the digging of cables anymore, it is subcontracted to specialized companies with the right machines" (TI HR manager, May 14, 2012). The company's main subcontractor was Sielte which used to belong to Ericsson. Sielte applied the metal agreement until April 2011, when it switched to the telecom sectoral agreement. Most of its workers were on permanent and full-time contracts, but it often used short-time work arrangements (*cassa integrazione*). Telecom Italia also subcontracted network maintenance and repair to Sirti, which was under the metal agreement and had lower pay and working conditions. An HR manager observed, "It is clear that these companies do not have second-level [company-level] agreements and so they have lower labor costs than Telecom Italia. And they can use workers with precarious working arrangements" (TI HR manager, May 14, 2012).

Telecom Italia's unions did seek to reduce precarity associated with subcontracting technician work. However, their campaigns in this area were not as public (and also not as successful) as in call centers. The unions had long tried to negotiate clauses requiring subcontracting companies to hire workers who were made redundant from client companies and to apply the same sectoral agreement as their clients. Italian unions find it difficult to say publicly that one sectoral agreement is worse than another, as their confederation statutes require them to achieve similar bargaining results. However, the terms of agreements always differ because power relations are uneven at the sectoral level. Thus, unions saw the goal of extending sectoral agreements across a company's value chain as an important part of strategies to reduce wage dumping:

> Unionist A: "Because, at least, we eliminate doubt about labor costs and then it would allow us to represent all the...."
> Unionist B: "All the value chain."
> Unionist A: "The ambition to represent all workers along the value chain is clearly very strong." (SLC-CGIL officials, March 23, 2012)

A second reason for extending agreements from the client company to its subcontractors was to ensure that the same sectoral union (for each of the three union confederations) represented workers carrying out the same jobs, to reduce competitive benchmarking of wages and conditions. Union representatives recognized that the division of responsibility across different sectoral unions (even if coordinated within a confederation) created communication challenges, as well as real conflicts of interest that could undermine solidarity. An SLC unionist observed:

> If the subcontractor is under the same contract, you [as a union] also have more responsibility regarding what happens in Telecom Italia, which might affect the subcontractor. It happened recently with Sielte that we internalized the maintenance of poles. That was positive for Telecom Italia but very negative for Sielte workers, who were in *Cassa integrazione* [short-time work arrangements]. If everyone is under the same collective agreement, you also feel in charge to redefine the order with Telecom Italia for ensuring employment at the subcontractor. (SLC-CGIL official, March 23, 2012)

One example of a challenge associated with this division across unions and agreements was the difficulty in mobilizing Telecom Italia technicians when subcontractors faced redundancy:

> Telecom Italia workers see them [technician subcontractors] as unfair competition. And when we go to meetings with Telecom Italia workers, their request is always to re-internalize the jobs. And on this point, in comparison with an autonomous union which can focus only on Telecom Italia, we are a confederal

union so we have to watch out, because we defend all workers not only the workers at Telecom Italia. (SLC-CGIL official, March 23, 2012)

While the unions recognized that this was an important goal, efforts to establish a framework for bargaining across the value chain had not yet been successful. Negotiations of the telecom agreement in the early 2010s stopped because the unions and management could not reach agreement on the subcontracting provisions the unions wanted to introduce. According to an HR manager at Telecom Italia:

> There is an attempt by the unions to put obstacles to the company in its use of an external workforce. This is one of the main difficulties in the ongoing negotiation round. From a union perspective, this is a necessity; from a company perspective, this is a serious limitation to the strategic freedom of the employer. Setting limitations for us is very difficult. There are some companies such as ours with some commitment to inform the union. But one thing is informing the union, another is to limit us in our freedom of action. (TI HR manager, May 14, 2012)

Summary

Both France Telecom and Telecom Italia outsourced a portion of their call center and technician jobs, while Telecom Italia shifted call center work to a lower cost subsidiary. In both cases, subcontractors and subsidiaries were covered by sectoral collective agreements, but generally with lower pay and conditions and (in Italy) heavy use of more precarious non-standard contracts. Unions in both cases sought to approach the problem of precarity and inequality associated with these strategies through re-internalizing work, with some success in both cases for call center jobs. However, unlike in the cases of AT&T, BT, Deutsche Telekom, and TDC (which also re-internalized jobs), these were not associated with major concessions by unions. This may be in part attributed to unions' greater institutional presence across the value chains of companies, with the same union confederations organizing workers in, or at least negotiating sectoral agreements covering, subcontractors and temporary agencies. Thus, externalization did not move work outside of union confederations' representation domains. There were also weaker cost-based incentives to externalize jobs, particularly in France, where strong formal job security gave companies less leverage for demanding concessions.

Put in the terms of my framework, constraints on exit from encompassing collective agreements and support for collective worker voice across vertically disintegrated value chains increased worker power to resist market-based benchmarking of employment terms and conditions. A further important factor was the relative strength of more militant unions known for their class-based ideologies, in multi-union bargaining systems. Both the France Telecom and Telecom Italia cases showed that these unions were unwilling to compromise on concessions within the incumbent. This could bring them into conflict with more conservative or partnership oriented unions.

A more significant difference between the two cases concerns union efforts to organize externalized workers and companies. In both countries, unions stated that bringing up conditions across the value chain was a central goal. However, Telecom Italia's unions were more directly involved in mobilizing their members across organizational boundaries, with the goal of improving conditions for temporary, freelance, and subcontracted workers. Unionists at Telecom Italia also reflected more on the challenges and longer-term objectives associated with building solidarity across unions and the different groups of workers they represented. They saw the challenge as one of overcoming what were often structural labor divides along value chains, and they were seeking solutions that tackled those divides through collective bargaining, legal action, and court cases. Thus, compared to the French case, where unions overcame their ideological differences to mobilize jointly against forced mobility and "management by stress" at France Telecom, Italian unions developed more creative and often militant strategies of inclusive solidarity outside of the incumbent. They faced many challenges, but were using a wide range of institutional, legal, and organizational resources to pursue greater equity across Telecom Italia's increasingly disorganized value chains.

Structural Inclusive Solidarity: Austria and Sweden

Both A1 and Telia were in countries and sectors where encompassing institutions constrained employer exit, through extending agreement terms or legislated social standards to subcontractors, temporary agencies, and subsidiaries. Both cases had strong support for collective voice in those workplaces. They also had low "union representation domain overlap" (Table 2.4), with either a clear division of responsibility between unions (A1) or all unions present in the incumbent and sector (Telia)—in both cases underpinning highly coordinated collective bargaining. These conditions were most favorable to ensuring that employers were less able to exploit outsourcing to increase precarity across the networked workforce. Management did externalize jobs, in some cases finding loopholes that allowed lower pay and conditions. However, unions were able to draw on coordinated bargaining to close these loopholes and re-regulate work.

Austria (A1)

At A1, the combination of encompassing collective bargaining through a sectoral agreement and inter-union cooperation between the incumbent's union GPF and the service sector union GPA constrained opportunities for employers to externalize work. Within A1, agency workers were widely used to gain flexibility in hiring and firing, as the permanent workforce enjoyed strong job security due to the large number of civil servants. Nearly 70% of the call center workforce were on temporary contracts, which were often renewed indefinitely. These temporary workers, however, were both unionized and entitled to the same employment terms and conditions as the permanent in-house workforce because of strong equal pay and treatment provisions in national law and collective agreements.

A1 still gained some savings from agency workers' lower dismissal costs and less generous pensions and benefits. However, the labor cost differential was significantly smaller than that associated with outsourcing or offshoring at many of the other incumbent companies. Management was not able to benchmark costs between external and internal groups of workers to argue for concessions because these cost differences were marginal. In addition, external workers were not widely perceived as undermining standards, because they were covered by strong institutional and negotiated protections.

In interviews, worker representatives noted that they were not happy with the high use of agency work, particularly the practice of keeping workers on these contracts for long periods of time: "For me, this is not satisfactory, because I think it's sick that you need agency workers at all. But when you're in the stock market, financially driven, it looks better, as though you were slimmer" (works councilor A1, October 26, 2011). At the same time, the union and works council were able to represent agency workers' interests, organizing them to join the union and intervening on their behalf in employment disputes. In one case described by the works councilor cited above, a temporary worker was dismissed "because management did not like him" (works councilor A1, October 26, 2011) and the works council succeeded in getting him reinstated.

Many services that telecom companies subcontracted were in GPA-represented industries, which also ensured their coverage through existing bargaining structures. Call center subcontractors were incorporated into the "miscellaneous business services" agreement in the late 1990s. This established a parallel structure of wage increases to those in the telecom sector, in line with productivity growth (Holst 2008, 36).

This collective bargaining system was not free of exit options. Sectoral collective agreements in subcontracted service industries like call centers did typically have lower pay and conditions compared to established industries like telecommunications. In addition, service employers made extensive use of a special category of freelance contracts to introduce more varied terms and conditions. A survey in the mid-2000s showed that 34% of the call center workforce in Austria was on these contracts (Shire et al. 2009, 445). These workers were considered self-employed and thus were not covered by collective agreements.

The GPA placed a high priority on closing this legal loophole, and had the capacity to do so as the major union responsible for "nearly all private sector white-collar employees" (Pernicka 2005, 215). The union set up the interest group work@flex to represent freelance workers and other employees on atypical contracts and to campaign for extending legislated employment protections to these workers. The GPA worked together with the regional health insurers, which began to investigate freelance contracts from 2005, conducting a nationwide audit. The audit established that the contracts were often used to evade social security contributions and minimum terms and conditions defined in collective agreements. Employers found to be abusing freelance contracts had to make retroactive social security contributions and wage payments. The union also persuaded the WKÖ to give up its resistance to legislative change, and in 2008 the national insurance law was amended to require most freelance contracts to be converted into standard employment contracts. This contributed to a radical decline in their use. In call centers, according to one interviewee, "they practically don't exist anymore. We have done away with this almost entirely. There may still be 10% where that still exists, but as soon as we find them, we'll change that" (GPA official, January 27, 2015).

Encompassing bargaining and strong inter-union cooperation were also resources for the GPF in preserving centralized collective bargaining at A1. The GPF and GPA negotiated a provision in both A1's company agreement and the telecom sectoral agreements that extended their terms automatically to subsidiaries and spun-off subcontractors:

> We wanted to prevent a flight from the collective agreement, where there would be different agreements. And so, in the first or second collective agreement [...] we negotiated a passage that the GPF also adopted, which says that collective agreements are also valid for companies that have been spun off and that provide services chiefly for the parent company. (works councilor A1, June 23, 2014)

This provision made it difficult for all telecom companies to introduce varied terms and conditions across their production chains—thus establishing encompassing rules across subsidiaries and major subcontractors.

Sweden (Telia)

In Sweden, unions could not rely on automatic extension mechanisms as in Austria, but traditionally used high membership rates and recourse to strikes and secondary boycotts to encourage employers to follow agreements. Telia was a member of the employer association Almega IT&Telecom, which negotiated one encompassing sectoral agreement. Major service subcontractors working for telecom companies were also members of either Almega IT&Telecom or employer associations affiliated with the larger Almega organization.

Similar to Austria, encompassing bargaining in the Swedish telecom and subcontractor industries both supported and was supported by a union structure that promoted inter-union cooperation at both levels. Telia employees were members of Seko in the blue-collar LO confederation, Unionen in the white-collar TCO confederation, and several small unions in the academic and professional confederation Saco. However, each union formally represented different occupational groups, limiting competition for members. The presence of one sectoral agreement for telecommunications and a central agreement with Telia at the corporate group level provided a strong platform for cooperation.

These unions also represented employees in other industries providing subcontracting services to the major telecom companies. IT and technician service subcontractors followed the telecom agreement or a similar IT agreement negotiated by Unionen and Saco. Call center subcontractors were members of an Almega association negotiating an agreement with Unionen. This structure allowed close coordination, with pattern bargaining focused on similar jobs. For example, negotiation over the telecom agreement occurred in the spring, and then Unionen would seek to achieve similar gains (with a high degree of success) in its negotiations with call center subcontractors later in the year. Most staffing agencies were also covered by collective agreements, and union representatives in telecom companies typically negotiated local agreements requiring identical terms and conditions for these workers. Union representatives observed that shop stewards at major telecom and call center companies were able to demand that all agency workers be covered by collective agreements.

Other employers applied the terms of industry agreements to both attract employees and to avoid public scrutiny and conflict with the unions. This also gave employers an incentive to either join the employer association, or to negotiate company-level agreements with the major unions, applying similar terms. Union officials noted that the threat of strikes served to maintain high bargaining coverage in sectors with weaker union presence, such as call center subcontractors. This, in turn, increased the reluctance of large employers to contract with companies that did not adhere to agreements: "The bigger the call centers become ... they are as well demanding that they have to have something that is going to make the peace so there won't be a strike" (Unionen official, February 14, 2014)

Unionen helped to organize a large strike in 2013, in a call center subcontractor that had refused to negotiate a collective agreement. Although the center was closed and its workers laid off, the campaign was viewed as a success by the union, gaining wide media attention and the intervention of the Swedish Ministry of Industry and Trade. This subsequently became an example for other companies that might be tempted to avoid collective bargaining.

The labor cost differences were also low between internal and external call center workers because of encompassing legislation and collective bargaining. Temporary agency workers were covered by strong equal pay and treatment rules, as well as by collective agreements, with high union density in this sector overall. In addition, most major call center subcontractors were signatories to their industry's sectoral collective agreement and had strong local union representation. Union representatives estimated that the pay difference between call center workers at Telia and at major subcontractors was between 2,000 and 5,000 krona/month, or US$1.40 to US$3.40/hour lower base pay. However, subcontractors also typically had a higher sales commission component that narrowed this gap. In addition, the broader terms of the agreements were similar, with some stronger provisions in the call center agreement, such as prohibitions on split schedules.

These relatively small differences meant that management could not easily use the benchmarking of labor costs to demand pay concessions. Because externalized workers were covered by collective agreements, the union did not view externalization as a major threat to broader equity goals or to sustaining union membership. At the same time, union representatives at Telia were concerned with the expansion of subcontracting and agency work in different time periods, and so also tried to encourage some re-internalization.

Around 2,000 call center employees were transferred to subcontractors between 1998 and 1999, when the company went through a major consolidation of its call center operations. Telia then gradually replaced subcontractors with temporary agency workers. By 2011, 40% of the workforce in customer service jobs and 30% in sales or support jobs were on temporary contracts. The union tried to convince management to internalize these workers, using the business case that the permanent workforce's customer service quality and productivity were higher:

> Three to four years ago we had perhaps a thousand or more by Manpower for instance. We of course wanted them to be employed by the company. [...] We said, employ them in-house instead. I think they, the management, decided to

do that because they noticed that the quality that they get from the employees was bigger if they are employed by us. [. . .] The company said: we are getting much higher customer satisfaction if we employ them ourselves, even if it costs a little bit more. (Unionen rep Telia, October 27, 2014)

By 2015, the proportion of agency workers in Telia's call centers had declined to 18% as more of these workers were shifted to permanent contracts.

Another constraint on exit concerned provisions in central collective agreements that did not permit the company to alter pay and conditions of employees who were moved to subsidiaries, or to introduce systematic differences in conditions across subsidiaries—similar to A1. In addition, when workplaces were sold or spun off, the terms of collective agreements were typically extended, while the union responsible for the spun-off employees remained unchanged.

Telia engaged in a series of spin-offs involving business and technician services. In 2001, Telia formed two separate units made up of business areas or companies that they planned to sell off as "non-core" businesses: the Telefos Group with business services and the Orbiant Group with field and network technician services. These business units were then sold and spun off as separate companies, many of which continued to contract with Telia. For example, Eltel and Relacom became the two largest subcontractors responsible for network construction, repair, and servicing.

These spin-offs transferred close to 11,000 employees to subcontractors between 2001 and 2007. However, the process was carried out in a largely cooperative way, preserving pay, conditions, and union representation. According to a union official, the local trade unions were closely involved at all stages:

> All these persons, they were moving from Telia to the new companies. And they looked after it so everyone would have a job after they . . . when Telia sold it, all the people had these possibilities. But if they worked for Telia and were moved to this new company, and they don't want to move to this new company, they had special solutions for them. For instance, early retirement, they had possibilities to be educated. And they also could receive money to go out of the company and have [. . .] two years of payment. (SEKO rep Telia, May 28, 2012)

The collective agreements moved with employees—under Swedish law, employees continued to be covered by agreements for one year following a transfer of ownership—and then they could be moved onto new company agreements (but with the same basic pay scale, pension rights, etc.—under the Almega telecom sector agreement). In addition, Telia required its subcontractors to sign up to the central collective agreement:

There is an agreement, for example, at Telia, they say: "if you're going to work for us a subcontractor, you have to sign the agreement, so that we know working conditions are in order." So they call us and tell us they want the agreement. [. . .] Telia is so powerful and if they put that in as a condition for subcontractors, they will make sure to fulfill that requirement to please them. (SEKO rep Telia, June 17, 2015)

At the time of my main field research, in 2010–2012, Telia divided up its network and field technician work across four subcontractors: Eltel, Relacom, Npower (Finnish), and MTS (owned by Ericksson). While each company used to specialize, either by service or by region, they were all competing with each other for a larger share of Telia's business—trying to sell the company complementary services as "bundles." Eltel and Relacom were particularly dependent: for example, around 40%–50% of Eltel's business was from Telia. This put pressure on union representatives and employees, who were expected to help their company compete through cost reduction and quality improvement.

As a result, there was some increase in precarity associated with a move from internal employment to externalized, subcontracted jobs. A Seko shop steward working for one of the technician subcontractors observed that job content and opportunities for advancement had changed:

There have been a lot of changes, we also see pressures. We can see that when we were state-owned, we could be more flexible in our work: a technician could start out doing work that was not so advanced, then we can work up to be more advanced and more flexible. There were opportunities in a big company for further training, career advancement, for doing different kinds of jobs. Now the companies are smaller, they have more of a division of labor: I just repair copper cables, I can't get a better salary or work up to a better job, so it is not as good as it was before. And we can also see that we do the work much faster there and don't need the same amounts of people doing the work. So it has gotten more efficient, but at the cost of the workers. (SEKO rep subcontractor, August 9, 2011)

It was difficult for interviewees to compare the pay structure at the new companies with the previous pay structure for technicians. A shop steward at another of Telia's subcontractors estimated that starting salary for "new technicians" without experience was slightly lower than it had been under Telia, while experienced technicians had similar pay levels. "We are not the same technicians that we were ten years ago. But in principle we have the same pay, it is not different in that way" (SEKO rep subcontractor, May 10, 2012).

Employees also experienced some reduction in job security. One way that this occurred was through the replacement of permanent contracts with temporary contracts. In 2005, the temporary staffing agency Manpower launched "Manpower Network Services," and Relacom downsized its staff—many of whom got jobs at Manpower and then were sent back to Relacom as agency employees on temporary contracts (Geary et al. 2010). This appeared to be a model that all of the subcontractors followed. A shop steward from one subcontractor estimated that 25%–30% of their workforce were employed through temporary agencies (SEKO rep subcontractor, May 10, 2012). Another was working for a temporary staffing company through this arrangement but was posted almost exclusively at her former employer: "[Subcontractor] let me go, and then I took a job with [staffing company] who rent me back to the company that sacked me" (SEKO rep subcontractor, August 9, 2011).

She explained that this model had been adopted because the volume of work changes over the year. There was a particularly large decline in labor demand during the winter in her area of network repair, as it is difficult to repair or replace buried network cables when the ground is frozen. However, the collective agreement required the company to pay temporary workers the same salary as permanent workers doing similar work. The union also was able to negotiate a new collective agreement at her employer in 2010–2011 in response to concerns with the large number of employees made redundant and then rehired through temporary staffing agencies: "the new rule is that after a while when you've been laid off, if the company needs a worker, they need to ask you first." At some companies, there was an agreement stating that the company could not hire temporary agency workers until nine months had passed after layoffs; and within that time period, employees who were laid off had to be rehired if there was a need for additional staff.

Agency employees also had some degree of job and salary security, as they were on "permanent contracts" with their temporary agency and received 90% of their salary during the time when no work was available in their area—again based on a collective agreement. These were the "pay between assignment" contracts that had been envisioned by the European Union's Swedish derogation from equal pay rules. However, unlike the UK case described above, in Sweden these contracts actually provided strong job security and a possibility of equal conditions. This meant that the agency shared some of the risk of business fluctuations or seasonal changes in labor demand with the employee. The union official working for the temporary agency explained that her employer and its competitors were able to do this because the agencies were often large and diversified, providing a range of services to client companies. One important service in the Swedish context is managing retraining and job placement for companies going through downsizing. This allowed them to absorb some of the risk associated with permanent contracts and salary guarantees, while providing "flexible" labor to their clients.

Summary

The Austrian and Swedish cases both show some degree of increased precarity associated with the externalization of call center and technician jobs. But they also stand out among the ten cases as those where unions had the greatest success in extending encompassing institutional protections to workers in these externalized jobs and across value chains. This effectively prevented employer exit from union agreements and strengthened collective worker voice for internal and externalized workers. In both cases, strong and sustained inter-union cooperation played a central role in outcomes—within collective bargaining systems supportive of what I have termed "structural inclusive solidarity." Although several major unions represented telecom employees in each country, these unions developed a relatively clear division of responsibility and coordinated their negotiations of company or sectoral agreements. This cooperation, in turn, was crucial to sustaining encompassing institutions in the face of the restructuring strategies of employers aimed at externalizing and differentiating employment contracts across companies and workplaces.

Comparing Strategies and Outcomes

The case study companies externalized call center and technician work through three alternative strategies: ownership of dedicated subsidiaries, use of temporary agencies, and subcontracting to third-party firms—with some use of offshore subcontracting in call centers. The shift of work to service subsidiaries is a partial form of externalization; although these subsidiaries were still owned by the incumbents, they typically were organized as internal subcontractors, responsible for selling call center services to their parent company and, in some cases, to other companies.

Figures 5.1 and 5.2 illustrate the proportion of call center and technician work externalized in the early 2010s through these different strategies by each company (where figures were available).

Figure 5.1 shows that TDC, Deutsche Telekom, Telecom Italia, and Orange Polska used dedicated subsidiaries for call centers, with all consumer-segment call center jobs at Deutsche Telekom and Orange Polska located in these

EXTERNALIZATION 235

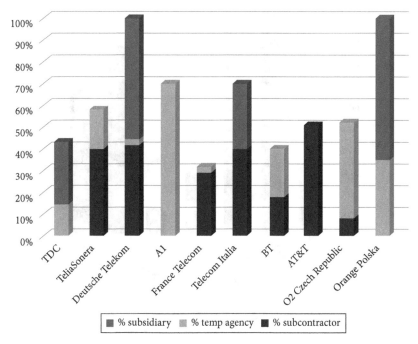

Figure 5.1. Estimated percentages of employees externalized in call centers (consumer segment), 2010–2012.

Notes: These figures are based on estimates provided by interviewees, who differed in their ability to give precise numbers of jobs externalized in each category. The reference year differs among the cases but is roughly in the 2010–2012 period. The percentage subcontracted at Telecom Italia is a conservative estimate, with up to 70% of call volume subcontracted in some areas of work. Temporary agency workers at Deutsche Telekom, Telecom Italia, and Orange Polska were used in the subsidiaries, whereas those at other companies were used in internal call centers. The figures for percentage subcontracted at France Telecom, BT, and AT&T include both domestic and offshore subcontracting.

subsidiaries. TDC, Telia, A1, BT, Orange Polska, and O2 Czech Republic used moderate to high numbers of agency staff in their internal call centers; Deutsche Telekom, France Telecom, and Telecom Italia used small numbers of agency staff; and AT&T did not use temporary agencies. Those companies that relied on moderate to high levels of subcontracting (20%–50% of jobs) primarily used either domestic subcontractors (Deutsche Telekom and Telecom Italia) or offshore BPO vendors (France Telecom, BT, and AT&T). TDC, Telia, A1, and Orange Polska did not subcontract (in this time period), and O2 Czech Republic subcontracted fewer than 10% of jobs.

In Figure 5.2 we see different patterns—with only Deutsche Telekom moving a substantial share of field technician work to a dedicated service subsidiary. Other companies, such as Telia, had established technician subsidiaries in the past, but

236   EXIT, VOICE, AND SOLIDARITY

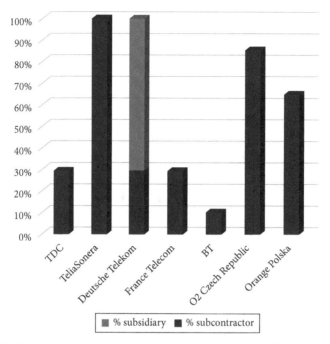

Figure 5.2. Estimated percentages of employees externalized in field technician services, 2010–2012.

Notes: These figures are based on estimates provided by interviewees, who differed in their ability to give precise numbers of jobs externalized in each category. The reference year differs among the cases but is roughly in the 2010–2012 period.

later spun off these jobs to subcontractors. Telia, O2 Czech Republic, and Orange Polska stand out as having subcontracted all or a majority of their field technician services to a third party. Interestingly, TDC, Deutsche Telekom, and France Telecom all used subcontractors for around 30% of jobs in field technician services, with BT the lowest at 10%—which unionists attributed to historic union strength in this part of the company. In the cases not shown in the figure (A1, Telecom Italia, AT&T), our interviews suggest that some portion of field technician work was outsourced—with lowest rates at A1, moderate at Telecom Italia, and high at AT&T.[6]

These figures illustrate the common trends described in the case studies: all incumbents adopted different combinations of these externalization strategies

---

[6] Outsourcing of technician services could also vary significantly by district at AT&T due to historic differences in collective agreements. For example, there was greater contractual jurisdiction over network construction at ATT Southeast and ATT West compared to ATT Midwest or ATT Southwest.

for both areas of service work. Many of the differences in the amount and form of externalization can be attributed to the specific institutional environment, with different opportunities to exit encompassing minimum standards, as well as to gain cost savings or flexibility not available in-house. For example, TDC was historically able to pay agency workers lower wage rates because they were covered by lower-cost collective agreements. In contrast, at Deutsche Telekom, the mostly non-union subcontractors had much lower pay and conditions compared to agency workers, who were covered by equal pay rules. Constraints on exit from internal employment could also affect the form of externalization. Deutsche Telekom's strong job security and location security agreements encouraged management to first shift call center and technician jobs into subsidiaries, in some cases later selling these to subcontractors. O2 Czech Republic represents a contrasting case in which weak job security allowed the company to externalize by downsizing its call center workforce while simultaneously increasing its use of temporary agencies, some of which hired former O2 Czech Republic workers, and to lay off most technicians when transferring their jobs to subcontractors. These types of institutionally influenced cost factors exerted some influence over externalization strategies at each of the companies.

The comparison also shows that all of the case studies kept a portion of call center work in-house (often a majority), or at least in a subsidiary controlled by the parent company (e.g., at Deutsche Telekom and Orange Polska). This suggests that service and sales are seen as having some strategic value. Technician services are more varied, with several companies outsourcing most or all of these jobs. However, the cases that spun off their technician units maintained strong control over companies that were often highly dependent on the incumbent. Most of the incumbents used a blended model, relying on subcontracting mostly for short-term projects and demand peaks, lower skilled work, or to service and install connections for competitors' customers on their networks.

In line with the broader concerns of this book, a central question in comparing the cases is how these externalization strategies—which moved jobs into more market-based employment relationships—affected worker precarity. This has several components. One is the precarity of internal employees, whose jobs are affected by spin-offs to subsidiaries or subcontractors, replacement by temporary or subcontractor employees, and concessions aimed at bringing more work back in-house. A second is precarity and inequality across the value chain: as work was externalized, how did pay and conditions compare to those in-house? The cases above show that these two outcomes were closely related, as a large gap in pay and conditions often drove concessions linked to exit threats by employers.

First, Table 5.1 compares restructuring measures that targeted existing in-house workers, through directly transferring call center and technician jobs to subcontractors and subsidiaries (either through transfer of undertakings or layoffs directly linked to the shift of jobs).

This comparison shows some variation across the four groups of cases, but also within each group. O2 Czech Republic, Orange Polska, Deutsche Telekom, TDC, and Telia all spun off part of their existing call center and/or technician workforce. While these measures led to downgrading of pay and conditions for affected workers in all cases, the negative impact was much less at Telia. At AT&T, BT, France Telecom, Telecom Italia, and A1, work was externalized more gradually, and thus outsourcing or use of agency workers was more difficult to directly connect to the ongoing redundancies at each company (see Chapter 3).

Another point of comparison concerns the inequality these externalization measures introduced across different groups of internal and externalized workers. We were only able to gather systematic data on pay for call centers to map these patterns of inequality. Figure 5.3 illustrates starting, typical, and top pay levels for in-house call centers, call center subsidiaries or second-tier contracts, and subcontractors where these figures were available. Pay levels for agency workers are included where these rates were allowed to deviate from those for equivalent permanent jobs. At A1 and O2 Czech Republic, we only had pay figures for in-house call centers, and we were not able to obtain pay data from Orange Polska.

This shows that two of the structural exclusive solidarity cases, AT&T and BT, and the representation domain divide cases, TDC and Deutsche Telekom, were distinctive in having very high pay for their in-house call center workers, as well as high inequality between in-house and externalized jobs. While we were not able to get comparative pay data for subcontractors in the Czech Republic and Poland, our interviews suggest that these similarly had lower pay rates compared to in-house workers. The ideological divide and structural inclusive solidarity cases had lower and/or more compressed pay scales for in-house staff, and smaller differences compared to pay rates for externalized groups of workers.

In addition, Figure 5.3 illustrates the large impact that concessionary or second-tier agreements had in reducing pay levels in these four high-inequality cases (at least for some groups of internal workers). TDC's subsidiary Call Center Europe had pay rates similar to those at subcontractors. Deutsche Telekom's call center subsidiary DTKS, BT's new lower-tier job titles, and AT&T's new call centers under the Internet Services Agreement all paid 30%–50% less compared to past agreements. As the case summaries above showed, all of these agreements were strongly influenced by employer benchmarking of labor costs and terms of collective agreements or individual contracts for similar externalized call center jobs.

Table 5.1 Worker Impact of Measures to Externalize Call Center and Technician Jobs (2000–2015)

Company	Measures to Externalize Call Center and Technician Jobs	Associated Changes in Pay and Conditions for Externalized Workers
Structural exclusive solidarity		
AT&T	Ongoing shift of work to subcontractors (including offshore)	N/A
BT	2003: 2,000 call center jobs offshored to India	Ongoing redundancies
O2 Czech Republic	2005–2011: 2,000 technician jobs outsourced	500 technicians transferred (maintained conditions for 2 years); others dismissed and often rehired by subcontractors at lower pay and without a union agreement
Orange Polska	(1) 2002: 6,000 technician jobs outsourced (2) 2010: all call center jobs transferred to subsidiary	(1) All technicians allowed to transfer at 15% wage cut + "financial inducements" from Orange Polska; majority took (generous) voluntary redundancy. Those transferred later experienced further wage cuts, layoffs, with no union agreement. (2) Two-year employment guarantee, no reduction in salary or pension (after union mobilization); new company-level agreement with Orange Polska unions
Representation domain divides		
Deutsche Telekom	(1) 2006–2008: 1,800 call center employees outsourced (2) 2008: 1,600 technicians outsourced (3) 2007: 50,000 technician and call center jobs transferred to subsidiaries	(1) Pay for transferred employees cut by one-third (immediately or after 2 years, depending on subcontractor); conditions also lower and some center closings; move to cheaper ver.di subcontractor agreement or no agreement (2) Pay and conditions secured for 3 years, with 1-year job security; move from ver.di to IG Metall agreement (3) 10% pay cut for existing employees; 30% lower starting pay; new company-level agreement with ver.di
TDC	2014: 800 call center employees outsourced	Reduction in pay and terms and conditions (after 1-year transition); shift to cheaper HK-negotiated agreement

(*continued*)

Table 5.1 Continued

Company	Measures to Externalize Call Center and Technician Jobs	Associated Changes in Pay and Conditions for Externalized Workers
Ideological divides		
France Telecom	Ongoing shift of work to subcontractors, temp agencies	N/A
Telecom Italia	Ongoing shift of work to subcontractors, temp agencies, subsidiaries	N/A
Structural inclusive solidarity		
A1	Ongoing shift of work to temp agencies	N/A
Telia	4,500 technicians outsourced	Transferred employees maintained terms and conditions; stayed under telecom sectoral agreement; some work intensification, reduced job security

Note: N/A, not applicable.

Table 5.2 compares the outcome of these negotiations between unions and management associated with re-internalizing call center jobs. Here I focus on the ten-year period from 2005 to 2015.

This shows that seven of the incumbents moved jobs that had been externalized back in-house. In four of these cases—AT&T, BT, TDC, and Deutsche Telekom—these changes were associated with negotiated concessions aimed at re-internalizing call center jobs or preventing further outsourcing. The remaining three cases—France Telecom, Telecom Italia, and Telia—show more minor or no concessions. Again, it is noteworthy that the cases with major concessionary agreements are those in which the unions faced both large gaps in pay, conditions, and union representation between in-house and subcontracted or agency workers and significant challenges in organizing these workers or extending agreements to them.

The best outcomes were at A1 and Telia. Encompassing institutions limited employer exit from minimum standards and collective agreements. Workers enjoyed strong collective voice resources to sustain these protections or re-internalize work. And the structure of union representation encouraged strategies of inclusive labor solidarity, with strong inter-union cooperation to maintain encompassing standards in the face of employer efforts to exploit loopholes.

At the same time, these structural or institutional factors did not fully determine outcomes. Worker representatives across the cases also adopted a range of

EXTERNALIZATION 241

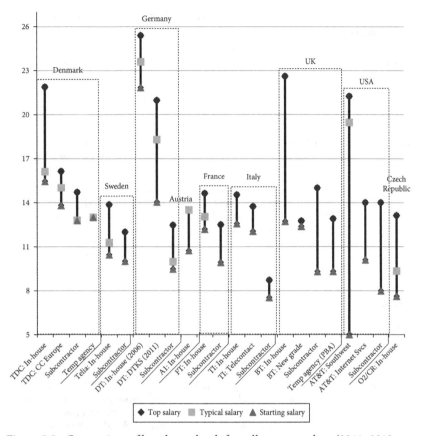

Figure 5.3. Comparison of hourly pay levels for call center workers (2011–2012, unless otherwise stated).

Source: Collective agreements, management/union surveys, and interviews.

Notes: All figures refer to customer service and sales, consumer segment; pay reported in US dollars, based on purchasing power parity. Comparison categories for each case include: (a) in-house; (b) subsidiaries and new pay grades (where present); (c) subcontractors (where used); and (d) temporary agencies (where used and where pay is allowed to deviate from in-house pay). Employees were no longer hired onto the AT&T Southwest reported "starting salary." We do not have figures for the "top salary" at A1; however, the typical salary is close to the top of the pay scale. Agency workers at Telia, DT, A1, FT, and TI are on the same pay scale as permanent workers—although they would typically be paid close to the starting salary level. The in-house pay rates at DT (2006) no longer apply, as all call center workers were moved onto a lower scale at the DTKS subsidiary.

strategies aimed at bringing up pay and conditions in externalized workplaces—essentially raising the market-based benchmark or establishing additional obstacles to or costs associated with outsourcing. At AT&T, unions bargained limits on the use of subcontracting, participated in global campaigns to improve conditions in the offshore BPO call center industry, and organized campaigns

Table 5.2 Measures to Internalize Call Center Work or Halt Externalization Plans and Associated Concessions (2005–2015)

Company	Measures to Internalize Work or Halt Externalization Plans	Associated Changes in Pay and Conditions for Internal Workers (Concessions)
Structural exclusive solidarity		
AT&T	2007–2013: 3,600 offshore jobs internalized	New pay grade with less favorable pay and conditions for jobs created through in-sourcing
BT	(1) 2007: Some temp agency workers made permanent (2) 2011: Management agreed to internalize 600–900 offshored jobs	(1) New pay grade with less favorable pay and conditions for internalized temp agency workers (2) New pay grade with less favorable pay and conditions for jobs created through in-sourcing
O2 Czech Republic	None	N/A
Orange Polska	None	N/A
Representation domain divides		
Deutsche Telekom	(1) 2007: Management agreed not to outsource new subsidiary (2) 2012–2014: Subcontracting reduced from 40% to 30%; percentage of temporary agency employment reduced; internal employment stabilized	(1) Pay reduced by 30% for new hires and working time increased for existing workers; more variable pay; weekend work introduced (2) Flexible working-time model introduced; part-time work increased; more intensive performance monitoring allowed
TDC	(1) 2011: All temp agency workers made permanent (2) 2012–2013: Management agreed to halt outsourcing plans (3) 2015: Management agreed to halt further outsourcing plans	(1) Unpaid lunches and reduced terms and conditions for new hires/internalized temps (2) Flexible working-time model introduced (3) Unpaid lunches for all employees; extra half-hour workday (with one-time payment); gave up overtime premiums for first 15 minutes; reduced holidays, holiday allowances, pensions
Ideological divides		
France Telecom	2010–2012: Amount of work outsourced decreased with declining call volume	None

EXTERNALIZATION   243

Table 5.2 Continued

Company	Measures to Internalize Work or Halt Externalization Plans	Associated Changes in Pay and Conditions for Internal Workers (Concessions)
Telecom Italia	(1) About 2005: 1,350 workers from a subcontractor moved to TI subsidiary; freelancers converted to training, probation, part-time, and temporary agency contracts (2) 2008–2012: All temporary agency workers in subsidiary made permanent	(1) Slightly lower initial pay grades for internalized temporary agency workers (2) Internalized workers on part-time contracts progressively moved into full-time contracts

Structural inclusive solidarity

| A1 | None | N/A |
| Telia | 2013–2015: Temp agency workers reduced from >30% to 18% of workforce | None |

Note: N/A, not applicable.

to pass legislation that discouraged call center offshoring. The unions at BT increased union membership rates among temporary agency workers through organizing and advocacy work and led a series of successful campaigns aimed at "closing the loopholes" in equal pay rules for these workers. At Orange Polska, unions successfully opposed management's plans to introduce lower pay rates for workers transferred to service subsidiaries, using member mobilization and protests to improve their bargaining position. Telecom Italia represents the most successful example of these strategies. Unions significantly improved conditions in the incumbent's largest call center subcontractor, while effectively banning them and others in their industry from hiring freelancers to bypass sectoral bargaining. In each of these cases, unions sought to broaden the scope of their efforts to constrain employer exit through strategies of inclusive solidarity that mobilized collective worker voice in creative ways.

6
Conclusions

This book started with a simple question: under what conditions do employers create and sustain good jobs with decent pay and conditions? After more than a decade of research in the telecommunications industry across ten countries, my answer is also a simple one: good jobs are more common where workers have power. Building collective power to insist that employers consider the social impacts of their management and restructuring policies has traditionally been a goal of labor movements worldwide. When market-based pressures encourage managers to shift risk onto workers, labor unions play an important role in pushing back, to make sure that they consider worker well-being and job quality alongside economic and financial objectives.

I have argued that worker representatives are most successful in building power to contest market-oriented restructuring where they can draw on three sets of ideal type conditions: constraints on employer exit from encompassing labor market institutions, support for collective worker voice in management decisions, and strategies of inclusive labor solidarity based on bridging divides among workers and in the labor movement. These are the building blocks for sustaining or strengthening workers' institutional and associational power. They are critical resources for asserting the legitimacy of social values and outcomes within workplaces, companies, industries, and the broader economy and society.

The chapters in this book trace the recent history of declining worker power in ten US and European incumbent telecommunications companies, connected to related trends of liberalization, financialization, and vertical disintegration. They all restructured work through downsizing, new performance management practices, and externalization of jobs, leading to intensified precarity and inequality for core workers and across increasingly networked workplaces. However, outcomes differed substantially across the cases. These outcomes broadly follow the model outlined in Chapter 2 (Figure 2.3)—based on the intersection of exit, voice, and solidarity in each case.

Unions and works councils had the most success contesting precarity in Sweden (Telia) and Austria (A1). Both came closest to ideal conditions supporting worker power: strong constraints on employer exit through encompassing employment standards and protections; strong legal and institutional support for collective worker voice in decision-making at workplace, company, and industry levels; and a labor movement composed of well-organized unions that cooperated with each other within the sector and across networked workplaces. Unions used these resources to maintain collective regulation and to fight back against attempts to bypass social rules. Inclusive labor solidarity was encouraged by union and bargaining structures that established reasonably clear boundaries between representation domains and supported union coordination along value chains—a set of conditions I have termed "structural inclusive solidarity."

In contrast, unions faced more substantial challenges as they sought to contest market-oriented restructuring in the United Kingdom (BT), United States (AT&T), Czech Republic (O2 Czech Republic), and Poland (Orange Polska). More fragmented institutions with low bargaining coverage and limited employment protections enabled employer exit through downsizing, punitive dismissal policies, or externalization of jobs to subcontractors, service subsidiaries, and temporary agencies. Countries had different legal participation rights and structures, with stronger supports for collective voice in the Czech Republic and Poland. But these were generally more limited than in the other European cases—giving workers fewer opportunities to participate in organizational decision-making.

Unions across the four cases were able to use associational power from their well-organized members to fight for some negotiated protections (or against their erosion) inside the incumbents—particularly through generous redundancy policies. However, they had fewer resources to fight precarity outside of these companies. This opened up labor cost differences within the telecom sector and between internal and externalized jobs. It also increased pressure on management to cut costs, and on unions to agree to concessions that brought these costs down closer to the external market. Solidarity among different unions representing telecom workers was less of a concern, with the exception of the Polish case, which did have multiple, ideologically divided unions within the incumbent and the sector. However, all four cases shared the bigger problem of improving conditions beyond the well-organized incumbent, with few institutional resources to extend bargaining to its largely non-union competitors, subcontractors, and temporary agencies—a pattern that I have called "structural exclusive solidarity."

The incumbents in Denmark (TDC), Germany (Deutsche Telekom), France (France Telecom), and Italy (Telecom Italia) had more mixed outcomes, as unions experimented with different combinations of resources to strengthen constraints on exit or to mobilize behind expanded collective voice. Unions in all four cases improved conditions for the incumbents' internal workers—for example, through favorable downsizing policies and limits on discipline-oriented performance management. However, regulating the externalization of work proved more challenging, particularly at TDC, Deutsche Telekom, and Telecom

Italia, where employers faced weaker constraints on their ability to exit through spin-offs or shifting work to subcontractors, and strong cost-based incentives to do so. Labor power in these four cases could be undermined by often bitter divides and open conflict among unions competing across unclear representation domains (TDC and Deutsche Telekom) or based on ideological divides in multi-union bargaining systems (France Telecom and Telecom Italia). Union success in asserting social demands was often dependent on overcoming these divides to cooperate on campaigns. These proved most successful where they were based on inclusive, solidaristic goals to bring up wages and conditions outside of core employers, either through collective bargaining, the courts, or legislative action.

This last point suggests that structure was not destiny. Constraints on exit and supports for voice were often strongly dependent on existing institutions, which had been established under historically contingent conditions. However, they were also constantly changing in the face of employer efforts to exploit institutional loopholes or exit options, and union efforts to mobilize their members, allies, and the public to close those loopholes. Across the ten cases, unions developed new strategies to fight for strengthened social regulation within their distinctive spheres of influence, based on solidaristic organizing and a concerted attempt to identify and overcome labor divides within their employers and across different groups of workers. In France, unions overturned punitive downsizing and relocation policies through a coordinated campaign to draw worker and public attention to the negative impact of these policies on workers' psychosocial health—leading to national legislation requiring worker consultation over these impacts. In the United Kingdom, telecom unions fought for over a decade for equal pay and treatment for temporary agency workers, eventually succeeding in closing off exit options associated with the use of pay between assignments contracts. In Italy, unions secured legal changes in the status of and protections for freelance workers, encouraging subcontractors to move thousands of jobs onto permanent contracts covered by collective bargaining.

The cases in this book clearly show that there is not one best-practice approach to collective bargaining and worker mobilization, even in the same industry and similar workplaces. The elements of a successful strategy differed depending on the context. Worker representatives had most success in challenging market-oriented restructuring where they made creative use of existing resources. In the French, UK, and Italian cases described above, public campaigns focused on both putting external pressure on management and strengthening pro-worker laws. But the specific targets of these actions were based on distinctive legal frameworks and opportunities: for example, a French legal principle that employers' responsibility for health and safety extended to psychosocial health; or the United Kingdom's transposition into law of a European Union directive on equal treatment of temporary workers. In other cases, social dialogue or partnership institutions were repurposed for new challenges. The works councils at Deutsche Telekom increasingly came under pressure to compete for jobs with subcontractors. However, they used their strong co-determination rights to negotiate new practices that balanced employer demands for flexibility with worker control and security: improving the fairness of variable pay, restricting intrusive monitoring, and developing a new working-time model that allowed workers to choose among more fixed or flexible schedules.

Finally, strikes and other forms of industrial action could be a powerful tool for challenging market-oriented restructuring across the cases, but the form they took and how they were used again depended on distinctive laws and traditions. At AT&T, strikes had strong member support, and helped to win new job-security provisions and restrictions on outsourcing. At Orange Polska, unions organized both a controversial nationwide strike and a hunger strike, and they won a more favorable package of voluntary redundancies with high severance pay and training investments. In countries or companies with less of a tradition of striking, employers' shift away from a social partnership orientation has also encouraged unions to adopt more conflictual tactics. Workers at Deutsche Telekom, A1, and TDC participated in strikes or major demonstrations in the period following liberalization, which were often among the first in their history. In other cases, such as Telia or BT, union representatives and shop stewards increasingly debated whether their strong partnership traditions were sustainable in the face of employer attempts to bypass collective regulation.

While labor unions used a range of different tactics, these had a shared logic and set of objectives—focused on sustaining or strengthening the social regulation of work. Across the cases, inclusive labor solidarity was an essential tool in fights to assert the value of worker voice over employer exit. Unions played a central role in mobilizing and channeling worker power to fight precarity, internalize jobs, and re-establish a balance between social and market values in the employment relationship.

Contribution to Debates: Conditions for Reversing Precarity

There is broad agreement that a growing number of workers in the wealthy economies of the Global North are experiencing precarious employment conditions—characterized by some combination of growing income and employment insecurity, more short-term or non-standard employment, and a declining social wage associated with more limited access to state benefits and entitlements (Kalleberg and Vallas 2017). The reference point for analyzing the extent and form of precarity is often the historic ideal of the standard employment relationship, with permanent contracts, a steady income, and predictable hours. As these conditions are available in a shrinking number of jobs, workers across the labor market—but particularly those in lower skilled, lower wage, or more easily rationalized jobs—experience what Castel (1995) described as a "destabilization of the stable." The growth of precarious work is thus connected with expanding labor market inequality, and in particular unequal access to high-quality jobs.

Debates concerning how these trends can be reversed start with different analyses of their causes. I consider two ways the problem has been framed in popular and policy debates. The first, which I term the "enlightened management" thesis, sees the challenge as one of encouraging better, more informed strategic choices by management that rest on recognizing mutual gains from investing in their workers. The second "technology-driven globalization" thesis sees the challenge as one of designing policies that help individuals and markets adjust more fluidly to politically neutral trends of globalization and technological change. Below I critique each of these perspectives, in light of the findings and arguments presented in this book.

High-Performance Work Systems and Enlightened Management

One popular argument holds that employers have a strong self-interest in designing more human-centered management models. Put more simply, investing in high job quality is "good for business"—producing mutual gains in terms of both better working conditions and expanding profits. Thus, the problem of precarious work is one that can be solved through better management education and transfer of best practices.

This "enlightened management" thesis has inspired a large body of research on high-performance or high-involvement work systems. The particular models studied have different features, but they typically involve a combination of high road practices that are argued to complement each other: e.g., job security, discretion, high pay, investment in skills, promotion opportunities, and opportunities to participate in decision-making or teams (Appelbaum et al. 2000; Shin and Konrad 2017). Researchers have found that these practices can improve performance in a range of industry and occupational settings—including in the telecom sector (Batt and Colvin 2011; Wood, Holman, and Stride 2006). Companies face higher costs when they take the low road, such as burnout, absenteeism, and turnover (Conway et al. 2016; Hancock et al. 2013). They also benefit from worker voice and engagement, which improve motivation, innovation, and problem-solving (Jiang et al. 2012).

A key puzzle in this literature is why so few employers use these practices, despite their proven benefits. If investing in better jobs raises the bottom line, why is job quality deteriorating along so many dimensions and for so many workers? In *Dying for a Paycheck: How Modern Management Harms Employee Health and Company Performance—and What We Can Do about It*, Pfeffer (2018, 5) laments the low take-up of high road management models in US workplaces, despite "many decades of research and teaching by both myself and colleagues around the effect of high-commitment or high-performance work practices on productivity and other dimensions of organizational performance." His answer is to try another tack, focusing on escalating organizational and social costs from poor (and declining) worker health and well-being. The logic remains similar, however: if only companies had the right data, and could see the economic benefits of investing in their workers, they would "do the right thing" and create good jobs with more security, better pay, and higher autonomy at work.

Kelly and Moen (2020) advance a similar argument—and even use a similar subtitle—in their book *Overload: How Jobs Went Bad and What We Can Do about It*. The book is organized around findings from an experiment they helped to design and implement at a large US company. Workers were given more control over their work and schedules, while managers were encouraged to adopt more developmental performance-management practices. They found, again consistent with decades of research, that taking the high road produced strong mutual gains: well-being improved, turnover declined, and employees were more motivated and satisfied. They similarly argue that the kinds of changes they observe generalize well beyond their case study setting. These interventions can and should be made "on a wide scale"—and corporate leaders have a central role to play in encouraging and implementing them.

This perspective has been influential within the management profession—particularly among human resource (HR) practitioners and executives. When I was at the London School of Economics, the then-head of People Operations at Google, Laszlo Bock, came to talk to our HR students about his book, *Work Rules! Insights from Inside Google That Will Transform How You Live and Lead* (Bock 2015). He confidently described Google's HR model as one that was grounded in a culture of worker voice, that valued debate, discussion, and employee participation at all levels. Together with generous benefits, hierarchy-busting teams, and agile working practices, Google has been seen as an employer that profits from investing in job quality (Grant and Russell 2020).

However, Google is also a good example of why enlightened management is not sufficient to create and sustain good jobs across the economy. Temps, vendors, and contractors, with typically lower pay and more insecure jobs, made up over half of Google's workforce by 2021 (Wong 2021). Even for core, internal workers, many of the practices described by Bock in his book were scaled back or cut over time (Tiku 2019). As a multinational company trying to satisfy shareholders, compete for contracts, and expand into new markets, it became increasingly difficult to balance these demands with workers' social values and voices. Google employees have started to fight back through protests, walk-outs, and union organizing (Conger 2021).

This example from Google resonates with the findings in this book. First, even where employers invest in their core workers, they face strong incentives to adopt cheaper and more precarious employment practices for other groups of workers. Decades of research on labor market segmentation have established the widespread use of these strategies for matching labor with fluctuating market demand, generating cost savings, and weakening potential organizing or coalitions across different groups of workers (Grimshaw et al. 2017). As shown in Chapter 5, externalizing jobs can lead to downgrading pay and conditions for both external and internal employees via benchmarking and concessions.

Second, even in those workplaces where employers adopt high road practices, and realize gains from these practices, they often have trouble sticking to them. The reasons are many. Sometimes middle managers resist more democratic or decentralized decision-making because they fear a loss of status and control (Batt 2004). Other times, pressure to cut costs—coming from investors, shareholders, or market competition—overwhelm longer-term commitments to a trust-based employment relationship resting on job security and employee voice (Godard 2004).

Perhaps most simply, most companies can motivate the bulk of their workforce quite effectively through some combination of short-term incentives, frequent monitoring, and fear of job loss. Put in the terms of this book's argument, investing in employee voice can be costly, with uncertain returns. Where exit options are available, they are attractive—and, as my findings show, can be an effective strategy for reducing labor costs and disciplining workers. Institutions that make it more difficult to take the low road are the best hope for encouraging more widespread adoption of the high road practices that generations of management researchers have sought to promote.

Technology-Driven Globalization

An alternative set of "technology-driven globalization" arguments start with the assumption that trends in precarity and job quality are connected to economy-wide changes in the supply of and demand for different skills or tasks. Just as management scholars and practitioners are responsible for the conventional wisdom that better managerial strategy can solve the problem of deteriorating job quality, economists and economic pundits frame the solution as supply-side investments in skills to offset market failures or social spending to ease market adjustments.

One influential argument holds that skill-biased technological change has led to declining demand for workers at the bottom of the skill distribution, at the same time that economic globalization and offshoring have increased the supply of workers competing to perform lower skilled work (Acemoglu and Autor 2011; Levy and Murnane 2004). Outsourcing is likewise a market-based response to shrinking information and monitoring costs, allowing for a more efficient allocation of labor across specialized organizations—and subsequently wage setting based on marginal demand for certain skills (Heshmati 2003). Recent analyses of the employment impact of digitalization and artificial intelligence (AI) predict further polarization, as new technologies substitute for workers performing routine tasks while pulling a growing supply of global service workers into competition with each other (Adermon and Gustavsson 2015; Böhm 2020). This may be contributing to a different process of "routine-biased" technological change, in which even higher skilled tasks can be automated (Goos, Manning, and Salomons 2014), potentially leading to a smaller number of experts guiding the mass provision of professional services (Susskind and Susskind 2015).

This strain of conventional wisdom in academic debates can also be found across popular media and policy discussions. At root, it holds that "there is no alternative"[1] to increasingly liberalized and globalized markets—facilitated by digital technologies, cloud computing, platforms, and rapidly advancing artificial intelligence. Friedman (2007) in *The World Is Flat* is perhaps the most well-known early cheerleader for the transformative potential of accelerating globalization and digitalization—as they enable "the sharing of knowledge and work—in real time, without regard to geography, distance, or, in the near future, even language" (p. 176). More recently, popular books are exploring the impact of artificial intelligence and advanced robotics on these trends. Baldwin (2019) describes a *Globotics Upheaval*, in which new technologies lead to intensified global competition across denationalized production networks. Brynjolfsson and McAfee's (2014) *Second Machine Age*, Frey's (2019) *The Technology Trap*, and Susskind's (2020) *A World Without Work* describe the effects of AI-based technologies in more balanced tones, anticipating alongside their benefits a slew of political and social problems associated with accelerating job loss, uneven wealth creation, and deepening economic divides.

While the enlightened management thesis is evoked to make the case that management can solve its own bad jobs problem, adherents of the technology-driven

---

[1] This phrase was originally used by the Victorian philosopher Herbert Spencer defending classical liberalism, or laissez-faire government, in responding to critics of free markets. It was used as a slogan in the United Kingdom by Conservative prime minister Margaret Thatcher to defend the inevitability of market-based reforms.

globalization thesis recommend public investments that give employers the tools to create more good work and broadly distribute its benefits via training and technology investments, perhaps combined with government transfers to ease dislocations (Broecke 2016). Friedman (2007, 277) envisions "a Great Society that commits our government to building the infrastructure, safety nets, and institutions that will help every American become more employable in an age when no one can be guaranteed lifetime employment" (p. 277). Brynjolfsson and McAfee (2014) and Frey (2019) also see the need for investments in infrastructure, education, or mobility vouchers targeted to the changing needs of business (and location of jobs). But they emphasize that this should be combined with policies such as universal basic income or negative income taxes for displaced employees.

These proposals all see public policy as a tool to correct market failures or ease social dislocations "after the fact"—when the trajectory of market-driven technology investments have run their course. What is missing in this literature, and the public debates surrounding it, is an understanding of the power dynamics within companies, industries, and economies that have been central to the analysis in this book. The strength and independence of collective worker voice can influence the weight given to market or social outcomes when companies decide how to adopt and use new technologies. The relative power of organized labor also plays an important role in government choices between different policies to redistribute resources in the economy or power in the employment relationship.

As Wajcman (2022, 18) observes, "All these authors shy away from addressing the extent to which the pursuit of profit, rather than progress, shapes the development of digital technologies on an ongoing basis, and the ways in which these very same technologies are facilitating not less work but more worse jobs." Management and investment decisions are guided by a range of considerations, including possibilities for not only accessing skills but also reducing labor costs. Digital and AI-based technologies are often used as a new set of tools to pursue an established set of strategies, not simply to automate but also to restructure and segment jobs in a way that enables new exit options (Holtgrewe 2014). This may take the form of further breaking up and internationalizing coding and programming tasks through crowd sourcing (Wood et al. 2019), shifting service work to freelance gig contracts in the growing platform economy (Collier, Dubal, and Carter 2018), and controlling worker effort and performance through new algorithmic management tools (De Stefano 2019; Moore 2017).

Certainly public investments in training and infrastructure, progressive taxation, and government transfers are important policy tools. However, missing in this literature are considerations of the role that collective bargaining and labor market institutions can play in encouraging employers to adopt fundamentally different approaches to restructuring. Constraints on employer exit and support for collective worker voice bring workers and their representatives into the equation, as key actors capable of applying more democratic processes to companies' strategic choices. Inclusive labor solidarity is the backbone to establishing these institutional conditions for socially motivated restructuring decisions, which are based on both sustainable investments in worker skills and more equitable redistribution of the gains from technological innovation. It is also a necessary ingredient for the broad-based political coalitions that hold the best hope for bringing about the policies many scholars and pundits in this literature recommend, from more generous financing of high-quality public education to redistributive public spending.

Reversing Precarity through Strengthening the Social Regulation of Markets

The argument I have advanced in this book is based on a different set of theoretical assumptions, grounded in the multidisciplinary field of comparative employment relations. And it also leads to a different set of recommendations aimed at solving the problem of expanding precarity at work. The starting point is a Polanyian concern with the "market-correcting" role of social and labor movements (Polanyi 1944). Exit through markets can often be a socially inefficient mechanism for expressing preferences or making decisions on resource allocation, reinforcing the power and interests of those able to exit over those with fewer choices. However, it can save costs in the short term and is often the easiest (and most lucrative) option for companies under pressure to rationalize work and maximize profits. The alternative is broadening access to democratic mechanisms for the exercise of collective voice, to encourage a more equal balance of power between workers and their employers and to increase the legitimacy of worker interests in organizational decision-making.

This argument connects most directly to two streams of recent research in employment relations. First, researchers have sought to theorize and empirically document the role of labor market institutions in encouraging high road employer strategies (Kalev, Dobbin, and Kelly 2006; Osterman 2018). There are clear connections here with the high-performance work systems literature, in that investments in less precarious management practices are often seen as part of an efficient or productive approach to the employment relationship (Budd 2004). However, employment relations scholars argue that the high cost of these investments, combined with the need for sustained cooperation from the workforce, means they are more likely where regulations and minimum employment standards close off the option of low road practices. Recent authors have continued to look to Europe for evidence that encompassing social regulation, employment protections, and generous welfare states can reduce inequality and stem the growth of precarious work (Adamson and Roper 2019). For example, Carré and Tilly's (2017) comparative study of retail jobs attributes differences in job quality between the United States, France, and Germany to social norms and labor market institutions. Kalleberg (2018) argues that active labor market policies and more generous social welfare systems are needed to fight precarity, based on a comparison of the United States and five European countries.

The findings in this book suggest that these kinds of policy interventions do play an important role in worker outcomes, as they help to constrain employer exit. However, these constraints are fragile and ultimately easy to bypass without collective worker voice and strategies of solidarity. Inclusive labor market institutions depend on strong and solidaristic labor movements both for their effectiveness and sustained strength (not to mention their existence in the first place). This is consistent with recent comparative research attributing current trends of growing precarity to the decline of unions and the associated shrinking level and coverage of wage-setting institutions (Kristal and Cohen 2017; Thomas, McArdle, and Saundry 2020). As activist nation-states increasingly pursue neoliberal labor market reforms demanded by employers (Howell 2021; Schulze-Cleven 2018), and as companies use their own political and organizational power to change laws and weaken unions (Kinderman 2017; Milkman 2020), sustaining or strengthening social regulation depends on labor power.

This leads to the second stream of research I build on, focused on labor union responses to precarious work. Here a central concern is with explaining why unions succeed or fail in fights to prevent downsizing and outsourcing, to internalize jobs, or to improve pay and conditions for low wage, temporary, or informal workers (Carver and Doellgast 2021; Doellgast, Lillie, and Pulignano 2018; Eaton, Schurman, and Chen 2017). Some recent examples of these studies include Benassi et al.'s (2019) comparison of collective bargaining over the use of agency work in the Italian and German metal sectors; O'Brady's (2021) study of union efforts to resist precarious work in the Canadian, German, Swedish, and US retail industries; Krachler et al.'s (2021) research on mobilizing nurses in the United States and Germany; and Trif et al.'s (2021) analysis of union actions to address precarity in multiple sectors across nine Central and Eastern European countries (see also Helfen, Sydow, and Wirth 2020; McCallum 2020; Refslund 2021; Samaluk and Greer 2021).

This literature documents the numerous challenges unions face as they fight to defend or improve job quality. Consistent with my research findings, outcomes are best where institutions are already more encompassing or where unions and other worker organizations cooperate with each other to extend existing protections to new groups. Their success depends on some combination of recognizing and using existing institutional power; and responding with creative strategies to mobilize associational power—often based on some degree of "institutional experimentation" (Ferreras et al. 2020; Wright et al. 2019).

A stream in this literature that is particularly resonant with this book's argument focuses on contests over legitimacy and identity within the labor movement, as worker representatives adjust to declining formal regulation or the loss of traditional institutional resources (Doellgast, Bidwell, and Colvin 2021). Rothstein (2022) shows that US and German tech workers were more successful in mobilizing where they "recoded" management discourse—convincing workers that market-oriented restructuring was not inevitable, and so could be contested through collective action. Reich and Bearman's (2018) study of worker mobilization at Walmart in the United States shows the importance of collective identity formation among workers, with social ties contributing to social change.

A related set of findings focus on new labor actors, such as alternative unions, worker organizations, or worker centers, both for their distinctive strategies and relationship with traditional unions. Fine and Bartley (2019) examine "co-enforcement" approaches in the United States, based on partnerships between governments and worker and community organizations to improve enforcement of employment law. Bondy (2021) studies "conflictual forms of complementarity" between new actors and corporatist unions in Israel. Azzellini and Kraft (2018, 6) describe the rise of new, shop-floor based worker organizations "rooted in self-activity" in a wide range of countries, from Europe to the Global South. These different examples represent what Meardi et al. (2021) refer to as "new voices claims" or "deeper roots claims" on behalf of precarious workers (see also Fischer-Daly 2021; Pannini 2021).

The findings and arguments in this literature suggest that strategies of inclusive labor solidarity require two kinds of supports—particularly outside of the kinds of large, unionized employers that are the focus of my study. On the one hand, they increasingly rely on creative discursive strategies aimed at building a shared belief that strengthening social regulation at work is both possible and desirable. On the other hand, they require cooperation among diverse labor and social movement organizations to bring about that vision.

However, my analysis shows that the improvements won in these campaigns are likely to be fragile and short-lived where they do not also establish institutions that close off employer exit, support expanded worker voice, and encourage more durable forms of inclusive labor solidarity. While building a strong collective identity is an important step on the path to institutionalization, conflicts are likely to persist or re-emerge if unions and other labor organizations are competing for a shrinking pool of members. Thus, tackling the organizational or structural problem of aligning interests within the labor movement must accompany struggles for recognition and legitimacy (Rathgeb 2018; Thelen 2014).

Employment relations researchers broadly agree that enlightened management or supply-side investments in skills and transfers will not on their own create broadly shared prosperity in a brave new "future of work." However, different streams within this literature each miss an important piece of the puzzle concerning how to build institutions capable of strengthening the collective and social regulation of employment, across economies that have experienced an erosion of these institutions over the past several decades. Collective bargaining and labor market institutions, democracy at work, and new approaches to worker mobilization each are unlikely to have a sustainable impact on worker outcomes in isolation from the others. All three factors are needed because they support and reinforce each other.

Lessons for Labor Unions

The book's findings also suggest lessons for labor unions. Given the diverse national contexts I cover in my case studies, I reserve my observations here to a few general points.

First, inclusive solidarity is essential to contesting market-oriented restructuring. It also can be extremely difficult to achieve, particularly where union density is declining and coordinated bargaining is weak or nonexistent. Worker representatives and labor activists need to identify the divides that undermine cooperation between different groups of workers and figure out how to bridge them. This means investing time, energy, and resources in building labor organizations that pull together workers with more or less labor market power, within industries and across vertically disintegrated value chains. It also means focusing on longer-term goals that place members' interests within a broader framework and agenda, centering on improving conditions for the most precarious workers to establish more encompassing regulation for all.

This leads to the second point, that solidarity is likely to be short-lived where it is not institutionalized. Perhaps increasingly, labor unions cannot build sustainable power without stronger pro-worker laws and enforcement of those laws. Based on the framework in this book, the target of these efforts should be policies that both constrain employer exit and support collective worker voice.

At a basic level, employment standards such as minimum wages and protections from discrimination or arbitrary dismissal should apply to all workers, including those with different contract types. The cases in this book also show vividly the need for sectoral collective bargaining institutions, with mechanisms that extend agreements to all employers and workers in an industry. Increasingly important are mechanisms to include subcontractor or agency workers under these agreements, and within the same unions' representation domains. Laws that bind companies to upholding social standards internally or across their production chains also reduce incentives to compete based on low pay and poor conditions. For example, several European countries have recently adopted laws that hold employers legally responsible for labor standards or human rights violations committed by subcontractors.

These kinds of legal and policy changes are more likely in the first place where labor unions and other worker representatives are strong and well-organized within major companies and industries. Not coincidentally, collective voice at these levels has often translated into greater influence over regional or national policy decisions, based on tripartite social dialogue institutions. Most basically, workers need to be able to organize unions free from employer intimidation, based on threats of firing or disinvestment. Campaigns to strengthen basic organizing rights are an essential starting point, as these rights have been rolled back or gutted in many countries. Built on top of this are then formal, legally protected participation and bargaining rights at workplace level and rights to worker representation on corporate boards. The cases in this book show many examples of how these institutions can be structured, with Germany providing the most comprehensive model. However, the example of Germany also shows that legal rights to voice need constraints on exit to be effective. Employers' capacity to bypass voice institutions inevitably weakens the power of worker representatives to propose and implement alternatives to more narrowly market-oriented restructuring strategies.

This book has focused primarily on contests over precarity within countries. However, the cases showed that even in a historically nationally bounded service industry, most companies relied on offshoring as part of their externalization strategies, particularly for call center and back-office work. Of course, most employers' exit options are not limited just to local subcontractors, subsidiaries, or staffing agencies. Uneven access to worker voice and divisions that undermine labor solidarity are also global challenges facing the labor movement, as unions and NGOs seek to bind employers to encompassing social standards. In Chapter 5, I gave examples of union campaigns to address these challenges in the telecom industry, such as solidarity actions by US unions in support of worker organizing in the Philippine BPO vendor industry. There have been many further campaigns not detailed here, often organized through the global union UNI-ICTS—from global agreements at France Telecom to coordinated organizing campaigns at Deutsche Telekom's T-Mobile international subsidiaries. The framework in this book is just as relevant at this international scale. However, the challenges to building comprehensive constraints on employer exit, support for collective worker voice, and strategies of inclusive labor solidarity are many times steeper. Building power and strengthening institutions often starts from the bottom up, but increasingly requires a vision of economic democracy as a global rather than an exclusive and nationalist project.

Final Thoughts

In 2013, I was invited to the Communications Workers of America's (CWA) headquarters in Washington, D.C., to present my book *Disintegrating Democracy at Work*, which was based on research at US and German call centers in the mid-2000s. Several audience members told me that the most striking impression from reading the book was how much worse conditions had gotten at their employers since my research. I have certainly seen more examples of losses than gains in close to two decades of studying restructuring in the telecom industry. Workers and union representatives complain of near constant downsizing, intensifying performance monitoring, and externalization of jobs to cheaper, often non-union firms and contracts.

At the same time, the CWA, like the other unions in this study, has continued to fight for good jobs, both for their own members and more broadly across different industries and worker groups. The campaigns at AT&T documented here give only a small window into these efforts. Early in the COVID-19 pandemic the CWA negotiated agreements with Verizon, Frontier, AT&T, CenturyLink, and American Airlines that included temporary telework arrangements and emergency paid leave (Labor Notes 2020). Employees diagnosed with COVID-19 or with underlying health conditions had the right to paid time off. Those facing other obstacles to coming in to work also could take this leave: for example, if they were in states with shelter in place orders or if their children's schools were closed. At a time when "essential service workers" in many industries were forced to walk out in protest against unsafe conditions and unsupportive company policies, CWA members could negotiate through their union, bringing concerns directly and collectively to management.

The COVID-19 pandemic also brought attention to inequality in access to broadband services, particularly in rural and low-income communities. A recent federal infrastructure package includes $65 billion for broadband investment. The CWA has used this as an opportunity to organize parallel campaigns in multiple states to pass legislation restoring "public utility commission oversight of broadband in public safety, network resiliency and consumer protection"—including collection of service quality and cost data across regions and providers (CWA 2021). This would reverse a trend toward deregulation, re-establishing the principle that telecommunications infrastructure is a shared public good and putting in place mechanisms to enforce this principle.

This kind of campaign is typical of the union's commitment to Bargaining for the Common Good—a movement to connect labor organizing and bargaining to broader public and social concerns. Another example is the Committee for Better Banks, which has brought together bank workers, community and consumer advocacy groups, and labor organizations to win just wages, career paths, and job security for front-line bank workers. A related Take on Wall Street coalition does activist training, voter education, and policy work focused on strengthening regulation of the financial sector (Jacoby 2021). These efforts are linked to CWA's campaigns to organize collective agreements in major banks, in coordination with UNI-Finance—drawing connections between unionization and more democratic oversight of the practices and political influence of the US financial industry.

Another set of initiatives focus on connecting economic and racial justice, centering on member-led political education. CWA helped develop a Runaway Inequality training program in 2015, organized in coalition with other unions and labor, environment, and social justice organizations (DiMaggio 2017). I talked with workers who had participated in these workshops, and they described the goal as building a shared understanding of the root causes of inequality, and talking about how their own workplace or employer battles fit into this bigger picture of financialized capitalism. More recently, the CWA developed a series of workshops on Building an Anti-Racist Union, organized through its national Committee on Civil Rights and Equity and based on the Paulo Freire Spiral Model of popular political education. Several activists talked to my class about their efforts to use these workshops both as an organizing tool and to get members involved in the union's political campaigns.

I give these examples by way of illustrating the broad field of union action that is often built out from the many workplace- and industry-specific struggles that are the focus of my analysis in this book. A comparison of the bargaining dynamics and outcomes within incumbent telecom companies and across their value chains gives an important window into why specific fights against precarity and inequality are won or lost. Over the longer term, labor movements help to build the institutional and ideational conditions for winning these fights, based on broader goals of balancing market demands with social objectives. Efforts to improve job quality require better management strategies and public policies. But most centrally and essentially, they require democracy at work based in solidarity, built from the ground up by workers and their unions. The challenges are significant. But approaching them with a clearer view of their scale and scope can help in organizing creative responses that advance contested goals of social justice.

References

Abboud, Leila. 2006. "At France Télécom, Battle to Cut Jobs Breeds Odd Tactics: Company Offers Money, Advice on Starting New Business if Employees Will Leave." *Wall Street Journal*, August 14, 2006. http://online.wsj.com/article/SB115551492597434704.html.

Acemoglu, Daron, and David Autor. 2011. "Skills, Tasks and Technologies: Implications for Employment and Earnings." In *Handbook of Labor Economics*, edited by Orly Ashenfelter and David Card, 1043–1171. Amsterdam: Elsevier.

Adamson, Maria, and Ian Roper. 2019. "'Good' Jobs and 'Bad' Jobs: Contemplating Job Quality in Different Contexts." *Work, Employment and Society* 33(4): 551–559.

Adema, Joop, Yvonne Giesing, Anne Schönauer, and Tanja Stitteneder. 2019. *Minimum Wages across Countries, ifo DICE Report*. ifo Institut—Leibniz-Institut für Wirtschaftsforschung an der Universität München (München).

Adermon, Adrian, and Magnus Gustavsson. 2015. "Job Polarization and Task-Biased Technological Change: Evidence from Sweden, 1975–2005." *The Scandinavian Journal of Economics* 117(3): 878–917.

Alberti, Gabriella, Jane Holgate, and Maite Tapia. 2013. "Organising Migrants as Workers or as Migrant Workers? Intersectionality, Trade Unions and Precarious Work." *The International Journal of Human Resource Management* 24(22): 4132–4148.

Alimahomed-Wilson, Jake, and Ellen Reese. 2021. "Surveilling Amazon's Warehouse Workers: Racism, Retaliation, and Worker Resistance Amid the Pandemic." *Work in the Global Economy* 1(1–2): 55–73.

Allen, Matthew M. C. 2020. "Hirschman and Voice." In *Handbook of Research on Employee Voice*, edited by Adrian Wilkinson, Jimmy Donaghey, Tony Dundon, and Richard B. Freeman, 38–53. Cheltenham, UK: Edward Elgar.

Almond, Phil, Tony Edwards, Philipp Kern, Kyoungmi Kim, and Olga Tregaskis. 2021. "Global Norm-Making Processes in Contemporary Multinationals." *Human Resource Management Journal*. Early view. https://doi.org/10.1111/1748-8583.12350

Anderson, Benedict. 1983. *Imagined Communities: Reflections on the Origin and Spread of Nationalism*. London: Verso Books.

Anner, Mark. 2011. *Solidarity Transformed: Labor Responses to Globalization and Crisis in Latin America*. Ithaca, NY: Cornell University Press.

Anner, Mark, Matthew Fischer-Daly, and Michael Maffie. 2021. "Fissured Employment and Network Bargaining: Emerging Employment Relations Dynamics in a Contingent World of Work." *ILR Review* 74(3): 689–714.

Appelbaum, Eileen, Thomas Bailey, Peter Berg, and Arne L. Kalleberg. 2000. *Manufacturing Advantage: Why High Performance Work Systems Pay Off*. Ithaca, NY: Cornell University Press.

Appelbaum, Eileen, and Rosemary Batt. 2014. *Private Equity at Work: When Wall Street Manages Main Street*. New York: Russell Sage Foundation.

Arendt, Hannah. 1963. *On Revolution*. London: Penguin Classics.

Arnholtz, Jens, and Nathan Lillie. 2019. *Posted Work in the European Union: The Political Economy of Free Movement*. Milton Park, UK: Routledge.

Atesia, Info. 2008. "Sciopero articolato di un'ora—20 febbraio 2008." http://infoatesia.blogspot.de/2008/02/sciopero-articolato-di-unora-20.html.
Avdagic, Sabina, Martin Rhodes, and Jelle Visser. 2011. *Social Pacts in Europe: Emergence, Evolution, and Institutionalization*. Oxford: Oxford University Press.
Azzellini, Dario N., and Michael Kraft. 2018. *The Class Strikes Back: Self-Organised Workers' Struggles in the Twenty-First Century*. Leiden, NL: Brill.
Baccaro, Lucio, and Chiara Benassi. 2017. "Throwing out the Ballast: Growth Models and the Liberalization of German Industrial Relations." *Socio-Economic Review* 15(1): 85–115.
Baccaro, Lucio, and Chris Howell. 2017. *Trajectories of Neoliberal Transformation: European Industrial Relations since the 1970s*. Cambridge: Cambridge University Press.
Baccaro, Lucio, and Jonas Pontusson. 2016. "Rethinking Comparative Political Economy: The Growth Model Perspective." *Politics & Society* 44(2): 175–207.
Baldwin, Peter. 1990. *The Politics of Social Solidarity: Class Bases of the European Welfare State, 1875–1975*. Cambridge: Cambridge University Press.
Baldwin, Richard. 2019. *The Globotics Upheaval: Globalization, Robotics, and the Future of Work*. Oxford: Oxford University Press.
Bamber, Greg, Jody Hoffer Gittell, and Thomas Kochan. 2009. *Up in the Air: How Airlines Can Improve Performance by Engaging Their Employees*. Ithaca, NY: ILR Press.
Batt, Rosemary. 2004. "Who Benefits from Teams? Comparing Workers, Supervisors, and Managers." *Industrial Relations* 43(1): 183–212.
Batt, Rosemary, and Alexander J. S. Colvin. 2011. " An Employment Systems Approach to Turnover: Human Resources Practices, Quits, Dismissals, and Performance." *Academy of Management Journal* 54(4): 695–717.
Batt, Rosemary, Alex Colvin, and Jeffrey Keefe. 2002. "Employee Voice, Human Resource Practices, and Quit Rates: Evidence from the Telecommunications Industry." *Industrial and Labor Relations Review* 55(4): 573–593.
Batt, Rosemary, David Holman, and Ursula Holtgrewe. 2009. "The Globalization of Service Work: Comparative International Perspectives on Call Centers." *Industrial and Labor Relations Review* 62(4): 453–488.
BBC. 2016. "France Télécom Suicides: Prosecutor Calls for Bullying Trial." *BBC News*, July 7, 2016. http://www.bbc.com/news/world-europe-36733572.
Behrens, Martin, and Andreas Pekarek. 2021. "Divided We Stand? Coalition Dynamics in the German Union Movement." *British Journal of Industrial Relations* 59(2): 503–531.
Bellego, Maxime. 2013. "Relation au travail et identité professionnelle du monde technique chez France Télécom." Doctoral thesis, Aix-Marseille Université.
Bellego, Maxime. 2021. *Le travail est malade, il nous fait souffrir: Il est urgent de soigner les pathologies du travail!* Louvain: De Boeck Supérieur.
Benassi, Chiara, Virginia Doellgast, and Katja Sarmiento-Mirwaldt. 2016. "Institutions and Inequality in Liberalizing Markets: Explaining Different Trajectories of Institutional Change in Social Europe." *Politics & Society* 44(1): 117–142.
Benassi, Chiara, and Lisa Dorigatti. 2015. "Straight to the Core—Explaining Union Responses to the Casualization of Work: The IG Metall Campaign towards Agency Workers." *British Journal of Industrial Relations* 53(3): 533–555.
Benassi, Chiara, and Lisa Dorigatti. 2020. "Out of Sight, Out of Mind: The Challenge of External Work Arrangements for Industrial Manufacturing Unions in Germany and Italy." *Work, Employment and Society* 34(6): 1027–1044.
Benassi, Chiara, Lisa Dorigatti, and Elisa Pannini. 2019. "Explaining Divergent Bargaining Outcomes for Agency Workers: The Role of Labour Divides and Labour Market Reforms." *European Journal of Industrial Relations* 25(2): 163–179.

Benassi, Chiara, and Tim Vlandas. 2016. "Union Inclusiveness and Temporary Agency Workers: The Role of Power Resources and Union Ideology." *European Journal of Industrial Relations* 22(1): 5–22.

Benvegnú, Carlotta, Bettina Haidinger, and Devi Sacchetto. 2018. "Restructuring Labour Relations and Employment in the European Logistics Sector." In *Reconstructing Solidarity: Labour Unions, Precarious Work, and the Politics of Institutional Change in Europe*, edited by Virginia Doellgast, Nathan Lillie, and Valeria Pulignano, 83–103. Oxford: Oxford University Press.

Berggren, Christian. 1993. *Alternatives to Lean Production: Work Organization in the Swedish Auto Industry*. Ithaca, NY: Cornell University Press.

Berman, Sheri. 2006. *The Primacy of Politics: Social Democracy and the Making of Europe's Twentieth Century*. Cambridge: Cambridge University Press.

Bernaciak, Magdalena. 2015. "All Roads Lead to Decentralization? Collective Bargaining Trends and Prospects in Central and Eastern Europe." *Transfer: European Review of Labour and Research* 21(3): 373–381.

Bernhardt, Annette, Rosemary Batt, Susan N. Houseman, and Eileen Appelbaum. 2016. "Domestic Outsourcing in the United States: A Research Agenda to Assess Trends and Effects on Job Quality." (March 24, 2016). Upjohn Institute, Working Paper No. 16-253.

Bernstein, Mary. 2005. "Identity Politics." *Annual Review of Sociology* 31: 47–74.

Béthoux, Élodie, and Patrice Laroche. 2021. "Employment Relations in France." In *International and Comparative Employment Relations: Global Crises and Institutional Responses*, edited by Greg Bamber, Fang Lee Cooke, Virginia Doellgast, and Chris Wright, 159. Newbury Park, CA: Sage.

Béthoux, Élodie, and Arnaud Mias. 2021. "How Does State-Led Decentralization Affect Workplace Employment Relations? The French Case in a Comparative Perspective." *European Journal of Industrial Relations* 27(1): 5–21.

Biggart, Nicole W., and Thomas D. Beamish. 2003. "The Economic Sociology of Conventions: Habit, Custom, Practice, and Routine in Market Order." *Annual Review of Sociology* 29(1): 443–464.

Blais, Marie-Claude. 2007. *La solidarité: Histoire d'une idée*. Paris: Gallimard.

Bock, Laszlo. 2015. *Work Rules!: Insights from Inside Google That Will Transform How You Live and Lead*. New York: Twelve.

Boes, Andreas, and Barbara Langes, eds. 2019. *Die Cloud und der digitale Umbruch in Wirtschaft und Arbeit: Strategien, Best Practices und Gestaltungsimpulse*. Freiburg: Haufe-Lexware.

Bohle, Dorothee, and Béla Greskovits. 2007. "Neoliberalism, Embedded Neoliberalism and Neocorporatism: Towards Transnational Capitalism in Central-Eastern Europe." *West European Politics* 30(3): 443–466.

Böhm, Michael J. 2020. "The Price of Polarization: Estimating Task Prices under Routine-Biased Technical Change." *Quantitative Economics* 11(2): 761–799.

Bondy, Assaf S. 2021. "Conflictual Complementarity: New Labour Actors in Corporatist Industrial Relations." *Work, Employment and Society*. Online First. https://doi.org/10.1177/0950017020981557

Bormann, Sarah, and Karl-Heinz Brandl. 2019. "Kundendienst mit Cloud und Crowd: Eine Highroad-Strategie für den Kundenservice." In *Die Cloud und der digitale Umbruch in Wirtschaft und Arbeit: Strategien, Best Practices und Gestaltungsimpulse*, edited by Andreas Boes and Barbara Langes, 221–238. München: Haufe Group.

Boroff, Karen, and Jeffrey Keefe. 1994. "Telecommunications Labor-Management Relations: One Decade after the AT&T Divestiture." In *Contemporary Collective Bargaining in the Private Sector*, edited by Paula Voos, 303–371. Madison, WI: Industrial Relations Research Association.

Bosch, Gerhard, Ken Mayhew, and Jerome Gautié. 2010. "Industrial Relations, Legal Regulations and Wage Setting." In *Low Wage in the Wealthy Work*, edited by Jerome Gautié and John Schmitt, 91–146. New York: Russel Sage Publications.

Brenner, Johanna, and Nancy Fraser. 2017. "What Is Progressive Neoliberalism?: A Debate." *Dissent* 64(2): 130–140.

Brinkmann, Ulrich, and Oliver Nachtwey. 2010. "Krise und strategische Neuorientierung der Gewerkschaften." *Aus Politik und Zeitgeschichte* (13–14): 21–29.

Broecke, Stijn. 2016. "Do Skills Matter for Wage Inequality?" *IZA World of Labor*. https://wol.iza.org/articles/do-skills-matter-for-wage-inequality/long.

Brookes, Marissa. 2019. *The New Politics of Transnational Labor: Why Some Alliances Succeed*. Ithaca, NY: ILR Press.

Brynjolfsson, Erik, and Andrew McAfee. 2014. *The Second Machine Age: Work, Progress, and Prosperity in a Time of Brilliant Technologies*. New York: W. W. Norton.

Budd, John. 2004. *Employment with a Human Face: Balancing Efficiency, Equity, and Voice*. Ithaca, NY: ILR Press.

Budd, John, and Devasheesh Bhave. 2008. "Values, Ideologies, and Frames of Reference in Industrial Relations." In *The Sage Handbook of Industrial Relations*, edited by Paul Blyton, Edmund Heery, Nicolas Bacon, and Jack Fiorito, 92–112. London: Sage.

Carré, Françoise, and Chris Tilly. 2017. *Where Bad Jobs Are Better: Retail Jobs across Countries and Companies*. New York: Russell Sage Foundation.

Carver, Laura, and Virginia Doellgast. 2021. "Dualism or Solidarity? Conditions for Union Success in Regulating Precarious Work." *European Journal of Industrial Relations* 27(4): 367–385.

Castel, Robert. 1995. *Les Métamorphoses de la question sociale*. Paris: Fayard.

Chabrak, Nihel, Russell Craig, and Nabyla Daidj. 2016. "Financialization and the Employee Suicide Crisis at France Telecom." *Journal of Business Ethics* 139(3): 501–515.

Chandler, Alfred. 1977. *The Visible Hand: The Managerial Revolution in American Business*. Cambridge, MA: Harvard University Press.

Colclough, Christina J., Malene Nordestgaard, and Søren Kaj Andersen. 2003. "Faglige strategier og forandringer indenfor den danske telekommunikationsbranche." In *Liberalisering, globalisering ogfaglige strategier i nordisk telekommunikation: En analyse af de faglige organisationers udfordringer og udvikling i Danmark, Norge, Sverige og Finland*, edited by Chrstina J. Colclough, 78–106. National Institute for Working Life, Report No 4: 2003.http://nile.lub.lu.se/arbarch/saltsa/2003/wlr2003_04.pdf

Collier, Ruth Berins, V. B. Dubal, and Christopher L. Carter. 2018. "Disrupting Regulation, Regulating Disruption: The Politics of Uber in the United States." *Perspectives on Politics* 16(4): 919–937.

Commons, John. 1909. "American Shoemakers 1648–1895." *The Quarterly Journal of Economics* 24(1): 39–84.

Conger, Kate. 2021. "Hundreds of Google Employees Unionize, Culminating Years of Activism." *New York Times*, January 4, 2021. Accessed November 26, 2021. https://www.nytimes.com/2021/01/04/technology/google-employees-union.html.

Conway, Edel, Na Fu, Kathy Monks, Kerstin Alfes, and Catherine Bailey. 2016. "Demands or Resources? The Relationship between HR Practices, Employee Engagement, and Emotional Exhaustion within a Hybrid Model of Employment Relations." *Human Resource Management* 55(5): 901–917.

Culpepper, Pepper D. 2010. *Quiet Politics and Business Power: Corporate Control in Europe and Japan*. Cambridge: Cambridge University Press.

Culpepper, Pepper D., and Aidan Regan. 2014. "Why Don't Governments Need Trade Unions Anymore? The Death of Social Pacts in Ireland and Italy." *Socio-Economic Review* 12(4): 723–745.

Curcio, Anna. 2018. "Italy: The Revolution in Logistics." In *The Class Strikes Back: Self-Organised Workers' Struggles in the Twenty-First Century*, edited by Dario Azzellini and Michael Kraft, 259–275. Leiden, NL: Brill.

Curwen, Peter, and Jason Whalley. 2004. *Telecommunications Strategy: Cases, Theory and Applications*. London: Routledge.

Cushen, Jean, and Paul Thompson. 2016. "Financialization and Value: Why Labour and the Labour Process Still Matter." *Work, Employment and Society* 30(2): 352–365.

CWA. 2019. "CWAers Build Global Solidarity to Lift Working Conditions for Everyone," September 5, 2019. https://cwa-union.org/news/cwaers-build-global-solidarity-lift-working-conditions-for-everyone.

CWA. 2020. *AT&T's Web of Subcontractors: Building Next Generation Networks with Low-Wage Labor*. Communications Workers of America. https://cwa-union.org/sites/default/files/20201005attsubcontractorreport.pdf.

CWA. 2021. "With Biden's Infrastructure Bill Promising Nationwide Broadband Access and Good Jobs, Communications Workers of America Launches Multi-State Effort to Regulate Broadband, Close Digital Divide," April 12, 2021. https://cwa-union.org/news/releases/cwa-launches-state-broadband-regulation-effort.

Czarzasty, Jan, and Adam Mrozowicki. 2021. "Unilateral Crisis Prevention and Crumbling Social Partnership in Poland." In *The Role of Social Partners in Managing Europe's Great Recession: Crisis Corporatism or Corporatism in Crisis?*, edited by Bernhard Ebbinghaus and J. Timo Weishaupt, 121–143. London: Routledge.

Dardot, Pierre, and Christian Laval. 2014. *The New Way of the World: On Neoliberal Society*. Brooklyn: Verso Trade.

De Stefano, Valerio. 2019. "'Negotiating the Algorithm': Automation, Artificial Intelligence, and Labor Protection." *Comparative Labor Law & Policy Journal* 41: 15.

Diedrich, Andreas, and Olga Bergström. 2006. *The Job Security Councils in Sweden*. Göteborg University, School of Business, Economics, and Law/Institute of Management of Innovation and Technology (IMIT). https://ec.europa.eu/employment_social/anticipedia/document/show.do?id=2641.

Diehl, Bruno, and Gérard Doublet. 2010. *Orange: Le déchirement: France Télécom ou la dérive du management*. Paris: Editions Gallimard.

DiMaggio, Dan. 2017. "Building an Army to Fight Runaway Inequality." *Labor Notes*, April 4, 2017. https://labornotes.org/2017/04/building-army-fight-runaway-inequality

Doellgast, Virginia. 2012. *Disintegrating Democracy at Work: Labor Unions and the Future of Good Jobs in the Service Economy*. Ithaca, NY: ILR Press.

Doellgast, Virginia, Maxime Bellego, and Elisa Pannini. 2021. "After the Social Crisis: The Transformation of Employment Relations at France Télécom." *Socio-Economic Review* 19(3): 1127–1147.

Doellgast, Virginia, and Peter Berg. 2018. "Negotiating Flexibility: External Contracting and Working Time Control in German and Danish Telecommunications Firms." *ILR Review* 71(1): 117–142.

Doellgast, Virginia, Matthew Bidwell, and Alexander J. S. Colvin. 2021. "New Directions in Employment Relations Theory: Understanding Fragmentation, Identity, and Legitimacy." *ILR Review* 74(3): 555–579.

Doellgast, Virginia, and Ian Greer. 2007. "Vertical Disintegration and the Disorganization of German Industrial Relations." *British Journal of Industrial Relations* 45(1): 55–76.

Doellgast, Virginia, Nathan Lillie, and Valeria Pulignano. 2018. *Reconstructing Solidarity: Labour Unions, Precarious Work, and the Politics of Institutional Change in Europe*. Oxford: Oxford University Press.

Doellgast, Virginia, and David Marsden. 2019. "Institutions as Constraints and Resources: Explaining Cross-National Divergence in Performance Management." *Human Resource Management Journal* 29(2): 199–216.

Doellgast, Virginia, Katja Sarmiento-Mirwaldt, and Chiara Benassi. 2013. *Alternative Routes to Good Jobs in the Service Economy: Employment Restructuring and Human Resource Management in Incumbent Telecommunications Firms*. London: London School of Economics and Political Science.

Doellgast, Virginia, Katja Sarmiento-Mirwaldt, and Chiara Benassi. 2015. "Union Campaigns to Organize across Production Networks in the European Telecommunications Industry: Lessons from the UK, Italy, Sweden, and Poland." In *The Outsourcing Challenge: Organizing Workers across Fragmented Production Networks*, edited by Jan Drahokoupil, 177–198. Brussels: ETUI.

Doellgast, Virginia, Katja Sarmiento-Mirwaldt, and Chiara Benassi. 2016. "Contesting Firm Boundaries: Institutions, Cost Structures, and the Politics of Externalization." *ILR Review* 69(3): 551–578.

Doellgast, Virginia, and Lisa Sezer. 2012. *Making the Right Call: Redesigning Call Centres from the Bottom Up*. UNI Global Union.

Dore, Ronald Philip. 2000. *Stock Market Capitalism: Welfare Capitalism: Japan and Germany versus the Anglo-Saxons*. Oxford: Oxford University Press on Demand.

Dorigatti, Lisa. 2017. "Trade Unions in Segmented Labor Markets: Evidence from the German Metal and Chemical Sectors." *ILR Review* 70(4): 919–941.

Dörre, Klaus, Hajo Holst, and Oliver Nachtwey. 2009. "Organising—A Strategic Option for Trade Union Renewal?" *International Journal of Action Research* 5(1): 33–63.

Drahokoupil, Jan, ed. 2015. *The Outsourcing Challenge: Organizing Workers across Fragmented Production Networks*. Brussels: ETUI.

Dribbusch, Heiner. 2004. "Working Time Cuts Agreed in Exchange for Job Guarantees at Deutsche Telekom." EIRO. http://www.eiro.eurofound.eu.int/2004/05/feature/de0 405205f.html.

Dribbusch, Heiner. 2019. "New Militancy in a Changing Industrial Landscape: The Migration of Industrial Action to the German Service Sector." *WSI Mitteilungen*. Special Issue 2019, 95–124.

Durazzi, Niccolo, Timo Fleckenstein, and Soohyun Christine Lee. 2018. "Social Solidarity for All? Trade Union Strategies, Labor Market Dualization, and the Welfare State in Italy and South Korea." *Politics & Society* 46(2): 205–233.

Durkheim, Emile. 1893. *The Division of Labor in Society*. New York: Simon and Schuster.

Eaton, Adrienne E., Susan J. Schurman, and Martha A. Chen. 2017. *Informal Workers and Collective Action: A Global Perspective*. Ithaca, NY: Cornell University Press.

Edwards, Tony, Paul Marginson, and Anthony Ferner. 2013. "Multinational Companies in Cross-National Context: Integration, Differentiation, and the Interactions between MNCS and Nation States: Introduction to a Special Issue of the ILRReview." *ILR Review* 66(3): 547–587.

Eichhorst, Werner, and Paul Marx. 2021. "How Stable is Labour Market Dualism? Reforms of Employment Protection in Nine European Countries." *European Journal of Industrial Relations* 27(1): 93–110.

Eidlin, Barry. 2018. *Labor and the Class Idea in the United States and Canada*. Cambridge: Cambridge University Press.

Emmenegger, Patrick. 2010. "The Long Road to Flexicurity: The Development of Job Security Regulations in Denmark and Sweden." *Scandinavian Political Studies* 33(3): 271–294.

Emmenegger, Patrick. 2014. *The Power to Dismiss: Trade Unions and the Regulation of Job Security in Western Europe*. New York: Oxford University Press.

Engels, Friedrich. 1845. *The Condition of the Working Class in England*. Oxford: Oxford University Press.

Erixon, L. 2008. "The Rehn-Meidner Model in Sweden: Its Rise, Challenges and Survival." *Journal of Economic Issues* 44(3): 677–715.

Esping-Andersen, Gøsta. 1990. *The Three Worlds of Welfare Capitalism*. Princeton, NJ: Princeton University Press.

Esping-Andersen, Gøsta, and Walter Korpi. 1984. "Social Policy as Class Politics in Post-War Capitalism: Scandinavia, Austria, and Germany." In *Order and Conflict in Contemporary Capitalism: Studies in the Political Economy of Western European Nations*, edited by John H. Goldthorpe, 179–208. Oxford: Oxford University Press.

ETUC. 2006. *The European Social Model*. European Trade Union Confederation. https://www.etuc.org/en/european-social-model.

ETUI. 2020. *Strikes Map*. European Trade Union Institute. https://www.etui.org/sites/default/files/2020-06/Strikesmap_20200407_1.pdf.

Eurofound. 2002. *Pacts for Employment and Competitiveness Case Studies: Telia*. European Foundation for the Improvement of Living and Working Conditions. http://www.eurofound.europa.eu/areas/industrialrelations/pecs/pdf/french/pecs_telia.pdf.

European Commission. 2010. *Progress Report on the Single European Electronic Communications Market—15th Report*. Brussels, Belgium. http://ec.europa.eu/information_society/policy/ecomm/library/communications_reports/annualreports/15th/index_en.htm.

Fantasia, Rick. 1989. *Cultures of Solidarity*. Berkeley: University of California Press.

Ferreras, Isabelle. 2017. *Firms as Political Entities: Saving Democracy through Economic Bicameralism*. Cambridge: Cambridge University Press.

Ferreras, Isabelle, Ian MacDonald, Gregor Murray, and Valeria Pulignano. 2020. "Introduction: Institutional Experimentation for Better (or Worse) Work." *Transfer: European Review of Labour and Research* 26(2): 113–118.

Fine, Janice, and Tim Bartley. 2019. "Raising the Floor: New Directions in Public and Private Enforcement of Labor Standards in the United States." *Journal of Industrial Relations* 61(2): 252–276.

Fischer-Daly, Matthew. 2021. "Human Dignity and Power: Worker Struggles against Precarity in US Agribusiness." *Labor Studies Journal* 46(4): 369–393.

Foucault, Michel. 1979. *The Birth of Biopolitics: Lectures at the Collège de France, 1978–1979*. New York: Picador.

France Telecom. 2001. *France Telecom Annual Report*.

Freeman, Richard B., and James L. Medoff. 1984. *What Do Unions Do?* New York: Basic Books.

Frey, Carl Benedikt. 2019. *The Technology Trap: Capital, Labor, and Power in the Age of Automation*. Princeton, NJ: Princeton University Press.

Friedman, Thomas L. 2007. *The World Is Flat: A Brief History of the Twenty-First Century*. New York: Farrar, Straus & Giroux.

Galant, Michael. 2020. "Philippine Call Center Workers Are in Danger: It's Our Problem, Too." *In These Times*, May 27, 2020. https://inthesetimes.com/article/philippine-call-center-workers-covid-cwa-unions-corporate-globalization

Gautié, Jérôme, and John Schmitt, eds. 2009. *Low Wage Work in the Wealthy World*. New York: Russell Sage Foundation.

Geary, John, Johan Martin-Löf, Claes-Göran Sundelius, and Bertil Thorngren. 2010. *The History of Telia*.Stockholm. https://thorngren.nu/wp-content/uploads/2014/03/The-History-of-Telia.pdf

Giry, Benoit. 2014. "La faute, la panne et l'insatisfaction: Une socio-histoire de l'organisation du travail de traitement des réclamations dans les services du téléphone." *Sociologie du Travail* 57(3): 277–298.

Givan, Rebecca Kolins, and Adrienne E. Eaton. 2021. "Mobilizing to Win in Europe: Change to Win and the Diffusion of Union Strategy." *British Journal of Industrial Relations* 59(3): 617–642.

Givan, Rebecca Kolins, and Amy Schrager Lang. 2020. *Strike for the Common Good: Fighting for the Future of Public Education*. Ann Arbor: University of Michigan Press.

Godard, John. 2004. "A Critical Assessment of the High-Performance Paradigm." *British Journal of Industrial Relations* 42(2): 349–378.

Goldman, Debbie J. 2021. *Resistance in the Digital Workplace: Call Center Workers in Bell Telephone Companies, 1965–2005*. PhD dissertation, University of Maryland, College Park.

Goos, Maarten, Alan Manning, and Anna Salomons. 2014. "Explaining Job Polarization: Routine-Biased Technological Change and Offshoring." *American Economic Review* 104(8): 2509–2526.

Gospel, Howard, and Andrew Pendleton, eds. 2005. *Corporate Governance and Labour Management: An International Comparison*. New York: Oxford University Press.

Gospel, Howard, and Andrew Pendleton. 2014. "Financialization, New Investment Funds, and Labour." In *Financialization, New Investment Funds, and Labour: An International Comparison*, edited by Howard Gospel, Andrew Pendleton, and Sigurt Vitols, 53–85. Oxford: Oxford University Press.

Gramsci, Antonio. 1919. "Workers' Democracy." *L'Ordine Nuovo*, June 21, 1919.

Grant, Christine, and Emma Russell. 2020. *Agile Working and Well-Being in the Digital Age*. New York: Springer.

Greer, Ian. 2008. "Organized Industrial Relations in the Information Economy: The German Automotive Sector as a Test Case." *New Technology, Work and Employment* 23(3): 181–196.

Greer, Ian. 2016. "Welfare Reform, Precarity and the Re-commodification of Labour." *Work, Employment and Society* 30(1): 162–173.

Greer, Ian, and Virginia Doellgast. 2017. "Marketization, Inequality, and Institutional Change: Toward a New Framework for Comparative Employment Relations." *Journal of Industrial Relations* 59(2): 192–208.

Greer, Ian, and Marco Hauptmeier. 2008. "Political Entrepreneurs and Co-Managers: Labour Transnationalism at Four Multinational Auto Companies." *British Journal of Industrial Relations* 46(1): 76–97.

Greer, Ian, and Marco Hauptmeier. 2012. "Identity Work: Sustaining Transnational Collective Action at General Motors Europe." *Industrial Relations: A Journal of Economy and Society* 51(2): 275–299.

Greer, Ian, and Marco Hauptmeier. 2016. "Management Whipsawing: The Staging of Labor Competition under Globalization." *ILR Review* 69(1): 29–52.
Grimshaw, Damian, Colette Fagan, Gail Hebson, and Isabel Tavora. 2017. *Making Work More Equal: A New Labour Market Segmentation Approach.* Manchester: Manchester University Press.
Grimshaw, Damian, Jill Rubery, Dominique Anxo, Maya Bacache-Beauvallet, László Neumann, and Claudia Weinkopf. 2015. "Outsourcing of Public Services in Europe and Segmentation Effects: The Influence of Labour Market Factors." *European Journal of Industrial Relations* 21(4): 295–313.
Gumbrell-McCormick, Rebecca, and Richard Hyman. 2013. "Mapping the Terrain: Varieties of Industrial Relations and Trade Unionism." In *Trade Unions in Western Europe: Hard Times, Hard Choices*, edited by Rebecca Gumbrell-McCormick and Richard Hyman, 2–29. Oxford: Oxford University Press.
Hall, Peter A. 2017. "The Political Sources of Social Solidarity." In *The Strains of Commitment: The Political Sources of Solidarity in Diverse Societies*, edited by Keith Banting and Will Kymlicka, 201–232. Oxford: Oxford University Press.
Hall, Peter A., and Michèle Lamont. 2009. *Successful Societies: How Institutions and Culture Affect Health.* Cambridge: Cambridge University Press.
Hall, Peter A., and David Soskice, eds. 2001. *Varieties of Capitalism: The Institutional Foundations of Comparative Advantage.* Oxford: Oxford University Press.
Hall, Peter A., and Kathleen Thelen. 2009. "Institutional Change in Varieties of Capitalism." *Socio-Economic Review* 7(1): 7–34.
Hancock, Julie I., David G. Allen, Frank A. Bosco, Karen R. McDaniel, and Charles A. Pierce. 2013. "Meta-Analytic Review of Employee Turnover as a Predictor of Firm Performance." *Journal of Management* 39(3): 573–603.
Hassel, Anke. 2014. "The Paradox of Liberalization—Understanding Dualism and the Recovery of the German Political Economy." *British Journal of Industrial Relations* 52(1): 57–81.
Hauptmeier, Marco, and Edmund Heery. 2014. *Ideas at Work.* Milton Park: Taylor & Francis.
Heckscher, Charles, and John McCarthy. 2014. "Transient Solidarities: Commitment and Collective Action in Post-Industrial Societies." *British Journal of Industrial Relations* 52(4): 627–657.
Heinisch, Reinhard. 2000. "Coping with Economic Integration: Corporatist Strategies in Germany and Austria in the 1990s." *West European Politics* 23(3): 67–96.
Helfen, Markus, Jörg Sydow, and Carsten Wirth. 2020. "Service Delivery Networks and Employment Relations at German Airports: Jeopardizing Industrial Peace on the Ground?" *British Journal of Industrial Relations* 58(1): 168–198.
Hermann, Christoph, and Jörg Flecker. 2013. *Privatization of Public Services: Impacts for Employment, Working Conditions, and Service Quality in Europe.* Milton Park: Routledge.
Heshmati, Almas. 2003. "Productivity Growth, Efficiency and Outsourcing in Manufacturing and Service Industries." *Journal of Economic Surveys* 17(1): 79–112.
Hirschman, Albert O. 1970. *Exit, Voice, and Loyalty: Responses to Decline in Firms, Organizations, and States.* Cambridge, MA: Harvard University Press.
Hoffmann, Jürgen. 2006. "The Relevance of the Exit Option: The Challenge for European Trade Unions of Post-Fordism, Internationalisation of the Economy and Financial Market Capitalism." *Transfer: European Review of Labour and Research* 12(4): 609–620.

Hofmann, Julia, Carina Altreiter, Jörg Flecker, Saskja Schindler, and Ruth Simsa. 2019. "Symbolic Struggles over Solidarity in Times of Crisis: Trade Unions, Civil Society Actors and the Political Far Right in Austria." *European Societies* 21(5): 649–671.

Holst, Hajo. 2008. "The Political Economy of Trade Union Strategies in Austria and Germany: The Case of Call Centres." *European Journal of Industrial Relations* 14(1): 25–45.

Holst, Hajo 2014. "Commodifying Institutions: Vertical Disintegration and Institutional Change in German Labour Relations." *Work, Employment and Society* 28(1): 3–20.

Holtgrewe, Ursula. 2014. "New New Technologies: The Future and the Present of Work in Information and Communication Technology." *New Technology Work and Employment* 29(1): 9–24.

Holtgrewe, Ursula, and Virginia Doellgast. 2012. "A Service Union's Innovation Dilemma: Limitations on Creative Action in German Industrial Relations." *Work, Employment and Society* 26(2): 314–330.

Hooker, Juliet. 2009. *Race and the Politics of Solidarity*. Oxford: Oxford University Press.

hooks, bell. 1984. *Feminist Theory: From Margin to Center*. Boston: South End Press.

Höpner, Martin, and Gregory Jackson. 2003. "Entsteht ein Markt für Unternehmenskontrolle? Der Fall Mannesmann." In *Alle Macht dem Markt? Fallstudien zur Abwicklung der Deutschland AG*, edited by Wolfgang Streeck and Martin Höpner, 147–168. Frankfurt: Campus Verlag.

Howell, Chris. 2021. "Rethinking the Role of the State in Employment Relations for a Neoliberal Era." *ILR Review* 74(3): 739–772.

Hirsh, Barry, and David Macpherson. 2013. *Union Membership and Coverage Database from the CPS (Union Stats.com)*. http://www.unionstats.com

Hyman, Richard. 2001. *Understanding European Trade Unionism: Between Market, Class, and Society*. London: Sage.

Hyman, Richard. 2010. *Social Dialogue and Industrial Relations during the Economic Crisis: Innovative Practices or Business as Usual?* Geneva: ILO Geneva.

Ibsen, Christian Lyhne. 2016. "The Role of Mediation Institutions in Sweden and Denmark after Centralized Bargaining." *British Journal of Industrial Relations* 54(2): 285–310.

Ibsen, Christian Lyhne, and Kathleen Thelen. 2017. "Diverging Solidarity: Labor Strategies in the New Knowledge Economy." *World Politics* 69: 409.

Ikeler, Peter. 2016. *Hard Sell: Work and Resistance in Retail Chains*. Ithaca, NY: Cornell University Press.

Ilsøe, Anna. 2012. "CSC-konflikten og den danske model." *FAOS forskningsnotat*. https://faos.ku.dk/pdf/forskningsnotater/forskningsnotater_2012/Fnotat122.pdf

Iversen, Torben. 1996. "Power, Flexibility, and the Breakdown of Centralized Wage Bargaining: Denmark and Sweden in Comparative Perspective." *Comparative Politics* 28(4): 399–436.

Jacoby, Sanford M. 1985. *Employing Bureaucracy*. New York: Columbia University Press.

Jacoby, Sanford M. 2021. *Labor in the Age of Finance: Pensions, Politics, and Corporations from Deindustrialization to Dodd-Frank*. Princeton, NJ: Princeton University Press.

Jaehrling, Karen, Mathew Johnson, Trine P. Larsen, Bjarke Refslund, and Damian Grimshaw. 2018. "Tackling Precarious Work in Public Supply Chains: A Comparison of Local Government Procurement Policies in Denmark, Germany and the UK." *Work, Employment and Society* 32(3): 546–563.

Jansson, Jenny. 2020. *Crafting the Movement: Identity Entrepreneurs in the Swedish Trade Union Movement, 1920–1940*. Ithaca, NY: Cornell University Press.

Jiang, Kaifeng, David P. Lepak, Jia Hu, and Judith C. Baer. 2012. "How Does Human Resource Management Influence Organizational Outcomes? A Meta-Analytic Investigation of Mediating Mechanisms." *Academy of Management Journal* 55(6): 1264–1294.

Johnston, Alison, Gregory W. Fuller, and Aidan Regan. 2021. "It Takes Two to Tango: Mortgage Markets, Labor Markets and Rising Household Debt in Europe." *Review of International Political Economy* 28(4): 843–873.

Johnstone, Stewart, and Tony Dobbins. 2021. "Employment Relations in the United Kingdom." In *International and Comparative Employment Relations: Global Crises and Institutional Responses*, edited by Greg Bamber, Fang Lee Cooke, Virginia Doellgast and Chris Wright. Newbury Park, CA: Sage.

Jørgensen, Carsten. 2012. *Denmark: Industrial Relations Profile*. Eurofound: European Industrial Relations Observatory Online. http://www.eurofound.europa.eu/eiro/country/denmark.pdf.

Kalev, Alexandra, Frank Dobbin, and Erin Kelly. 2006. "Best Practices or Best Guesses? Assessing the Efficacy of Corporate Affirmative Action and Diversity Policies." *American Sociological Review* 71(4): 589–617.

Kalleberg, Arne L. 2018. *Precarious Lives: Job Insecurity and Well-Being in Rich Democracies*. New York: John Wiley & Sons.

Kalleberg, Arne L., and Steven P. Vallas. 2017. *Precarious Work*. Bingley, UK: Emerald Group.

Kapeller, Jakob, and Fabio Wolkenstein. 2013. "The Grounds of Solidarity: From Liberty to Loyalty." *European Journal of Social Theory* 16(4): 476–491.

Katz, Harry C., Rosemary Batt, and Jeffrey H. Keefe. 2003. "The Revitalization of the CWA: Integrating Collective Bargaining, Political Action, and Organizing." *Industrial and Labor Relations Review* 56(4): 573–589.

Katz, Harry C., and Alexander J. S. Colvin. 2021. "Employment Relations in the United States." In *International and Comparative Employment Relations: Global Crises and Institutional Responses*, edited by Greg Bamber, Fang Lee Cooke, Virginia Doellgast, and Chris Wright, 49–74. Newbury Park, CA: Sage.

Katzenstein, Peter. 1985. *Small States in World Markets: Industrial Policy in Europe*. Ithaca, NY: Cornell University Press.

Kellogg, Katherine C., Melissa A. Valentine, and Angele Christin. 2020. "Algorithms at Work: The New Contested Terrain of Control." *Academy of Management Annals* 14(1): 366–410.

Kelly, Erin L., and Phyllis Moen. 2020. *Overload: How Good Jobs Went Bad and What We Can Do about It*. Princeton, NJ: Princeton University Press.

Kelly, John. 1998. *Rethinking Industrial Relations: Mobilization, Collectivism, and Long Waves*. London: Routledge.

Kinderman, Daniel. 2017. "Challenging Varieties of Capitalism's Account of Business Interests: Neoliberal Think-Tanks, Discourse as a Power Resource and Employers' Quest for Liberalization in Germany and Sweden." *Socio-Economic Review* 15(3): 587–613.

Kochan, Thomas A., Adrienne E. Eaton, Robert B. McKersie, and Paul S. Adler. 2009. *Healing Together: The Labour-Managment Partnership at Kaiser Permanente*. Ithaca, NY: ILR Press.

Kochan, Thomas A., and Paul Osterman. 1994. *The Mutual Gains Enterprise*. Boston, MA: Harvard Business School Press.

Krachler, Nick, Jennie Auffenberg, and Luigi Wolf. 2021. "The Role of Organizational Factors in Mobilizing Professionals: Evidence from Nurse Unions in the United States and Germany." *British Journal of Industrial Relations* 59(3): 643–668.

Krippner, Greta R. 2011. *Capitalizing on Crisis: The Political Origins of the Rise of Finance.* Cambridge, MA: Harvard University Press.

Krippner, Greta R. 2017. "Democracy of Credit: Ownership and the Politics of Credit Access in Late Twentieth-Century America." *American Journal of Sociology* 123(1): 1–47.

Kristal, Tali, and Yinon Cohen. 2017. "The Causes of Rising Wage Inequality: The Race between Institutions and Technology." *Socio-Economic Review* 15(1): 187–212.

Labor Notes. 2020. "Verizon Unions Win Model Paid Leave Policy for Coronavirus—Will Other Unions Demand the Same?" *Labor Notes*, March 18, 2020. https://labornotes.org/blogs/2020/03/verizon-union-wins-model-paid-leave-policy-coronavirus-will-other-unions-demand-same

Lazonick, W., and M. O'Sullivan. 2000. "Maximizing Shareholder Value: A New Ideology for Corporate Governance." *Economy and Society* 29(1): 13–35.

Lee, Tamara, and Maite Tapia. 2021. "Confronting Race and other Social Identity Erasures: The Case for Critical Industrial Relations Theory." *Industrial and Labor Relations Review* 74(3): 637–662.

Lévesque, Christian, and Gregor Murray. 2010. "Understanding Union Power: Resources and Capabilities for Renewing Union Capacity." *Transfer: European Review of Labour and Research* 16(3): 333–350.

Levy, Frank, and Richard J. Murnane. 2004. *The New Division of Labor: How Computers are Creating the Next Job Market.* Princeton, NJ: Princeton University Press.

Lillie, Nathan. 2006. *A Global Union for Global Workers: Collective Bargaining and Regulatory Politics in Maritime Shipping.* New York: Routledge.

Lin, Ken-Hou, and Donald Tomaskovic-Devey. 2013. "Financialization and US Income Inequality, 1970–2008." *American Journal of Sociology* 118(5): 1284–1329.

Lukes, Steven. 1974. *Power: A Radical View.* London: Macmillan.

Luxemburg, Rosa. 1899. *Reform or Revolution.* Oxnard, CA: Pathfinder Press.

Marchington, Mick, Jill Rubery, and Fang-Lee Cooke. 2005. "Prospects for Worker Voice across Organizational Boundaries." In *Fragmenting Work: Blurring Organizational Boundaries and Disordering Hierarchies*, edited by Mick Marchington, Damian Grimshaw, Jill Rubery, and Hugh Willmott, 239–260. New York: Oxford University Press.

McCallum, Jamie K. 2013. *Global Unions, Local Power: The New Spirit of Transnational Labor Organizing.* Ithaca, NY: Cornell University Press.

McCallum, Jamie K. 2020. *Worked Over: How Round-the-Clock Work Is Killing the American Dream.* New York: Basic Books.

McCarthy, Michael A. 2017. *Dismantling Solidarity: Capitalist Politics and American Pensions since the New Deal.* Ithaca, NY: Cornell University Press.

Meardi, Guglielmo, Melanie Simms, and Duncan Adam. 2021. "Trade Unions and Precariat in Europe: Representative Claims." *European Journal of Industrial Relations* 27(1): 41–58.

Mias, Arnaud. 2008. "La configuration européenne d'une branche: Les télécommunications." In *Le nouveaux cadres du dialogue social: Europe et territoires*, edited by Annette Jobert, 129–187. Brussels: PIE Peter Lang.

Milkman, Ruth. 2020. *Immigrant Labor and the New Precariat*. New York: John Wiley & Sons.
Moisander, Johanna, Claudia Groß, and Kirsi Eräranta. 2018. "Mechanisms of Biopower and Neoliberal Governmentality in Precarious Work: Mobilizing the Dependent Self-Employed as Independent Business Owners." *Human Relations* 71(3): 375-398.
Moore, Phoebe V. 2017. *The Quantified Self in Precarity: Work, Technology and What Counts*. Milton Park: Routledge.
Mori, Anna. 2017. "The Impact of Public Services Outsourcing on Work and Employment Conditions in Different National Regimes." *European Journal of Industrial Relations* 23(4): 347-364.
Murhem, Sofia. 2003. "Telekomservice i Sverige." In *Liberalisering, globalisering ogfaglige strategier i nordisk telekommunikation: En analyse af de faglige organisationers udfordringer og udvikling i Danmark, Norge, Sverige og Finland*, edited by Chrstina J. Colclough, 78-106. National Institute for Working Life, Report No 4: 2003. http://nile.lub.lu.se/arbarch/saltsa/2003/wlr2003_04.pdf.
O'Brady, Sean. 2021. "Fighting Precarious Work with Institutional Power: Union Inclusion and its Limits across Spheres of Action." *British Journal of Industrial Relations* 59(4): 1084-1107.
O'Brady, Sean, and Virginia Doellgast. 2021. "Collective Voice and Worker Wellbeing: Union Influence on Performance Monitoring and Emotional Exhaustion in Call Centers." *Industrial Relations: A Journal of Economy and Society* 60(3): 307-337.
OECD and AIAS. 2021. *Institutional Characteristics of Trade Unions, Wage Setting, State Intervention and Social Pacts*. Paris: OECD. www.oecd.org/employment/ictwss-database.htm.
Ost, David. 2018. "Workers and the Radical Right in Poland." *International Labor and Working-Class History* 93: 113-124.
Osterman, Paul. 2018. "In Search of the High Road: Meaning and Evidence." *ILR Review* 71(1): 3-34.
Palier, Bruno, and Kathleen Thelen. 2010. "Institutionalizing Dualism: Complementarities and Change in France and Germany." *Politics & Society* 38(1): 119-148.
Palpacuer, Florence, and Amélie Seignour. 2020. "Resisting Via Hybrid Spaces: The Cascade Effect of a Workplace Struggle against Neoliberal Hegemony." *Journal of Management Inquiry* 29(4): 418-432.
Panici, Chiara. 2013. "La vicenda Atesia. Il dilagare della precarietà e l'operato del parlamento, dei governi e dei sindacati." *Quaderni San Precario*, February 2013.
Pannini, Elisa. 2021. "Winning a Battle against the Odds: A Cleaners' Campaign." *Economic and Industrial Democracy*. Early view.
Paparella, Domenico. 2000. "Sectoral Agreement Signed in Telecommunications." Eurofound. http://www.eurofound.europa.eu/eiro/2000/07/feature/it0007158f.htm.
Pateman, Carole. 1970. *Participation and Democratic Theory*. Cambridge: Cambridge University Press.
Peck, Jamie. 2017. *Offshore: Exploring the Worlds of Global Outsourcing*. Oxford: Oxford University Press.
Pernicka, Susanne. 2005. "The Evolution of Union Politics for Atypical Employees: A Comparison between German and Austrian Trade Unions in the Private Service Sector." *Economic and Industrial Democracy* 26(2): 205-228.

Pfeffer, Jeffrey. 2018. *Dying for a Paycheck: How Modern Management Harms Employee Health and Company Performance—and What We Can Do about It*. New York: HarperBusiness.

Pignoni, Maria-Teresa, and Émilie Raynaud. 2013. *Les relations professionnelles au début des années 2010: Entre changements institutionnels, crise et évolutions sectorielles*. DARES Analyses. http://travail-emploi.gouv.fr/IMG/pdf/2013-026-2.pdf.

Piore, Michael, and Sean Safford. 2006. "Changing Regimes of Workplace Governance, Shifting Axes of Social Mobilization, and the Challenge to Industrial Relations Theory." *Industrial Relations: A Journal of Economy and Society* 45(3): 299–325.

Polanyi, Karl. 1944. *The Great Transformation: The Political and Economic Origins of Our Time*. Boston: Beacon Press.

Pontusson, Jonas. 2005. *Inequality and Prosperity: Social Europe vs. Liberal America*. Ithaca, NY: Cornell University Press.

Pontusson, Jonas. 2011. "Once again a Model: Nordic Social Democracy in a Globalized World." In *What's Left of the Left: Democrats and Social Democrats in Challenging Times*, edited by James Cronin, George Ross, and James Shoch, 89–115. Durham, NC: Duke University Press.

Poole, Michael, Russell Lansbury, and Nick Wailes. 2001. "A Comparative Analysis of Developments in Industrial Democracy." *Industrial Relations: A Journal of Economy and Society* 40(3): 490–525.

Rathgeb, Philip. 2018. *Strong Governments, Precarious Workers: Labor Market Policy in the Era of Liberalization*. Ithaca, NY: ILR Press.

Refslund, Bjarke. 2021. "When Strong Unions Meet Precarious Migrants: Building Trustful Relations to Unionise Labour Migrants in a High Union-Density Setting." *Economic and Industrial Democracy* 42(2): 314–335.

Reich, Adam, and Peter Bearman. 2018. *Working for Respect: Community and Conflict at Walmart*. New York: Columbia University Press.

Rifkin, Jeremy. 2001. *The Age of Access: The New Culture of Hypercapitalism*. London: Penguin.

Rothstein, Sidney A. 2022. *Recoding Power: Tactics for Mobilizing Tech Workers*. New York: Oxford University Press.

Royle, Tony. 2004. "Employment Practices of Multinationals in the Spanish and German Quick-Food Sectors: Low-Road Convergence?" *European Journal of Industrial Relations* 10(1): 51–71.

Rubinstein, Saul. 2000. "The Impact of Co-Management on Quality Performance: The Case of the Saturn Corporation." *Industrial and Labor Relations Review* 53(2): 197–218.

Rueda, David. 2007. *Social Democracy Inside Out: Partisanship and Labor Market Policy in Advanced Industrialized Democracies*. Oxford: Oxford University Press.

Sako, Mari, and Gregory Jackson. 2003. "Enterprise Boundaries and Employee Representation: Deutsche Telekom and NTT Compared.: Paper presented at Society for the Advancement of Socioeconomics Conference, June 26–28, 2003, Aix-en-Provence.

Samaluk, Barbara, and Ian Colling Greer. 2021. "Organised by Transitions: The Self-Organisation of Next-Generation Welfare Professionals in Slovenia." *Work in the Global Economy* 1(1–2): 95–117.

Scharpf, Fritz Wilhelm. 1987. *Sozialdemokratische Krisenpolitik in Europa*. Vol. 7. Frankfurt am Main: Campus.

Schmitter, Phillipe, and Gerhard Lehmbruch, eds. 1979. *Trends Towards Corporatist Intermediation*. Beverly Hills, CA: Sage.

Scholz, Sally J. 2008. *Political Solidarity*. Philadelphia: Penn State Press.
Schulze-Cleven, Tobias. 2018. "A Continent in Crisis: European Labor and the Fate of Social Democracy." *Labor Studies Journal* 43(1): 46–73.
Schwan, Michael, Christine Trampusch, and Florian Fastenrath. 2021. "Exploring Changes in the Management of Public Debt and Assets across Europe." *Review of International Political Economy* 28(4): 840–842.
Seifert, Hartmut, and Heiko Massa-Wirth. 2005. "Pacts for Employment and Competitiveness in Germany." *Industrial Relations Journal* 36(3): 217–240.
Sheridan, Richard. 2015. *Joy, Inc.: How We Built a Workplace People Love*. New York: Portfolio.
Shin, Duckjung, and Alison M Konrad. 2017. "Causality between High-Performance Work Systems and Organizational Performance." *Journal of Management* 43(4): 973–997.
Shire, Karen, Annika Schönauer, Mireia Valverde, and Hannelore Mottweiler. 2009. "Collective Bargaining and Temporary Contracts in Call Centre Employment in Austria, Germany and Spain." *European Journal of Industrial Relations* 15(4): 437–456.
Sil, Rudra. 2017. "The Battle over Flexibilization in Post-Communist Transitions: Labor Politics in Poland and the Czech Republic, 1989–2010." *Journal of Industrial Relations* 59(4): 420–443.
Silver, Beverly J. 2003. *Forces of Labor: Workers' Movements and Globalization since 1870*. Cambridge: Cambridge University Press.
Skorupińska, Katarzyna. 2018. "The Failure of a New Form of Employee Representation: Polish Works Councils in Comparative Perspective." *European Journal of Industrial Relations* 24(2): 163–178.
Sørensen, Ole Henning, Vassil Kirov, and Ursula Holtgrewe. 2018. "Social Partners' Levers: Job Quality and Industrial Relations in the Waste Sector in Three Small European Countries." *Industrial Relations Journal* 49(3): 242–258.
Sørensen, Ole Henning, and Claudia Weinkopf. 2009. "Pay and Working Conditions in Finance and Utility Call Centres in Denmark and Germany." *European Journal of Industrial Relations* 15(4): 395–416.
Sorge, Arndt, and Wolfgang Streeck. 1988. "Industrial Relations and Technical Change: The Case for an Extended Perspective." In *New Technology and Industrial Relations*, edited by Richard Hyman and Wolfgang Streeck, 19–47. Oxford: Blackwell.
Sorge, Arndt, and Wolfgang Streeck. 2018. "Diversified Quality Production Revisited: Its Contribution to German Socio-Economic Performance over Time." *Socio-Economic Review* 16(3): 587–612.
Stjernø, Steinar. 2009. *Solidarity in Europe: The History of an Idea*. Cambridge: Cambridge University Press.
Streeck, Wolfgang. 1992. "Revisiting Status and Contract: Pluralism, Corporatism and Flexibility." In *Social Institutions and Economic Performance: Studies of Industrial Relations in Advanced Capitalist Economies*, edited by Wolfgang Streeck, 41–75. London: Sage.
Streeck, Wolfgang. 1997. "Beneficial Constraints: On the Economic Limits of Rational Voluntarism." In *Contemporary Capitalism: The Embeddedness of Institutions*, edited by Robert Boyer and Roger J Hollingsworth, 197–219. Cambridge: Cambridge University Press.
Streeck, Wolfgang. 2009. *Re-Forming Capitalism: Institutional Change in the German Political Economy*. Oxford: Oxford University Press.

Streeck, Wolfgang, and Kathleen Thelen, eds. 2005. *Beyond Continuity: Institutional Change in Advanced Political Economies*. Oxford: Oxford University Press.
Susskind, Daniel. 2020. *A World without Work: Technology, Automation and How We Should Respond*. London: Penguin UK.
Susskind, Richard E., and Daniel Susskind. 2015. *The Future of the Professions: How Technology Will Transform the Work of Human Experts*. New York: Oxford University Press.
Tapia, Maite, Tamara L. Lee, and Mikhail Filipovitch. 2017. "Supra-Union and Intersectional Organizing: An Examination of Two Prominent Cases in the Low-Wage US Restaurant Industry." *Journal of Industrial Relations* 59(4): 487–509.
Tapia, Maite, and Lowell Turner. 2013. "Union Campaigns as Countermovements: Mobilizing Immigrant Workers in France and the United Kingdom." *British Journal of Industrial Relations* 51(3): 601–622.
Taylor, Charles. 2004. *Modern Social Imaginaries*. Durham, NC: Duke University Press.
TDC. 2003. TDC Annual Report 2003. https://tdcgroup.com/en/investor-relations/announcement-list/2004/3/tdc-annual-report-2003-13365764
TDC. 2004. TDC Annual Report 2004. https://tdcgroup.com/en/investor-relations/announcement-list/2005/2/tdc-annual-report-2004-13365690
TDC. 2005. TDC Annual Report 2005. https://tdcgroup.com/en/investor-relations/announcement-list/2006/2/tdc-annual-report-2005-13365626
TDC. 2006. TDC Annual Report 2006. https://tdcgroup.com/en/investor-relations/announcement-list/2007/2/tdc-annual-report-2006-13365573
TDC. 2008. TDC Annual Report 2008. https://tdcgroup.com/en/investor-relations/announcement-list/2008/2/tdc-annual-report-2008-13365243
TDC. 2010. TDC Annual Report 2010. https://tdcgroup.com/en/investor-relations/announcement-list/2010/2/tdc-annual-report-2010-13365892
Tele Danmark. 1997. Tele Danmark Annual Report 1997.
Thelen, Kathleen. 2014. *Varieties of Liberalization and the New Politics of Social Solidarity*. Cambridge: Cambridge University Press.
Thomas, Mark P., and Steven Tufts. 2020. "Blue Solidarity: Police Unions, Race and Authoritarian Populism in North America." *Work, Employment and Society* 34(1): 126–144.
Thomas, Pete, Louise McArdle, and Richard Saundry. 2020. "Introduction to the special Issue: The Enactment of Neoliberalism in the Workplace: The Degradation of the Employment Relationship." *Competition & Change* 24(2): 105–113.
Thompson Financial. 2012. Thompson Banker One Database.
Thompson, Paul. 2003. "Disconnected Capitalism: Or Why Employers Can't Keep Their Side of the Bargain." *Work, Employment and Society* 17(2): 359–378.
Thompson, Paul. 2013. "Financialization and the Workplace: Extending and Applying the Disconnected Capitalism Thesis." *Work, Employment and Society* 27(3): 472–488.
Tiku, Nitasha. 2019. "Three Years of Misery Inside Google, the Happiest Company in Tech." *Wired*, September 13, 2019. https://www.wired.com/story/inside-google-three-years-misery-happiest-company-tech/
Trappmann, Vera. 2012. *Trade Unions in Poland*. Friedrich Ebert Stiftung. https://library.fes.de/pdf-files/id-moe/08949.pdf.
Traxler, Franz. 2002. *Industrial Relations in Posts and Telecommunications Examined*. European Foundation for the Improvement of Living and Working Conditions. http://www.eurofound.europa.eu/eiro/2002/03/feature/at0203202f.htm.

Trif, Aurora, Valentina Paolucci, Marta Kahancova, and Aristea Koukiadaki. 2021. "Power Resources and Successful Trade Union Actions That Address Precarity in Adverse Contexts: The Case of Central and Eastern Europe." *Human Relations*. Early view. https://doi.org/10.1177/00187267211020189

Van Hoyweghen, Ine, Valeria Pulignano, and Gert Meyers. 2020. *Shifting Solidarities: Trends and Developments in European Societies*. London: Springer Nature.

Vitols, Sigurt. 2001. "Varieties of Corporate Governance: Comparing Germany and the UK." In *Varieties of Capitalism: The Institutional Foundations of Comparative Advantage*, edited by Peter A. Hall and David Soskice, 337–360. Oxford: Oxford University Press.

Vlandas, Tim. 2013. "The Politics of Temporary Work Deregulation in Europe: Solving the French Puzzle." *Politics & Society* 41(3): 425–460.

Voß, Gerd Günter, and Hans J. Pongratz. 1998. "Der Arbeitskraftunternehmer. Eine neue Grundform der Ware Arbeitskraft?" *Kolner Zeitschrift fur Soziologie und Sozialpsychologie* 50: 131–158.

Wagner, Ines. 2018. *Workers Without Borders: Posted Work and Precarity in the EU*. Ithaca, NY: ILR Press.

Wajcman, Judy. 2022. "Automation: Is it Really Different This Time?" In *Marx and the Robots: Networked Production, AI and Human Labour*, edited by Florian Butollo and Sabine Nuss, 12–21. London: Pluto Press.

Wearden, G. 2010. "Union Cancels BT Strike Ballot." *The Guardian*, July 5, 2010. http://www.guardian.co.uk/business/2010/jul/05/union-cancels-bt-strike-ballot.

Webb, Sidney, and Beatrice Webb. 1902. *Industrial Democracy*. London: Longmans, Green.

Weber, Max. 1922. *Economy and Society: An Outline of Interpretive Sociology*. Berkeley: University of California Press.

Weil, David. 2014. *The Fissured Workplace: Why Work Became So Bad for So Many and What Can Be Done to Improve It*. Cambridge, MA: Harvard University Press.

Wilkinson, Adrian, Tony Dundon, Jimmy Donaghey, and Richard B. Freeman. 2020. "Employee Voice: Bridging New Terrains and Disciplinary Boundaries." In *Handbook of Research on Employee Voice*, edited by Adrian Wilkinson, Jimmy Donaghey, Tony Dundon, and Richard B. Freeman, 2–18. Cheltenham, UK: Edward Elgar.

Wong, Julia Carrie. 2021. "Google Workers Demand Back Pay for Temps Company Underpaid for Years." *The Guardian*, September 15, 2021. https://www.theguardian.com/technology/2021/sep/15/google-underpayment-wages.

Wood, Alex J., Mark Graham, Vili Lehdonvirta, and Isis Hjorth. 2019. "Good Gig, Bad Gig: Autonomy and Algorithmic Control in the Global Gig Economy." *Work, Employment and Society* 33(1): 56–75.

Wood, S., D. Holman, and C. Stride. 2006. "Human Resource Management and Performance in UK Call Centres." *British Journal of Industrial Relations* 44(1): 99–124.

Wright, Chris F., Alex J. Wood, Jonathan Trevor, Colm McLaughlin, Wei Huang, Brian Harney, Torsten Geelan, Barry Colfer, Cheng Chang, and William Brown. 2019. "Towards a New Web of Rules: An International Review of Institutional Experimentation to Strengthen Employment Protections." *Employee Relations* 41(2): 313–330.

Index

For the benefit of digital users, indexed terms that span two pages (e.g., 52–53) may, on occasion, appear on only one of those pages.

Tables and figures are indicated by *t* and *f* following the page number

AFL-CIO (American union), 85–86
agency work. *See also specific company*
   generally, 19, 190–91
   collective bargaining and, 254
   representation domain divides and, 207–8, 212–14
   solidarity, effect of, 190–91
   structural exclusive solidarity and, 197–99
   structural inclusive solidarity and, 227, 230–31, 233–34
alienation, 22–23
alternative unions, 255
A1 (Austrian company)
   call center employees
      externalization and, 234–35, 235*f*, 238, 239*t*
      freelance contracts, 227–28
      hourly pay levels, 241*f*
      reinternalization, 240–43, 242*t*
   civil servants at, 60*t*
   collective worker voice and, 56*t*
   contesting precarity at, 244–45
   downsizing and, 129–31
      generally, 106, 141
      redundancy policies, 129–31, 139–41, 140*t*
      tables, 140, 140*t*
   exit constraints and, 56*t*, 60, 63
   externalization and
      generally, 226, 234
      agency work, 227
      call center employees, 234–35, 235*f*, 238, 239*t*
      outsourcing and subcontracting, 227, 228
      structural inclusive solidarity, 227–28, 239*t*
      subsidiaries, 228
      technicians, 235–36, 236*f*
   labor-management cooperation at, 75*f*
   participation rights and structures at, 67–71, 79
   percentage of union membership at, 74*f*, 74–75

   solidarity and, 91, 101–2
   strikes at, 76–77, 247
   structural inclusive solidarity and
      generally, 102–3, 190–91, 227–28, 239*t*
      externalization, 227–28, 239*t*
      technicians, externalization and, 235–36, 236*f*
   Telekom Austria Personalmanagement GmbH (subsidiary), 129
artificial intelligence (AI), 251, 252
associational power, 4, 244, 245. *See also specific company*
AT&T (American company)
   AT&T Mobility (subsidiary), 100
   call center employees
      externalization and, 234–35, 235*f*, 238, 239*t*
      hourly pay levels, 238, 241*f*
      outsourcing and subcontracting and, 194
      reinternalization, 240–43, 242*t*
   collective worker voice and, 56*t*
   contesting precarity at, 245
   downsizing and, 115–18
      generally, 106, 126
      mergers and acquisitions (M&A), 115
      no-layoff clauses, 116–17
      redundancy policies, 108–25, 108*t*, 125*t*
      strikes, 117
      tables, 108–25, 108*t*, 125*t*
   exit constraints and, 56*t*, 61, 63
   externalization and, 192–95
      generally, 191–92, 202–3
      call center employees, 234–35, 235*f*, 238, 239*t*
      outsourcing and subcontracting, 192–95
      structural exclusive solidarity, 192–95, 238, 239*t*
      technicians and, 235–36, 236*f*
   labor-management cooperation at, 75*f*
   ownership structure of, 107–8
   participation rights and structures at, 71, 79

AT&T (American company) (*cont.*)
  percentage of union membership at, 74*f*, 74–75
  Regional Bell Operating Companies (RBOCs), 100, 106–7
  Sitel (subcontractor), 213
  solidarity and, 98–99, 100, 101–2
  strikes at, 78, 117
  structural exclusive solidarity and
    generally, 103, 190–92
    externalization, 192–95, 238, 239*t*
  technicians, externalization and, 194, 235–36, 236*f*
  Workplace of the Future Agreement (WPOF), 78
Austria. *See also* A1 (Austrian company)
  AK (Chamber of Labor), 52–53
  Collective Agreement Act of 1949, 52–53
  collective worker voice in, 56*t*
  exit constraints in, 52–53, 56*t*, 60–61, 62, 63
  Federal Economic Chamber, 91
  Federation of Austrian Industry, 130
  Ministry of Labor, 52–53
  participation rights and structures in, 79
  privatization in, 107
  Social Democratic Party, 130
  solidarity in, 83–84, 88, 91, 101
  strikes in, 72, 76–77
  structural inclusive solidarity, 88, 91, 101–3
  structure of workplace representation in, 65
  union mobilization resources in, 72
  unions in, 52–53, 55, 61–62
  welfare state in, 52
  WKÖ (Chamber of Business), 52–53, 83, 91, 228
  works councils, 65

"Bargaining for the Common Good" movement, 259
benchmarking, 35–36
BPO industry, 61, 193, 195, 196–97, 257–58
BPO Industry Employees Network (BIEN), 195
BT (British company)
  call center employees
    discipline and, 147
    externalization and, 234–35, 235*f*, 238, 239*t*
    hourly pay levels, 238, 241*f*
    performance management and, 146–48, 185*t*
    quarterly performance reviews, 147–48
    reinternalization, 240–43, 242*t*
    warnings, 147

  collective worker voice and
    performance management, effect on, 145–46
    table, 56*t*
  contesting precarity at, 245
  debt and, 109
  downsizing and, 113–15
    generally, 106, 126
    redundancy policies, 108–25, 108*t*, 125*t*
    retraining, 114–15
    tables, 108–25, 108*t*, 125*t*
  exit constraints and
    generally, 61, 63
    performance management, effect on, 145–46
    table, 56*t*
  externalization and, 196–99
    generally, 191–92, 202–3
    agency work, 197–99
    call center employees, 234–35, 235*f*, 238, 239*t*
    outsourcing and subcontracting, 196–97
    structural exclusive solidarity, 196–99, 238, 239*t*
    technicians, 235–36, 236*f*
  labor-management cooperation at, 75*f*
  market share of, 107
  mergers and acquisitions (M&A) and, 110
  Openreach (subsidiary), 100
  ownership structure of, 107–8
  participation rights and structures at, 71, 79
  percentage of union membership at, 74*f*, 74–75
  performance management, 145–51
    generally, 144, 145–46, 150–51, 184–87
    call center employees and, 146–48, 185*t*
    collective worker voice, effect of, 145–46
    exit constraints, effect of, 145–46
    technicians and, 148–50, 186*t*
  solidarity and, 98–99, 100, 101–2
  strikes at, 78
  structural exclusive solidarity and
    generally, 103, 190–92
    externalization, 196–99, 238, 239*t*
  technicians
    externalization and, 235–36, 236*f*
    GPS monitoring, 149
    performance management and, 148–50, 186*t*
business unionism, 41

call center employees. *See also specific company*
  generally, 16
  externalization and, 234–35, 235*f*, 237–38
  performance management and, 144

case studies. *See also specific company*
  generally, 4–5, 18
  case selection, 16–17
  comparative model, 102f, 102–4
  mapping, 50–51
  methodology, 16–17
Český Telecom (Czech company), 100, 101, 108–9, 111. *See also* O2 Czech Republic (Czech company)
CFDT (French union), 84, 96
CFE-CGC (French union), 84, 96, 132–33, 217
CFE-FO (French union), 96
CFTC (French union), 84, 96
CGB (German union), 84
CGIL (Italian union), 85, 96, 219, 221–22
CGT-FO (French union), 84
CGT (French union), 84, 96, 132–33, 217
CISL (Italian union), 85, 96, 221–22
class unionism, 41
ČMKOS (Czech union), 87
collective bargaining
  agency work and, 254
  exit constraints and, 24–25
  importance of, 256–57
collective worker voice
  generally, 48–49
  alternative economic models and, 33
  case studies, 50, 63–80, 68t
  change in industrial relations and, 31
  comparative model, 102f, 102–4
  contesting precarity and, 3–4, 14
  decline of, 34–36
  democracy and, 30–31
  economic benefits of, 32–33
  as education, 31
  employers and, 21
  exit constraints, relation to, 21, 48–49
  financialization and, 34–35
  forms of, 31–32
  incumbent companies, percentage of union membership in, 73–75, 74f
  institutional power and, 4, 244
  labor-management cooperation, 75f
  legal and state support for unions, 72–73
  liberalization and, 34–35
  participation rights and structures, 64–71, 68t
  performance management, effect on, 144, 188–89
  representation on corporate boards, 67
  strikes, 73–79
  structure of workplace representation, 64–67
  theory of, 30–36
  union mobilization resources, 68t, 72–79
  vertical disintegration and, 34, 35–36
Committee for Better Banks, 259
commodification, 23
contesting precarity. *See also specific company*
  generally, 3–4, 17–18
  collective worker voice and, 3–4, 14, 30–36
  conditions for
    generally, 247–48
    enlightened management, 248–50
    high-performance work systems, 248–50
    technology-driven globalization, 250–53
  creative approaches, 246–47
  exit constraints and, 3, 4, 14, 22–30
  ideological divides and, 246–47
  representation domain divides and, 246–47
  social regulation of markets, strengthening, 253–56
  solidarity and, 4, 14, 36–48
  strikes and, 247
  theory of, 4
Courtin, Pascal, 131
COVID-19 pandemic, 258
CWA (American union), 10, 78, 99, 116–18, 192, 193–95, 258–59
CWU (British union), 78, 99, 114, 145–46, 147–48, 196–99
Czech Republic. *See also* O2 Czech Republic (Czech company)
  collective worker voice in, 56t
  exit constraints in, 54–55, 56t, 60–61
  incumbent companies, percentage of union membership in, 73–74
  privatization in, 107
  representation on corporate boards in, 67
  solidarity in, 86, 87–88, 98–99, 100–1
  strikes in, 73, 79
  structural exclusive solidarity in, 98–99, 100–2, 103
  structure of workplace representation in, 67
  union mobilization resources in, 73
  unions in, 54, 61–62
  welfare state in, 54
  works councils, 67
Czech Union of Postal, Telecommunications, and Press Distribution Employers (Czech employer association), 100–1

Dansk EL-Forbund (Danish union), 208, 212
Dansk Metal (Danish union), 75–76, 92–93, 119–20, 163–64, 208, 209–10, 211, 212–13
DBB (German union), 84

Denmark. *See also* TDC (Danish company)
  AC (Danish Confederation of Professional Associations), 82
  Act on Salaried Employees, 52
  collective worker voice in, 56t
  cooperation committees, 64
  DA (Confederation of Danish Employers), 82
  DE (Danish Chamber of Commerce), 82–83
  DHS (Danish Commerce and Services), 82–83
  DI (Confederation of Danish Industries), 82–83, 92–93
  exit constraints in, 51–52, 56t, 59–60, 61, 63
  flexicurity in, 118
  incumbent companies, percentage of union membership in, 73–74
  LH (Danish Association of Managers and Executives), 82
  LO (Danish Confederation of Trade Unions), 82
  privatization in, 107
  representation domain divides in, 92–93, 101–2, 103–4
  solidarity in, 81–83, 87–88, 92–93, 101
  strikes in, 72, 75–76
  structure of workplace representation in, 64–65
  union mobilization resources in, 72
  unions in, 51–52, 55, 61–62, 72
  wages in, 52
  welfare state in, 51–52
Deutsche Telekom (German company)
  generally, 8–10
  apprenticeships at, 172
  associational power and, 14–16
  call center employees
    absenteeism and, 177
    externalization and, 238, 239t
    hourly pay levels, 238, 241f
    monitoring, 173–74
    pay at risk, 174–75
    performance management and, 173–78, 185t
    prizes and, 177
    reinternalization, 240–43, 242t
    sales goals, 175
    stress and, 177–78
    time controls, 175
    variable pay, 173, 175–76
  civil servants at, 60t
  collective worker voice and, 56t
    performance management, effect on, 184
  contesting precarity at, 14, 245–46
  downsizing and, 126–29
    generally, 106
    redundancy policies, 126–29, 139–41, 140t
    tables, 140, 140t
  DTKS (Deutsche Telekom Kundenservice) (subsidiary), 173, 174, 177–78, 183, 184, 206, 207–8
  DTTS (Deutsche Telekom Technischer Service) (subsidiary), 178–81, 183, 184, 205–7
  exit constraints and
    generally, 60, 62, 63
    performance management, effect on, 184
    table, 56t
  externalization and
    generally, 203, 213–14
    agency work, 207–8
    call center employees, 238, 239t
    outsourcing and subcontracting, 9, 203–4, 206–8, 236–37
    representation domain divides, 203–8, 238, 239t
    subsidiaries, 13, 204–6, 236–37
    technicians, 235–36, 236f
  institutional power and, 14, 15–16
  labor-management cooperation at, 75f
  mergers and acquisitions (M&A) and, 110
  participation rights and structures at, 67–71, 79
  percentage of union membership at, 74f, 74–75
  performance management, 171–84
    generally, 144, 171–72, 183–84, 187, 188
    call center employees and, 173–78, 185t
    collective worker voice, effect of, 184
    exit constraints, effect of, 184
    technicians and, 178–83, 186t
    works councils and, 171–72, 173–74, 175, 178, 180–81, 182, 183
  precarity and, 13
  representation domain divides and
    generally, 190–91, 203–8
    externalization, 203–8, 238, 239t
    outsourcing and subcontracting and, 203–4, 207–8
  solidarity and, 14–16, 93–94, 101–2
  strikes at, 76–77, 247
  technicians
    generally, 9
    autonomy of, 180
    externalization and, 235–36, 236f
    goals, 181–83
    parity commission, 182

pay at risk, 181
pay reductions, 179–80
performance management and, 178–83, 186t
variable pay, 181, 182–83
Telekom Training, 172
T-Mobile (subsidiary), 257–58
T-Service (subsidiary), 205
unions and, 8, 9–10, 14
Vivento Customer Service (VCS) (subsidiary), 204–5
Vivento Personal Service Agentur (PSA) (subsidiary), 127, 128
Vivento Technische Service (VTS) (subsidiary), 205
Walter Services (subcontractor), 204
works councils and, 246–47
generally, 9–10, 15–16
performance management and, 171–72, 173–74, 175, 178, 180–81, 182, 183
DGB (German union), 62, 84
diversified quality production, 32–33
double movement, 25–26
downsizing. *See also specific company*
generally, 18, 105–6, 141–42
exit constraints, effect of
generally, 106
strong exit constraints, 126–41, 140t
weak exit constraints, 111–26, 125t
financialization and, 109–10
liberalization and, 106–7
ownership structure and, 107–9
DPG (German union), 126–27

enlightened management, 248–50
entrepreneurship, solidarity and, 45–46
European Trade Union Confederation (ETUC), 33
European Union
Acquired Rights Directive, 63
privatization in, 107
exclusive pay-setting, 25
"exit, voice, and loyalty" framework, 3–4, 14, 20
exit constraints
generally, 48–49
case studies, 50, 51–63
collective bargaining and, 24–25
collective worker voice, relation to, 21, 48–49
comparative analysis, 56–63, 56t, 60t
comparative model, 102f, 102–4
contesting precarity and, 3, 4, 14
downsizing, effect on
generally, 106

strong exit constraints, 126–41, 140t
weak exit constraints, 111–26, 125t
employers versus unions, 20–21
financialization and, 27–28, 29
institutional power and, 4, 244
internal employment relationships, exit from, 56t, 59–60
labor legislation and, 24
liberalization and, 26, 28, 29
minimum standards, exit from, 56t, 61–62
national differences, 51–56
neoliberalism and, 26
outsourcing and subcontracting and, 29
performance management, effect on, 188–89
social policy and, 23–24
theory of, 22–30
unions and, 24–25
vertical disintegration and, 28–29
welfare state and, 23–24
externalization. *See also specific company*
agency work (*see* agency work)
call center employees and, 234–35, 235f, 237–38
comparative analysis, 234–43
ideological divides and, 214–26
outsourcing and subcontracting (*see* outsourcing and subcontracting)
precarity, effect on, 237–43
representation domain divides and, 203–14
structural exclusive solidarity and, 191–203
subsidiaries (*see* subsidiaries)
technicians and, 234, 235–36, 236f, 237–38

feminism, 38
financialization
collective worker voice and, 34–35
downsizing and, 109–10
exit constraints and, 27–28, 29
FISTEL (Italian union), 96, 221–22
flexicurity, 118
FO (French union), 131
France. *See also* France Telecom (French company)
collective worker voice in, 56t
exit constraints in, 53, 56t, 60–61, 63
France Telecom Law, 131
ideological divides in, 94–95, 96–97, 101–2, 103–4
Ministry of Labor, 53
National Rally Party, 47
participation rights and structures in, 71
privatization in, 107
representation on corporate boards in, 67

France (cont.)
   RST (employer association), 95
   solidarity in, 84–85, 87–88, 94–95, 96–97, 101
   strikes in, 73, 77
   structure of workplace representation in, 65–66
   union mobilization resources in, 73
   unions in, 53, 55, 61–62
   welfare state in, 53
   works councils, 65
France Telecom (French company)
   generally, 5–8
   associational power and, 14–15
   call center employees
      absenteeism and, 154–55
      discipline and, 152
      externalization and, 234–35, 235*f*, 238, 239*t*
      hourly pay levels, 241*f*
      incentives and, 151, 152
      monitoring, 155
      outsourcing and subcontracting and, 214–15
      performance management and, 152–57, 185*t*
      reinternalization, 240–43, 242*t*
   civil servants at, 60*t*
   collective worker voice and
      performance management, effect on, 151–52
      table, 56*t*
   contesting precarity at, 14, 245–46
   debt and, 109
   downsizing and, 131–34
      generally, 106, 141, 142
      redundancy policies, 131–34, 139–41, 140*t*
      tables, 140, 140*t*
   exit constraints and
      generally, 60, 63
      performance management, effect on, 151–52
      table, 56*t*
   externalization and, 214–17
      generally, 214, 225–26
      call center employees, 234–35, 235*f*, 238, 239*t*
      ideological divides, 214–17, 239*t*
      outsourcing and subcontracting, 8, 214–17
      technicians, 235–36, 236*f*
   ideological divides and
      generally, 190–91
      externalization, 214–17, 239*t*
   institutional power and, 14, 15
   market share of, 107
   mergers and acquisitions (M&A) and, 108–9, 110
   moral harassment at, 6–7, 134
   Nouvelle Expérience des Télécommunications (NExT), 6, 132
   Observatory of Stress and Forced Mobility, 6
   ownership structure of, 108
   participation rights and structures at, 71, 79
   percentage of union membership at, 74–75
   performance management, 151–63
      generally, 144, 151–52, 162–63, 184–87, 189
      call center employees and, 152–57, 185*t*
      collective worker voice, effect of, 151–52
      exit constraints, effect of, 151–52
      technicians and, 157–62, 186*t*
   precarity and, 13
   promotions based on performance evaluations, 153–54
   prosecutions of, 134
   solidarity and, 14–15, 95, 96–97, 101–2
   strikes at, 77
   suicides at, 6, 15, 133, 134, 155
   technicians
      generally, 7–8
      collective identity of, 158–59, 162
      externalization and, 235–36, 236*f*
      GPS monitoring, 157–58
      individual monitoring, 158
      multi-skilled teams, 159–60
      outsourcing and subcontracting and, 214–16
      performance improvement programs, 160–61
      performance management and, 157–62, 186*t*
      stress and, 159
   unions and, 6–7, 14
   variable pay, 155–57
FZZ (Polish union), 86–87
FZZPT (Polish union), 98

Germany. *See also* Deutsche Telekom (German company)
   collective worker voice in, 56*t*
   dual system of training, 172
   exit constraints in, 52–53, 56*t*, 60–61, 62, 63
   incumbent companies, percentage of union membership in, 73–74
   job protection in, 171–72
   participation rights and structures in, 67–71
   privatization in, 107
   representation domain divides in, 92, 93–94, 101–2, 103–4
   solidarity in, 83, 84, 87–88, 92, 93–94, 101
   strikes in, 72, 76–77

structure of workplace representation in, 65
union mobilization resources in, 72
unions in, 52–53, 55, 61–62
welfare state in, 52
Works Constitution Act, 10
works councils in, 65, 171–72
Ghent system, 72
globalization
　alternatives to, 251
　solidarity and, 44
　technology-driven globalization, 250–53
GMB (British union), 85–86
Google, 249–50
GPA (Austrian union), 62, 84, 91, 94, 227, 228
GPF (Austrian union), 91, 227

hedge funds, 27–28
high-performance work systems, 248–50
HK (Danish union), 92–93, 163–64, 208–9, 213

IBEW (American union), 99
identity politics, solidarity and, 46–47
ideological divides. *See also specific company*
　generally, 94–98
　contesting precarity and, 246–47
　externalization and, 214–26
　outsourcing and subcontracting and, 214–22, 223–25
　subsidiaries and, 222–23
IG BCE (German union), 43–44
IG Metall (German union), 43–44, 93–94
inclusive pay-setting, 25
individualism, solidarity and, 45–46
industrial disputes. *See* strikes
institutional power, 4, 244. *See also specific company*
Italy. *See also* Telecom Italia (Italian company)
　collective worker voice in, 56t
　Confindustria (employer association), 95
　Damiano Ordinances, 220
　exit constraints in, 53, 56t, 60–61, 63
　ideological divides in, 94–95, 96, 101–2, 103–4
　incumbent companies, percentage of union membership in, 73–74
　Ministry of Labor, 135
　participation rights and structures in, 71
　privatization in, 107
　representation on corporate boards in, 67
　RSAs, 66
　RSUs, 66
　solidarity in, 84, 85, 87–88, 94–95, 96, 101
　strikes in, 73, 77–78

structure of workplace representation in, 65, 66
union mobilization resources in, 73
unions in, 53, 61–62
welfare state in, 53

labor legislation, exit constraints and, 24
labor solidarity. *See* solidarity
liberalization
　collective worker voice and, 34–35
　exit constraints and, 26, 28, 29
　privatization and, 106–7, 108, 108t
　solidarity and, 43–44

Manpower (staffing agency), 198–99, 233
market-oriented restructuring
　generally, 2–3
　politics of, 13–14
　precarity and, 14
Marx, Karl, 22–23
mergers and acquisitions (M&A), 108–10
methodology of study, 16–17

neoliberalism
　exit constraints and, 26
　solidarity and, 45–47
NIDIL (Italian union), 219, 221
NSZZ Solidarność (Polish union), 86–87, 98

ÖGB (Austrian union), 84
OPZZ (Polish union), 86–87
Orange plc, 109
Orange Polska (Polish company)
　call center employees
　　externalization and, 234–35, 235f, 238, 239t
　　hourly pay levels, 241f
　　reinternalization, 240–43, 242t
　collective worker voice and, 56t
　contesting precarity at, 245
　debt and, 109
　downsizing and, 111–13
　generally, 106, 126, 142
　redundancy policies, 108–25, 108t, 125t
　strikes, 112
　tables, 108–25, 108t, 125t
　exit constraints and, 56t, 63
　externalization and
　　generally, 191–92, 202–3
　　call center employees, 234–35, 235f, 238, 239t
　　outsourcing and subcontracting, 201
　　spin-offs, 201–2

Orange Polska (Polish company) (*cont.*)
    structural exclusive solidarity, 201–2, 239*t*
    subsidiaries, 201–2
    technicians, 235–36, 236*f*
  labor-management cooperation at, 75*f*
  mergers and acquisitions (M&A) and, 108–9
  Orange Customer Service (OCS) (subsidiary), 202
  participation rights and structures at, 71, 79
  percentage of union membership at, 74*f*, 74–75
  solidarity and, 95, 97–98, 101–2
  strikes at, 79, 112
  structural exclusive solidarity and
    generally, 103, 190–92
    externalization, 201–2, 239*t*
  technicians, externalization and, 235–36, 236*f*
Organisation for Economic Co-operation and Development (OECD), 53, 54
OSZPTNS (Czech union), 99, 100–1
O2 Czech Republic (Czech company)
  call center employees
    externalization and, 234–35, 235*f*, 238, 239*t*
    hourly pay levels, 241*f*
    outsourcing and subcontracting and, 199, 200
    reinternalization, 240–43, 242*t*
  collective worker voice and, 56*t*
  contesting precarity at, 245
  debt and, 109
  downsizing and, 111
    generally, 236–37
    overview, 106, 126
    redundancy policies, 108–25, 108*t*, 125*t*
    tables, 108–25, 108*t*, 125*t*
  exit constraints and, 56*t*, 63
  externalization and, 199–201
    generally, 191–92, 202–3
    call center employees, 234–35, 235*f*, 238, 239*t*
    outsourcing and subcontracting, 199–201
    structural exclusive solidarity, 199–201, 239*t*
    technicians, 235–36, 236*f*
  labor-management cooperation at, 75*f*
  mergers and acquisitions (M&A) and, 108–9
  participation rights and structures at, 71, 79
  percentage of union membership at, 74*f*, 74–75
  solidarity and, 98–99, 100, 101–2
  structural exclusive solidarity and
    generally, 103, 190–92
    externalization, 199–201, 239*t*

  technicians
    externalization and, 235–36, 236*f*
    outsourcing and subcontracting and, 199
  outsourcing and subcontracting. *See also specific company*
    generally, 19, 190–91
    employer liability for acts of, 256–57
    exit constraints and, 29
    ideological divides and, 214–22, 223–25
    representation domain divides and, 203–4, 206–12, 213–14
    solidarity, effect of, 190–91
    structural exclusive solidarity and, 192–97, 199–201
    structural inclusive solidarity and, 227, 228–30, 232

performance management. *See also specific company*
    generally, 19, 143–45, 188–89
    call center employees and, 144
    collective worker voice, effect of, 144, 188–89
    comparative analysis, 184–88, 185*t*, 186*t*
    exit constraints, effect of, 188–89
    solidarity, effect of, 145
    technicians and, 144
    unions and, 143–44
    works councils and, 143–44
Poland. *See also* Orange Polska (Polish company)
    collective worker voice in, 56*t*
    exit constraints in, 54–55, 56*t*, 59–60, 61
    ideological divides in, 94–95, 97–98, 101–2, 103–4
    incumbent companies, percentage of union membership in, 73–74
    privatization in, 107
    representation on corporate boards in, 67
    Social Dialogue Council, 54
    solidarity in, 86–88, 94–95, 97–99, 101
    strikes in, 73, 79
    structure of workplace representation in, 67
    union mobilization resources in, 73
    unions in, 54, 61–62
    welfare state in, 54
    works councils, 67
precarity
    externalization, effect of, 237–43
    market-oriented restructuring and, 14
private equity funds, 27–28
privatization, 5, 106–7
PROSA (Danish union), 210
Prospect (British union), 145–46, 196–97

representation domain divides. *See also specific company*
  generally, 92–94
  agency work and, 207–8, 212–14
  contesting precarity and, 246–47
  externalization and, 203–14
  outsourcing and subcontracting and, 203–4, 206–12, 213–14
  subsidiaries and, 204–6, 209–10, 213–14

SACO (Swedish union), 82, 88–91, 229
SEKO (Swedish union), 88–91, 229, 232, 233
SKPT (Polish union), 98, 112, 202
SLC-CGIL (Italian union), 221–22, 224–25
social dialogue institutions, 257
social policy, exit constraints and, 23–24
social regulation of markets, strengthening, 253–56
solidarity
  generally, 48–49
  agency work, effect on, 190–91
  associational power and, 4, 244
  case studies, 51, 80–102, 89t
  commodification versus, 23
  comparative model, 102f, 102–4
  contesting precarity and, 4, 14
  defined, 22, 36–38
  difficulty in achieving, 256
  entrepreneurship and, 45–46
  exclusive solidarity, 39
  globalization and, 44
  identity politics and, 46–47
  ideological divides (*see* ideological divides)
  ideology and, 41, 42
  importance of, 256
  individualism and, 45–46
  insider-outsider divides and, 43–44
  institutionalization, necessity of, 256
  liberalization and, 43–44
  loyalty compared, 22
  national differences, 81–88
  neoliberalism and, 45–47
  outsourcing and subcontracting, effect on, 190–91
  performance management, effect on, 145
  political solidarity, 37–38
  representation domain divides (*see* representation domain divides)
  shared identification, 38–39
  social solidarity, 37–38
  structural exclusive solidarity (*see* structural exclusive solidarity)
  structural inclusive solidarity (*see* structural inclusive solidarity)

  subsidiaries, effect on, 190–91
  theory of, 36–48
  vertical disintegration and, 41
strikes. *See also specific company or country*
  collective worker voice, 73–79
  contesting precarity and, 247
structural exclusive solidarity. *See also specific company*
  generally, 98–101, 103
  agency work and, 197–99
  externalization and, 191–203
  outsourcing and subcontracting and, 192–97, 199–201
  subsidiaries and, 201–2
structural inclusive solidarity. *See also specific company*
  generally, 39–41, 88–91, 102–3
  agency work and, 227, 230–31, 233–34
  outsourcing and subcontracting and, 227, 228–30, 232
  subsidiaries and, 228, 231–32
subsidiaries. *See also specific company*
  generally, 19, 190–91
  ideological divides and, 222–23
  representation domain divides and, 204–6, 209–10, 213–14
  solidarity, effect of, 190–91
  structural exclusive solidarity and, 201–2
  structural inclusive solidarity and, 228, 231–32
SUD (French union), 84–85, 96, 132–33, 217
SUD-PTT (French union), 132–33
Sweden. *See also* Telia (Swedish company)
  Almega IT&Telecom (employer association), 82–83, 91, 228, 231
  CN (Confederation of Swedish Enterprises), 82
  Co-determination Act, 64
  collective worker voice in, 56t
  Employment Protection Act, 59–60, 138
  exit constraints in, 51–52, 56t, 59–60, 61, 63
  incumbent companies, percentage of union membership in, 73–74
  LO (trade union confederation), 82
  participation rights and structures in, 79
  privatization in, 107
  PTK (Council for Negotiation and Cooperation), 12
  representation on corporate boards in, 67
  SAF (employer association), 91
  Security of Employment Act, 137
  solidarity in, 81–83, 88–91, 101
  strikes in, 11, 72, 75–76

288　INDEX

Sweden (*cont.*)
　structural inclusive solidarity in, 88–91, 101–3
　structure of workplace representation in, 64–65
　union mobilization resources in, 72
　unions in, 51–52, 55, 61–62, 72
　VF (employer association), 82–83
　wages in, 52
　welfare state in, 51–52

TDC (Danish company)
　call center employees
　　commissions, 166–67
　　discipline and, 165
　　externalization and, 234–35, 235*f*, 238, 239*t*
　　hourly pay levels, 238, 241*f*
　　performance management and, 163–67, 185*t*
　　reinternalization, 240–43, 242*t*
　　sick leave, 166
　　team-building, 164–65
　　training, 167
　　variable pay, 166
　Call Center Europe (subsidiary), 163–64, 165, 166, 167, 209, 212
　civil servants at, 60*t*
　collective worker voice and
　　performance management, effect on, 163
　　table, 56*t*
　contesting precarity at, 245–46
　debt and, 109
　downsizing and, 118–24
　　generally, 106, 126
　　redundancy policies, 108–25, 108*t*, 125*t*
　　restructuring, 119–21
　　strikes, 124
　　tables, 108–25, 108*t*, 125*t*
　exit constraints and
　　generally, 60, 63
　　performance management, effect on, 163
　　table, 56*t*
　externalization and, 208–13
　　generally, 213–14
　　agency work, 212–13, 236–37
　　call center employees, 234–35, 235*f*, 238, 239*t*
　　outsourcing and subcontracting, 122, 208–12, 213
　　representation domain divides, 208–13, 238, 239*t*
　　subsidiaries, 209–10
　　technicians, 235–36, 236*f*
　Go Excellent (subcontractor), 208–9
　labor management cooperation at, 75*f*
　market share of, 107
　mergers and acquisitions (M&A) and, 109–10
　NetDesign (subsidiary), 209
　participation rights and structures at, 67–71, 79
　percentage of union membership at, 74*f*, 74–75
　performance management, 163–71
　　generally, 144, 163, 171, 187–88
　　call center employees and, 163–67, 185*t*
　　collective worker voice, effect of, 163
　　exit constraints, effect of, 163
　　technicians and, 167–71, 186*t*
　representation domain divides and
　　generally, 190–91
　　externalization, 208–13, 238, 239*t*
　solidarity and, 92–93, 101–2
　strikes at, 76, 124, 247
　technicians
　　externalization and, 235–36, 236*f*
　　GPS monitoring, 170–71
　　performance management and, 167–71, 186*t*
　　stress and, 169
　　targets, 168, 169
　　variable pay, 169–70
technicians. *See also specific company*
　generally, 16
　externalization and, 234, 235–36, 236*f*, 237–38
　performance management and, 144
technology-driven globalization, 250–53
Telecom Italia (Italian company)
　Atesia (subcontractor), 219–21
　call center employees
　　externalization and, 234–35, 235*f*, 238, 239*t*
　　hourly pay levels, 241*f*
　　outsourcing and subcontracting and, 219–22, 223
　　reinternalization, 240–43, 242*t*
　　subsidiaries and, 222–23
　collective worker voice and, 56*t*
　contesting precarity at, 245–46
　downsizing and, 134–36
　　generally, 106, 142
　　redundancy policies, 134–36, 139–41, 140*t*
　　strikes, 135–36
　　tables, 140, 140*t*
　exit constraints and, 56*t*, 63

externalization and
  generally, 214, 225–26
  call center employees, 234–35, 235f, 238, 239t
  ideological divides, 217–25, 239t
  outsourcing and subcontracting, 217–22, 223–25
  subsidiaries, 222–23
  technicians, 235–36, 236f
ideological divides and
  generally, 190–91
  externalization, 217–25, 239t
  labor-management cooperation at, 75f
  mergers and acquisitions (M&A) and, 108–9
  participation rights and structures at, 71, 79
  percentage of union membership at, 74f, 74–75
  SIELTE (subcontractor), 223
  solidarity and, 95, 96
  strikes at, 77–78
technicians
  externalization and, 235–36, 236f
  outsourcing and subcontracting and, 223–25
Telecontact (subsidiary), 222–23
Wind (subsidiary), 95
Tele Danmark (Danish company), 92, 119, 120–21. See also TDC (Danish company)
Telekom Austria (Austrian company), 91, 129. See also A1 (Austrian company)
Telekomunikacja Polska (Polish company), 97–98, 108–9. See also Orange Polska (Polish company)
Televerket (Swedish company), 91, 107. See also Telia (Swedish company)
Telia (Swedish company)
  generally, 10–13
  associational power and, 14–16
  call center employees
    externalization and, 234–35, 235f, 238, 239t
    hourly pay levels, 241f
    reinternalization, 240–43, 242t
  civil servants at, 60t
  collective worker voice and, 56t
  contesting precarity at, 14, 244–45
  downsizing and, 136–39
    generally, 106, 141
    redundancy policies, 136–39, 140, 140t
    tables, 140, 140t
  Eltel (subcontractor), 231, 232
  exit constraints and, 56t, 60, 63
  externalization and, 228–34
    generally, 226, 234

agency work, 230–31, 233–34
  call center employees, 234–35, 235f, 238, 239t
  outsourcing and subcontracting, 11–12, 15–16, 228–30, 232
  spin-offs, 231–32
  structural inclusive solidarity, 228–34, 239t
  subsidiaries, 11–12, 231–32
  technicians, 235–36, 236f
institutional power and, 14, 15–16
labor-management cooperation at, 75f
layoffs and, 12–13
mergers and acquisitions (M&A) and, 108–9, 110
MTS (subcontractor), 232
Npower (subcontractor), 232
Orbiant Group (subsidiary), 231
ownership structure of, 107–8
participation rights and structures at, 67–71, 79
percentage of union membership at, 74f, 74–75
precarity and, 13
Relacom (subcontractor), 231, 232, 233
solidarity and, 14–16, 101–2
strikes at, 230
structural inclusive solidarity and
  generally, 102–3, 190–91
  externalization, 228–34, 239t
  technicians, externalization and, 235–36, 236f
Telefos Group (subsidiary), 231
unions and, 12–13, 14
theory of contesting precarity, 4
  generally, 17–18
  collective worker voice, 30–36
  exit constraints, 22–30
  solidarity, 36–48
TKF (Danish union), 92, 119
TUC (British union), 85–86, 199

UGL (Italian union), 96
UIL (Italian union), 85
UNI-ICTS (global union), 10, 12, 17, 195, 257–58
Unionen (Swedish union), 88–91, 229
unions. See also collective worker voice; specific union
  generally, 4–5
  alternative unions, 255
  lessons for, 256–58
Union syndicale Solidaires (French union), 84–85

Unison (British union), 85–86
Unite (British union), 85–86
United Kingdom. *See also* BT (British company)
  Agency Regulations, 199
  Agency Workers Regulations 2010, 62
  collective worker voice in, 56*t*
  exit constraints in, 53–54, 56*t*, 59–60, 61, 62
  participation rights and structures in, 71
  privatization in, 107
  representation on corporate boards in, 67
  solidarity in, 85–86, 87–88, 98–99, 100, 101
  strikes in, 73, 78
  structural exclusive solidarity in, 98–99, 100, 101–2, 103
  structure of workplace representation in, 66–67
  Transfer of Undertakings, Protection of Employment Rules, 196
  Union Learning Fund, 78
  union mobilization resources in, 73
  unions in, 53–54, 55, 61–62
United States. *See also* AT&T (American company)
  "at will" employment in, 54
  Bargaining for the Public Good, 86
  Black Lives Matter, 46–47, 86
  collective worker voice in, 56*t*
  exit constraints in, 53–54, 56*t*, 59–60, 61, 62, 63
  incumbent companies, percentage of union membership in, 73–74
  National Labor Relations Board (NLRB), 66, 194
  participation rights and structures in, 71
  privatization in, 106–7
  representation on corporate boards in, 67
  solidarity in, 85–86, 87–88, 98–99, 100, 101
  strikes in, 73, 78
  structural exclusive solidarity in, 98–99, 100, 101–2, 103
  structure of workplace representation in, 66–67
  union mobilization resources in, 73
  unions in, 53–54, 55, 61–62

Varieties of Capitalism, 33
ver.di (German union), 84, 93–94, 126–27, 128, 180, 204
vertical disintegration
  collective worker voice and, 34, 35–36
  exit constraints and, 28–29
  solidarity and, 41
voice. *See* collective worker voice

welfare state, exit constraints and, 23–24
whipsawing, 35–36
works councils, performance management and, 143–44. *See also specific company or country*

Printed in the USA/Agawam, MA
July 24, 2023

813455.028